POMPEY

POMPEY

The Island City with a
Football Club for a Heart

NEIL ALLEN

ICON

Published in the UK in 2020
by Icon Books Ltd, Omnibus Business Centre,
39–41 North Road, London N7 9DP
email: info@iconbooks.com
www.iconbooks.com

Sold in the UK, Europe and Asia
by Faber & Faber Ltd, Bloomsbury House,
74–77 Great Russell Street,
London WC1B 3DA or their agents

Distributed in the UK, Europe and Asia
by Grantham Book Services,
Trent Road, Grantham NG31 7XQ

Distributed in Australia and New Zealand
by Allen & Unwin Pty Ltd, PO Box 8500,
83 Alexander Street, Crows Nest, NSW 2065

Distributed in India
by Penguin Books India,
7th Floor, Infinity Tower – C, DLF Cyber City,
Gurgaon 122002, Haryana

Distributed in South Africa
by Jonathan Ball, Office B4, The District,
41 Sir Lowry Road, Woodstock 7925

Distributed in the USA
by Publishers Group West,
1700 Fourth Street, Berkeley, CA 94710

ISBN: 978-178578-669-3

Typeset by Cecile Berbesi Rault

Printed and bound in Great Britain
by Clays Ltd, Elcograf S.p.A.

For John Jenkins and Basher Benfield.
They loved Pompey and Pompey loves them.

CONTENTS

FOREWORD

Ian Darke

Football commentators are supposed to be neutral, so let's start with a confession: I'm not. Pompey are my hometown club and I have never been ashamed to admit it. Is it tricky when I have to cover my favourite club on TV? Not usually.

You have to leave your passion at the commentary box door but there was one occasion when the mask slipped. Pompey were playing Brian Clough's talented Nottingham Forest team in an FA Cup quarter-final in March 1992. Everyone thought that Forest would be too classy for a mid-ranking second-tier team, but Alan McLoughlin grabbed a deserved winner at a packed Fratton Park. I have to admit, my voice was cracking with emotion a bit when the final whistle blew and I said: 'Pompey roll back the years to produce one of their most famous victories against all odds.'

Of course, that was the year Pompey nearly upset Liverpool in the semi-final, only to be denied by a Ronnie Whelan equaliser three minutes from time at Highbury. An agonising penalty shoot-out defeat in the Villa Park replay left me in near despair as I walked back to my car. Those two games perfectly sum up the whole emotional roller coaster of supporting this club through thick and, it seems, mostly thin. Many a Saturday has been ruined along the way.

And that brings me to that certain something that makes Pompey fans special, if not unique. They are at their best in adversity, when the team needs them most. Maybe that's because, to use Alan Ball's famous line, 'People went to war from this city.' As a kid I can remember playing on the many bomb sites left by German raids, especially near the Dockyard. That has perhaps bred a city of fighters who can come through hard times to bounce back. In that regard, the football club matches the people it represents. It is England's only island city and you don't see too many kids wearing Manchester United or Liverpool shirts. Most are proud to be Pompey.

My dad took me to Fratton Park when I was six years old. As a schoolboy right-winger for Francis Avenue Junior School half a mile from the ground, I marvelled at the brilliance of Peter Harris, who got all five goals one late summer evening against Aston Villa. What can I tell younger fans about him? He was like an early version of Cristiano Ronaldo. Quick and deadly. Jimmy Dickinson was also in that team, all graceful elegance at wing-half with not a hair out of place. Capped 48 times by England and a survivor of the team that twice won the title for Pompey. Imagine that now. Pompey, champions of England!

Since then I have seen Pompey through eight relegations and six promotions. I worked out that I've watched them in all four divisions, twice over. Even though my work prevents me from seeing all the games, I buy a season ticket for the North Stand Lower every season and go every time I can. But when commentating elsewhere, I have a phone in front of me with text messages from my sons, Adam and Rob, updating me on the scores. If I suddenly sound depressed on air, you will know why.

But through the decades I have somehow always managed to be there when it mattered most. The promotion from League Two at Notts County which ended four years in the basement left me quite tearful, bearing in mind the club nearly died and was saved by its own supporters. It felt like the first step out of hell. I bought a bottle of champagne at St Pancras station on the way home and shared it with some Pompey fans on the concourse.

Winning the FA Cup in 2008 was surreal. I had given up hope of ever seeing that happen. Better still though was the shock 2-0 win over Harry Redknapp's Spurs in that Wembley semi-final two years later. A brilliant display from a doomed team. It seemed to be written in the stars that day. On the flip side, play-offs are just a sea of heartbreak for Pompey. Can anyone recall a single lucky break in any of those games? Me neither. My favourite Pompey season was the one in which Paul Merson's creative playmaking orchestrated an unlikely promotion to the Premier League, playing some fabulous football. 'Merse' even got clapped off by home fans after a 5-0 win at Millwall, he was that good.

But one game sums up Pompey and their fans for me. That midweek match at home to Stockport with the team cut adrift at the bottom of the table and looking relegation certainties. That night was incredible. It is the only time I have seen a crowd win a game on its own. From start to finish, the fans produced a deafening wall of noise and you could see the Stockport players thinking 'What the hell Is going on here? This lot are bottom and the fans are going bananas.' Those opposition players froze and Pompey won 1-0, going on to escape relegation that year. I sat in the Fratton End just marvelling at what I was witnessing. I've never seen anything like it, before or since. Just as the Liverpool fans could not believe it when 13,000 of us turned up at Anfield to support a Division Three team in a midweek League Cup tie. Just as Thierry Henry was incredulous that the Fratton End were belting out songs despite Arsenal holding a 5-1 lead. Henry turned to Pompey's Arjan De Zeeuw, laughed and said: 'Your fans are crazy, but amazing.' He was right.

Jobs, relationships and colleagues come and go but Pompey is a life-long love affair and sentence rolled into one. The best of times and the worst of times, as a famous son of the city, Charles Dickens, once wrote. Let's hope one day soon we are back on the pitch celebrating another promotion. Get the ticker tape ready just in case.

August 2020

The city on an island has a football club for a heart, and as time goes on that heartbeat will sound throughout football. We may have a notoriously disreputable recent past, there is no denying that. Our future though, will be an example to the rest of football; this is what a football club really should be.

Micah Hall, November 15, 2012

JOHN JENKINS

10 August 2019

Queen Elizabeth II joined the chorus of approval, rising to her feet to unite in a poignant standing ovation. John Jenkins could not be certain, despite his vantage point, unable to pick out individual faces from the crowd, regal or otherwise. Thankfully the moment was snapshotted for perpetuity as the media observed the unfolding of a story which would populate global headlines.

Portsmouth's Southsea Common had reunited 300 Operation Overlord brothers for the D-Day 75 commemorations in June 2019. Ushered from the wings to occupy centre stage was Jenkins, the self-effacing 99-year-old born in Collingwood Road, at the city's heart. Addressing an audience whose eminent presences included the Queen, Donald Trump and then-Prime Minister Theresa May, Jenkins' touching delivery recounted his role as a 23-year-old company sergeant major in the 1944 Normandy landings which would turn the tide in the Second World War. That evening, Jenkins was toasted in homes across the country he served so heroically, as news programmes aired their coverage.

The former trolleybus driver needs no introduction in the city of Portsmouth which has served as home to him since 1919, particularly to those of a Pompey persuasion. As the League One club's boardroom ambassador, he is an instantly recognisable presence, an ageless obelisk standing on permanent Fratton Park duty. Since his footballing enlightenment at the age of eight, Jenkins has witnessed six promotions and eight relegations, along with two Division One titles, two FA Cups and a Checkatrade Trophy. Now his 91st Pompey season is under way.

'My late wife would ask: "Why don't you take your bed up Fratton Park?" said Jenkins. 'My response was that it wouldn't fit through the turnstiles!

'I had four uncles who were Pompey fanatics, Fratton Park enthusiasts and dyed-in-the-wool supporters. From the moment they took me to watch us play against Sheffield Wednesday in October 1928, I was hooked. Dave Watson scored a hat-trick in a 3–2 win – and, as far as I was concerned, I wanted to go to Fratton Park whenever there was a game.

'That included the reserves, with very good gates for those matches back then, around eight or nine thousand. At half-time, you would hear the bell ring in the South Stand and knew the phone message had come through revealing the first-team score, which was then put up on a scoreboard.

'I never saw my dad because he passed away when I was a baby. I'm not even sure how he died. I think he was in the army in India and something happened out there. I can remember seeing a photograph of him dressed in khaki drill, with a big black moustache and black hair. So my mother, Lily, had to raise me and my brother George.

'My four uncles – George, Will, Frank and Albert – were her brothers and treated me like their son. I was well looked after, particularly when it came to Pompey, and I owe them plenty of thanks for taking me there.

'Pompey was my team, no doubt about that. I suppose I have been associated with the club ever since, one way or another.

'I grew up watching Freddie Worrall; he was always one of my favourites. He played in the era before the Second World War and would run in from the wing and jump about ten feet to head the ball. Another was Jimmy Dickinson, of course, while Jack Smith was an inside-right who played for England in the early 1930s.

'I was at Wembley to see us win the FA Cup in 1939 and then 2008, but probably the 2008 victory under Harry Redknapp hit me more as something to savour, even at my age.

'This is a wonderful club. When you mention Pompey everyone knows who you are talking about.

'I'm still a boardroom ambassador, and I'm lucky to have a seat in the directors' box with my name on. There is so much about Fratton Park which is special to me.'

A weather-lashed Union flag, the remnant from celebrations marking the Queen's Golden Jubilee, clings to the balcony outside Jenkins' Milton flat. Within living room comforts, a photograph of the monarch, bedecked in white hat, inhabits the first shelf of a cluttered bookcase. Elsewhere, a picture of Diana, Princess of Wales, rubs shoulders with framed family photos, positioned atop a teak-chiselled nest of tables. The widower's esteem for the Royal Family is striking, as is his pride at serving his country, including 28 years in the Territorial Army. Decorated with the MBE in recognition of services to the military, during his investiture the Queen asked whether he was still serving. She was informed that Jenkins' retirement involved working in the Portsmouth Dockyard, probing the engine rooms of boats for traces of asbestos – the Royal Yacht Britannia among those receiving his attention. The MBE features among eight medals which regularly accompany Jenkins on public duty, others consisting of the Legion of Honour, the 1939–1945 Star, the France and Germany Star and the Imperial Service medal. Then, in the summer of 2019, he received another accolade from the Queen – applause.

'I was fourteen when I left school and wanted to join the Navy but, because of my age, instead I signed up for Cunard and went to sea as a bellboy on an ocean liner.

'My first ship was the RMS *Mauretania*, once the world's largest ship. She was so fast, holding the Blue Riband for twenty years in recognition of record average speed in the Atlantic Ocean.

'At 5.30am every day someone would bang on the door to wake us up to carry out the morning scrub. You were allocated a special part of the ship, such as the stairwell, which had to be scrubbed by hand.

'After that I would change into my black tunic, with buttons all the way down the front, and put on a peaked cap with the Cunard badge on, then stand by the saloon doors in first class, opening them for guests.

'The funny thing was, many years later, I was on a course with the Navy and went into Bristol town centre, where we stumbled across a pub called The Mauretania – and the saloon doors I used to open were there!

'I asked the barman if he minded me opening and closing them and, when he looked confused, had to explain my reasons. He couldn't believe they were the same doors.

'We would sail from Southampton to New York, reaching Pier 54, West 14th Street, and from there carried out fortnight-long cruises to the West Indies. I worked there for three to four months before the *Mauretania* came home to Southampton, being taken out of service in September 1934. We were the final crew.

'The *Mauretania* was scrapped, but they should have preserved her. She was launched in 1906 and getting a bit old, rattling a bit. We slept down below in what was called the 'glory hole' and there were bumps all around the sides.

'After that I worked on the RMS *Alaunia*, travelling to Halifax in Nova Scotia, Canada, and New York. When the Second World War broke out, the Navy took her over and she became the HMS *Alaunia*, surviving the war before becoming a repair ship.

'When I was called up to the Army, my basic training was carried out in Liverpool, then I served in Northern Ireland for two years before being dispatched for training in Scotland at one of the lochs.

'Next we were stationed at a camp in Glyndebourne, East Sussex, which stages an opera festival every year. Then, one day, following a service at a lovely church with a lychgate, we were marched to Newhaven, where we caught a landing craft. That night we left for a piece of sea the Navy nicknamed Piccadilly Circus, which was a rendezvous point. From there we landed on Gold Beach in Normandy.

'I was what they called a pioneer sergeant and my main job was ammunition, although I wouldn't say I was an expert! You had the 25-pounder shells for the guns, the ordinary boxes of .303 rifles and the stuff for the rocket launchers, with my responsibility involving setting up the dumps of ammunition.

'Our next objective was Bayeux, but the Germans had already gone, leaving it completely intact. Their cathedral now contains stained-glass windows in tribute to the Allies who landed in Normandy.

'On our way to Caen, we arrived at a farmhouse with breeze-block pigsties around the back, containing no pigs because the Germans had eaten them all. It was extremely wet and heavy that day, so we crowded into these pigsties and slept there that night.

'Then the American bombers came overhead and bombed the area to bits, leaving rubble everywhere, which made it more difficult to get through. The city of Caen was practically obliterated during the fighting.

'One of the worst places I saw was Fallingbostel, in northern Germany. Bergen-Belsen was the big concentration camp, and then this little one at Fallingbostel was almost an overflow. The first thing I saw upon arrival were three skeletons on the ground. I was informed by a Canadian Red Cross chap that they had just died. They'd had no food and starved. That place was awful. We didn't stop there too long.

'My war ended on 8 May 1945. I can remember being just outside of Bremen, Germany, and a Sherman tank began firing his gun into the air, its driver shouting that it was all over. That date, 8 May – it sticks in the mind.

'From that moment I travelled all over Germany for a good eighteen months, sent to different places, but eventually ended up in a coal mine at a village called Dorstfeld, west of Dortmund.

I wasn't anything to do with coal but, with the need to get everything back up and running again, coal was required for the railways, coal was required for electricity, coal was required for everything.

'At the coal mine, the miners had a canteen to cook their food in while on duty. It was our duty to ensure they were supplied with the ingredients to make a hot meal every day.

'On one occasion, a miner had been killed in an accident down below and my sentry approached me and said: "I don't know what's going on down the road, but you had better come up and have a look."

'So I did and there was a horse wearing black plumes pulling a carriage – it was the funeral of the miner. There were three of us, so I told them: "When it comes towards us, we will present arms as a mark of respect. The war is over."

'After it had passed, we went back to normal, never thinking any more about it, but the next morning my sentry said: "Sarge, you had better come down and have a look what's outside the guardroom." There were cucumbers, tomatoes, lettuce and spring onions – it was the villagers' way of thanking us for showing respect towards the deceased miner.

'For a long time there was a fraternisation ban, so we weren't allowed to be friendly with the villagers. We also had a message through to say any visits from the Russians should be reported immediately.

'When the miners finished a shift, we had to tap their billy cans to check they weren't taking any soup home. But if you are a miner with a drop left and have kids at home, what are you supposed to do? Sometimes, I let them get away with it.'

Pompey's 2019–20 campaign is anticipated to once again produce a challenge for a Championship return, following an eight-season absence. It kicked off inauspiciously, with Shrewsbury Town's Ryan Giles' stunning 30-yard left-footed strike inflicting a 1–0 away defeat for Kenny Jackett's side. It represented a debut goal in the teenager's maiden Football League appearance, on loan from Wolverhampton Wanderers. The Blues unveiled four debutants in their starting XI, of which Rangers loanee Ross McCrorie was dismissed following the second of two bookable offences, nine minutes from time. At that juncture they were already chasing a leveller at Montgomery Waters Meadow, yet ultimately were unable to capitalise on 63 per cent possession, fifteen goal attempts and ten corners. Crucially, the dogged Shrews scored with their sole effort on target.

Pompey's response was swift, banishing Championship Birmingham City from the Carabao Cup three days later with a heartening 3–0 triumph at Fratton Park. It yielded two goals for summer signing Ellis Harrison on his full debut, a welcome return having failed to register during the pre-season friendly programme. The approaching Saturday's visit of Tranmere Rovers signified the opening Fratton Park fixture of the League One campaign – and an opportunity for Jenkins to commence his latest season of support. Pompey's long-serving receptionist, Debbie Knight, hand-delivered the club's fixture list to the pensioner's home earlier in the week, while former England, Ipswich Town and Blues striker Ray Crawford was standing by to supply transport. The encounter with newly promoted Rovers lured a crowd of 18,575, their fourth-highest Fratton Park attendance in 2019, with owner Michael Eisner among those present, along with directors from his investment group, The Tornante Company. Such was the level of demand, with a boardroom creaking at full capacity, Portsmouth chief executive Mark Catlin sacrificed his place at the pre-match hospitality in favour of seating Jenkins. The club continue to rally around their treasured employee.

Adding to the gravitas of the fixture was the curious presence of Will Ferrell in the directors' box, Hollywood royalty regarded affectionately for a string of popular comedies, including timeless favourites *Anchorman* and *Elf*. Ferrell's interest in football is not superficial, possessing a minority stake in Major League Soccer side Los Angeles FC, who feature Cardiff City chairman Vincent Tan among their primary owners. The actor's south-coast presence at Fratton Park was secured through his friendship with Eisner's son and Blues board member Breck, a television and film director who sat alongside Ferrell during match proceedings.

Not since George Best, the enigmatic yet brilliant Manchester United and Northern Ireland artisan, had Fratton Park attracted a figure of such significant standing to a directors' box. Best was a close companion of former Pompey owner Milan Mandarić, having signed for his North American Soccer League franchise, San Jose Earthquakes, at the start of the 1980s. When Best sought residency at the Sporting Chance Clinic, in nearby Liphook, he became a fixture at Pompey home games. Through their frequent boardroom encounters, Jenkins would also strike up a friendship with the man who appeared 470 times for the Red Devils, to the extent Best felt compelled to present him with his autobiography *Blessed* one Christmas. It was inscribed 'Best Wishes, Happy New Year, 2005, George Best'. Best passed away eleven months later, at the age of just 59. A silver-framed photograph of the pair resides on a table at the 99-year-old's home.

'I became Pompey's boardroom steward many years ago; now they treat me like a friend more than a steward. They let me sit down to dinner with them as well, sometimes,' added Jenkins.

'George Best was one of my favourites in the boardroom. I knew him very well. I served in Northern Ireland for two years and was familiar with where he grew up in East Belfast, so I could talk to George about lots of places he knew. We became very good friends.

'He was a great player, no doubt about that, and would come down to every home game as Milan's guest. He used to say to me: "Are you going to put my bets on, John," but Milan never liked him betting!

'Then one day he came up to me and said: "I think I've got some money to come back, John. Will you go and collect it, please?" It was worth about £400 and he gave me £20 of his winnings. He was a lovely man, George.'

Jenkins, along with fresh directors' box colleague Ferrell, witnessed a 2–0 victory for Pompey over Micky Mellon's Tranmere, signifying their first points of the season. Ben Close, an unused substitute in the opening-day defeat at Sunderland, had netted against Birmingham on his return to the side during the week, subsequently retaining his place against Rovers. Born and raised in the city, the home-grown talent handed his club a 27th-minute lead with a magnificent strike, lashing a first-time right-footed shot into the top corner from 30 yards. Chosen as Sky Sports' goal of the day, it represented a tenth goal in 22 matches for the 23-year-old as his blossoming progress continued until the tutelage of boss Jackett. Skipper Tom Naylor sealed the win on 75 minutes, steering the ball home from close range after Paul Downing's header had been cleared off the line by David Perkins following a Lee Brown right-wing corner.

Brown himself was denied a place on the scoresheet two minutes from time having pounced from close range after keeper Scott Davies had failed to cling on to substitute Brett Pitman's stinging shot. During emotional celebrations, the left-back, also marking his 29th birthday, gazed towards the heavens and dedicated his first Pompey goal in 54 appearances to his grandad, who had passed away earlier that week. The linesman's flag cut short the touching tribute, along with the sound of Jackett screaming for him to resume defensive duties, with play having already recommenced.

The triumph was the result of fine work by the Blues, whose buoyant dressing room subsequently misplaced its voice when a beaming Ferrell entered, jokingly demanding a greater awareness of the offside rule, before willingly posing for photographs. Goalscorer Naylor, who rigidly refuses to subscribe to the chattering of social media, had been unaware of the Hollywood superstar's Fratton Park presence until the startling moment of his post-match entrance. As for boss Jackett, usually so impressively impervious to distractions, he couldn't resist the opportunity for a photographic keepsake with the distinguished guest. Ferrell's Fratton Park return may be indeterminable, but Jenkins will certainly return, with a Tuesday evening encounter against Coventry City next booked in at the famous old ground.

It was four years previous when Jenkins abseiled down the Spinnaker Tower to raise money for Rowans Hospice, while, ahead of the 2012 London Olympics, he carried the Olympic torch around Fratton Park. These days he relies on a walking stick to aid his progress but retains his independence by remaining in the Eastern Road home once shared with his beloved Peggy, their marriage spanning 74 years before they were parted. Jenkins turns 100 in November, an occasion to invariably prompt more communication with the Queen, courtesy of the birthday card customarily sent to centurions.

'Someone once told me, I don't know whether it's true, that when I spoke at the D-Day commemorations even the Queen stood up to applaud,' he added.

'That's something, isn't it.'

Ian Chiverton, Eric Coleborn and Jay Sadler

18 August 2019

Geoffrey Chiverton was a modest man, unconcerned with pursuing plaudits. Work mattered, with on-call commitments to Godalming Fire Station intertwining with the day job at car body builders King & Taylor. Such was the hectic schedule, it usually deprived the family of his presence at their Christmas meal, pager notifications dragging him away at the most inopportune of moments. Yet Chiverton's dedication to his work and the wider Godalming community did not go unnoticed, as evidenced in 1993 when Chiverton's young family had watched on from the upper gallery at Buckingham Palace as the Queen bestowed on him the MBE, recognition for his outstanding service to the Godalming community, a proud moment which has lived on in the memory. Following his Surrey homecoming, the fire-station stalwart banished his commendation from the public eye, relegated to a living room drawer, albeit granted an annual outing to fulfil Remembrance Day parade duty. Such was the strength of Chiverton's humility, he rebuffed the standard opportunity to embellish credit and debit cards with his newly acquired additional three letters.

For son Ian, the pride at his father's lofty standing within the community which remains the family home is understandable, a high regard undiminished following the fireman's passing with pneumonia in December 2014 at the age of 65. There remain regrets. Chiverton senior's admirable dedication to his work meant that he spent just two and a half seasons accompanying his son as a Fratton Park season-ticket holder. These late-life moments are cherished by Ian, yet balanced by sorrow that their Pompey connection was so heartbreakingly brief.

Today, the 36-year-old is partnered by eight-year-old daughter Abby, regulars at Pompey matches spanning both the men's and women's games. The pair totalled 147 Blues matches during the previous two seasons – and intend on maintaining that fervent support during the campaign ahead.

'Growing up, I never had a shared hobby with my dad – and I so wanted to. He didn't follow football until I got him into Pompey later in his life, then he started to come to a few games,' said Chiverton.

'Dad was out all the time, working in his day job, yet also on call for the fire service. Sometimes I'd be walking home from school with my friends and we would see him running past, heading towards the fire station with his alarm sounding.

'We can't have shared more than a couple of Christmas Day dinners together during my childhood. It was a running joke in the family that the second my mum placed the meal on the table, his alerter sounded. He'd return an hour and a half later. It was a massive commitment from him towards both jobs.

'As a consequence, I did so few things with my dad. As a kid, it was always on my mind that one day, when an adult, I would share a hobby with my child; I wanted that more than anything.

'When I had a daughter, it occurred to me it would be a bit tricky because I didn't know what to do with girls. It's different now. Abby has become used to football and will sit through the men's game as well as the women's. It's amazing to have that shared hobby, and for away games we can spend hours of a journey talking football.

'It took me years to actually get my dad into the game; he never understood. I would say: "Dad, I want a Portsmouth shirt," and the reply was: "What, like a T-shirt with Portsmouth written on it?" He just did not get it at all, and it took me years of pestering, hassling him. "Please, Dad, just come to a game with me." Even my mum would get on his back to agree.

'He was very dismissive of it, not that bothered, but when I eventually got him to attend a match after many, many years of trying, he caught the bug instantly. People do, don't they.

'I had a season ticket alongside a friend, Ben Hudson. Then Ben joined the police force and was instructed to work weekends, affecting his attendance, so on one occasion I finally convinced my dad to accompany me, using that ticket. Now he would never admit he was wrong, but on the way home, he turned to me and said: "I guess I could come again."

'Following a few visits using Ben's seat, Dad enquired about season-ticket availability – and we ended up regularly going to Fratton Park together. Before he died, we had finally managed to share a few years of Pompey.

'I was really adamant I wanted something to share with my children. Apart from the last few years, I didn't have anything with my dad, so creating that joint experience was really important; that's why I tried getting Abby into football.

'It has worked maybe a bit more than I expected, to the point where on one occasion the men and women played on the same day, which was ridiculously annoying. I chose Oxford United away to take in Kenny Jackett's team, leaving my wife to take Abby to the women's game. Then she shut my son's foot in the car door and instead had to take him to hospital. Abby was crying down the phone to me for an hour because she couldn't go. It did occur to me: "Have I got her too much into it?" I don't think so!

'Now she has started playing the game herself as a defender. I would ask why she couldn't take it up and she would respond: "Girls don't play football, only boys." Her grandma is a traditionalist and made her do ballet and gymnastics, but she wasn't very good at them, and I was thinking: "I wonder if she would be good at football?" When she started watching the women's game, she wanted to try it herself.

'In each of the last two seasons, we have attended more than 70 games. Having started to support the women, we don't want to let either side down, so have ended up doing both. It just developed into a habit.

'When there's a weekend with no football, we get bored and my wife quickly becomes sick of us around the house, especially on a Sunday! If we don't have a women's game, Abby is climbing the walls by 10am because we're just so used to it. She is treated like a squad player; they invite her into the dressing room and she feels so accepted.

'I took her to a few men's games, but she was restless during the match, so bored, asking for food, calling for her iPad, it wasn't working. Then a friend of mine, Sam Bowers, mentioned the women's team and advised me to take that approach. It intrigued me.

'Knowing Abby, I needed a player for her to meet or she wouldn't have any early connection, so I found Lauren Peck on Twitter and messaged her. It was basically: "I'm bringing Abby to her first game. Would you mind just saying hello to her, please?" It was no problem.

'When we arrived, Lauren was warming up and, upon noticing Abby, came straight across to speak to her. I saw my daughter's face – and from that moment she fell in love with football.'

Ian and Abby's maiden Pompey Women fixture occurred in August 2017, with Cardiff City the visitors to Havant & Waterlooville's Westleigh Park home on the opening day of the 2017–18 campaign. The hosts ran out 4–1 winners.

In the two years that followed, the pair have been absent from just six matches in all competitions, their continued presence embraced by manager Jay Sadler and his players. They showed their appreciation at Christmas 2018, Sadler's playing squad orchestrating a whip-round, resulting in a pair of blue Adidas boots decorated with a white stripe, wrapped up and handed over to Abby as a festive gift. Younger brother

William wasn't left out either, with the toddler given sweets. In Abby's room at the family's Godalming home hangs a framed pink away shirt autographed by the squad, a present from boss Sadler in recognition of her first season following the Blues.

Elsewhere among her burgeoning collection are Lauren Peck's medal and shirt from the 2018 Hampshire Cup final victory over Southampton. Similarly, Gemma Hillier, the only female presence in Pompey's Hall of Fame, alongside the likes of Paul Merson, David James and Alan Knight, posted a shirt and cup final medal following her departure from the club.

Chiverton added: 'When someone looks after your child, you naturally form a bond with them – and the manager and players are unbelievable with Abby.

'When we arrive at matches, I'll set up my equipment for filming our vlogs and Abby disappears. She is either at the turnstiles selling tickets and programmes, in the changing room with the players, or warming up on the pitch alongside them. Jay lets her join in with the final drill, which is amazing. She is very, very lucky to have such access.

'There are probably about ten of us hard-core fans who attend all Pompey Women home games, although the pair of us are the only ones present at away fixtures. I genuinely think they are grateful and they pay that back by looking after Abby on a match day, which is beyond anything we could expect.

'In her first season of playing football, Abby was really nervous about the opening training session, so Lauren Peck, who is with Fulham now, came along to watch and lend support.

'When my daughter made her debut for Milford Pumas Youth under-8s, Ellie Kirby, Daisy McLachlan and Carla Perkins drove over to Surrey to watch. It's a fair trek just to see a small kid's game. They also gave her advice beforehand.

'When the match got under way, there was a boy having a worldie and he scored in the top corner, which really upset Abby as she had literally just gone in goal. At that point, with the game still being played, Ellie went onto the pitch to console her, putting her arm around the shoulders saying: "Come on Abby, you can do it." That meant so much.

'I suppose our approach to supporting the women's game is a bit of a new concept for them. Of course they've had kids as mascots before, but with Abby it's different; she literally hero worships these players and they are not used to that.

'Interaction with fans is quite a new concept to the girls. Among the first thing I noticed when attending was how, when they scored, they'd just walk off, Where the men would race over to the fans, the women hug each other and walk away with the minimum of fuss. It's not their fault as they're used to playing in pretty much empty stadiums with the only people present being their parents.

'Last season I had a word with the manager and some of the players about celebrating with the supporters and, when Emma-Jane May scored in the Portsmouth District Football Association Cup final win against Horndean, she ran over to us and produced a mini-crowd jump, leaping over the advertising boards into our arms. That was brilliant, and the first time I had seen that happen at this level.

'Some of them are quite shy and we don't want to bother them too much. They are not paid footballers and they don't owe us anything. Initially, some were a little overwhelmed by a young girl running up to them and giving a hug – now Abby high-fives them.

'Can you imagine a random kid grabbing a Sunday League bloke, patting his belly saying: "Have a good game today, mate." The girls' reaction was the same at first, yet are now used to it, and I have become friends with some of them.

'In our first season of following them, they won the Hampshire Cup at Alton and invited Abby onto the pitch. When the trophy was presented to the skipper, Amelia Southgate, she lifted it before passing it onto the next person – Abby! None of the other players, it was straight to her.

'Last season in the Hampshire Cup final 3–1 victory over Southampton Women FC, she was again invited onto the pitch for the presentation ceremony, only this time Katie James hauled Abby onto her shoulders and gave her the trophy. Then Jay Sadler came over and handed my daughter his medal in recognition of her support. That's a lot more personal than the men's game.'

The pair's devotion to Pompey Women earned them a nomination for a national award. Abby's brainchild, Pompey Women's Vlogs, began life as a phone attached to a selfie stick, attracting 300–400 views during its infancy. Today, they position a GoPro attached to a tripod behind each goal on a match day, uninhibited by the copyright issues associated with filming the men's game.

The coverage made the shortlist in the prestigious 2019 Football Blogging Awards, in the Best Women's Football Content Creator category. With the awards being held at Manchester City's Etihad Stadium, Ian's mum paid for them to savour overnight attendance, while Abby was granted permission from Godalming Junior School to attend.

They were beaten by the Liverpool-centric The Redmen TV's *Women's Football Show*, a product with a mammoth 386,000 YouTube subscribers, but for Ian and Abby, the nomination felt like a prize in itself.

Chiverton said: 'Women's football can be quite a hard sell and, because I have got to know the Pompey players, I genuinely felt for them. They don't get any recognition and to me that represented a massive injustice. By creating a vlog and putting it out there, maybe one or two people would watch and give games a go themselves.

'Each vlog takes four to five hours to put together. It is a real push to complete before the next match. At the end of last season I was thinking: "I really don't know whether I can do this any more" – then you receive a nomination for a national award! Earning such recognition for my work spurred me on – and it's important I continue to highlight the women's game.

'Mind you, some people just don't want to listen. If you are going to judge the quality of football based on what you see on *Match of the Day* and then watch Pompey Women in the third tier, don't expect it to be of that standard, you're not going to get it. If you just relax your attitude a little and take the game for what it is, you'll realise it's good to watch. I've encouraged people to attend at times and they've come up to me at the end of the match and said: "Do you know what, I was wrong; that was pretty good."

'Don't compare the women's game with the men's. If you expect the same thing then you might as well leave because you're not going to get it. That doesn't make it rubbish you know, it's just a different type of game.

'What I've learnt from watching the women's game is that it's ridiculously competitive, especially some of the tackles which fly in. I remember our first game watching Pompey play. Three minutes in against Cardiff there was a ridiculously bad challenge inside the box and I thought: "My God, what is this?" I thought the girls would be pulling out of tackles, but no, there's none of that. It's really competitive.

'It's worse than the men. In the men's game you receive a red card straight away, but in the women's there's more leniency, like Sunday League. Even if I didn't have my daughter alongside me, I would still happily attend their games because it's worth watching.

'The stuff I am starting to dislike about the men's game isn't actually there [in the women's game]. Money, overpaid players who don't care about the club, no access to footballers, VAR coming in, there's none of that.

'The women's game is pure football. They go out there and give their all. There are some really skilful players in our league and challenges are flying in, but no diving, you don't get it. There's a Chichester City Ladies player who likes to fall over a lot, but that's the only time I have seen it – and even then it was just the once.'

The 2019–20 Pompey Women season kicked off at home to Watford, seeking to build on the previous campaign's final position of eighth in the twelve-team FA Women's National League South Premier Division. Greeting supporters outside the home of Baffins Milton Rovers was Blues chairman Eric Coleborn, decked in yellow high-vis jacket and equipped with a warm handshake and a message of thanks for each arrival's attendance on a glorious south-coast afternoon. The ground's sole turnstile was overseen by the ever-welcoming Sarah Ferre, a former gate woman at Fratton Park and familiar face around the men's club since accompanying her uncle to a first game in 1979. Sarah's mum, Janet, was positioned as sentry at the neighbouring gate, on call to aid those with bikes, the disabled and, on some occasions, supporters arriving with prams, emphasising the family-friendly environment. At the far end of the ground, the bottom gate adjacent to the Langstone Harbour football pitches was, on this day, manned by Simon Colebrook, the chairman of Pompey Supporters' Trust. He and wife Jane had insisted on each paying the £5 fee for their own entrance, irrespective of match-day volunteer roles. Gate duty is rotated between Colebrook and Steve Hatton, the Trust's long-standing membership secretary, who frequents matches with wife Christine.

Elsewhere, Ian Chiverton and Abby had been busy pre-match, decorating the stadium with two large Pompey banners draped over hoardings, while nine small flags, liberated in opportunist fashion by Abby from the previous day's men's fixture against Tranmere Rovers, also stood to attention from new vantage points.

'I think it's nice to invite people in. We are trying to encourage them to come to matches, that's the bottom line,' said Coleborn, now in his second season as chairman of Pompey Women.

'I enjoy welcoming people and, as they leave, thanking them for coming and supporting the team. If anybody wants to give me feedback on anything we can improve on, then I am there to listen and potentially act upon their opinion. At the end of the day, we want them to return.

'As chairman of this club, I possibly see things a little bit differently. It's not like Fratton Park, where you have thousands of people in attendance and the vast corporate side to it. Here we are very much focused on fans coming to support the team – and it's important they see somebody trying to work for them.

'We are attempting to create a good experience for people at what is a lovely venue to stage football. We want those who arrive to have a good time, to enjoy themselves in an extremely relaxed atmosphere where you can walk around the ground, have a drink, sit down on the terracing or go into the clubhouse. This is a friendly club which plays in a family atmosphere.

'We possess a phenomenal group of volunteers. My match-day staff do an excellent job, looking after the turnstiles, the car park, clearing the ground, and they do this for the love of the club, which is fantastic. Even I will go and retrieve the balls which fly out of the ground – we are one.

'As a club, we are run sustainably and what earns you revenue is the support delivered by people coming to the games; that's what I am desperately trying to make certain can happen.

'I think we are doing the right things. It's no good sitting on your laurels; you have to keep improving and improving and improving – and that's what I'm trying to do, looking at what we are doing, seeing where we can raise our game.

'We are slowly building. This is the beginning of my second season and it does take time.'

Coleborn was parachuted into his role in June 2018, following the decision to bring Pompey Women under the umbrella of the men's club. The move was initiated to preserve the team's survival in the face of escalating losses which had already cost previous owner Mick Williams approximately £35,000 during his three-year chairmanship. During Williams' final season at the helm, the club were forced to take on a nomadic existence, using eight different home venues, including Havant & Waterlooville, Littlehampton, Bognor, Gosport and Petersfield. On occasions they had to secure a pitch 24 hours before a fixture. The lack of a consistent ground for Pompey Women inevitably impacted upon crowd numbers – and finances. Williams, previously an instrumental figure in the Portsmouth Supporters' Trust capture of Pompey to prevent liquidation, was regretfully confronted with the prospect of wrapping up the women's team in the summer of 2018. The precarious situation prompted chief executive Mark Catlin to orchestrate a union under the club banner, with Baffins Milton Rovers chairman Steve

Cripps providing a home for the Blues, earning a place on the Pompey Women's board in the process.

As for the role of chairman, Coleborn represented a natural fit. A highly respected Trust board member and club president, he also possesses a long-standing business presence in the city through his Glass & Mirror Centre premises in North End. It's a responsibility the local businessman has set about with admirable ardour.

'Pompey Women were going to fold. Mick Williams was using his own money and it was costing him a lot. This standard of football is not cheap to put on,' he said.

'It's not a local league. Our fixture list contains Yeovil, Plymouth, Cardiff, Gillingham and MK Dons, involving travel all over the place, while we use two training pitches a week, which require paying for, so costs spiral to say the least. It's an expensive game.

'Coming under the roof of Pompey was crucial – and Michael Eisner and his board didn't take any convincing. They immediately saw the benefits and it makes good sense all round. This is one club with two teams.

'We run it sustainably, and what we take is what we can spend, but we're always working on how to cut costs sensibly, while seeking methods to increase revenue, like any club does. It's a simple business format.

'Not only do Pompey let us use their gym facilities at Roko once a week, but they supply the kit and share the University of Portsmouth as first-team sponsors, while also organising other commercial deals for our benefit. To be honest, we wouldn't be able to survive without such support and I thank them for that.

'Everything is looked at and has to be costed, and it's about being realistic. For example, our match-day programme has this season doubled in price to £2, which was necessary. The decision was made that it had to be more realistic price-wise for what we are producing; it is a good-quality programme, not just a team sheet.

'It is an expensive game and we must ensure we are looking after the pennies. Nobody at the club is paid, not even the manager, although we do pay travelling costs.

'I am a businessman with a business plan – I will make certain we don't attract losses. To aid that we need to increase the gates, get more people along, which adds to the income. On top of that there's programme sales and money spent inside the ground, all of which will help to build the football club moving forward.

'We want to create the best team we possibly can to give our supporters the best experience they can possibly have. We are trying to build an infrastructure, making things better for the girls that play and improving the product on the pitch.

'That's my job and it is slow progress – but I believe we are getting there.'

Pompey Women endured an opening-day 2–0 defeat to the Hornets, watched by a healthy crowd of 207.

Both goals arrived in the first half courtesy of Helen Ward's right foot. The Watford striker is Wales skipper and all-time leading scorer for her country, with 42 goals in 70 matches. Employed full-time, she combines playing duties with work in the club's media and marketing departments, serving as the face of the self-styled 'Golden Girls' in the local community.

In contrast, Pompey's nineteen squad members and eleven backroom and media staff work on a voluntary basis. In addition to matches, the players are required to train three evenings a week, including Wednesday night gym work at Pompey's Hilsea training ground.

Travel costs for training sessions are met by the club, however, at a rate of 15p a mile, while a 30-mile radius offers recruitment boundaries focused on identifying talent from the Reading, Portsmouth, Southampton and Brighton areas.

Such are the financial discrepancies between women's sides, Watford were chaperoned to the season opener by coach, whereas a minibus hired from Pompey in the Community transports Pompey Women to their encounters. Such is its restrictive size, it cannot accommodate backroom staff, who drive separately in a six-seater van.

Cost monitoring has been essential in preserving the existence of a club on the brink of going under before Pompey chairman Michael Eisner stepped forward, a necessity acknowledged by Sadler.

Arriving as assistant manager in July 2016, rapid personal progression resulted in his appointment as first-team boss merely four months later. The subsequent readjustment to a self-sustainable model has been challenging, but not without hope.

Following the dismantling of their development and youth groups after the 2018 change in ownership, Pompey in the Community now provides the grass-roots pathway into the club, an independent charitable trust affiliated to the club which oversees teams from under-10s upwards.

Opportunity also exists through the University of Portsmouth shirt sponsorship and doors have been opened for Sadler to attend the university's September football trials to scout talent for the Pompey Women set-up.

And the 27-year-old remains encouraged by the ongoing affiliation with the main football club.

Sadler said: 'We have recently promoted Mia Adaway into the first team, who has been at the club since she was under ten. She has been training with the seniors since the age of fourteen, but legal requirements have prevented her from representing us until reaching sixteen.

'Losing our development group was not ideal, and it has left us with a bit of a hole, preventing us from bringing players up for training or dropping them down for match minutes, so that has been a challenge.

'There remains an ambition to reintroduce a development team. I tried to push for its return this season, but I think we're probably another year off, although we're able to link up with Pompey in the Community and the University of Portsmouth.

'This is short-term pain for long-term gain. Overall, the vision brought into the women's club by Pompey is really exciting; it just needs a bit of time and patience – and hopefully we will see the rewards on the pitch as well as off it.

'The key is becoming self-sustainable, to stand on our own two feet. We know where we are and we have an understanding of the resources we possess – but we must get the best out of them. As long as you have the basics – a training ground, training equipment and hungry players wanting to win games of football – then you are quite happy. We are lucky, we have all three.

'In terms of bringing in players, we are looking at a smaller area and a smaller pool of players which we believe are good enough and it has truly tested our recruitment strategy, but the outcome has been phenomenal, probably my best at the club.

'With players on a twelve-month registration, the summer usually brings a high turnover, yet this has actually been the first season in which we have been able to retain a large majority of the squad. There are thirteen players remaining from last year, with five fresh faces added and Mia brought up from the youth set-up, which is the smallest amount of newcomers we've had in my three years at the club.

'Slowly, but surely, things are piecing together well in this partnership. Pompey's media team have been unbelievable integrating with us, promoting the women's team over their vast social media reach, and, with Eric as chairman, you can see the vision where they want to take the club.

'Not only that, we have established a link with Kenny Jackett and his assistant Joe Gallen. Earlier this month, Joe invited me and my staff to watch the first team train, then afterwards sat around a table with their backroom people, including the head of sports science, and we were allowed to pick their brains, the session lasting about an hour. The information was excellent, something to take away and implement into our environment.

'At the end of it, Kenny Jackett handed me his mobile number and said if ever I needed anything then to contact him, while I was welcome at any time to watch them train.

'On the following Thursday evening, after our training, I messaged Kenny thanking him for the opportunity and wished him the best of luck against Sunderland that weekend. He replied with "No problem" – and wished us well against Watford in our opening game. Wow, I was like a child at Christmas!

'It's small steps, but small steps in the right direction.'

Sadler welcomed second son, Archie, into the world in March 2019, a wonderful moment but one that stopped him from accompanying his side to Plymouth Argyle, with Pompey drawing 2–2 in his absence. As a consequence, ever-present Chiverton and his daughter totalled more Blues fixtures than the manager that season, a fact which raises a chuckle from the Pompey Women boss.

Yet Chiverton also retains devotion towards the men's team, remaining a season-ticket holder since first settling into his Fratton End seat for a chaotic 2000–01 campaign, in which Tony Pulis, Steve Claridge and Graham Rix all served as managers. The Blues remained in Division One that season, following a 3–0 final-day win over Barnsley.

With Abby accompanying him in recent years, the pair participated in the good-natured pitch invasion at Meadow Lane to mark Pompey's promotion to League One in April 2017. When Paul Cook's team clinched the League Two title three games later – courtesy of a 6–1 Fratton Park mauling of Cheltenham Town – they once more descended upon the pitch.

Moments of success for the pair to cherish, although Chiverton admits his growing affection for the women's game has impacted upon his regard for the men's format.

He said: 'During the last two seasons, I have attended three-quarters of the men's away games, but it has reached the point where my son is approaching three and I can no longer disappear all day. I now have to be a bit more selective, but I guess that's what comes of growing up.

'I still enjoy watching the men, but following women's football has taken the edge off it. If Pompey men lose I'm really annoyed, as we all are, but I know if the women win the following day then I will completely forget that defeat.

'If both teams lose then you don't want to speak to me for a few days – and my work colleagues know that! Don't talk to me, I'm really bad. I can't even go home and forget about it as I have four to five hours of match footage to edit for our vlogs, so have to relive it!

'When Pompey reached the Checkatrade Trophy final against Sunderland in March 2019, we didn't attend because the women were playing Loughborough on the same day.

'It prompted a couple of not-so-nice messages from people on Twitter telling me I had made the wrong decision and would regret it – as would Abby. A lady even very kindly offered to take Abby with her daughter, but I declined. People thought I was forcing Abby, but I would have had to drag her kicking and screaming to attend Wembley that day.

'It simply wouldn't have sent the right message to my daughter if we had joined those 40,000 Pompey fans along Wembley Way on that afternoon. You are loyal to a women's team which doesn't get much attention and then, when the men have a glory day, you suddenly ditch them and instead travel to that game? That scenario didn't sit right with me in any way, shape or form and I don't regret our decision, not even for a second.

'We had a big choice to make – and had to show loyalty to Pompey Women. We wanted to remind the girls that we're always there to support them, no matter what, even if it meant missing out on a Wembley trip.

'Mind you, at the match against Loughborough, it was like tumbleweed blowing through – there was no one there! A lot of staff who volunteer their time had gone to the final, including the stadium announcer, so we had to play the music and announce the line-up, while Abby helped sell programmes at the gate.

'We won 2–0 – and got home in time to watch Pompey win 5–4 on penalties against Sunderland to collect the Checkatrade Trophy. It was definitely the right decision.'

It was the setting of Godalming Junior School which initiated the creation of a Pompey association which has now stretched to three generations of the Chiverton family.

As a ten-year-old, Ian and his friends gathered in the school hall keen to satisfy a fledgling interest in football. On the agenda was the selection of a team to pledge allegiance. In his case, this entailed avoiding the larger, more popular clubs so fashionable among those outside natural catchment areas.

Noting that the dad of my friend Jamie Pollard supported Pompey, he swiftly established his affiliation. Given Chiverton family holidays were often spent in Southsea, a regular destination largely dictated by his mum's fear of flying, the rubber stamp was applied to his application.

Eventually luring his reticent dad into enlisting as a member of the Fratton faithful, it became inevitable that mum, Ann, would also sign up. Ill health these days deprives her of matches, but a family WhatsApp group keeps her in touch with the Blues' progress through Ian's goal updates. Once the final whistle sounds in Pompey Women fixtures, she can expect a phone call from her son, enthusiastically poring over proceedings.

Ann's knitting talents have also adapted a Blues tinge, yielding cuddly clones of goalkeeper Hannah Haughton and Danielle Rowe, in addition to long-serving men's midfielder Gareth Evans. As for the youngest, two-year-old William, he has already established himself as a regular at Pompey Women matches and made his Fratton Park bow in the 2–0 victory over Tranmere Rovers earlier in August, sitting in the Milton End with mum, Susie.

The legacy continues to gather momentum, despite the passing of the family's head.

'In 2014, my dad entered hospital with pneumonia,' said Ian. 'They put him in a coma to regulate his breathing and he never awoke. Within three days he had passed away. It happened so quickly – he had been retired for just a year.

'Having been a public servant for so many years, he deserved his retirement, even buying the car he always wanted – a Nissan Qashqai. He got a year, that was it. Life's pretty cruel; it wasn't fair.

'When I started watching Pompey Women, taking Abby along too, we were made to feel so welcome.

'For a couple of hours you forget about your problems because football is giving you a good time, and that's what it's about.

Even now, if I miss a football match, I'm really grumpy and feel unbalanced because I haven't had my weekend treat.

'I recall watching the 2008 FA Cup quarter final victory against Manchester United on the television around my parents' home. When the full-time whistle sounded, I started crying, prompting my dad to ask what the matter was.

'I never thought I would see Pompey at Wembley, and the next step was the semi-finals held there, and I became emotional. Do you know what? My dad hugged me and started to cry himself. That was the first time I ever saw him shed tears; the other occasion was in 2011 when Abby was born.

'Both my parents came with me to the semi-final against West Bromwich Albion because they knew how much it meant to me. That's football. It brings families together – and I'm now sharing those special memories with Abby.'

JACK WHATMOUGH

15 September 2019

The Southampton number fifteen caught the eye of Jack Whatmough, who duly registered the performance in his black notebook. Amid the wreckage of a 4–0 home defeat to Chelsea under-16s at the Staplewood training complex a month earlier, the influential central midfielder's bravery on the ball sufficiently stirred the onlooker's interest. Whatmough's desire to reintegrate with football prompted the volunteering of his scouting services to Pompey's head of youth recruitment, Neil Sillett, who gladly accepted. The first assignment took him to the club he walked out on as a disillusioned thirteen-year-old and the Blues' fiercest rivals, Southampton. Not that the central defender is preoccupied with such trifling tribalism these days.

A cartilage tear sustained against Doncaster Rovers in February 2019 signalled a third operation on his left knee by the age of 23 and the start of a familiar fight for fitness. Wretched misfortune has impeded the progress of a once prodigiously talented teenager honoured with England youth recognition, listing Dele Alli, Ben Chilwell and Ruben Loftus-Cheek among international team-mates. The Gosport-born Whatmough has battled back with admirable fortitude to revive his Pompey career, demonstrating mental strength belying his years.

However, the latest setback saw him resort to excessive drinking and betting on horse racing to alleviate loneliness that arose from being deprived of competing in the sport he loves. Having reached out to the Sporting Chance Clinic for guidance, Whatmough has learnt how alternative focus, such as football scouting, can offer constructive distractions during ongoing recuperation. Encouragingly, he is adamant that he has now emerged through the darkest times of his career.

'Imagine somebody's favourite hobby is drawing. How would they feel if you told them to stand outside the room and instead watch others draw?' said Whatmough. 'Well, that's how it felt for me with football; mentally it takes everything out of you.

'It's difficult watching it on TV, having to look at the lads in day-to-day training, to sit up in the stands on a match day seeing the game. It's unbelievably tough. I've come through that now, thanks to help from others. I've been looking for something to do during my recovery, finding ways to fill my time. I just want to be involved in football again, so carrying out a bit of youth-team scouting has been ideal. I watched Southampton against Chelsea under-16s, taking a little notebook Neil Sillett gave me to write down observations. I think I have an eye for a good player and it was what I really needed at that stage of my recovery.

'I've had dark times – which is something I'm no longer afraid to admit – as it's mentally tough going through three long-term injuries before the age of 23. For a lot of footballers, stepping across that white line is their escape from something. You may be having the worst time at home, but when you enter that pitch everything is forgotten. There is no escape when you are injured. It's mentally the most draining thing you will ever suffer as a footballer. I've had incredibly tough times during this lay-off in particular, sitting in a dark room not wanting to talk to anyone. You never get used to injuries.

'I was in a bad place, but men can't be upset, it's an ego thing. We can't possibly talk about it, just put it to one side and carry on as if nothing is wrong. I changed that, I had to, otherwise I would still be low, struggling mentally. I owe so much to the PFA and the Sporting Chance Clinic.'

In July 2019, Whatmough confided in fiancée Demi and his parents about the demons plaguing his rehabilitation. Demi, a sales executive at Pompey for three years, spoke to Fratton Park colleague Ashleigh Emberson about her concerns, who in turn located a number for the Liphook-based Sporting Chance Clinic. Then the footballer made the crucial phone call.

'The first week or two following my injury I was fine. I thought: "I'll get over this, I'll be okay." We have a three-storey house in Port Solent and our bedroom is on the top floor, but being on crutches for the first three months, I was unable to climb stairs. A bed was instead moved into the gaming room on the bottom floor, so I slept there.

'Each morning I would come to the training ground for rehabilitation for an hour, then return to that room. I spent 23 hours a day in there: sleeping, eating, and I couldn't even have a shower for eight weeks. It was mentally draining – these are the things people don't see. There was a two- or three-month period when I was on the floor. I had no motivation to come into the club and carry out the work. I had no motivation for anything; I didn't want to leave the house. My girlfriend would ask if I wanted to go out for a nice meal. I didn't. I had no interest.

'I had to replace my buzz of football with something, which became gambling on horses. It wasn't for thousands of pounds, but it was completely out of character. Previously I wouldn't set foot in a casino. I craved a bit of happiness from sport, so it was horses. It started as £10 on phone betting apps, but escalated; next there were visits to casinos and betting shops. Then I began drinking.

'I'm not a drinker. The occasional beer is nice, and if others are having a drink then I will, socially, but never at home when on my own. That changed. If I'd had a bad day at the training ground during my recovery, I'd pick up some cans of Carling on the way home, drinking them in the afternoon or with dinner in the evening. I wouldn't think anything of it. It was my way of forgetting about things. Depending on my mood, I would drink between four and eight cans a day; it did me no favours and I put on weight. I was scared of opening up and admitting I needed help.

'People don't see what you have to go through. After the injury initially occurred, I was probably sleeping two hours a day. There was pain in my knee and it was uncomfortable keeping my leg constantly straight. My fiancée had to do everything. It felt as though I was piling all this pressure on her, and I couldn't even walk my dogs Lily and Teddy for twelve weeks. I saw what Demi was going through and it eats away at you a little.

'At least now I'm in a situation where I can see light at the end of the tunnel. I have no doubts whatsoever I will be back playing football, no doubts.'

Whatmough was seventeen years, three months and eight days old when handed his first-team debut against Southend United in a League Two encounter in November 2013. His present appearance tally of 96 matches and one goal has been devastated through a succession of serious injuries, depriving a procession of Pompey managers of the defender's ability on a consistent basis. In March 2015, he suffered anterior cruciate ligament damage to his left knee during a League Two match with Cheltenham Town, sidelining him for almost ten months. The former Neville Lovett Community School pupil returned strongly and would later start the opening seven matches of Kenny Jackett's reign as Pompey boss, the former Wolves boss having replaced Paul Cook in the summer of 2017. Another cruel setback once more intervened, with cartilage damage to his left knee collected during a training session signalling another five months laid low following knee surgery. With inevitability, Whatmough again forced his way back into Jackett's side, starting 35 of 41 Pompey League One fixtures before that fateful Fratton Park afternoon against Doncaster in February 2019.

Owner Michael Eisner sanctioned pioneering surgery at the Princess Grace Hospital in Marylebone, London, utilising a procedure which involved positioning an artificial membrane over the top of his problematic knee area to serve as a blocker once the repair had taken place. Injected with Whatmough's blood, the membrane now serves as a cartilage.

'I had reached 30 matches by February, the most I'd ever played in a season, holding conversations with the gaffer throughout. He kept asking: "Do you need a rest, do you need a game off?" Yet I had that mentality of playing regularly, in good form, confident and convinced I didn't require a break, I was fine. Looking back, I should have taken a game or two off, but didn't want to. Then, against Doncaster, I went to make a tackle and caught my studs in the ground. I felt it straight away, a bit of a pop, so booted the ball into the North Stand and sat down calling for the physio.

'A scan showed it was double the size of the previous tear. The one I previously fought back from was 1.5 cm – this was 3 cm and wiping out the original one in the process. I was playing the best football of my career, establishing a really good partnership with Matt Clarke and Pompey were chasing promotion. Then it all came crashing down. One of the best decisions I've ever made was to pluck up the courage to seek help through the Sporting Chance Clinic during those dark times.

'The gaffer and the boys were away on a week-long training camp in Dublin, so I called him to explain what was happening. He told me he understood; he had been injured long-term himself and provided his full support, which was so important to me.

'It was never on my mind to carry out an eight-week residential, I wasn't at that stage – I just wanted to know whether I was drinking and gambling for a buzz. In truth, I knew I wasn't enjoying it; it wasn't enjoyable one bit. At the Sporting Chance Clinic I spoke to Barry, who told me that everything stemmed from struggling mentally with being injured. "It's not you as a person," he reassured me.

'I was asked about sleeping patterns and admitted I wasn't dropping off until around 2am as I couldn't switch off. Apparently drinking can be connected with breathing patterns. It felt as if I'd had the weight of the world lifted off my shoulders after the first session. I immediately stopped drinking and gambling. I've been five times now and we are getting to the stage where talk isn't about negative things, it is focused on planning for the future, which is enjoyable.

'I genuinely thought that if I walked into that place they would batter me – *don't gamble, don't drink, don't do this*. It wasn't like that at all. It is explained that you drink because you aren't happy and are trying to forget. You gamble to receive a buzz, then you lose and aren't buzzing – it's a repeated cycle. "Yes," I thought. "That's actually it." I wasn't an alcoholic, far from it actually. I've had a drink since, but not anything silly, just one or two, and I've barred myself from betting apps and feel in a much better place. The truth was, I was mentally suffering.

'Now I didn't know this bloke from Adam, yet there I was talking to him and he was coming back with things I would never have thought of. They were points of view my missus would never say, that my mum would never say. It was fantastic getting a conversation with someone away from football and away from your actual life. During injury rehabilitation, there are times where you have the best day ever and walk away feeling a million dollars. The next day is the worst you've ever had; you simply never know what's coming around the corner. For instance, the other day I was running inside in the gym and felt a pinch in the knee and thought: "What's that?" I had been running for a month, then one day I didn't feel great, so I had a week off. There's no point getting too high or too low. I can now look at it that way, whereas before I would take the lows low and the highs high – and you can't.'

Whatmough was born in Portsmouth's St Mary's Hospital, but Gosport was home to him, growing up in The Parkway. The youngster would kick a ball around playing fields at Holbrook Leisure Centre, often while training with his brother, Tom. Following a trial at Gosport FC, a youth team, the coach informed his mum, Sarah, that the seven-year-old 'won't be a footballer'. However, Whatmough was handed his opportunity at Gosport Falcons, a group of friends managed by his dad, Gary.

Whatmough said: 'I went to Rowner Junior School and, when my dad left the Royal Marines, he took up a caretaker role at the school, just to keep an eye on me as I was a bit naughty! He'd come in every day and, as soon as he walked through the gates, the head teacher would say: "I need to talk to you about Jack." My dad turned around and replied: "Look, I'm here for work and running the school football team as a favour. Any problems, call Jack's mum!" They never called my mum, though. She has a presence which makes everyone scared of her, even me now!

'Anyhow, when I was around nine, I represented the year above against Gomer Junior School in the local schools final. During the game I had a nosebleed – the ball struck me right on it and it was pouring. I put two tissues up there and carried on. After the final whistle, a scout named Kev Neal told my mum and dad he would like me to go to the club he worked for – Southampton. Then Jan Rowles at Pompey contacted us, so I had two trials on the table.

'The first was for Pompey, held at the King George V Playing Fields in Cosham, and you had to wear all white. All I had remotely close was my Real Madrid kit, which my parents didn't think was appropriate, so we went to Asda and bought a plain white kit for about £5. Among those present were the Da-Costa brothers, Curt and Claude, at the time billed as the next big thing in Pompey. I played alongside Curt in defence and thought he was miles ahead of everyone; he was unbelievable.

'While the Pompey trials lasted a day, Southampton's stretched to six weeks, and, following a month, they wanted to sign me for their under-10s. The facilities at Southampton were very good, although it wasn't a big family club like Pompey. They had favourites in each age group and those favourites were looked after. I rose to under-14s, with Steve Moss as manager and, one Saturday following an 8–0 defeat to Chelsea, he stood in the dressing room and asked who thought they should get a contract for the next year. Nobody put their hand up, to which he responded: "That's wrong; everybody should put their hand up."

'The following week we lost 4–0 to Tottenham Hotspur and again he put forward the same question. Recalling what he had said the previous Saturday, me and another lad put our hands up. Then he told us: "No, nobody's getting a contract." Immediately, I questioned why I was wasting my time being there. The next day, my mum called those in charge of the Academy to query the situation and whether it was worth spending hundreds of pounds driving me around on Southampton duty if there was nothing at the end of it. She was reassured it was something said in the heat of the moment. Still, they offered to meet us.

'Taking up the offer, we were subsequently told Southampton had yet to decide on contracts, it was too early. Then Steve Moss looked at me and said: "Do you want to be here?" I told him I didn't and it was agreed I would leave. That Sunday night, Jan Rowles called and informed me Pompey were keen.

'The under-14s manager was Steve Stone, not the former England player, mind! It was agreed I would train on the Tuesday night at Admiral Lord Nelson School on the artificial pitch. I enjoyed it from the opening minute. It was the way he trained us, while the boys were a lot better, and I loved every second. I had played against Ben Close loads of times as a kid and he was there, as were Claude and Curt Da-Costa. I felt so much happier in footballing terms. After my second training session I was told a trial was no longer needed – and I signed. In the space of a week I had gone from Southampton to Pompey.'

Although he would eventually grow to 6ft 2in, concerns over Whatmough's height during youth set-up residence saw him held back a year by head of youth operations Paul Smalley to aid his development, dropping down from under-15 level. That decision was reversed by Andy Awford, shortly after taking over as Academy boss and, before the season was out, the defender was lining up for the Blues' under-18s. His first year as an apprentice involved a substitute appearance for Michael Appleton's side in a Capital One Cup fixture at Plymouth Argyle in August 2012. Following a purge of the first-team squad's senior players to slash the wage bill of a club embroiled in administration, the Blues named a fourteen-man squad featuring twelve teenagers, among them the lad from Gosport.

He said: 'They were bad days during administration and, as a first-year scholar, one month I didn't receive my wage, instead handed £10, although it was settled by the end of the month. We were quite lucky as apprentices though, and considering we lived in digs around the area, we didn't really need money. I didn't think anything of it at the time, but now I'm more grown up and knowing bills, looking back I understand the impact the club's financial issues had on the senior players. Imagine missing a mortgage repayment; you don't realise how deep things were. I know it's not the biggest thing, but when we trained at the Wellington Sports Ground, the food suddenly went downhill, from being served lovely meatballs to eating dry chicken, and that's when, as kids, we started to notice.

'Later, when the club were forced to leave our Eastleigh training base, we'd get changed at Fratton Park and travel to different places to train. On occasions, us Academy kids had to use the big car park next to the ground, now a Tesco supermarket, as there was nowhere else.

'We also had Tal Ben Haim drop down to train with us for a period as he was in dispute with the club and didn't want to leave. He was horrible, going around kicking us on purpose – it was toxic. We tried to have a laugh with him one day. Kane Cook, who lived in digs with me in Kirby Road, North End, once saw Ben Haim walking upstairs at Eastleigh and shouted: "Your laces are undone." They weren't, it was a little childish joke, but Ben Haim stood and glared at him. I thought he was going to beat him up!

'There wasn't even a gym for the first-team players to use. They'd have to pay for membership out of their own pocket, around £40 a month, and carry out the work in their own time. As a scholar, at least we had membership at Roko! In my second month of being a first-year scholar, I travelled with the first team for the first time, which was at Plymouth.

'On 34 minutes, our player-coach, Ashley Westwood, was forced off injured. I was warming up and the call came across. "Jack!" No way – I was coming on for my debut aged fifteen! Then I realised they were referring to Jack Maloney, who was next to me on the touchline. Of our three substitutes, I was the one unused in that 3–0 defeat.

'Dressing rooms can be intimidating places at times, particularly at that age, and the words of Ash Westwood before the game stick with me even now. He was geeing us up saying: "Be the best player on the pitch. I know *I'm* going to be the best player." He possessed confidence, and he could actually voice that in front of people. Wow. In contrast, I was naturally nervous putting the shirt on.

'It wasn't until September 2013 – thirteen months later – that I was next named in a Pompey squad, among the substitutes for the League Two trip to York City. For the coach journey, I sat at a table with Jed Wallace, Ricky Holmes and Simon Ferry, with Jed tipping me off that I had to ask the squad whether they wanted cups of tea. Apparently, it was the protocol, the duty of the youngest player. Not only that but you had to go around offering to make toast as well. I was pretty much the chef. They don't ask, you offer, every half an hour!

'Adjusting to the first-team environment was also helped by Dan Butler, who lived with me in Magdalen Road, Hilsea, and was two years older. He talked to me the entire time, settling me down, and even now we speak every other day. I have just asked him to be joint best man at our wedding in June 2021, along with Clark Denford, our assistant kit man. Jed also helped, such a massive character around the place. If the boys attempted to batter me with comments, he would batter them back for me!

'We lost that York match 4–2, a fixture memorable for the mistakes from our goalkeeper John Sullivan, who later apologised in the dressing room and then had a bit of a row with our first-team coach Alan McLoughlin! On the coach journey back, Jed read out a Tweet from a fan who had got in touch with Sullivan: "I heard you put your head into your hands after the game – and dropped it." We were all laughing.

'My debut arrived in November 2013 against Southend United – Andy Awford's first as caretaker boss following the dismissal of Guy Whittingham. It was brave of Awfs to put me in, to be fair, and years later I spoke to him about that decision and he was unaware I was only aged seventeen! We trained at Fratton Park on the morning of the game and, while carrying out laps of the pitch during the warm-up, he pulled me aside and asked how many tickets I wanted for that evening. I was starting! Unable to drive at that point, I walked to the train station and, on the way, called my dad to ask if he wanted to come to the match, without revealing the full details. He said he didn't! Being a Manchester City fan, he had never before attended Fratton Park. When I told him the reason, he came along among eight of my family.

'That night I partnered Sonny Bradley in the centre of defence and was up against the 6ft 3in Barry Corr, a big strong striker, and we lost 2–1. Afterwards, both Shaun Cooper and Johnny Ertl reassured me: "You did really well tonight, you should be proud of yourself." The following month, we travelled to St Mary's in the

FA Youth Cup and suffered a 7–0 defeat. I skippered a side which included Ben Close, Conor Chaplin, Brandon Haunstrup and Alex Bass. The next day, I was in a taxi heading to Gunwharf Quays to meet a few of the lads for tenpin bowling and a game of pool, just a bit of fun to take our minds off what had happened, when Awfs rang. He informed me he had good news and bad news. Then added: "The bad news is we lost last night and I wanted to see how you feel. That's football – when you suffer a heavy defeat you must deal with it." And the good news? I had been called up for an England under-18 training camp!

'I was actually driven to St George's Park in a black S-Class Mercedes sent by the FA and, upon arriving, saw Dele Alli and Ruben Loftus-Cheek. I was thinking: "Wow, I've made it!" In March 2014, I made my debut against Croatia in a side containing Ben Chilwell and future Pompey team-mate Bryn Morris, with Alli and Demarai Gray among the substitutes. Awfs and Richie Barker, along with my parents, watched us lose 2–1 at St George's Park. After the game, the Croatian lads wanted to swap shirts. Not a chance! It was my first England appearance and I was keeping mine – to this day it is framed and on the wall at home.'

Richie Barker's forgettable Pompey tenure ended following a dismal 3–0 defeat at League Two high-flyers Rochdale in March 2014. Whatmough played in central midfield for a third consecutive match, on this occasion partnering Toumani Diagouraga, a loanee from Brentford. The result left the Blues 90th in the Football League. Unsurprisingly, Barker departed by mutual consent within 48 hours, with Andy Awford taking over as caretaker boss for the remainder of the campaign. Immediately, the then seventeen-year-old Whatmough was restored to his customary position at the centre of defence for a remarkable late-season surge which would see Pompey retain their league status with three matches to spare. Success was on the horizon and, three years later, Whatmough started at Notts County in April 2017, a 3–1 win that yielded promotion on the way to capturing the League Two title three games later.

He said: 'After that Rochdale defeat under Barker, the changing room was horrible, the worst I have ever been in. The club was in a bad place. Awfs came in once again, initially as caretaker boss, and kept us up. He didn't do anything differently, training wasn't changed, he simply got the players onside, utilised the experienced heads and gave everyone the boost of confidence they required.

'When Paul Cook replaced him, it was a really good spell for the club. I know I didn't play too much, but what a changing room, with massive characters such as Kyle Bennett and Gary Roberts. His first campaign was 2015–16 and ended with elimination in the League Two play-offs at Plymouth. The bus journey home from Devon was the worst I have ever been on. No one spoke; not a word was said to each other.

'The following season we again challenged at the top of the table but, in March 2017, lost 1–0 at home to Crewe. There were those who thought we were done, that automatic promotion was over, but we were fifth with a game in hand and the changing room was well aware of that. Our next match was a midweek trip to Crawley Town and, the previous day, skipper Michael Doyle pulled us in for a team meeting in the training ground's common room. His address was basically: "Lads, it's in our hands. There are games coming up and if we win them we'll be in the top three. It's only us who can let this go now." It was mostly the older boys who spoke, before Amine Linganzi stood up and talked about his Christian beliefs. He explained that he had been in a Blackburn Rovers changing room which had all the money in the world and added: "But none of them possess the heart and passion of you." It was a lift which was probably needed.

'Following six wins in our subsequent eight matches, we headed to the County Ground in the knowledge that we could be promoted that day. We felt untouchable; we knew we were leaving League Two. With Matt Clarke struggling with a knock, I was handed my third league start of the season and a 3–1 win over Notts County earned us a return to League One. The team coach on the way home was full of alcohol, with Kyle Bennett on the microphone at the front, conducting us through old-school classics such as 'Take Me Home, Country Roads' and 'Wonderwall'.

'When we arrived back at Fratton Park, while getting off the bus with a beer in my hand I considering hiding it in case fans took exception, but one passed me a Budweiser, so I walked into a packed Victory Lounge with two drinks! Then I saw Michael Doyle on somebody's shoulders. After that, every single Saturday was win the game and go out and celebrate – it felt like four weeks of drinking!

'We thought Doncaster had won League Two, so were battling for the remaining two spots during the final three matches. Besides, there was that big rivalry with Plymouth in those days. They had knocked us out of the play-offs the previous season and we wanted to finish ahead of them; that was our priority. When we were crowned League Two champions, with Argyle in second place, it was probably more of a buzz to end the season ahead of them than topping the table.

'None of us expected to beat Cheltenham on that final day to clinch the title. It wasn't in our thoughts. During that 6–1 victory, Noel Hunt, who was injured, was at the back of the substitutes' bench keeping track of scores elsewhere on his mobile phone, informing us of updates. However, after our game finished there was a wait for final whistles elsewhere. It was only when the television in the home changing room showed the League Two table with a 'C' next to our name that we realised what had just happened. To stand in the directors' box and see pretty much every Pompey fan present on the pitch celebrating and singing was a special moment.

'Then, before the month was out, Cook left for Wigan. We had been discussing him being linked there in our players' WhatsApp chat, and I can even remember seeing one of the lads assure us the manager wouldn't go: "We've just got promoted and he'll get a bigger budget." We know how that turned out!'

Contracted until the summer of 2021, having signed an extended deal seventeen days before his latest long-term injury, Whatmough is fortunate to possess such security during ongoing rehabilitation. His continuing absence is being felt by the Blues, who have employed four different central defensive partnerships during the opening nine fixtures of the 2019–20 campaign. Among them is midfielder and newly appointed skipper Tom Naylor, while striker Oli Hawkins has been identified for centre half duty for the foreseeable future following a previous stint there nineteen months earlier. The uncertainty surrounding team selection at the heart of Jackett's defence reflects a poor start to the season which has left the Blues seventeenth in League One. Whatmough has been pencilled in for a return before the campaign ends, although is reticent to publicly declare his target date.

He said: 'I would advise anyone going through an injury to actually speak to someone, just for the opportunity to hear a different voice and receive a different opinion on how to deal with matters. I was told to take up different hobbies: snooker, golf, whatever. My routine was watching the boys train, carrying out some gym work, then returning home to watch football on the TV. I needed to take my mind off it. So I now play at Fareham Snooker Club and have taken up golf at Swanmore Golf Centre, and it really worked.

'My missus has known me since the age of eighteen and she knows what I'm like. I put on this massive front of being fine, but that's what men do, because apparently it's weak to not be all right. The truth is, there's no reason not to admit you are mentally struggling. I look at things differently now. I don't view myself as just a footballer any more; I'm a person as well. I feel healthier, happy within myself and all from a simple chat getting rubbish off my chest.

'My girlfriend tells me I'm a different person to the Jack she first met – and that's what I want. My family have seen a change too. I am a right lazy so-and-so at home, I really am, but now I do a little hoovering – it's therapeutic. It sounds stupid, but it's something to get involved in rather than sitting watching TV and thinking about rubbish.

'I don't know when I'll be back this season. There is a rough idea, but I certainly don't want to be putting out dates. It's important not to pile pressure onto myself to meet public deadlines. I will be back, I have no doubt about that, it's just whether the knee holds up and they have used one of the best surgeons around to make sure it does. The club have given me every opportunity. Mark Catlin is always there for me and one of our owners, Eric Eisner, texted his support. It is now down to me and I'm working hard to be back soon.'

Mark Catlin

16 September 2019

The rebuild was constructed from within, an indefatigable workforce supervised by a car salesman, an IT manager, an electronics manufacturer and a plumbing wholesaler. Bonded by Pompey passion, they galvanised thousands of like-minded folk, unskilled in the footballing field but prepared to gather up trowels to reassemble a club crumbling into the ground. Outsiders had almost demolished the club, devastating the valuable commodity they were entrusted with preserving. The Blues started afresh with foundations dug by their own, appointing a trusted Pompey Hall of Famer in Guy Whittingham as permanent manager. They had been failed by outlanders, so the subsequent siege mentality was entirely understandable.

There was one stranger among friends, an East Ender of West Ham United persuasion who once ran a Romford market stall selling albums and videos before shaping a Spanish telecommunications company. Upon the accession of fan ownership in April 2013, Mark Catlin was delegated chief executive responsibilities. Predecessors had perished while taking sides in the boardroom, crucial political miscalculations condemning them never to be welcomed back. The role had become toxified, a club figurehead to distrust – yet, six and a half years later, he remains at the helm.

Catlin represents an anomaly in football, an anchored presence in a transient industry. His longevity at a club previously known for its volatility is testament to the 53-year-old's commendable effectiveness. Outgoing and approachable, his impact was instant, re-establishing lines of communication torn down by previous owners. This fresh approach continues to be applauded. No longer a suspicious newcomer in their midst, Catlin has established himself as a popular figure at Fratton Park, a thirst for accessibility which even stretches to personally answering each email that lands in his inbox. Such engagement has drawn his attention to gathering discontent among supporters towards manager Kenny Jackett, following a fitful start to the 2019–20 campaign.

A return of five points from their opening five League One matches has dictated a seventeenth placing for the Blues, a disappointing start compounded by the cancellation of three fixtures before mid-September. Pompey's latest Fratton Park league outing was the 3–3 draw with Coventry City, an outcome which prompted many to turn on their manager. The visit of Burton Albion looms with increased pressure piling on Jackett who, for the first time in a two-year tenancy, finds his position publicly questioned among the Fratton faithful.

'Last year, I felt results exceeded the performances. This year, results haven't matched our performances,' Catlin admitted.

'You can't get away from the fact we have lost a couple of early games and it has put everyone under pressure because expectations are so high. We have to deal with it calmly, otherwise, should that pressure seep through into the manager and he starts making decisions alien to him such as coming out of his comfort zone to appease the fans, then things can unravel very quickly. We have seen it before at Fratton Park.

'The fans are very frustrated at the moment. They see the players we possess, but we aren't getting the results to match up to the management team and the footballing talent.

'As much as I defend Kenny – and I will defend him because he is such a great manager – ultimately, we are all judged by results. You don't want your team at the bottom of the league yet playing an attractive brand of football. People don't care about that, they want results. To a degree, I believe people will put up with a more direct style if positive results are forthcoming.

'Using my West Ham background, I can remember Sam Allardyce in charge, and when the team were doing well there were no complaints – but it unravels very quickly if you're not obtaining results. Having said that, there was a huge section of our fan base that didn't like Paul Cook's style of football, criticising it for being too possession-based tippy-tappy. After five minutes, you could hear people screaming to get the ball into the box.

'In the current situation, I believe we are looking at one particular game as the focal point of a lot of supporter frustration – Coventry. At Shrewsbury Town we were on top and unfortunate to lose to a wonder goal, while Sunderland was a pretty even game. Having said that, you can keep making excuses but games are won and lost in boxes – we've made some stupid mistakes in defence and not been clinical enough in the opposition penalty area.

'Yet the Coventry match, in the eyes of a lot of fans, has brought Kenny's leadership into question. Whether you are sitting on a till at Tesco or McDonald's, or chief executive or manager [of a football club], people make mistakes. Assessing the Coventry fixture, if Kenny had seen the game out for a victory then his decision to bring on a defender was vindicated, if he didn't then he made a mistake. You learn and get on with the next game; you can't dwell on it.

'The best snooker players are capable of producing a bad shot, but when they are next at the table must put that behind them. The poorer players dwell on it and, before you know it, they've lost a few frames and are out of the game.

'I am not making excuses for that Coventry draw, but I had a horrible, sickly feeling watching that match progress. They put us under pressure and we looked like nervous wrecks. You could feel the goal coming. You had the nagging feeling that was going to happen.

'Kenny has the ability to shut the criticism out. You must focus on what you believe to be right – if you do it consistently enough then you will get the right results.

'Some supporters these days can be very fickle and, whether you are a player or a manager, you can become a hero after a good game – and go from hero to zero on the back of a poor one.

'We know where we want the club to be, whether this year, next year or the year after. We won't make rash decisions.'

Jackett is the longest-serving manager of Catlin's chief executive reign. Following Paul Cook's decision to join Wigan in May 2017, just 26 days after capturing the League Two title with a 6–1 final-day demolition of Cheltenham Town, attention immediately switched to the former Wolves boss. In the final days of fan ownership, Jackett dominated the shortest of shortlists, with rising managerial talent Danny Cowley and brother Nicky who were impressing with Lincoln City also among the small number. As prime candidate, Jackett was invited to interview at the Godalming home of board member John Kimbell, a two-to-three-hour dialogue with Catlin, chief operating officer Tony Brown and club director Mike Dyer.

Jackett was unveiled in June 2017, with incoming owners Tornante in full support of the appointment. Once their takeover was completed two months later, they honoured an early pledge by handing their manager a two-year extension – 23 matches into his Pompey reign. It was a remarkable show of faith by chairman Michael Eisner, whose belief remains strong in a manager who has so far delivered League One finishes of eighth and fourth place, in addition to winning the Checkatrade Trophy.

Catlin added: 'We know what we are doing. We are built on stability, consistency, hard work and, ultimately, if you keep ticking those boxes regularly enough you will be successful. You must remain resolute in your beliefs. When running a business, you recruit someone, get them to do a particular job and, whether they have a bad month, two months or three months, if you still believe in that person you stick by them.

'We still believe strongly in Kenny, so you continue trying to assist, supporting, doing what you can to turn it around, because we certainly aren't changing for change's sake.

'We're striving to earn promotion, I have always said that, and I'm proud of the fact we're constantly seeking to improve on and off the pitch. Last season we finished fourth, so our default target this term is to finish higher than that.

'That's not to say if we finished sixth we would get rid of Kenny, because we wouldn't. Should he ever come to us and say: "Look, I think it's time for a change," then that's different, but at this moment it's not something we would look to initiate. There is zero pressure from the owners and board on Kenny. Kenny puts pressure on himself, the fans add to that, but he is a very experienced manager who has managed big clubs with high expectations. I believe he will come through it.

'If we appointed a new manager and he lost two games on the trot, supporters would call for him to be sacked as well; that is the nature of football these days. I don't agree with it and we are not going to buckle under it. Our first year back in League One was Kenny's honeymoon period. There was a new ownership, we had lost Paul Cook, quite a few players had departed and the new man at the helm was rebuilding. Last season was an improvement, finishing fourth and winning the Checkatrade Trophy.

'You can't argue with the fact that we are improving, but is it at the rate which is going to please all fans? That has always been the question for me. In my six full seasons previous to this, we have regressed just once in terms of league position, which was our second campaign under fan ownership.

'Our growth chart has been pretty much constantly upwards, on and off the pitch. We are reaping the rewards of stability and not making rash decisions. You look at clubs embroiled in a cycle of sacking their managers. They are the ones that keep going down and down and down – generally, the ones that stick with managers for long periods are those that achieve success.'

While Catlin's focus is on Pompey, flourishing business interests outside of football ensure his ongoing presence as chief executive is motivated by passion rather than financial necessity. As an eleven-year-old, he established a pitch at Dagenham's Sunday market, selling decorative dried flowers set in miniature wheelbarrows and wishing wells constructed out of sandpapered and varnished lolly sticks. The Barking-born entrepreneur later graduated to producing clothing, before obtaining a permanent stall on Romford market selling albums and videos. Yet it would be the foundation of what has become one of Spain's largest independent telecommunication companies, Telitec, that empowered Catlin to explore his footballing interests, the Alicante-based business providing a crucial financial bedrock.

Recruited as commercial director at Spanish football club CD Jávea, he climbed to the position of president, before returning to England in November 2009 to serve at Bury as a commercial director and board member for almost three years. Then, in October 2012, he volunteered his services at a club in administration and unable to offer a working wage – Portsmouth Football Club.

'As a very young kid, I always wanted to be prime minister because I wanted to make a difference in people's lives. Football has that same effect,' Catlin said.

'I am very lucky. I have a great business in a lovely Spanish coastal village called Moraira, which funds how I want to live. One of the first conversations when we came out of administration at Pompey involved the chairman Iain McInnes forcing a salary on me, as I was not receiving a wage. He was adamant there had to be a level of accountability and, if working for free, this couldn't be achieved.

'I have never been motivated by money, either here at Pompey or anywhere else. I've always been success-driven. When I arrived at Fratton Park it wasn't about the salary – there wasn't one – but how passionate Pompey fans were. As a West Ham fan, it took me back to how loyal and passionate my own club's fans were when growing up in the seventies and eighties.

'I always had a begrudging admiration for Pompey supporters, so to see the club's demise from afar compelled me to get involved and help.

'I have grown businesses, sold them and then moved on to the next one. I had a retail chain which was twice ranked in *The Sunday Times* Fast Track 100, selling CDs and DVDs in shops nationwide.

It was a huge business, called Music Box, but I could see the advent of the internet and the dangers it would pose to retail, so I sold it in the late 1990s.

'Then I moved to Spain, initially for a break, but stayed for twelve years, starting Telitec. Predominantly dealing with ex-pats living in Spain, it was inspired by my own experiences. As I found out, there was difficulty connecting to the internet and paying crazy costs to call back home. I remember it was the old internet dial-up at the time and very, very expensive, costing around a pound a minute to call the UK.

'It's not like that now, of course, but back then mobile phones were starting to find their feet and, with the deals I negotiated with the big carriers, I felt I could undercut and grow the market – it has since developed into one of Spain's largest independent telecommunication companies covering the whole of Spain and its islands. What started as selling cheap minutes back to the UK has grown into a national wireless network, offering mobile, wireless and fibre connections throughout Spain.

'I have very little to do with it now, but a great chief executive runs the business for me, although my stake remains 100 per cent. You can ask if I'm a millionaire and, while I would struggle this minute to write out a cheque for £1m, should I sell my company, like most people with successful businesses, the net assets would probably be worth far more than £1m. That provides a platform to carry out my role at Pompey through love, rather than being driven by money. I always believe that gives you a wonderful advantage and makes you better at it – it has never been a chore.

'Mind you, you think you're wealthy until you get involved in football. I was running CD Jávea, a club in the fifth tier of Spanish football, equivalent to the National League, with ex-West Ham defender Kenny Brown serving as my manager. He memorably scored the Hammers' winner against Manchester United in April 1992 to hand Leeds United the impetus in the race for the old Division One title.

'He is a thoroughbred when it comes to football and his dad, Ken, is a bit of a legend at Norwich City where he won the Milk Cup as manager in 1985, and he played alongside Bobby Moore,

Martin Peters and Geoff Hurst during the glory years for West Ham in the sixties. They once told me: "Mark, we love you, you are like family to us, but we must give you some advice. Become the chief executive at a football club – you get to make all the decisions but don't have to put the cash in! We don't want to see you losing all your money!"

'It's easy to do; you think you are rich, then you get involved in a football club and it can suck your money away very quickly. It's a beast, growing and growing, and the bigger it gets the more feeding it needs – and money is the food. That's a football club. It has always been a rich man's sport. The Championship has run away from League One and League Two, a gap influenced by parachute payments mixed with clubs desperate to get into the Premier League. It's widely known as a basket case of a league in financial terms. Owners think they can rewrite the rules in regards to how to run a football club – yet realise pretty quickly that they can't. Statistically, your playing budget dictates, to a large degree, where you finish in the league that season. It's not everything, but it is a huge contributing factor.

'The challenge at Pompey has always appealed. Initially it was great to help save the club and amazing to be part of a team containing the likes of Ashley Brown, Iain McInnes, Micah Hall, Mark Trapani and Mick Williams. It was difficult at times but, upon reflection, I look back fondly at that period.

'The day we exited administration it was a shambles of a club. There were still massive debts, it was continuing to leak huge sums of money, we had no kit deal in place, no training facilities, a demoralised workforce; you name it, we had every problem imaginable.

'For the first two years it was difficult on and off the pitch. We operated with a limited playing budget, not much bigger than clubs such as Accrington Stanley and Newport County, as we were still paying off debts and sorting the club out for the long term, while at the same time trying not to kill the ambitions of our fan base.

'We didn't have a rich owner to pick up the phone to ask: "Can you please throw in another couple of million this month?" We had to become disciplined – and the biggest movable feast at a football club is the playing budget. It's the only thing you have real flexibility in and can manipulate it to such a degree that it has a massive impact on your profit and loss and cash flow.

'We were under fan ownership and had just asked fans to each put in £1,000. Then there was the Tifosi crowdfunding scheme for our new training pitches. You can't keep going back to supporters, always wanting more.

'I actually have a lot of sympathy with those managers from the opening two years. The perception was that we possessed one of the biggest budgets in League Two – but we didn't. We kept hammering out the message to make sure people understood that. We were Pompey, but it didn't mean we had more money than Newport, for example, who at the time had a lottery winner as owner pumping millions in. We had debts and losses inherited as part of the deal to buy the club and they required addressing before turning our full financial attention to the playing budget.

'We had sorted out the losses and debts by the time Paul Cook arrived as manager in May 2015, allowing us to invest heavily in him and the team – and two years later we won League Two.'

Prospective owner Michael Eisner was present at an emotional Fratton Park for that title win, witnessing the escape from the division that had shackled the Blues for four years. Seventeen days later shareholders delivered the green light for Tornante's £5.67m takeover, with an emphatic 81.4 per cent of the club's equity holding agreeing to the sale. However, ahead of the August 2017 completion, Catlin contemplated an exit, his mission accomplished. Those who appointed him were preparing to relinquish control – and the chief executive agonised over whether to accompany them through the door.

'When Michael expressed an interest in buying the club, knowing his history and upon meeting him, I felt he was the perfect fit for us,' added Catlin. 'The feedback I received from fans centred on them wanting us to be sustainable, to have somebody engage with supporters, to care for them and respect the club's history and traditions. He ticked all the boxes.

'During the period of Michael attempting to buy the club, I'd made up my mind to leave for a fresh challenge. For me, it was about getting the deal over the line and waving goodbye, departing on an absolute high. Having arrived at a club on the verge of liquidation, I would walk away leaving it in profit, with money in the bank, in a league higher and a billionaire owner striving towards a bright future.

'Possibly on the back of Michael coming in and the feeling he would want to appoint his own person, I received some really attractive offers, from one top Premier League club in particular. Out of confidentiality I won't name them, but headhunters representing them called on more than one occasion. They explained that the club in question operated through an interview process and were keen on two other candidates. "We have done a lot of digging in football, and you seem to tick a lot of boxes," I was told.

'As they weren't offering me the job, I didn't feel there was anything to talk about. If I had gone for an interview and not been taken on, I'd have completely betrayed Portsmouth Football Club, even though at the time I was in a mindset to move on. Football's a small world, and it eventually gets out. In my time at the club I've had many offers, but can honestly say never once have I expressed an interest in pursuing or going after any of them. I think people within football pretty much know my loyalties are to Pompey.

'Still, on the eve of his takeover, I met Michael and he said: "Look, we need to sort you out with a contract." I informed him I thought it best if I leave, allowing him to recruit his own choice of chief executive.

'To be fair, Michael spent an hour talking about his history, using the analogy of chapters within the book. I felt I'd written my last chapter at Pompey, the book was finished, we had won the League Two title, were debt free, in profit – and now under new ownership. Michael explained these were still the book's early chapters, others required writing, and wanted me to be a part of them.

'That stuck with me and I've subsequently had two years with Michael as chairman – and I don't regret staying. I love the area, I love the club, and, despite not always agreeing with some of them all the time, I love my connection with the fans.'

The fracturing of Peter Storrie's relationship with the Fratton faithful heralded his bristling exit in March 2010, with escalating levels of abuse cited as the driving factor. As chief executive, Storrie had overseen Pompey becoming the first Premier League club to enter administration. With the Blues remaining in financial dire straits, three months later David Lampitt was appointed as Storrie's successor ahead of the 2010–11 season, their first campaign outside of the top flight for seven years. Lampitt's standing among supporters and club staff deteriorated significantly during his 21-month tenure. On his watch, following the passing of club great Len Phillips, twice winner of the old Division One title with the Blues and an England international, his family were quoted £1,575 for the wake to be held at his beloved Fratton Park. The event was instead staged at nearby Moneyfields Football Club, free of charge. Pompey were placed into administration by the High Court in February 2012 and six days later Lampitt was among 30 staff members handed redundancy. His replacement was Catlin, whose own stamp on the chief executive role continues to retain supporter respect.

'During my first couple of years, when the club was struggling, I said that should the time arrive where I felt I'd lost the fan base then I would leave, but I don't yet sense that. I walk around on match days and pretty much every person wants to come up and shake my hand, passing on messages to ignore moaners on social media,' said Catlin.

'If ever I believe I've lost that trust with the fans, I'll be the first to hold up my hands and move on. I try to be as honest and open within the realms of professionalism as I can be – I attempt to do things the right way.

'Sometimes doing the right thing isn't always popular, but the monthly question and answer session through our website helps my accessibility. Recently I've had criticism for my defence of Kenny, but I will continue running Q & As. Unfortunately, in life and society these days, a few people can spoil what most seem to enjoy.

'We've had to stop fans bringing drinks into matches, one of the reasons being that some were sneaking alcohol into their Coca-Cola bottles and getting drunk and causing trouble. Probably that is 0.0001 per cent of our support, but unfortunately that spoils it for everyone else. You can't stand there sipping everyone's drink to test for vodka or gin!

'During my time at Bury, I always attended fans' forums. I set up as many as I could as engagement is so important, and it's common decency. At Pompey we have instilled a 48 working hours policy for responding to emails from supporters. If the answer isn't from me, it will be a member of the relevant department, so everyone is accountable. When that was introduced, I believe it was unique in football. Previously fans would never receive any response, as clubs felt they didn't need to – but it's just decency. You can never take the support of fans for granted.

'I've been a football supporter all my life, and I treat people how I want to be treated. On a match day I can walk from the club shop to the South Stand and if someone asks for an autograph or to pose for a photo, then I will oblige. Growing up as a West Ham fan, if Trevor Brooking or whoever walked by and ignored me, I would be devastated. It means a lot to people and I hold a privileged position.

'I know that approach is different to most chief executives – and there are some good chief executives out there, mind. You must have a thick skin and, when things are not going as well as you hoped, maintain that approachability as some go into their shell and refuse to come out again. It happens to owners, too. They put money in, receive abuse and withdraw from the public eye.

'I come from the East End. I had a pretty rough background generally, and deep down that is who I am. I don't want to be someone I'm not, I want to be me. I like how I am and I don't ever want that to change; you are what you are. Be honest, be truthful, never put on any airs or graces attempting to be something you're not – fans always respect that.

'It's how I am as a person: I'm a fan, I love football, it's a passion, I like the highs and the lows, and it's an adrenaline rush for me. It affects people's lives.

'We are what we are, and this is a tough, working-class city. People don't earn huge money down here, but they like to watch a game of football and want passion, honesty and transparency – and I hope that's what they receive from me.

'There are clubs I would fit in at, and there are clubs I wouldn't fit in at – and I definitely fit in with Pompey because of my background.

'I love this club and always will, genuinely. It is a privilege and an honour to be chief executive of Portsmouth Football Club. I travel the country, I go to every away game, I wear a blue suit and put on the tie and am proud to represent this club.'

The escalating pressure on Jackett is a reminder of the level of demands within a supporter base now witnessing an eighth season outside the Championship. The last decade has seen nine different managers occupy the Fratton Park hot seat on a permanent basis. Catlin's own executive team includes chief operating officer Tony Brown and chief commercial officer Anna Mitchell, two key figures whose long-term presence has created essential stability during Pompey's renaissance off the field of play. Such patience does not endure on the pitch. The immense burden of expectation on a club perceived to still be below its rightful league position can weigh down on managers and players alike. From his vantage point, Catlin has witnessed casualties, robust characters crumbling under the strain of serving the Blues. Only the strong survive the Fratton roar.

He added: 'I believe my long association with Pompey provides me with an inner strength. You become battle-hardened. I have that experience of managing a club equipped with bigger expectations. I'm a lot calmer and less emotional than during the opening two or three years in the job.

'It's a little-known fact that after the 1–0 defeat to Crewe Alexandra at Fratton Park in March 2017, Paul Cook received absolute dog's abuse from fans immediately around the dugout and I felt was on the verge of calling it a day. It was a period when, for a number of games, the vitriol aimed at Paul had increased significantly, and no manager or player should have to put up with that, especially one who, like any diehard Pompey fan, wanted promotion.

'After the game, I went down to his office to check if he was okay, as I always do with our managers, and he was raging. We had quite an emotional meeting, and I reminded Paul how much I and the silent majority of fans thought of him and asked that he didn't do anything rash at the post-match press conference.

'He's very emotional, wears his heart on his sleeve, and I asked him to give things time, at least until after the trip to Crawley Town a few days later.

'To me, it was touch and go at that time whether Paul had had enough of the pressure he was under. People don't realise defeats hurt me and managers like Paul just as much as the fans, but we travelled to Crawley and won – and the rest was history. In the first minute, Michael Doyle flew in with a tackle and I knew we were well up for it. There was a big French flag among the fans and the 'On Our Way' song was born.

'We had probably reached rock bottom against Crewe, yet that seemed to lift us and we went on that remarkable run, picking up 31 points out of the final 36 to win the League Two title. What went on in that room after Crewe should remain confidential, but it was quite an emotional time.

'When any club finds itself in a league lower than it is accustomed to, it can create a difficult situation, whether you are the chairman, chief executive, and definitely if you are the manager or players. That's a key point I've learned during my time here: you must get people into the club who can manage that expectation and can manage that pressure.

'I have seen managers come here and completely fold. Good managers and good coaches have struggled with the pressure. I was at Bury when Richie Barker was boss and the players loved him. They would have run through brick walls for him, he was one of them, but it didn't work at Fratton Park. He has since moved to other clubs and, in differing roles, achieved success. I saw a completely different Richie Barker during his time at Fratton Park; it just didn't click. He is genuinely one of the brightest coaches around – you ask players at other clubs he's worked at – but it doesn't always fit. I have probably spoken to Richie twice since he left, which is a shame, but it just didn't work out. He has achieved success as a coach since, at MK Dons, Charlton Athletic and Rotherham United, and I still think could go on and become a manager elsewhere. Just not here.

'While the fans are extremely supportive, they are also very demanding. If we were in the Premier League or Championship, you would get a lot more leeway – but in League One, there is always the anticipation that, and with the greatest respect, we should be beating the likes of Burton Albion, Rochdale or Accrington Stanley.

'Let's not forget, it didn't work for Tony Pulis here either, yet he achieved success elsewhere. A number of managers have been at this club and, for whatever reason, it didn't click – yet they've gone on to achieve amazing achievements elsewhere.

'One thing I have learned since arriving at Fratton Park is that the character of players and managers is so important. There's a particular player this season – I am not going to name him – whose talent is unbelievable, but I did worry before we signed him whether he possessed the psychological strength; was he strong enough mentally to play for us? So far I have been very pleased.

'Look at some of the players we've had whom our fans haven't really taken to. Not naming names, I can think of one now in the Premier League and another in the Championship, yet our supporters weren't having them at the time. It's a demanding place. The role of Pompey manager is a pressure position and, given my experience now, I would never advocate bringing in a rookie boss here. You need someone who has managed at a big club, who has coped with pressure and expectation from the fan base.

'I now try to keep away from social media, yet very early on at Bury regarded it as a great tool, enabling me to judge the fan base's opinions – now I don't think you can. There's a minority of people always angry for whatever reason. Pompey could win the Champions League and the following year again reach the final, but they'll probably want to sack the manager and sack the chief executive, because they failed to win it once more – it's just how it is.

'People can have an opinion – I never have an issue on that – but when it is vitriolic and/or contains blatant lies which are clearly not factual, then it becomes hurtful. Hurtful to the point where you think: "Why do I bother?"

'Although I'm on Facebook, I now rarely go on there. I have to constantly tell my wife, Elaine, not to read out things people are saying – I just don't want to know. That's a shame, but there are plenty out there with agendas. I hate using the word, yet there's a lot of trolls as well, setting up fake accounts because they don't like you and are intent on hammering you. In fairness, I believe it's worse at other football clubs.

'Although, I have to state, one of my big selling points to managers and players is that you will never experience supporters like this at any other club.'

In the build-up to Burton's visit, Catlin has taken up the case of well-known Blues fan John Westwood, who the previous week had been refused admittance to England's Euro 2020 qualifier against Kosovo at St Mary's. Stewards at Southampton's stadium had prevented his entry on the basis of The Petersfield Bookshop owner wearing a Pompey shirt, in this instance the purple-coloured third strip. Renowned for his outrageous match-day attire, on this occasion Westwood sported an England hat, long black leather jacket and jeans, his standard uniform for international fixtures. Other supporters were granted leniency and simply instructed to cover up their Blues shirts, yet the 56-year-old's offer to turn his inside out was rejected because stewards felt he would still be recognisable and his safety could not be guaranteed.

Following additional reports of Pompey flags within St Mary's being removed by stewards, it prompted Catlin to seek an explanation from Southampton, who subsequently issued an apology.

Catlin said: 'In the strongest possible terms, we have spoken to Southampton, the Football Association and Hampshire police.

'As an England fan and the chief executive representing Portsmouth Football Club, I think the whole situation was handled very poorly.

'If, long before the game, they had taken the decision to prevent fans wearing Pompey shirts from entering the ground, they should at least have had the decency to contact us and allow us to deliver that message to our own fan base – whether we agreed with it or not.

'Sometimes John is right in what he says, sometimes he is wrong in what he says. In this particular instance, he was absolutely blameless. The definition of being advised prior to the game was actually him advised as he tried to gain access to St Mary's.

'We weren't best pleased with the treatment of many Pompey fans that evening. There were other instances where I believe stewards on the day used common sense and turned a blind eye to most of our fans, telling them to cover up their shirts, which was a sensible approach. It does seem, however, that on this occasion John Westwood was victimised.

'To be clear, for England games the stadium safety and security is passed over to the home club. It is supposed to be a neutral venue – so how it was handled has left a bitter taste in my mouth.

'I am very proud to be a chief executive and director of Pompey, and Michael is very proud to be chairman of the club, and we class fans as our own family. While we can have disagreements internally, we will protect any of our family in the wider football environment, if warranted. In this instance, I felt a member of our family was badly treated.

'Once we heard what had happened to John and others, we wrote to the FA and Southampton expressing our concerns. The FA responded and explained that, as all England games are held at a neutral venue, the decision was taken locally by Southampton – and I wasn't happy with Southampton's response.

'It does raise a bigger question about taking England matches on the road. The host club must remember this isn't a club game, it's an England game, and England attract people from different football backgrounds. If you can't cope with it or are unable to handle it, don't stage an England fixture.

'What happens when England play at Old Trafford? Do they stop Liverpool fans going in? I know we didn't prevent Southampton fans coming to Fratton when we hosted a Lionesses game in 2013.'

✳ ☾ ✳

Boos greeted the culmination of Burton's visit to Fratton Park. Brett Pitman's match-levelling penalty five minutes into added time may have left an impression on the scoresheet, but it was not enough to satisfy the Fratton Park crowd. Having fallen two goals behind after six minutes through strikes from Joe Sbarra and Kieran Wallace, shell-shocked Pompey's rescue mission was aided by John-Joe O'Toole's second yellow card, both cautions collected for impeding John Marquis, with 64 minutes remaining. Shortly before half-time, Ronan Curtis reduced the arrears with a close-range left-footed finish. That far-post effort tempered criticism among the home faithful when the interval was signalled, certainly vocally.

Gareth Evans was introduced for Ryan Williams on the right flank at the break, immediately injecting some much-needed drive with a string of quality crosses into the penalty area. The substitute earned recognition as *The News'* man of the match. How the lacklustre Blues had cried out for his energy and directness as they laboured in pursuit of Burton's lead, an alarming absence of invention made for a comfortable evening for visiting keeper Kieran O'Hara, regardless of the numerical advantage. Then, deep into stoppage time, Evans' corner was delivered from the right and, in the ensuing scramble, Pompey substitute Ellis Harrison cleverly controlled the ball high on his chest, only to be knocked to the ground by Jake Buxton, prompting referee Craig Hicks to point to the spot, with Pitman customarily clinical in his duties.

It proved to be the penultimate kick of the match. At the final whistle many of the home element of the 16,610 crowd vented their frustration, a substantial proportion directed towards the boss. A return of one victory from Pompey's opening six League One fixtures represented an unconvincing start to Jackett's third campaign in charge. As questions were raised over the manager's destiny, a contemplative Catlin mulled over his own Fratton Park future.

'My next challenge might not be in football,' the Blues' chief executive admitted. 'In all cases, I'd like to continue working with Michael, his family, Andy Redman and the board moving forward, but it may not necessarily be in the game.

'I have done a lot in football now and, while still desperate to get Pompey promoted, there are other opportunities presenting themselves away from the game, chances I've always sacrificed for football, but you can never say never.

'For me, it's always good to get out of anything on a high rather than a low. Should we get to the Championship, it would be difficult to leave, having worked so hard to achieve it, but maybe that's the time, who knows?

'You cannot pre-plan these things, they tend to happen naturally, something which feels right at that particular time.

'I'm just focused on getting this fantastic club back into the Championship and then, at that great moment, perhaps saying: "My work is done." From where we were, to potentially delivering the club to one division outside the Premier League with an amazing owner might just be a fitting end to my story.

'Michael [Eisner] uses the analogy that the Championship is another chapter, the sequel to this current story, so who knows? As long as I feel the fans, Michael and the board still want me here and I believe we are progressing, then I'll probably stay. However, if in my heart I feel I've lost the fans and the club isn't progressing, then I would take the decision to leave Pompey.

'I have acted – and always will – with the best interests of the club at heart.'

JOHN WESTWOOD
AND SAM MATTERFACE

24 September 2019

John Westwood's meticulously assembled hit list exceeds more than 1,000 entries, each phone number prefaced with a single word – 'Scum'. There have been a flurry of recent inclusions, unwanted intruders spewing vitriol down the line, but the ever-expanding tally of culprits' phone numbers has been maintained with chuckling diligence.

It is no longer personal – fifteen years of phone calls have numbed initial offence, outrage displaced by a desire for a spot of sport, serving as delicious retribution. The Petersfield Bookshop owner winces at staff exposed to abuse, understandably protective of those innocents caught in the crossfire during his running battle with Southampton supporters. With his mobile number systematically posted on message boards, Westwood largely remains the target, a burden he accepts with cheery countenance. The frequency of the phone calls has ramped up in recent weeks, a Carabao Cup pairing between the fierce south-coast rivals drawing John Anthony Portsmouth Football Club Westwood to the forefront of hostilities as a consequence.

In the build-up, Pompey's most recognisable supporter suffered the ignominy of being refused entry to St Mary's for England's Euro

2020 qualifier with Kosovo on account of wearing his beloved club's purple-coloured third kit. His plight, depicted in *The News*, drew little sympathy from those of Southampton preference – and the volume of phone calls multiplied considerably. The 56-year-old, however, exacts revenge by retaining the offending numbers, seizing on the complacency of those failing to withhold their identity, before taking the opportunity to exact his own brand of vengeance.

'The bizarre thing is these Southampton lads give it all that but know I am not a troublemaker. I am just a football fan,' he said.

'If they want a scrap, there are hundreds of people in Pompey that will give them a fight, so why go for me? I can't get my head around it. They've rung threatening to burn my shop down, stab me, hurt my mum and my kids, I've had all that, going back fifteen years. It's water off a duck's back, but I will never change my number though; I don't give into anything.

'My number is often put up on a Scummer website, so everyone rings it, but I save them, every single one. There's now more than 1,000 entered into my phone, while double or treble that amount have withheld their numbers. What I do, which works brilliantly, is initially respond with a text reading: "Your number has been noted, recorded and handed into the police to be monitored. Have a nice day." I don't hear back from 99 out of 100 of them; it's funny that!

'Best of all, using the numbers I've kept, I hand them out to the boys I know from following England around the world. We're a football family, we stick together and, as well as Pompey mates, there's boys from Liverpool, Millwall, Leicester City, Chelsea, Wolverhampton Wanderers, Bolton Wanderers, Exeter City, Charlton Athletic, Middlesbrough and Sheffield Wednesday. Proper fans. There's also ultras from France and Spain, and they're all happy to help me. You'd be surprised how many of those phone numbers later change. If Southampton fans want to play these games then that's their problem – they started this.

'The next tattoo I'm getting will be a parrot dressed up as me with a speech bubble coming out of it, which refers to an absolutely true story about a phone call I once received. There used to be a tattoo studio below my flat, which I had to go through to reach where I lived. Living there was a scruffy African Grey parrot called Compo and, one night, when I returned home a bit boozy, my phone rang and it was one of those Scum numbers.

'So I answered it, put it on loudspeaker and could hear this bloke saying "Westwood this" and "Westwood that", which caught the attention of the parrot, who started talking to him. Now Compo knows only so many words, which are sort of in the right context, but still spoken in parrot fashion, yet was now involved in a conversation with a ranting bloke on the phone. I stood there, taking in this surreal 30–40 seconds, then the bloke shouted: "Westwood, you are an idiot," before hanging up. To think he called me an idiot – he was the one talking to a parrot!

'The frustrating thing is when they ring up the shop and swear at members of my staff. What has that to do with football? Then there's giving us bad Google reviews, trying to affect my business.

'I don't do the internet, I never look; social media is not in my life, and I don't do Facebook. About fifteen years ago, I would visit message boards, but nobody likes reading bad words written about them. No matter who you are, that's going to play with your head, so I thought: "What's the point?", although I get letters every now and again.

'I have friends who are Scummers. Believe it or not, my solicitor, Richard Bayliss, is a Southampton fan and season-ticket holder, a lovely bloke who helps me with my football problems.

'I love the banter and all that sort of stuff. Admittedly some of our supporters take it to extremes, but I don't ever want to get involved in that sort of rubbish. I'm a football fan, and I enjoy the chat between the two groups.

'I look at this Carabao Cup game in two ways. The outcome will depend on how seriously Southampton take it, in terms of what team they put out, and whether they can handle the atmosphere. The close proximity of our fans and the actual hatred that will come from those terraces can be venomous, and in the past I've seen legs go on their teams.'

In the build-up, Westwood received an email from Southampton's Supporters Relations Team offering an apology for denying entry into the England fixture they had staged, citing a 'communication oversight'.

A club statement released to the media almost a week earlier had read: 'The police and safety plan around the game stipulated that any fan in this scenario would not be admitted for safety and security reasons. This was communicated to the fan in question on multiple occasions ahead of his arrival at the stadium.'

The Premier League club's claim of a prior warning was refuted by Westwood, with Pompey chief executive Mark Catlin taking up his case. Southampton soon admitted fault.

'Mark, bless him, chased it up. He asked if I minded him giving my number to Southampton – well I thought they were meant to have it! Then he told me they would prefer to email their response, so wanted my email. So much for having "communicated" with me before that England game.

'For the past 40 years, I've worn my Pompey shirt and an England hat to every England match. England represents England, but my Pompey colours represent what part of England I'm from. Our national side is meant to reflect every single football club in the country, from the professional level to non-league; it is for everyone, regardless of the club you support.

'I've seen Liverpool and Leeds United shirts worn at England games at Old Trafford, I've seen Manchester United shirts worn at the Etihad Stadium. I've been to Leicester City and seen the tops of their rivals. It's England. Fans mix at Wembley, they mix abroad.

'I have to accept that the way I dress for football may get me noticed. It's my own fault. It's not something I do to attract attention, it's because of my love for the club, but if I dress like that then I have to accept the flak that goes with it. It's one of those things.

'I wear my Pompey shirt at every other England ground, so why not St Mary's? I didn't go there to cause any problems, and I even offered to turn my shirt inside out, but was basically told I was too well known to be let in with the ticket I had bought.

'Some of their supporters have since said I am banned from St Mary's for peeing on the seats for a Carling Cup game in December 2003, which isn't true. What actually happened was, with eight minutes to go, I was dying for a wee but was told by stewards I couldn't as Manchester City fans had smashed up the toilets during a game the previous month. So, I went against the wall instead – it wasn't the seats.

'We're all looking ahead to meeting them at Fratton Park now, but in reality I can't see us winning, I really can't. They have too much, especially considering the problems we're having defensively at present; they're going to rip us to shreds.

'I can handle losing, it doesn't matter, as there is no pressure on us. They can't take the mickey if they win because they should do, it's expected. I just hope we don't get stuffed.'

Since 1958, The Petersfield Bookshop has been a fixture on Chapel Street, its Royal Warrant of Appointment balanced atop the crowded four-decked sign fixed above the entrance. His alter ego cavorts around football grounds in clown shoes, a stove hat and a blue-and-white dreadlock wig, playing a bugle and ringing a bell, but the authentic John Westwood resides at the family premises, overseeing business since dad Frank's passing in January 2006.

The shop's picture-framing facilities have seen it fulfil orders from the Queen and Prince Charles over the years, continued excellence recognised by the awarding of the Royal Warrant, making them one of only 816 holders across the world. Yet declining trade has threatened the shop's existence, a time-honoured profession devastated by the internet's emergence. At its peak, twelve staff were employed by The Petersfield Bookshop – today there are four, including Westwood.

In attempts to preserve its 61-year standing, parts of the premises have been converted into four retail units and utilised for rental opportunities, presently housing a pet shop, massage parlour, a Life Church and tattoo parlour. The next stage of development consists of planning permission to build four double flats above the shop, with additional proposals for an events area, sketched to hold 50–60 people, thereby offering theatre space for schools and groups.

Westwood said: 'I have two passions in life – football and the shop. It is a Jekyll and Hyde existence, from the tranquillity of the bookshop, which obviously has it stresses and strains, to the madness of football, which lets out your frustrations.

'I'm so proud of what my dad achieved, I love the book trade and love the people, but how we are still here I don't know. The book market has changed completely, and trade has dropped off an incredible amount.

'I am young to the trade at 56. There's not much young blood coming through, and you are not going to make money out of it. All I need is to have a few beers on Saturday and watch Pompey. If I can do that then I'm fine. I'm not worried about the hours I have to work, just as long as I can see my football.

'Our trade has been one of the hardest hit out of everyone. People get their information from the internet, so why would they need lots of books? Not only that, people's way of life has changed and fashions have altered. Now it's minimalist and people don't want rows of books in their home; now they prefer pictures and a plant – they want it to look like a doctor's waiting room.

'The next generation will probably reinvent it: "Books – what a great idea." You never know, things do change. LPs came back, flared trousers went out of fashion and returned, but it will never reach the levels it once was for obvious reasons.

'It's hard and we've had to diversify. We have lots of plans as you can't sit on your laurels, and I want to carry on my dad's legacy. He was known throughout the world, attending book fairs in Boston, New York, San Francisco and Japan. Hopefully my children – Marcus and Yasmin – can one day get involved in the business.

'And if the internet crashed tomorrow, we would be millionaires because people would want books again!'

Westwood sold his Station Road flat in Petersfield in 2013 to finance the shop's ongoing survival, a sacrifice which also involved giving away beloved cats Pompey, Fratton and Chimes. He moved in with friend Mark Murphy in Cosham.

For the last three and a half years he has lived in the shop's upstairs office, a foldaway camp bed crammed between a sauna, piles of books and his computer, while an unopened pack of Rat and Mouse Killer Block Bait lies adjacent to his sleeping arrangements, ready to combat the return of unwelcome visitors. There is no shower and the sink in the downstairs toilet suffices for a strip wash, while a camping stove and microwave provide eating options, although Westwood's preference is a hearty lunch at Poppins Cafe or the Tai Tong Chinese restaurant, with bananas, apples, cherry tomatoes and cashew nuts serving as a healthy dinner in the evenings. There is no television, but he recently discovered Amazon Prime can be accessed through his Acer computer, offering film opportunities never before considered. As for the infrared sauna, it represents residual from his former flat. A prized possession, Westwood excitedly swears by its 'health benefits'.

At weekends, he is allowed to stay at fiancée Jacqueline's house in Titchfield, which also provides opportunity to utilise his partner's shower. An Earl of Southampton Trust home, there is a stipulation that non-residents can stay only for up to twelve days a year. However, considering his own living circumstances, Westwood has struck an agreement that means he can visit for weekends.

'I'm not worried about myself. I have football and enjoy the job; I have never been materialistic about things.' he added.

'I do miss my flat. It had Pompey carpet, Pompey wallpaper, the ceilings were decorated with Pompey scarves and flags – now all my stuff is in storage and I am dreading checking on it. Most has been in a Leigh Park garage for six years, the other is in a friend's Portakabin near Chichester, which I know has leaked and my belongings are going to be ruined.

'I've become used to living in my office. At the end of the day I have always been adaptable to situations. You don't get anything in life without hard work and I've never been frightened to get my hands dirty.

'If I'm honest, I'm a bit of a wuss. I hate spiders and I have had rats up here. I've even bought some rat poison, but you've got to get on with it. I am lucky enough as there are other people so much worse than us, other countries, starving with nothing to drink. Us Westerners don't understand what real poverty is.

'We have people sleeping at night in the forecourt of the shop. It's enclosed so it protects them from the weather, and we take them out coffees. When you look at that, at least I've got somewhere to sleep. There is always someone worse off.'

It is time for the transformation once more, the bookshop owner's metamorphosis into football fan rendered through outrageous clothing and singular behaviour. The Carabao Cup fixture is tagged as the biggest-ever football police operation in Hampshire history, utilising riot police, helicopters and drones for the first encounter between the sides in seven and a half years.

Southampton have won once in 43 years at Fratton – and the man in the stove hat and clown shoes will take up usual residency at Row Z, seat 70 of the Fratton End hoping that statistic will not be amended in their fierce rivals' favour.

'I was a late starter,' added Westwood. 'I wasn't really a football fan for a long time, but into horse riding. I had my own New Forest pony called Grimmy. If anything, I was a Leeds United follower. They were the team in the day and I was the glory hunter watching them on *Match of the Day*.

'Then, on Boxing Day 1976, my dad took me aged thirteen to watch Pompey play Brighton & Hove Albion at Fratton Park. It wasn't the football, but the atmosphere – I was hooked. I loved the passion, the smell of the ground with the old cigarettes and, if I am honest, the danger. Being a young lad, I was fascinated seeing skinheads and dangerous people – and there really were dangerous people.

'In 1989 I changed my middle name to Portsmouth Football Club. It was the natural thing to do because Pompey's my life – it just seemed obvious to incorporate that into my name. I had been married for three months and hadn't told the wife!

'Then there's my instruments and clothes. I've had a few bugles, while the current bell is purpose-made, using the top of a fire extinguisher, which makes it last longer than others over the years. Mind you, I think I'm going deaf from using it so much.

'The clothes are a mishmash. We played Chelsea at home in the FA Cup in March 1997 and a friend of mine owned a tall hat, which I wore for the match rather than my usual cap. I liked it so much it remained, and a year later I bought the stove hat I currently wear. My ex-wife gave me the blue plastic wig for a Christmas present, while, for my 35th birthday, a friend, Lin Cowdrey, made me a waistcoat with BGO embroidered on it, standing for Blundering Great Oaf.

'Then, in a Norwich pub, Dave Anderson, who used to play the drums with us at matches, told me he had some blue-and-white chequered trousers and suggested I got some too. When I had tattoos done to my legs, I decided to turn the trousers into shorts.

'As for the shoes, kids said I looked like a clown, so I started wearing these cheap clown boots which soon fell apart, so I replaced them with proper £320 ones, with £40 import duty from the USA. After all, football is meant to be a laugh.'

Adrian 'Bunny' Redding immediately recognised the latest press patron approaching his Fratton End booth seeking to collect an allocated media pass for the evening's visit of Southampton.

'Didn't I send you off once?' he asked Sam Matterface.

It is almost twelve and a half years since the talkSPORT commentator last visited Fratton Park in a working capacity, an occasion which signalled his final match at radio station 107.4 The Quay. The May

2007 goalless draw against Arsenal, in which Darren Cann's flag ruled out Niko Kranjcar's potential match-winner for offside, deprived Harry Redknapp's side of a UEFA Cup place. That summer, Matterface departed for Sky Sports News before joining talkSPORT in July 2010, seeking a return to his cherished commentary roots. As a freelancer, the 41-year-old supplements income through football television work with ITV, while he is presently involved in commentary duties on the station's *Dancing on Ice*.

Yet it was The Quay which presented the Dartford-born Chelsea fan with the break he craved. At the age of 23, he arrived at the Twyford Avenue radio station which had replaced Radio Victory, establishing himself as a popular listening figure alongside co-commentator Mick Quinn and later Alan McLoughlin. During stints with five-a-side football team AFC 601, Matterface also encountered Pompey steward Bunny, a well-known local referee of 23 years' experience who once booked a Portsmouth Sunday League player who passed wind in his face as he examined the studs on the culprit's boots, a story which made national headlines in 2009.

A familiar face to greet the commentator upon that long-awaited return on a day which began with an irritated Matterface taking talkSPORT colleague Danny Mills to task live on air. The mocking Mills' belittling of that evening's south-coast clash as existing on 'page seven or eight' of world derbies had triggered some.

'I can't believe it has taken so long,' said Matterface. 'I've been back to Fratton Park to watch games, attended Hall of Fame evenings, visited friends in Portsmouth, I even had a house down here until 2016, but haven't been able to cover a match.

'We had to fight for this game, too. As soon as the draw came out I was off my seat at my Manchester home saying: "I'm going back, we're covering it." Then I had to ring the talkSPORT football editor and explain: "This is really big. At this round of the competition you won't get a better atmosphere, you won't get a better story. This is it."

'During the build-up, you read quotes from Ricardo Rocha, who played for Benfica against Sporting Lisbon and Porto, saying this runs deeper, while Lomana LuaLua, who has represented Olympiacos against Panathinaikos, claimed this derby is on another level.

'I don't think people on the outside realise that – and I started the morning by giving Danny Mills my opinion on talkSPORT because he suggested it wasn't a big derby. I got a bit emotional, and I let myself down. I have listened back to it and it sounds all right, but I got annoyed and I think that's wrong. I should have been a little more 'stand back', giving facts and backing up my argument rather than going in with a beating heart thinking: "This is my derby, it's the most important thing in the world." That's how it came across, and I don't think I put it into context as much as I should have.

'I was already scheduled to go on air this morning and, just before I opened my mouth, a producer, very cleverly I think, whispered in my ear: "By the way, Danny says he doesn't think it's really a derby."

'The producer wound me up enough, he got what he wanted, and I stupidly fell for it! I opened by saying: "Have you booked Danny a doctor's appointment because he seems to have lost his senses."

'If you've been involved in it and attended one, you know how tough it is. Danny Higginbotham also joined in saying it's the fiercest one he has played in – and he appeared in April 2005, also my favourite Pompey game covered.

'I can still recall it now: "LuaLua LuaLua and Portsmouth are thrashing Southampton", I've heard it so many times. The Quay played it over Queen's 'Don't Stop Me Now' every day for the next God knows how many days. Even now, whenever I hear that song, I think of that game.

'That was probably the best half of football I have ever commentated on. I can't even remember the second half, and I don't think anything happened.

'It's a ridiculous story, the whole thing, Harry Redknapp coming back, LuaLua scoring twice and then going off a minute later following a somersault celebration – it's ludicrous! It was a great occasion to be involved in. It was three days before my 27th birthday so I had either been out the night before or was going out afterwards – it was probably both, I was young at the time!

'I can remember it all. In the tunnel afterwards, my first question to Alain Perrin was: "How worrying is it for you that the best result you will achieve is so early in your Portsmouth career?"

'As for the opposition manager, it was always irrelevant to me, apart from on this occasion. I chased Harry down the tunnel and I got him to talk to The Quay live on air. I said: "Harry, how are you. You okay?" He went: "No, not really Sam, no."

'So I followed it up with "How difficult was it?" to which his response was: "It was horrible, I didn't like it, I didn't feel comfortable."

'He never really wanted to go to Southampton – he did it out of spite towards chairman Milan Mandarić following all the problems between them.

'It was crazy. It won't be as bad as that today – it won't be, it can't be, simply because those circumstances won't happen again. Hopefully there'll never be a situation where Portsmouth and Southampton are struggling against relegation in the same league in the same season. There won't ever be a situation where one manager leaves a club to go to their south-coast rivals. Those circumstances won't come together again, so that's the greatest story of a derby there has ever been in this area.'

Matterface's broadcasting pathway began at Orpington Hospital Radio in 1992 as a fourteen-year-old, branching out into mobile disco work at weddings and other occasions. At the age of twenty, he became McDonald's' youngest manager in UK history, overseeing firstly Bexleyheath and then Sevenoaks branches, culminating in an invitation to Chicago to commemorate the group's 25th anniversary of opening their first restaurant in the UK.

The media remained an irresistible lure, Matterface's relentless pursuit of entry consisting of firing off a CV and demo tape to almost every radio station in the country, yet receiving just two positive responses, from Radio Kent and Radio Suffolk, yet no offer. Eventually

Capital Gold supplied the opportunity, while he also produced in-house videos for Wimbledon Football Club during the course of a season. Then, in July 2001, Matterface joined The Quay for a six-year period of commentating on Pompey, coinciding with the Division One title under Harry Redknapp, four Premier League campaigns and six south-coast derbies.

'My first derby at St Mary's was in the Carling Cup in December 2003. I didn't know where I was going – I hadn't been there before – so parked my car not too far from the ground. When I returned following a 2–0 Pompey defeat, every vehicle on the road had been smashed up – apart from mine at the very end. It had The Quay logo plastered across the car doors, yet was untouched, so who do you think was responsible!

'In January 2005, again at St Mary's, it was the FA Cup and Greek goalkeeper Kostas Chalkias was making his debut having just signed. I had Pompey players Steve Stone and David Unsworth doing commentary with me and, when Chalkias dropped one in during a 2–1 defeat, Stone uttered: "Beware of Greeks bearing gifts."

'When Harry was unveiled as Southampton manager in November 2004, I was at the press conference, standing at the back of the room at St Mary's, just being busy. I waited until the very end, just when it looked like it was wrapping up, and asked: "Harry, after being at Pompey for as long as you were and involved in south-coast derbies previously, did you not think for one minute that it wouldn't be a very good idea to become the manager of Southampton?" He got annoyed, like he does, and blustered his way through it.

'A year later I received a call from him on the landline at his Sandbanks home and he was going: "Sam, Sam, there's a bloke in a boat at the bottom of my garden trying to take pictures of me through my windows." Once I advised him to shut the curtains, he carried on: "I can't believe this; all I want to do is just come back and they won't let me." That was Harry, floating things and getting me onside early on. It was clear he would return to Pompey.

'He and Milan had a horrible relationship on occasions. I have never told this story on record before, but at the end of the 2003–04 season, their first in the Premier League, Pompey had beaten Middlesbrough 5–1 at Fratton Park, with Yakubu netting four times.

'I was outside the tunnel having handed the microphone to Harry while Mick Quinn, sitting at the back of the stand, was asking the questions. About twenty yards to Harry's right was Mandarić, carrying out another interview.

'Now Harry would sometimes get distracted in the middle of a live interview and had noticed Milan. Holding the microphone while talking, he turned around, pulled the microphone down and pointed to Mandarić mouthing a very rude word – and you could sort of hear it, despite him not saying it vocally! To think at the time they were denying they disliked each other!

'With Harry, he would hate you one minute and love you the next; he would move on, and it was brilliant. You could have a row with him, stand up to him, and then he would just forget it; he didn't bear grudges for long.

'He was fantastic for Pompey and I spent so much time with him – I had the good, the bad and the ugly. Harry made the mistake of going to Southampton but had the balls to come back and take the flak and I was impressed by that.

'Unfortunately, I don't think he will ever get the status he deserves at Pompey because of that; it was a stupid thing he did.

'I attended the 2008 FA Cup final as a fan, as I had left to join Sky Sports the previous summer, so Chris Wise commentated on the game. He had rebuilt the team again, bringing in the likes of Lassana Diarra, Glen Johnson, Jermain Defoe, Sol Campbell, David James and Sylvain Distin – we are talking about Pompey here. That was the best side anybody had seen apart from going back to the early 1950s. An outstanding football team of renowned names.'

Matterface quit The Quay to join Sky Sports News in July 2007, the forthcoming campaign producing an FA Cup triumph and Pompey's highest top-flight finish for more than half a century. On the day of his departure, it was announced The Quay's owners had formed a joint venture company with Pompey, the club possessing a 26 per cent stake in a partnership which also consisted of Spirit FM in Chichester and Isle of Wight radio. Pompey, under new owner Sulaiman Al-Fahim, bought the station outright in August 2009, yet it was put into administration within twelve months and, in July 2010, was sold to Celador and replaced by The Breeze.

'In my eyes The Quay was incredibly important. I got really lucky as the people who owned the radio station were The Local Radio Company, who didn't have a clue about football, but they knew about broadcasting and they knew I could broadcast. They took a punt on me. I was a kid, 23 when I came down, and had free rein.

'I really wanted to get into the media and, having quit my job at McDonald's, was in Elephant and Castle, London, on my way to a seminar on leafleting as I was trying to get into digital marketing. I received a phone call from Mark Browning, programme controller for TLRC, who asked what I was doing. I made up a lie on the spot: "I'm just walking into Capital Radio to sort out my contract for the new season."

'Their response was: "Don't sign it. I want you to come down and talk to us before you sign that contract." I replied: "I can't just not turn up for a meeting." He said: "Tell them you are ill and come down to Portsmouth to see me." So I did – and moved down the next day.

'What we did really well was to make it local, make it just about Portsmouth. At the time there was nothing solely for the city, so we knew it was the golden ticket. We didn't care what was happening in Southampton or Winchester, we only cared about Portsmouth. Wave 105, Power FM, Ocean FM, Radio Solent, they had to straddle different cities, but we didn't, so that was our USP – and it worked.

'In the first year, football was making up just 10 per cent of the output, yet eventually became what The Quay was known for. Pompey were promoted to the Premier League in our second year, extra programmes were added, rising to a show every night from Monday to Friday, and basically football began to bring in all the money. We paid £42,000 for Pompey rights to begin with. That became £100,000 for the second contract for a team then in the Premier League, and then, for the final one while I was there, it had reached £125,000.

'Quinny was my best signing and that happened because I had free rein to do whatever I wanted. I couldn't find anybody I liked. I tried Paul Hardyman and Albert McCann in pre-season friendlies and wanted someone I knew.

'Our first game was at Wolverhampton Wanderers on the opening day of the 2001–02 season, with Shaun Derry as co-commentator as he was unavailable to play. He was also simply there because Quinny was driving a hard bargain! Initially he said no straightaway, so I kept bothering him and it got to the point where my group editor asked if I wanted him to get someone – basically it was "You've had your chance!"

'I knew I wanted Quinny, though – I just had to get the deal over the line and in the end agreed to £250 a game, which was huge money for us to pay, ridiculous. We couldn't do anything else as there was no other money apart from that – he had it all! However, he was brilliant and he made the coverage. You need someone who connects with the supporters and we were a good partnership who got on well. We still do.

'Steve Stone was given a show, but it was actually going to be 'Mickey Quinn's World of Football'. Quinny had left by then, yet we were going to pay him just to do that programme, putting an ISDN line into his house, but it didn't come to fruition.

'My worst moment was the day I left for Sky Sports – and discovered The Quay had been sold to Pompey. They sent me a note basically saying: "Thank you very much. We would never have been able to sell it if it hadn't been elevated to this status" and I was heartbroken. I had handed it over and walked out of the door, that's it. I never knew anything about the sale until after I had gone.

'We were an independent media outlet prepared to be critical and had an agenda different from the club's designs. Being sold to Pompey ended up diluting the product. You become the club media, and fans are going to see right through it. How could you continue being independent, giving objective criticism? They sold it for £1.2m.

'In 2000, they bought a loss-making radio station, which was the old Radio Victory, registering less in Portsmouth than BBC Radio 3, and it rose to earn a Sony Gold award for the best radio station in the country and registered a huge listenership. Well done to them, fantastic, but selling to Pompey ruined the radio station – it was dead within a few years.

'I love the area, I love the people, I love the time I spent here; it was the defining period of my career, and what a great time to be at Pompey. Oh and yes, I also love that Pedro Mendes commentary!'

Under the talkSPORT banner, Matterface would call his first Southampton victory at Fratton Park, the Premier League club cantering to a 4–0 success. Pompey's opening 21 minutes consisted of hitting the outside of the post, a flashing half-volley diverted over the crossbar by the slightest of deflections and Christian Burgess unable to convert from close range following a goalkeeping intervention.

Then, in their first attack, Ralph Hasenhüttl's side seized the initiative through Danny Ings. Raised in Netley and of Southampton persuasion, it marked the first of two first-half goals from the ex-Liverpool striker, with Cedric and substitute Nathan Redmond sealing the comprehensive outcome in the second half. The visitors may have been deserved victors, but the powerful performance of a Fratton faithful whose remarkable volume was undiminished by the scoreline earned praise, even from an impressed Hasenhüttl during post-match interviews.

Hampshire police reported five arrests at the game, including a 52-year-old Portsmouth fan on suspicion of animal cruelty, having swung a punch at Thames Valley police horse, Luna, in a curious moment captured by video.

'They will never compete with Pompey fans off the pitch,' said Westwood. 'Yes, they can beat us on the pitch, but they are not a proper football club in my eyes – and in the eyes of a lot of fans from neutral clubs.

'There is not a lot of respect for Southampton; nobody regards them as an old-school club. They are something of a nothing club, always have been.

'That's not just me looking at it through blue-tinted Pompey glasses, that is a conversation I have had with people. Play Up Pompey.'

LEE SMITH AND DINO NOCIVELLI

29 September 2019

The dreams are excruciatingly vivid. Infinite reruns of the same terrifying scenario which conclude with the screams of Lee Smith. The gun-wielding man of unfamiliar appearance can never be outrun. Smith's sprinting legs inexplicably seizing up as the escape route lingers longingly in the distance, his voice depleted, rendering pleas for assistance inaudible. Then it ends. This was supposed to be closure, yet Smith remains haunted.

In June 2019, former Southampton Football Club youth coach Bob Higgins was sentenced at Winchester Crown Court to 24 years and three months in prison on 45 counts of indecently assaulting 24 boys. He was convicted of sexually touching and groping victims between 1971 and 1996, among them Smith, who waved anonymity to reveal the grim details of his ordeal.

Despite Pompey allegiances established through his upbringing on a Landport council estate, he signed for Southampton's Centre of Excellence at the age of twelve as a striker with a prolific return. During the next three years, the former City of Portsmouth Boys' School pupil established himself as an outstanding prospect at The Dell and once scored 360 goals in a single season, playing for five different teams at the age of thirteen to fourteen, his rich promise rewarded with an invitation to England youth trials. Accompanied by Alan Shearer in attack, the youth team duo offered a tantalising glimpse of a goal-laden future.

Then, at the age of fifteen, Smith severed his ties with the Division One club, refusing to continue attending training sessions. When a letter demanded an explanation for his reasons, he cited cruel 'Scummer' jibes from fellow pupils in reference to his association with Southampton which was impacting his school work.

With his release eventually secured, the striker signed apprentice forms at Fratton Park in July 1988, alongside a golden crop of Blues talent, including Darren Anderton, Darryl Powell and Andy Awford. It wasn't until December 2016 that Smith revealed the truth behind that abrupt Southampton exit – Higgins. His testimony subsequently helped convict his tormentor, ensuring justice was served after more than 30 years, yet Smith remains imprisoned.

'I am still struggling today. You want to try to move on, but you can't. There are still flashbacks and nightmares. I get paranoid going out and I need to be with someone because I feel I'm being followed – I am always looking around,' said the Cosham builder.

'There was a time when I was paranoid about what people thought of me. Some made it clear that they doubted my claims about Higgins. I hated going to Fratton Park because everybody was looking at me.

'Now the paranoia centres on thinking somebody is following me, ready to kill me. I don't know if there is, I can't say whether anything like that could happen – I very much doubt it – but it's at the back of your mind. You are a crucial witness in a court case that put someone away for 24 years.

'There is no closure for me at the moment. I know Higgins is locked up, but there's no closure and I don't think there ever will be. There are always things going on at the back of your mind.

'After his conviction, I thought that would be the end, but it's not. It has been almost four months since the sentencing and it's still terrible. It has become a little easier knowing he's locked up every day and can't commit anything else to other children, but the whole court process plays on your mind, being there every day, listening to other players' stories, seeing him in that dock.

'I'm having bad nightmares at the moment. It began a couple of weeks after sentencing. The dream starts with this man visiting Higgins in prison. They are having a conversation and I can hear him being instructed to take me out. Then, when he eventually finds me, he starts pursuing, carrying a gun, wanting to kill me.

'Nothing changes in the dream. I'm trying to scream "Help, help" and there's nothing coming out. He is getting closer and closer, then I wake at exactly the same point, startled and sweating. My wife, Tracey, tells me she knows when I've had that dream as I'm kicking, lashing out, shouting.

'I've obviously had nightmares before, but nothing like this. It's not that I'm afraid to go to sleep – as soon as my head hits the pillow I'm gone. It happens on days when I haven't even been thinking about Higgins, he's not on my mind, but I've now had the same dream a dozen times.

'I'm not the only one of us having bad dreams. I've spoken to others, but theirs have been different. A few weeks ago, I saw a psychologist on Harley Street who told me that I'm suffering from post-traumatic stress disorder. Apparently it will go away in time, I don't know when.

'They offered me counselling, but I can deal with it myself, especially after what happened last time. The medication back then gave me suicidal thoughts, messing with my head, and I didn't know where I was. I don't want to go down that road again. They were my worst times, dark days.

'Counselling involved talking about things over and over and over again. I don't want to talk about it. We've done what we've had to, we've got justice, and I want to try to move on, but there's one thing stopping me – the dreams.

'If it wasn't for them I would be fine, absolutely fine, but the nightmares are holding me back. I can't get closure.'

Of all of Higgins' victims, Smith counts himself among the fortunate ones – he escaped. He recalls the exact moment he realised he had to get out, while carrying out heading drills at The Dell's gym, a standard routine involving jumping above Higgins in an attempt to win the header. Without explanation, the coach furtively seized Smith's genitals, squeezing and twisting them to send the youngster crumpling to the floor winded. The aggressor then stood over sneering: 'Get up Smithy, you puff.'

For the remainder of the session, the fifteen-year-old stood by the doorway, refusing to take part. Once changed, he never returned to the club.

He added: 'From what I heard in court, I feel quite lucky. I was groomed more than others – but they had more sexual contact with Higgins than I did. In contrast, I had just the one incident of a physical nature, which was in the gym.

'There were probably other occasions which I didn't realise, like when he gave us naked soap water massages, rubbing intimate areas and being incredibly intrusive. He could have abused me a dozen times without me even knowing. Every player had those massages, you go along with it, it doesn't even enter your mind what might be happening.

'Now I'm older, I look back on things and can recall two tournaments in Sweden when he carried out naked soap water massages, never in England, always abroad. An entourage of parents came to these tournaments, helping wash the kit and generally assisting.

'Higgins would call us into the gymnasium, announce the squad of fourteen or fifteen, and then we were instructed to get undressed and return with just a towel wrapped around our waist, naked underneath. There was a separate room with three or four gymnasium mats and a bowl of soap water laid out next to each one.

'Some of the parents massaged their own children, with Higgins and the other two or three coaches looking after the rest of us. I always had Higgins, always. He would select us from a line, hand-picking; it didn't matter who was next in the queue, he chose the one he wanted.

'You would lie down naked, facing the ceiling, and, firstly, he stood between your legs, basically seeing everything, then started rubbing your thighs, before between your groin. Next you had to turn over, he would begin with your calves, gradually moving into the hamstrings, then into your buttocks.

'In court, he claimed he got the idea from Don Revie, with the defence playing a 30-second video of the former Leeds United manager carrying out these massages on professional footballers. You could see how rough the actual treatment was – and that's what Higgins did with children. He also told the court it was down to our own discretion whether we came in naked or put shorts on, which is an absolute lie. As if any of us would have chosen walking around with nothing on in preference to wearing shorts.

'These massages would take place every day on tour and always before a match. It never happened to me in England, although I discovered in court there were a couple of instances of lads receiving them at one of his six or seven homes. I went to his house in Litchfield Road, Southampton, half a dozen times, staying there once with other players, but nothing happened on that evening.

'Higgins would also have naked showers or baths with us following training sessions in The Dell's gym.

'His father-in-law, Sid, had one lung and a hunched back and would help out at training by making us tea and soft drinks. In court, Higgins claimed that, after training, Sid would shower in the referee's room where the coaches changed and, wanting to give privacy to an old man, he would instead come into the away dressing room with us to wash. I never saw Sid have a shower – there would be no need for him to as all he did was make tea – so that was another lie and an excuse from Higgins.

'Instead he would join us in the away dressing room, wearing a towel, hanging it up on a peg and then coming into the big bath, if not the showers, standing there exposing himself while chatting to us, and always staying longer than he should have done.

'It didn't stop there. As we dressed afterwards, one of the coaches would come in and say: "Smithy, Bob wants to speak to you." It wasn't always me, but whoever it was had to join him in the referee's room to chat about tactics and how you could improve in training. During this conversation he would dress, drying himself with a towel, exposing himself. I was called into that room on at least a dozen occasions, with nobody else allowed in until the chat was over. It was how it worked.

'What he was doing was very clever. I don't think I even had sex education at school until I was thirteen or fourteen, and it might well have been later than that. I didn't know anything about sex at the time.

'The very first day he signed me, he drove me to training and started rubbing my leg in his car, touching inside my groin, asking about being the father figure I never had. I wasn't allowed to tell anyone, it was our little secret. The same with the kit he gave me, it was a special kit: "Don't tell anyone." In court I heard he gave lots of kit away – to everyone.'

Smith broke his silence in December 2016 after former Southampton colleagues Dean Radford, Jamie Webb and Billy Seymour stepped forward to lift the lid on Higgins' regime. Following 23 years of marriage, he decided to reveal his own disturbing experiences to wife Tracey towards the end of a family holiday in Tenerife. Returning to their Cosham home on the Friday evening, he contacted children's charity the NSPCC the next morning. It began a very public process, having spent three decades concealing his torment at the hands of Higgins, refusing to confide in a soul.

Smith remained in football until injury dictated his retirement at the age of 28, having featured at non-league level for Waterlooville, Fareham, Gosport, Newport (Isle of Wight), Worthing and Selsey. By that stage he had been converted into an attacking full-back, a change during an eye-catching two-year spell with arguably the finest youth team in modern Pompey history.

Smith operated as left wing-back for Malcolm Beard's side who famously toppled Liverpool in an FA Youth Cup quarter-final replay in March 1990. A bumper Fratton Park crowd of 4,285 forced the kick-off to be delayed, with Darren Anderton's deflected extra-time goal settling the encounter against a Reds team featuring Steve McManaman and Steve Harkness.

The Blues squad included future internationals Anderton and Darryl Powell, while Andy Awford later represented England's under-21s and occupies Pompey's Hall of Fame, with Stuart Doling, Micky Ross and Russell Perrett also progressing to the first team.

It was a scholarship treasured by Smith, a period when duties also involved cleaning the boots of Mark Kelly, Pompey's Academy manager, in addition to Kevin Ball, John Beresford and Gavin Maguire.

'God knows what would have happened to me if I hadn't walked out of Southampton,' said Smith.

'Higgins' attitude towards me changed after I turned up to training wearing a roll-neck jumper to cover up a couple of love bites on my neck. I didn't have a girlfriend, it was just a stupid Monday night at Fifth Avenue nightclub in Portsmouth, during a disco for youngsters. He noticed and called me into the dressing room before really ripping into me.

'From that point he was cold towards me, detached, then came that moment in the gym which saw me walk out on the club.

'I took a big risk too. Higgins had long threatened to ruin my football career because of something he held over me from when I was aged thirteen.

'On one occasion after training, I noticed a team-mate's pair of Farah trousers, which were exactly the same as mine but had an 'F' emblem on them. I wanted them as everybody was in designer clothes and mum couldn't afford much, which is no excuse. Being brought up in a single-parent family, money was tight – and I wanted them.

'So I swapped them for mine – and was found out. Higgins made a big deal about getting the police involved and said: "The player's parents want you out of the club, the manager Lawrie McMenemy wants you out of the club, but I have gone out of my way to keep you."

'I have since spoken to the player concerned and nothing of the sort was ever mentioned about the trousers, certainly not the police. It was Higgins frightening me.

'I was so embarrassed I didn't turn up training for three or four weeks, then, while sitting on the doorstep talking to a couple of friends, Higgins pulled up in his car and asked me to get in.

'He told me about McMenemy knowing, about what the police would do, how he would write to all football clubs telling them I was a thief – but that he was willing to have me back at Southampton. There was a training session that night and he took me to his home to give me Danny Wallace's England under-21 shirt. "I only give these to special players," he said. It was the grooming process in action.

'He held that over me for a long, long time and, when the sexual assault happened to me on that night a few years later, I knew straight away I had to leave.

'While on Southampton's books, I would get ribbed by the Pompey schoolboy players I knew. They called him "Uncle Bob", as they had heard bits and pieces, but I didn't believe them; I just thought they were jealous. I was well warned, but wouldn't have it.

'I was a vulnerable kid and he played on that. I never had a dad – I don't know where he is even now – and Higgins exploited that from the start. "I know you haven't got a father figure," he would say. "Would you like me to be a father figure?" I just thought he was being kind – you don't realise at that age what he was actually doing.'

While Smith and many of his youth-team colleagues have received justice, the fight continues for six other alleged victims of Higgins. Dean Radford and five other teenage boys were the first of the Southampton youngsters to step forward, yet, in the subsequent 1992 court case, Higgins was acquitted of sexual offence charges on the direction of a judge. The 'Forgotten Six' are subject to the double jeopardy principle which prevents a suspect being retried for the same criminal offence.

Dino Nocivelli is a senior associate solicitor at London law firm Bolt Burdon Kemp, specialising in abuse cases and the leading lawyer in relation to abuse in football and other sports. The firm represent five of the six in addition to those seeking compensation from Southampton.

He said: 'There are exceptions to double jeopardy. For sexual offences, the only one is for rape. It does not include non-penetrative offences or inappropriate touching, groping, masturbation, the list goes on.

'As it stands, the Forgotten Six will never be able to get closure, justice or resolution of these issues. Of those six, two have given evidence on the stand against Higgins on three separate occasions – the 1992 case, a second in 2018 and a third in 2019. All these boys also drafted impact statements, which couldn't be heard because Higgins can be sentenced only for crimes he committed. In the eyes of the law, he didn't commit crimes against these six.

'The result is, even though they helped to prosecute this man, in the eyes of criminal law they are not recognised and will never be classed as victims or survivors. It's horrendous. Higgins is behind bars, they helped put him there, yet they will never get the closure of justice for what he allegedly did to them. They must live with that.

'In the initial case, Higgins was acquitted. He wasn't found innocent because criminal law doesn't allow that. A jury didn't find him not guilty. It was at the judge's direction to find him not guilty.

'Higgins cannot be retried because the allegations do not reach the serious and severe level. We think that is incorrect. All forms of child sexual abuse are serious and severe. When the law was last changed, people didn't appreciate the impact of child abuse, and we feel it now fulfils other criteria for new compelling, substantial evidence. The man is a convicted child abuser – and that information was not present at the original trial.

'We have labelled them the Forgotten Six. That's how they feel: forgotten. They have been forgotten by the criminal justice system.'

Nocivelli, who is also ambassador of the Survivors Trust, is campaigning to make all sexual abuse offences exceptions under double jeopardy rules, thereby allowing those previously acquitted to be prosecuted again. That has prompted the launch of an online petition to the UK Parliament and government which needs to reach 10,000 signatures in order for the government to respond.

> He added: 'Data from a Freedom of Information request reveals that the number of people to come forward in relation to alleged child sexual abuse by Bob Higgins was 95. Since Higgins was originally reported in 1989, thirteen have come forward. That is thirteen boys who could have been saved. How many do we think there actually are?
>
> 'In general, we know that one in four disclose. It depends on the circumstances. We know females are more likely to disclose than males, we know white people are more likely to disclose than black people. These are white, male footballers.
>
> 'There is abuse in gymnastics, swimming, rowing, rugby, the list goes on, but football is the biggest area we are seeing at the moment. People always focus on the monsters – Higgins, Barry Bennell, Ted Langford, Jimmy Savile, the list goes on – but attention should be on the systems that allow this to happen.
>
> 'The fact is, these monsters operate in normal society but they don't look like monsters. If we can improve the system, the monster cannot operate within. It suffocates them, it takes away their air, that's why these cases are important.
>
> 'If checks were in place, could those boys have been saved? Would they have known who Bob Higgins was? No. Could they have been saved? I would say yes.'

In 2016, the Offside Trust was created to provide a support mechanism for those who have endured child abuse in sport, with a vision of working alongside football clubs and organisations to improve safeguarding.

Founded by Steve Walters and Chris Unsworth, who were both victims of Barry Bennell, the group has steadily established strong links with football clubs, holding various support events for survivors at the likes of Pompey, Crystal Palace, Everton, Bristol City and Wolverhampton Wanderers.

Among its eight ambassadors is Smith, who serves as the south-coast point of contact, a voluntary role which once saw him stopped in Farlington Sainsbury's by somebody keen for guidance. The 47-year-old remains dedicated towards ensuring others aren't subjected to the suffering he continues to experience.

Smith said: 'I have become stronger as a person through my work with the Offside Trust. I've received emails praising me for showing courage and bravery. I have been told: "If people like you didn't speak up then we wouldn't know anything." Awareness is crucial and I have learnt that through my work.

'In August, Crystal Palace played Aston Villa and they hosted ten of us, putting us in an executive box with a fantastic view, supplying free food and drink. After the game we had our photos taken with Gary Cahill and Mark Bright. More importantly, we attended an hour-and-a-half session with Palace's head of safeguarding and equality, Marcus Puddephatt, who talked us through their procedures, which were absolutely brilliant. Clubs are trying to make a difference.

'I also cannot fault the Football Association since the trial. Sue Ravenlaw, the head of equality and safeguarding, has been brilliant. Despite my initial reservations, they couldn't have been more supportive, putting me and Tracey in touch with the Sporting Chance Clinic, who have offered 52 weeks of counselling free of charge.

'There's also a benevolence fund ensuring that survivors who are struggling financially due to the court process can apply online and, if they qualify and are out of pocket, will be reimbursed. The people presently involved in the FA cannot be held responsible for the failure to deal with Higgins.

'I have been an Offside Trust ambassador for nine months and it was difficult for me when I started the role, but it was a distraction. I don't want people to go through what we did. It's about raising awareness and highlighting the signs.

'It still goes on, I have no doubt about it, and we are never going to stop it. The more awareness we raise, the more people look out for these things.

'A single mum, for instance, sending her son off for football practice with the coach picking them up. You don't know what's going on in the car, you haven't a clue. That was my experience. I thought Higgins was being kind, but that's the way these people operate.

'If people want to abuse children they will do anything. There are scout leaders, priests, you hear it going on all the time, and they shouldn't be left alone. The truth is, nobody knows who they are. You never know. We will never stop it completely.

'As survivors, though, we can get the message across to football clubs as well as parents. If I can stop one man abusing one child, then I have done a good job.'

There is a cabin positioned at the bottom of Smith's Cosham garden, supplying the sedate setting for moments of quiet contemplation. Constructed from leftover timber, it represents a two-year labour of love for the builder, keen to create a getaway to allow him to gather his thoughts. Inside, two beer pumps serve Carlsberg and Carling, although they are presently laid low with the cooling system broken. Still, a row of Smirnoff vodka, The Famous Grouse whisky and Southern Comfort provide the shots. On one wall hangs a Bournemouth shirt autographed by its original owner – Darren Anderton, who remains in touch with his former Pompey team-mate. Elsewhere, a signed white Pompey away shirt from the 2018–19 campaign can be seen. In the summer, upon the occasion of his 25th wedding anniversary, the sizeable garden catered for 200 people, with the cherished snug open for business and inevitably taking pride of place. For all the destructiveness that dominates his dreams, there exists a sense of serenity in this part of Smith's world.

He added: 'I call this my little snug, my getaway. Rather than going out and socialising in the pub where I don't feel safe, I can come down here and sit and think about things.

'I've been to Pompey once this season – the first Fratton Park game against Tranmere Rovers. Pompey's my club, I love them. I'm a Pompey boy. There are still people at the club who were there when I was on their books, which I like. I would like to move on from everything. To be honest, I don't think about Higgins at all now, which is a good thing.

'The support I've had is tremendous. People come up to me and ask me about it, although I find it quite difficult to explain and don't go into detail with individuals.

'I will answer them, though. I won't blank it out. Not any more.'

Kenny Jackett

6 October 2019

Kenny Jackett speaks of evolution, but change at Fratton Park has been driven by necessity rather than ambitious upgrading. Only four clubs in the Football League surpassed the 88 points registered by Pompey last season, while nobody could match the 109 goals scored across all competitions. A fine foundation for another tilt at promotion following League One play-off semi-final elimination at the hands of Sunderland in a devastating finale.

Then dawned a summer of transition, initiated by leading lights Jamal Lowe and Matt Clarke, whose desire to compete at a higher level hastened Fratton Park exits, the club recompensed through sizeable transfer fees. The highly regarded pair had been included in the PFA League One Team of the Year. Top scorer Lowe's outstanding campaign yielded seventeen goals from the right wing, including a sumptuous Wembley chip. Stylish centre-half Clarke, whose season consisted of a club record 60 appearances, was crowned *The News/Sports Mail*'s Player of the Season for a second successive year. There was a further setback for Jackett when another first-team regular, Nathan Thompson, enforced his post-Christmas pledge to walk away from Pompey in search of Championship football. Rejecting a fresh contract from Portsmouth, the first-choice right-back departed on a free transfer, a scenario Jackett had long played out publicly. Nonetheless, the inevitable outcome was no less disappointing.

Promotion shortcomings had deprived the Blues of three key performers, forcing an overhaul of personnel and the playing system, transformations designed to improve upon the 2018–19 season's fourth-placed finish. Yet while Clarke and Thompson's departures had been anticipated and accepted, the manner of Lowe's transfer to Wigan Athletic rankled significantly. Agitating for a move upon his pre-season return, the former Hampton & Richmond Borough player made little effort to hide his malcontent around the training ground, irritating a number of team-mates and infuriating a defiant club hierarchy. Following confusion over his listing on a team sheet for a July 2019 friendly at Havant & Waterlooville which he had not travelled to, Jackett declared a misunderstanding and handed the winger permission for a five-day absence to collect his thoughts. Significantly, there was to be no change of heart, and the wantaway Lowe was reunited with former boss Paul Cook at the DW Stadium in a transfer exceeding £2m, a deal which also emphatically raised the wages of one of Pompey's mid-range earners.

'I didn't really envisage Jamal leaving,' said Jackett. 'Nobody wanted him to go, but obviously he had his mind set on moving on. In the end, it's difficult to get somebody to do something they don't want to do. If somebody doesn't want to stay week after week after week, you become resigned to the situation and you may as well let that person go, particularly if the transfer fee is right – which it was.

'For us, it was then about signing John Marquis and Marcus Harness if we could, before letting Jamal go. We got both deals over the line – and I gave him his wish. We tried to get him to stay, but he had his mind set on a fresh challenge after two and a half years at Pompey. He wanted the move and it's hard to keep people who don't want to be there. You can dig your heels in, but, as the weeks and months go by, you come round to the fact you may as well let them go; that's my experience.

'As much as Jamal had high motivation the previous season, I don't think his motivation level was to stay here this term. The money offered for him was high, very high, and if you are trying to keep a player who is not necessarily going to perform to his best, then it comes to a point where you have to think of the club and take the cash. It was a tough one. Jamal was with us, but could he produce his best form? No. Did he want to move on? Yes, 100 per cent.

'At Brighton in a behind-closed-doors pre-season friendly, I decided to substitute him after ten minutes; he wasn't quite there on that particular day. It was a training ground game anyway, so both sides altered quite a lot as it progressed. We changed everyone at half-time and then put on another couple of kids halfway through the second half. The total substitutions were thirteen from us, with Brighton similar, and you have to put Jamal coming off into the context of the game – it wasn't a first-team match where you've got three subs. There was also his name being on the team sheet at Havant & Waterlooville, which was my fault, to be honest.

'I spoke to Jamal on the Friday and didn't think he was in the right frame of mind to play. It wasn't like he failed to turn up, that wasn't the case. His name did appear on the team sheet, but pre-season team sheets, particularly early on, are very vague, and you'll do well to get a team sheet most of the time. On that day, our team sheet wasn't accurate. I did say that at the time, but people didn't necessarily believe it because it got in the way of a good story. It was never my intention for Jamal to play; we agreed he wasn't going to. No way did he fail to turn up, that wasn't the case. We tried to keep him, but it wasn't something he wanted to do. In the end it was unfortunate and it was a shame, but football moves on and people move on. His wish was granted.'

Lowe completed his protracted switch to Wigan barely 48 hours before the 2019–20 campaign kicked off with a home fixture against Neil Warnock's Cardiff City, back in the Championship following relegation from the Premier League. He has subsequently featured in all of Wigan's opening ten matches, starting seven of them, yet still to open his goal account. Meanwhile, Clarke headed to Brighton & Hove Albion in a £4m deal, although six weeks later the Premier League club dispatched him to Derby County on a season-long loan. Denied immediate top-flight football, the 22-year-old was alternately offered a maiden Championship campaign to develop under new boss Phillip

Cocu. Clarke was immediately involved, starting seven matches by the start of October, with first-team opportunities escalated following a car crash which sidelined centre-half rival and captain Richard Keogh for fifteen months with damaged knee ligaments.

As for Thompson, a switch to QPR fell through when the Championship club opted instead to extend veteran right-back Angel Rangel's contract by twelve months. Consequently, the former Pompey full-back struggled to find a new employer, utilising Gosport Leisure Centre to maintain fitness and featuring in an under-23 pre-season friendly for Bristol City. Thompson was still without a club two matches into the season. Jackett was happy to help out his ex-player, allowing the defender to train with the Blues for almost a fortnight. Ultimately, midway through August, the 28-year-old signed a two-year deal with Peterborough United, remaining in League One. Boss Darren Ferguson had already recruited former Doncaster Rovers right-back Niall Mason that summer, restricting Thompson's involvement to four substitute appearances.

'We wanted Nathan to stay, but he informed us pretty early on he was going to wait and see what happened in the summer, which is his prerogative,' added Jackett.

'There's not a problem with that, we understand. He was straight with us and I didn't stop playing him. Yes, he was a loss, but he had his own reasons for moving on, which was to do what he thought was best for his career. He saw out his contract and always did his best for this club. I would have loved him to stay. Several times we offered a new contract, but it didn't fit into what he wanted. He was eager to see what was out there during that particular summer. From his point of view, you never know until you try. I suppose if your mind is made up, then you have to give it a go.

'If you are to have regrets, it's maybe not trying. Nathan felt it was worth the risk trying to get into the Championship and, in the end, it was totally his decision, which I respect. There's no hard feelings, he trained with us for nearly two weeks after leaving to keep him ticking over before signing for Peterborough. Nathan had two good years with us and I was pleased with him, both as a person and as a player. His only goal was our equaliser in the Checkatrade Trophy final to take it into extra-time, while his defensive reading of the game was very, very good – he's hard to beat in a one-v-one. A somewhat underestimated player, really.

'It was never an option to re-sign him once he left, as we had recruited James Bolton by then, so had our quota of right-backs. James has suffered injury and it has taken him a little while, but he's had a good week and his cross set up Brett Pitman for the winner against Bolton Wanderers. It will be interesting how he builds on this now. At 25 he's a younger guy coming into his time and there's no reason why he can't go on and emulate what Nathan has done.

'With Matt Clarke, we would have had more of a chance keeping him if promotion had been won; similarly it might still have been difficult depending on the type of offers on the table. In the end, Brighton secured his services. He did very well and it will be interesting to follow his career now. I have a lot of time for him as a player and a person; he's a fantastic professional, a really committed one. Matt was rock solid defensively and could bring the ball out – it was something we worked on and worked on. It was certainly eye-catching, but the main thing within our team was how solid he was defensively. He improved and, with the age he is, hopefully the fact he can put forward such a high amount of league games for a young guy can only stand him in good stead in the future as he tries to break into the Premier League with Brighton.

'Matt had a year left on his contract and, when Brighton started bidding, the obvious was going to happen – he was going to go. When a club like Brighton put good money on the table, it was then about getting the best deal for ourselves rather than whether he was leaving or not. For the opening six months of last season, Matt and Jack Whatmough were our centre-halves, a very, very good partnership and, looking at the age of them, it would have been great if they could have played in Pompey's central defence all the way through. For one reason or another it doesn't happen, one gets injured and the other moves on in the summer, but that's football.

'It was hard to keep Matt as nobody is able to turn down a Premier League club, and, in summing up the whole situation, everyone was very thankful for what he did for the club. I am sure we all wish him the best in his future career. Players move on, it happens at every club – it's about then replacing them.'

❊ ☽ ❊

It's early October and Jackett's third season at Fratton Park is enduring mounting criticism. After a mediocre haul of nine points from the opening eight league matches, supporter unrest has manifested in the stands since a 1–0 defeat at Wycombe Wanderers two games previous. League One finishes of eighth and fourth represented significant progress but with the promotion hopefuls floundering in nineteenth position, the 57-year-old is weathering his most challenging period as Blues boss.

Jackett arrived on the south coast in June 2017, following Paul Cook's departure for Wigan Athletic. The incoming manager inherited a successful side, a talented squad newly promoted from League Two as champions, albeit ageing, having largely been assembled to reap short-term goals. Jackett's most recent association with League One was as manager of a Wolverhampton Wanderers side which, in 2013–14, captured the title with a divisional points record of 103, representing his third career promotion. Having lost his Molineux position two years later upon the completion of Chinese conglomerate Fosun International's takeover, there was a 39-day spell at the helm of Rotherham United, before electing to walk away due to unfulfilled promises by the owners. By the summer of 2017, the former Wales international midfielder was involved in assisting Tottenham Hotspur's under-18s, while casting an eye over potential managerial roles. Then Pompey's call arrived.

Jackett said: 'I didn't have a full-time role at Spurs. I've friends among the youth side there and was allowed to observe training for six months, also helping out with some of the sessions. I was more of a floating coach, with no formal role. I wasn't an employee of Spurs, but was there with their under-18s every day. It was a case of observing and keeping my eye in while out of work. I wanted to get back into football and did have some enquiries and offers. Pompey was a great opportunity, a terrific club to be part of.

'Pompey has a great reputation from the outside – and inside it's everything you think it is going to be. There's a very passionate crowd and Fratton Park is a unique ground, which is a massive strength. The impressions I gathered from coming here as a player, coach and opposition manager are spot on – its reputation is justified and this is a terrific club.

'With it having just come out of League Two, I had the opportunity to build on that success, if possible, to continue taking Pompey forward. Whether the manager had stayed or not, there was going to be quite a natural evolution of that team. Maybe it needed refreshing a little as it was quite an older side, yet one which had done the job getting back into League One. Regeneration is something which happens from one season to the next, whether you are a new manager or have been there a number of years. It needed to regenerate and replenish. Maybe more athleticism is required as you move up higher, and that was certainly the case with that particular team. Those players had done an excellent job for Pompey, very good professionals who had served the club extremely well and contributed a lot. However, there were a few aged 33–34 and I felt some freshness was needed.

'As a manager, I try to recruit from below wherever you are as I believe that brings a hunger and also develops some saleable assets for the club, which is very important. There must always be one or two experienced players, but I don't generally go for a whole team of older performers and attempt to bring in some younger ones and develop them. We wanted promotion that first campaign, but every club would say that in pre-season because of the play-off system. Ultimately, eighth was more than respectable. We were involved in the race until the penultimate game, but just couldn't quite earn sixth spot. Last season we gave it a good go, but unfortunately couldn't quite get over the line. There was a high standard among the top five teams and I'm pleased to say we were one of them. We fell at the last hurdle in the play-offs. There was a lot we can be proud of in the league campaign, but similarly there was the FA Cup win at Norwich City and a fantastic day at Wembley in the Checkatrade Trophy.

'Reflecting on League One, the standard of the other teams was impressive, but they kept going and just edged us. We achieved 88 points and didn't do a lot wrong; it was a case of others having a little bit more. We were consistent until the end and gave it everything, but ultimately three other sides got those promotion places. We gave it a good go and I can't necessarily put what happened during the second half of the season down to one spell or a particular injury. Injuries happen over a ten-month campaign, but we just couldn't get our noses in front and over the line. In terms of promotion, I cannot put my finger on one reason why it didn't happen, or one person or losing this game or losing that game. You always seek those things but, looking back, I can't really see one.'

Buoyed by the bolstering of the Fratton Park coffers through the sales of Clarke and Lowe, Jackett recruited eight players this summer to drive the latest promotion crusade. James Bolton was the first to arrive, linking up on a free transfer from Shrewsbury Town to fill the right-back slot vacated by Thompson. Paul Downing and Norwich loanee Sean Raggett strengthened the central defender ranks following Clarke's exit and with Jack Whatmough still injured long term. Elsewhere, Australian international winger Ryan Williams, who had emerged through the Blues' Academy before being sold to Fulham in 2012, returned to the south coast as a free agent having turned down a new deal at Rotherham United. Meanwhile, combative central midfielder Ross McCrorie arrived on a season-long loan, an Ibrox decision criticised by a large proportion of Rangers fans who held him in high regard.

Jackett splashed out £450,000 on Ipswich Town striker Ellis Harrison, having twice been unsuccessful in pursuing the Welshman's signature over the previous two transfer windows. Marcus Harness was signed as Lowe's replacement for an undisclosed fee reported to be around £900,000, with the 23-year-old attacker having caught the eye when Burton Albion hosted the Blues in April 2019. Finally, a fee of around £1m was spent on Doncaster's John Marquis, whose 67 goals in 153 appearances established him among the most prolific marksmen in the lower divisions – and Jackett's final recruit of the transfer window.

Regardless of their summer strengthening, two victories from Pompey's opening eight league matches have left Jackett's men thirteen points adrift of the automatic promotion spots. For the previous weekend's visit of rock-bottom Bolton, Jackett surprisingly opted to rip up his trusted 4-2-3-1 system in favour of a 4-4-2. Boosted by the impressive Harness back from injury and introduced from the bench at half-time, Pompey ran out 1–0 winners through Brett Pitman's header, albeit in a largely lacklustre display.

'Coming off the back of the Wycombe game, the system and set-up just didn't work, so we have evolved,' said Jackett.

'Unfortunately Marcus came off at Blackpool with a thigh injury when he was doing well. He's back now and it would be lovely if he could build on that and go on to be as successful as Jamal was. They're different types of wide players. Jamal is more pace and power who gets in behind, while Marcus comes to feet and is perhaps more of a technical winger, getting around people, finding holes in pockets and is a very good crosser of the ball.

'We found a role for Jamal that was quite exclusively halfway between centre-forward and right wing, giving him the freedom to come in off the flank and find holes. He was hard to handle because of his pace, particularly going in and towards the goal, although not that much in terms of back to goal receiving it. He was very difficult to stop with any move forward which involved the ball in front of him and his finishing was good. That position suited him, it gained him confidence and was a key role for the team. The side were set up for wingers, with Jamal and Ronan Curtis on opposite flanks, and both delivered.

'During my first season, we were more a 4-4-2, with two forwards, and Jamal was asked to track back a lot, producing more midfield and defensive work, whereas last season we played 4-3-3 with him right up on the front line as much as possible. With the number nine as the focal point – mainly Oli Hawkins and sometimes Brett Pitman – Jamal had the licence to get right up with him and be there as much as possible. It was a role which probably developed as it went along, benefiting the team. You always play to the strengths of your best players and he was that, so we gave him the type of balls he needed. If Hawkins played back to goal, he brought Jamal into the game a lot, allowing that freedom to then be able to go right across the line and move into goalscoring positions, whereas maybe in the first season he didn't, as he was covering the right-back.

'Now we have Harness on the right and he has to put that injury behind him and hopefully can get back up to speed pretty quickly. He had half a game against Bolton on Saturday and I'm seeking for him to settle down and play the majority of the matches, if not all, because he looks like he will be strong for us. With a muscle injury, I didn't feel he would be ready to start that match. In the first game back following a muscle injury the best thing is coming off the bench, and he showed a lot of quality. Harness has confidence taking the ball – he's one of those players who can receive it and receive it very well. It was no secret that he developed really well for Burton in League One last season and was one of the standout performers against us, which was the reason we pursued him and, ultimately, were then pleased to get him.

'This year is heading towards a 4-4-2 again, because our forwards look strong. We haven't quite had the goals and, although Harness can score, he will be a provider. His delivery is very, very good, and probably he and Gareth Evans are our best crossers. It will swing towards our forwards, so that's where the majority of our goals are going to come from, as opposed to last year when it was set up for the wide men which is quite unusual.

'We operated with an out-and-out 4-3-3 at Wycombe and I don't think it particularly worked, whereas against Southampton and Bolton we fielded a 4-4-2, with the number ten a little closer to the number nine, resembling two up front. In that system, the wingers serve more as providers than scorers. If they get goals as well that's fine, but there are some different strengths this year and the team needs to work it out quickly so we can get winning. Last year we got the wingers into the game with quite a lot of early balls which suited both of them, and they scored the goals. Along with whoever played centre-forward, it provided a really strong front three. That hasn't necessarily worked this year and, now with a second forward, the wingers will be providers as we want more of a traditional approach to bring out our strengths. Whichever formation you use, you must utilise the talents of your best players.'

Pompey's stuttering start to the League One campaign had prompted the first airing of 'We want Jackett out' chants during the previous month's 1–0 defeat at Wycombe. Adebayo Akinfenwa's 83rd-minute penalty after new skipper Tom Naylor inexplicably handled while airborne at the far post saw patience snap among some of the 2,125 travelling support. For the first time, the fans publicly turned on their manager during a match in what could be a watershed moment for his Blues tenure. Afterwards, Jackett stopped to converse with a number of unhappy supporters gathered around the team coach outside the entrance to Adams Park. Conducted in a respectful and polite manner by all concerned, Pompey's boss subsequently received rounds of applause from two separate groups he engaged with. Nonetheless, the dissent fired towards the manager during fitful early-season progress is palpable, with Jackett also aware of the growing frustration.

'There is pressure and I understand that. It's a great club and a privilege to be here, so you must make sure you do your best. How do you do that? You win the next game, that's what you have to do,' he said.

'Through all of it, you must concentrate on the next match and do everything you can to win it; that's the only way. I don't like sweeping previous games under the carpet. You have to give an accurate assessment of where you are and what you did well because there'll be some things you have right, even in defeat. Bolton was an important win, but we need to build on that. As an experienced manager, you focus on your next game, put all your energy into that and do everything you can to win it.

'You don't ever want to lose your job. It's important to stay balanced and keep everything in perspective, but similarly you are just as desperate as anybody else to be successful, probably more so. Nobody wants to be successful, to win games and earn promotion more than I do. You hear supporter comments all the time; you can't say you blank it out. You don't. You hear it, of course you do, you pick it up. I stop for petrol in the week and know what the feelings are;

nobody knows more than you. It is part of football management, and if you want to be successful you have to come through it.

'I believe in this group of players, I do think wins are there, and hopefully Saturday was one building block to us becoming a consistent force in the division, climbing up the table and working hard at gaining confidence. After Wycombe, there was some conversation with fans waiting by the team bus, who had a few points and criticism. I talked to them and did say that, on that particular day, it had been a 50/50 game and we were poor. You can't say we played well, we didn't, and things needed to improve.

'Before that, you look at Coventry City. I thought we had broken the back of them at 3–1, and we deserved those three goals, but you need to close it out – on that particular day we didn't, for whatever reason. Firstly there was a mistimed challenge for a penalty. Then they equalised after a long throw has been launched into the box and the shot went through sets of legs to make it 3–3. I'm not putting that down as unlucky, we should have closed the game out – definitely, we should have. It was two points dropped.

The decision to bring on Christian Burgess at 3–2 was to enable us to go with three centre-backs and bring full width to our play. With the opposition down to less men, you must go as wide as possible, that was key, getting the full-backs into wide areas to be able to keep the ball. It didn't work. Straight after putting a centre-back on, there's a long throw coming in, but that change usually looks after you. It didn't on that particular occasion and we conceded a third goal. I don't know whether I regret that. It was Christian Burgess on for Gareth Evans, I don't think it had any real bearing, it was more about us not being able to open up from the back. We had to go full width, to keep the ball, I certainly didn't think that change would weaken us from the throw. Some substitutions have nothing to do with outcomes and I still feel putting Christian on just before a long throw didn't particularly weaken us – but the timing of it felt that way.

'I understand things get said about styles of play and there's a lot of opinions about football. My thinking is a good team always has the short pass and long pass – and the good players use the right one at the right time. When I have my teams right, at whatever club, there is a balance, a middle ground, and every option available. Good sides possess a Ben Close, whom the ball can go through, but, similarly, pace up front where you can go long and straight in as well; it's about picking the right pass. Similarly, the philosophy of playing it out from the back in League One every single time isn't going to work because people close you down, but there are times to play to use it. For Craig MacGillivray, whether it's a quick pass to a centre-half or a full-back, or going through the middle, it is the right pass at the right time. Our aim is to make sure they are set up with all of the options, all of the passing choices, and then for the players to select the right one at the right time.

'It's not a case of being unaware of supporter opinion, you are obviously aware, but the only thing you can affect is the next match and training sessions up to that particular game where you have the players. Ultimately, that's your best chance of being successful and turning things around. I believe in the club, it's a great club, and I believe in the players. We have enough good players to come good.'

Jackett is currently not the only target of supporter ire, with an out-of-sorts Ronan Curtis also coming under fire. The Republic of Ireland international's form is unrecognisable from that produced upon his Football League arrival twelve months earlier. Plucked from League of Ireland Premier Division side Derry City in May 2018, the left-sided winger's dazzling early-season performances swiftly attracted transfer talk. Despite a dip in effectiveness towards the end of the campaign, Jackett selected the youngster as his Player of the Season, following a magnificent year in which he netted twelve goals from 49 outings and earned full international recognition. However, Curtis has struggled to recapture that form, culminating in cheers greeting his substitution on 62 minutes against Bolton. Before that uncomfortable moment, the crowd's exasperation was evident as he struggled to influence the game, but nonetheless maintaining a willing attitude. Within an hour of the final whistle, the 23-year-old had tweeted 'Boys dug deep to get the three points. Hopefully the start of a good run. Could have done with the twelfth man today'. His pointed remark about the Fratton faithful's support inevitably irked many, the comment soon removed from social media as he scrambled around seeking damage limitation.

Jackett said: 'Ronan Curtis is putting 110 per cent into everything; his work rate has been phenomenal. He's probably looking for that goal which can spark off a good run for him. He is capable of it so he's maybe a little frustrated with his end product, but certainly the work rate and the effort is terrific from him.

'I did see that he put out a tweet and then deleted it. It's one of those where I am sure when he sees the response it prompted he will learn. He is very passionate and committed. As his manager, it's about channelling that, but he's had our full backing all the way and has to keep working away to produce those goals and assists he is still looking for.

'Now the wingers must track back and maybe come off in possession to shift the full-backs, so there are spaces in behind them. We will see whether I take him out this weekend for Doncaster – it depends on the type of competition around the wingers and how you want to play – but Ronan has deserved our backing after last year.

'Ronan was a surprise package last season, one of our better young players, and had a terrific year. The team was very much set up for him and Jamal – and they delivered. The wingers are slightly different this season – they must come off their full-backs. It is about moving opposition full-backs but not being right up against them, shifting the full-backs and supplementing the midfield slightly more, with the number ten now a second centre-forward.

'I do think the strength of the side is perhaps the strikers. That is probably where the goals are going to come from – Marquis, Pitman, Harrison. It's maybe a bit more traditional.

'We have Doncaster next which will be a hard game. They have started the season well and again we'll be looking at a front two. John Marquis isn't as strong in the air as Oli Hawkins, and the big one with John so far is he's made a lot of runs, very, very good runs, but we haven't necessarily played him in or been able to play through.

'He has needed either a partner or somebody close to him. He has been isolated too many times, which is why Pitman is now up there. Marquis' runs are very good, and if he keeps that up, we will learn how to bring out the best in him and spark a goalscoring run.

'In matches gone by, Brett has come too deep to get the best out of him and I understand why, because he is trying to get us playing and to get on the ball, but he needs to be up and around the goal as well.

'From Southampton onwards, we have worked on our number ten operating really close to our number nine, with those two forming a relationship on and off the ball. If you've got a partner close then it can work, Brett being a little bit more to feet and John's movement along the line bringing us some football and some shots.

'We have already lost three matches on our travels, whilst our away record last season was excellent. We have suffered defeat at Shrewsbury, Sunderland and Wycombe, all by a single goal but still losses. We have to address that and we must do better, which begins by building on last weekend as we have the capability.

'Our season is ahead of us, definitely, but we have needed to improve some of the performances. We have made a step in the right direction, but require more steps.'

As indicated, Jackett retained the 4-4-2 system for the trip to a Doncaster side positioned ninth in League One following a heartening beginning to ex-Pompey defender Darren Moore's tenure. The Blues once again partnered Marquis and Pitman in attack, with Harness fit to resume right-flank duties and Gareth Evans recalled to the left-hand side of midfield. However, Curtis was absent, a hamstring strain felt in training 24 hours earlier sidelining him and prompting his withdrawal from the Republic of Ireland squad for two Euro 2020 qualifiers.

For Marquis, it signified a Keepmoat Stadium reunion, having registered 67 goals in 153 appearances before departing for Fratton Park in July. Somewhat inevitably, his return was frostily greeted by a home support taking delight in every on-pitch error. The 27-year-old's indignity was completed with a half-time withdrawal in place of Ellis

Harrison, who would cap his opportunity with Pompey's stoppage-time winner.

A fluent Rovers were mightily impressive, yet crucially missed a cutting edge with injuries depleting striking options, prompting winger Kieran Sadlier to be thrust into attack. Throughout the one-sided encounter, Moore's men, conducted by the timeless James Coppinger, twice struck the bar and were denied by MacGillivray, while Sadlier improbably failed to convert at the far post during the first half.

In a breakaway following a Rovers corner, Ben Close surged upfield and pushed the ball into the path of Evans motoring down the left, who finished effortlessly to hand the visitors a surprise 60th-minute lead.

The equaliser arrived eight minutes from time, Alfie May's angled shot from the right beaten out by MacGillivray, with left-back Reece James following up to lash home a left-footed finish from inside the box. The hosts had eyes on the late winner their play warranted. However, one minute into time added on, James Bolton flung in a cross from the right – and Harrison cleverly steered a header into the top corner of the net from ten yards out to seal a 2–1 success. A smash-and-grab delivered without conscience, but nonetheless it represented successive League One victories, lifting Pompey into sixteenth spot. The result was the perfect antidote for Jackett, striving to change opinion among fans with faltering belief.

'I have regular contact with the owners. Eric Eisner was over to watch the Southampton and Bolton matches,' said Jackett. 'We have conference calls discussing overall thinking, recruitment and other aspects. They want to be kept up to speed in regards to where we are.

'They want a stable environment. This is a club which has had fantastic ups and downs, massive highs, but has almost been out of business as well. Wherever they are and whatever their ambitions, it's a great coup for Pompey to have these owners and I'm sure they will be very, very successful.

'There is always pressure. You have to speak to the board, in terms of their own views. I can't speak for them, but they have been very supportive of me – and I do think I have a very clear relationship with them.'

KEV MCCORMACK
AND BARRY HARRIS

11 October 2019

In the setting sun, Kev McCormack gazes ahead, drinking in a garden well nourished and evidently treasured, before allowing a wry smile to interrupt the contemplative moment.

> 'I get recognised more for being Kev the kit man who washes men's pants than I ever did for boxing. I sign autographs as Pompey's kit man, which is quite humbling to be honest, yet wasn't really asked as a title-winning boxer,' he reflects.

Certainly there is no telltale trace of indignation in the 52-year-old's voice, merely acceptance of a mid-life transformation that has largely eclipsed proud accomplishments. When inhabiting the world of boxing, his natural environment, McCormack is recognised as a Welsh sporting great, unequivocally lauded in amateur boxing circles.

Since the inauguration of the Amateur Boxing Association (ABA) Championships' super heavyweight division some 37 years ago, no boxer has surpassed the man from Cwmbran's remarkable haul of three titles. It's a feat equalled only by Olympic bronze medallist and

Commonwealth Games champion David Price, with other notable winners including Anthony Joshua, Audley Harrison, Tyson Fury and Dereck Chisora. McCormack's prolific period of success comprised of three triumphs during a four-year domination. When the great Joe Calzaghe, fellow Welshman and sometime sparring partner at a Newbridge gym, secured his maiden ABA Championships welterweight decoration at the Royal Albert Hall in 1991, that same evening, McCormack was present to register his third in the super heavyweight division.

Unlike contemporaries, the ex-Royal Marine didn't covet professional ranks, and instead his career was floored by amateur boxing regulations dictating retirement at the age of 31. He bowed out having represented his country in three Commonwealth Games, amassed a record-breaking ten Welsh titles and, of course, that trio of ABA Championship crowns, assuring a distinguished presence in the sport's annals.

This Pompey season represents McCormack's 21st as Fratton Park's kit man, an association initiated by the departure of the legendary Gordon Neave. His predecessor served the Blues for more than half a century, featuring as player, coach, trainer, physio and kit man, service which was rewarded with two testimonials. In May 1999, Neave's retirement party involved Pompey hosting West Ham United, attracting a healthy crowd of 4,285. Blues boss Alan Ball identified a replacement, a towering doorman routinely stationed outside the Chimes Bar on match days. Kev the kit man entered the Fratton faithful's consciousness, but the boxer forever fights beneath the surface.

'To this day I cannot stand Preston. I hate Preston because I got knocked out there twice, on the same day a year apart at the Preston Guild Hall,' said McCormack with a grin.

'It was 1986 and the semi-finals of the ABA heavyweight division, and I faced Eric Cardouza. I had just turned nineteen – I'm just a baby – and it is being shown on *Sportsnight*, with the great Harry Carpenter commentating. I was doing all right in the first round and then the next, gone, knocked out. I still have the video, with Harry Carpenter saying: "This Welshman is doing really… Oh my God, he's gone." In the changing room afterwards, my brother enquired: "You okay?" I responded: "Yeah. When am I fighting?" I couldn't remember being in there!

'The following year I was back, the semi-finals of the ABA, heavyweight division once more, and held in Preston. I was boxing six-foot-six Henry Akinwande and, in the first round, was spark out. Harry Carpenter's words were: "This Welshman had a bit of bad luck last year when he got knocked out, but he's doing really well… Oh my God, he's gone again."

'Akinwande went on to win the final, later becoming pro and crowned WBO heavyweight champion and Commonwealth heavyweight champion, while Cardouza won bronze in the 1986 Commonwealth Games. There was no shame losing against boxers of that calibre, yet doubts were setting in.

'After that second knockout, I sat in the dressing room conceding that I was finished; I was going to pack it in. My trainer, Chris Manley, insisted: "Don't be silly, we're going to move you up to super heavyweight next year. You are still a baby, you're boxing men. You haven't matured yet." They said I would never do it – my trainer just replied: "You watch him."

'The first year at my new level, I reached the ABA semi-finals again, now held at the Norbreck Castle Hotel in Blackpool. I faced a lad called Clifton Mitchell, from Derby. It was a ding-dong affair – he put me down twice and I put him down twice – then in the last round he bit me on the neck. I returned to my corner and my coach had seen the claret, but the ref hadn't – most importantly, the judges had and disqualified him.

'I was in the ABA final against Steve Wollaston, an opponent who had knocked out everybody en route. Previewing our bout at the Wembley Arena, *Boxing News* predicted a Wollaston victory – by knockout.

'I put him down in the second round and felt my hand being thrust into the air. I dropped to my knees and cried. I always liked proving people wrong – I was the 1988 ABA champion.

'It's a wonderful feeling having your arm raised by a referee like that; I've never come across anything better. I don't know why, I suppose it's adulation. You train hard for all that time, then there's that horrible nervous energy before fight nights, and the outcome is being crowned champion. It's special.

'Chris, God rest him, would say: "That walk to the ring is like waiting for death, isn't it?" And it is. There's that anxiety, the nerves, it's a horrible feeling, the worst feeling in the world. If my trainer was alive today, he would say: "Where would you find Kev before he fought? In the toilet." That's where I'd be, believing I needed to go for a wee, but actually I didn't, it was just nerves.

'I was the most nervous fighter you would ever see in your life, but once you get into the ring, they announce you, the bell goes – and you can't remember that anxiety.

'In March 2015, I came out of retirement to raise money for the Oakley Waterman Caravan Foundation through a charity boxing evening at the Mountbatten Centre. My son, Oliver, had never watched me box – I packed up when he was young – and he was in the changing room asking: "Are you all right, Dad, are you all right, Dad?"

'I eventually snapped: "Oliver, go away. No, I'm not all right, I have a 28-year-old in the other corner trying to rip my head off and I am aged 47 and haven't done this competitively since I was 31." Nerves got to me, everybody was there, including our former FA Cup-winning keeper David James.

'As I came out for the walk to the ring, they played the Pompey Chimes, which I wasn't expecting, and I felt awful, my stomach churning. When I reached the middle, they announced my name to a good cheer, and the only thing I heard while in my zone was my daughter, Kimberley, shout: "Knock him out, Dad." I won on points over the scheduled three rounds.'

McCormack represented Wales in the 1986 Commonwealth Games in Edinburgh and the 1990 Commonwealth Games in Auckland, New Zealand, progressing to the quarter-finals on each occasion. His third and final appearance came in Victoria, Canada, in 1994, where the boxer was asked by Wales to fulfil flag-bearing duties at the Centennial

Stadium's opening ceremony. The red vest alongside a photograph of the proud moment occupies a frame hung in the hallway of his Waterlooville home, an immediate talking point for any observant guest. Meanwhile, there was medal glory at the 1993 European Amateur Boxing Championships in Bursa, Turkey, claiming bronze.

Raised in South Wales, McCormack attended school with future Manchester City and Wales goalkeeper Andy Dibble, and he followed Newport County's progress with interest. As an aspiring footballer, he was on the books of Cwmbran Town's youth team, before prioritising boxing. At the age of eighteen, he gained work in Portsmouth as a bricklayer, tempted over from Wales by his boxing coach, Chris Manley, who had been employed as a scaffolder on the construction of Port Solent. Initially returning home at weekends, McCormack soon settled on the south coast, maintaining his boxing career and eventually joining the Royal Marines.

'My first footballing memory was watching the 1979 FA Cup final between Arsenal and Manchester United in the days when *Grandstand* would oversee a big build-up, lasting the day. That game saw Alan Sunderland net a last-minute winner for the Gunners – it remains one of the greatest finals I have ever seen.

'Then, 29 years later, I was on that coach being filmed. Pompey had won the 2008 FA Cup and I was sitting on the front seat as we drove away from Wembley.

'A mate rang as we pulled away. He was at The Dorallt Inn in Cwmbran, oblivious to how I was spending my day, and asked: "What are you doing?" I replied: "I'm just coming out of Wembley now." He repeated: "What are you doing?" I told him: "I'm sitting at the front of the bus with the FA Cup on my lap." He went: "Shut up" – and at that point the bus came into view of the cameras. I could hear him as he was watching the telly where he was, shouting: "There's my mate, there's my mate."

'This job has kept me in sport. I know the lads take the mickey because I am overweight and bald, but I was a half-decent boxer, and I did some decent things. I won ABA titles, and people don't realise that winning one is hard enough, but I took it three times. I don't think I received the recognition I deserved for achieving that, but that doesn't bother me because I gave credit to myself.

'I love that adrenaline rush. I love a match day, being around the players; that buzz they get I get because that's what boxing gave me. I remember carrying the Welsh flag for the opening ceremony of the 1994 Commonwealth Games in front of 30,000 people, but I will never, ever forget the goosebumps on my arms when Pompey were crowned First Division winners.

'It was May 2003. We had just beaten Rotherham United 3–2 at Fratton Park and were going to the Premier League. The players were being announced onto the pitch, one by one, then Harry Redknapp turned to me and said: "What are you doing here?"

'I thought he was giving me a rollicking for standing there, so close to these league title winners, then he added: "Kev, you are as much part of this team as anybody else." I was introduced to the crowd and there was that cheer and noise. The place was rocking. With that and the AC Milan game in November 2008, I have never heard atmospheres like them.

'I enjoyed boxing because it was a good discipline for me – and a way of staying out late as a kid! I had strict parents and had to be in bed by 7pm and hung around with these lads, who one day asked if I wanted to go with them to the gym. I was aged seven, and from that point I fell in love with the sport.

'My brother, Brendan, was also very good, but fractured his skull in a car accident in Liverpool, so had to pack it in. He came back, though, fighting at heavyweight, and on the night I won my tenth Welsh title, he claimed victory in his category.

'I retired at 31, back in those days, as an amateur, since they were the rules, although it was later increased to 40. I could have turned pro, and perhaps should have, but the World Boxing Association (WBA) was the only world title at that stage, with no super heavyweight division.

'Looking back, my boxing life gives me great satisfaction as I went around the world and met great people. I never got paid for it, I did it because I enjoyed boxing, enjoyed the thrill of it, enjoyed the winning. I've calmed down over the years, because I was an angry man. Why wouldn't I be an angry man? I am an ex-boxer and Royal Marine! It's very hard to get out of that set-up. I struggled when I finished boxing. Previously I'd go to the gym to release all the pent-up frustration, taking it out on the bags or sparring and getting a few rib-ticklers in.

'I don't like the recognition I get at times when people say: "There's Kev the kit man." I am just being myself, being a nice fella chatting away to fans because I like to hear their point of view.

'Boxing gave me a decent living and made me into a decent man, albeit an angry man at times, I suppose. I'm a great believer of your life being mapped out and, if I had become a professional boxer, I wouldn't have come down here, met my wife Sarah, had two beautiful children and experienced the adventures I've had with Pompey. It has been an adventure, and I've been kit man to some great managers.'

McCormack's Pompey affiliation began in the HMS *Nelson* gym, having been approached by Blues physio Neil Sillett to help train injured footballers. Overseeing the introduction of boxing as part of their rehabilitation, the twice-weekly schedule saw him befriend club stalwarts Andy Awford and Alan Knight. Soon McCormack earned a job heading match-day security for Fratton Park's Chimes Bar, a task which saw him recruit Marines and physical training instructors to carry out doorman duty armed with a steely glare. Then, in May 1999, manager Alan Ball offered him the job he still holds to this day. Despite an interview with chief executive David Deacon, during which he mistook him for Martin Gregory (the club's owner at the time) and addressed him as 'Mr Gregory', he started work.

'I don't know why Bally offered me the job, I couldn't tell you. I would like to think he saw a good man in me and knew I could do it,' added McCormack.

'My second game was a trip to Wolverhampton Wanderers in August 1999, when a Rory Allen goal had put us 1–0 up going in at the break – and there was claret everywhere after I had jumped up to celebrate and banged my head on the dugout roof!

'Now their right-back, Kevin Muscat, had kicked Jeff Peron all over the place and was still having a go at Jeff down the tunnel while returning to the dressing room at half-time. Attempting to intervene, I said: "Lads, lads, calm down," to which Muscat snapped: "Oi, if you don't clear off you'll get some."

'That set me off: "You what? You had better get in there before I give you a dig."

'At that point, Colin Lee, Wolves' caretaker boss, shouted: "What's your problem?" By this time, my Marine head was on: "Problem? You'll have a problem in a minute if you don't clear off."

'Then I spotted Bally down the tunnel. "Oi, get in here," he roared at me. My head was down as I headed towards him and he repeated: "Get in here."

'I entered the dressing room and he slammed the door behind me. "Right, you lot," he shouted. "That's the sort of balls I want to see!"

'In those days, teacups were in the dressing room and used to fly when Bally was about. If the cap came off and hit the floor you knew, you knew. He was such a lovely man, so passionate about Pompey, so passionate about football, you could listen to him for hours. I was in awe of him.

'We had Robert Prosinečki, one of the best players I've ever seen, and I loved listening to him. To think we had him when his legs had gone, but he was still a genius, an absolute genius, and funny. I should never have started smoking, but would have a few cigarettes and the first time Prosinečki came in he said: "Kev, fire, fire." I said: "What? Where?" He actually wanted a light for his fag! Every game I'd have a Marlboro Red lit for him, at half-time and the end of the match. Those cigarettes were like tarmac and he would smoke in my laundry room or the dressing-room toilets.

'On away trips, before the game, he would have a smoke and order either a double espresso or triple espresso, while telling me stories about Real Madrid and Barcelona. Rob once gave me a Rolex watch to look after. I asked: "What's this?" – and he replied it was worth £85,000 and Barcelona had given it to him as a present!

'We had Dario Silva here, a Uruguayan international striker who was as mad as a box of frogs and didn't speak much English.

Around Christmas 2005, he came into my room at Fratton Park and noticed half a bottle of brandy I'd been given. "Good?" he enquired. I replied: "Yes," – then he drank the lot in one go, right in front of me. "Very good," he said, before leaving.

'Peter Crouch was another here and I remember him buying this rather expensive settee, a huge three-seater, and he asked me to give him a hand lifting it into his Port Solent flat.

'I recognised the problem straight away: it wasn't possible to get it up to the third floor. There was a spiral staircase and it wasn't going to get in a lift. I should know – as a bricklayer by trade I did all the lifts when all that housing was being built.

'Crouchy replied: "I've spent a fortune on this, about £2–3,000, I can't take it back." So I told him to get me a ladder. I put the settee on my head, tied around my waist with ropes, and climbed up, with Crouchy, Courtney Pitt and Shaun Derry holding the ladder while I scaled it. After reaching the top, I threw it onto the balcony and through the open French doors. I think it's still there now – nobody would be able to get that out!

'We had Paul Merson for a season – he liked a gamble but he was a good lad. Back in those days they had to wash their own training kit, so Merse promised me £10,000 if I did his and we got promoted. As we were all in awe of him, I went: "Yeah, whatever." We won the First Division title that year – and he was as good as his word.

'When Crouchy first joined he told me he didn't have a washing machine and asked me to do it for £15 a week. Recently on his podcast he claimed it was £60 a week – was it hell! I never got it all the time anyway, footballers are tight!'

At Pompey's Copnor Road training ground, Lee Brown has been press-ganged into addressing the local media ahead of October's League One visit of Gillingham. A boisterous dressing-room presence armed with ready quips, the left-back was last month promoted to vice-captain, replacing Gareth Evans. Headlining Kenny Jackett's reshuffle, however, was Brett Pitman's removal as skipper in favour of Tom Naylor, following two seasons in office. Brown's chirpy pre-match patter is interrupted by Ellis Harrison mischievously querying the futility of zipped pockets on the arms of his tracksuit top, with McCormack soon aligning himself with the mocking striker. With footballing pride demanding a response, Brown identifies Barry Harris as a rich source of ammunition to fire in the direction of Pompey's kit man.

'Bazza, what are you doing tonight? Proper kit man doing a little Q & A,' prods the smirking 29-year-old. 'I would rather hear your stories, Bazza.'

Later that day, the man whose Pompey association stretches 67 years, serving a variety of roles on a voluntary basis and seeing 33 different first-team managers, is booked to appear at Fratton's Rifle Club for a charity fundraiser titled 'An Evening With Barry Harris'.

For the past twenty years, boot man Harris and McCormack have formed a back-room double act, the unlikely pairing bonding as travelling companions and room-mates, although close proximity has been known to spark bickering bouts, much to the amusement of those who happen to be in the vicinity. The Thursday night event, compered by Jake Payne and promoted by Dale Field, was a success, raising in excess of £1,000 for Macmillan Cancer Support, a total boosted by a raffle for Enda Stevens' Republic of Ireland shirt, donated by the former Blues full-back, and a signed Sergio Agüero Manchester City top. It was quite a night for the Harris family with his son, Pete, steering a band of three to triumph in the Pompey quiz stage of the proceedings, yielding a windfall of £80, although there was confusion when somebody not associated with the team, but positioned on a nearby table, had enthusiastically roared the answer to a tie-break, thereby earning them victory. Nonetheless, Harris was delighted with the outcome.

The 75-year-old said: 'When I knew I was doing the event, I rang Harry Redknapp, as well as my old friend Mike Summerbee, who does a couple of after-dinners every week. Harry stressed that people were coming to see me, so it was important I was myself. He also suggested that if there was something I wanted to say but could not remember, to write it on a big piece of paper and put it into my pocket. He always has time for you.

'I loved Alan Ball and Jim Smith, but he's my favourite Pompey manager. It's his man-management which stands out, the way he spoke to people – it was the right way, and he could tell you off without telling you off. As far as players went, he knew exactly what a player could do and wouldn't ask them to do anything else.

'If he had one weakness, it was that he didn't play kids. You had to be seasoned pros to work with Harry, but he got the best out of them. I class him as a friend. I ring him up and he always asks after my wife Sue – he's one nice bloke.

'I've never fallen out with any of our managers, although Tony Pulis wouldn't talk to me; he'd look at me as though I shouldn't be there, hardly ever saying a word. The funny thing was, a few years back when we were training at Eastleigh and he was manager of Stoke City, they came in to train after us as they had a match against Southampton. Kev and I were sitting in the van before travelling up north somewhere and Tony was all over me like a rash. It was all "Hello, big fella, how are you getting on?" I thought: "What's that all about?" Tony could be very rude, very abrupt, but I never really fell out with him.

'Ian St John was very arrogant. I was talking to a player once and he came in and said: "You don't get paid to sit and talk to players." Well, I didn't get paid at all, I work for nothing! He was distant as a manager, which is why the players didn't like him. He had been a great footballer, but his handling of people was very poor and a record of 27 wins in 119 league matches shows he wasn't a manager.

'Bally was a lovely man, and two weeks before his death in 2007, I cleaned the windows at his home in Hook Lane, Warsash. I had a cleaning business after leaving the dockyard in 1981 and he was a customer. I would go round every six weeks.

'Some managers don't want to talk football and I understand that, it's their job. I didn't want to talk about cleaning windows and floors! With Bally, though, you could stop him and chat football.

During his first spell, I'd get back from an away game with Gordon Neave and Bally would usually ask what we were doing. If not too late, Gordy would always get fish and chips for his wife and head home, while Bally said to me: "You're not going anywhere, let's get a drink," and we'd head off to the Chimes Bar at Fratton Park, which was open in the evening. He had some wonderful stories.

'When he was manager the second time around, I remember Fitzroy Simpson, who was very flamboyant, in the dressing room going on about being in the 1998 World Cup finals with Jamaica. Bally overheard him one day and said: "Your job is at Pompey. We pay your wages to go off and play for these teams around the world." Then Bally really put him in his place: "Come and talk to me when you've won the World Cup!"'

Born in February 1944 at his family home at Spurlings Farm, in the village of Wallington, Fareham, during an air raid, Harris had his first Pompey encounter at the age of eight, accompanying dad, Bill, and brother, Cyril, to an FA Cup fifth round fixture with Doncaster Rovers in February 1952, a match which saw Bob Jackson's Portsmouth side run out 4–0 winners. He was appointed team mascot for the following season, a responsibility bestowed by legendary Pompey defender Reg Flewin, who had struck up a friendship with the youngster. Asked to lead the players onto the pitch and shake hands with the captains, the visit of Stanley Matthews' Blackpool represented Harris' first day at work for the football club he cherished. Departing to serve in the merchant navy for six years, Harris re-established his Blues links upon his return by working as the Pompey Sailor mascot, travelling home and away with the club with the pre-match remit of parading a 'Play Up Pompey' placard and attempting to gee up the crowd.

Eventually he would graduate to working as a physio for the reserve and youth teams, volunteer responsibilities which he combined with operating in the back room, helping clean boots and moving skips of kit on match days. Not that the Harris influence was purely restricted to off-pitch matters as two of his sons, Clive and Pete, spent time on the books of Pompey's youth team, although they did not progress into the professional game. A generation later, grandson Charlie, the offspring of third son Wayne, was in the Academy set-up in recent years, only to leave to focus on rugby.

'I've never been paid at Pompey, but I get looked after. I receive kit, I don't have to pay to get into games and I stay at the team hotels. It doesn't bother me not being on the payroll; I am quite happy doing what I do.

'I enjoy mixing with footballers, listening to their chat, and it's just nice to be around the club, although football banter can be wicked sometimes! Don't get involved in football if you don't want to get the mickey taken out of you.

'I've fed players at my house too. Lee Brown and Ronan Curtis both arrived around the same time in the summer of 2018 and were staying at a local hotel, so I invited them round and made them chicken curry. I just wanted to help them settle in. I like having people around me and that's probably why I do what I do around the club.

'A few years ago we had Ben Chorley and, when not picked, he would drive from his Kent home to watch the match and have a full English breakfast round mine beforehand; he was another nice bloke. I treat them as friends, and if anyone wants to talk football, I will, 24 hours a day.

'I'm discreet, though. I would never tell anyone what is going on at the club or give my opinion on matters. If I said something and it got back to the manager, it would put me in real trouble, but I'm lucky on the whole, as people don't usually bother me. Sue and I have been out before and when asked what was said by the manager at half-time, I'll just respond with "I don't know, I was changing some studs!" You have to be discreet, which is probably why I have been at the club as long as I have.

'At one stage I was the physio for the reserve and youth teams, but had to give that up in the early nineties when it was decided you had to have hospital qualifications. Before that, I went to Lilleshall for six weeks over three years to qualify for the job. When the changes came in, the club offered to send me to university, but I didn't think I was brainy enough!

'When Jim Smith was manager, he started taking me on the team coach to do the food, which was basically tea and toast for the players on the way up and then getting the fish and chips on the way home. As players' diets changed, I would buy pasta from Marks & Spencer the previous day and cook it on the coach to feed them after a match.

'When we were in administration during Bally's second spell, the club was in a real mess so Sue and I would make sandwiches at home, using fillings such as chicken, ham or cheese, and take them on the coach for the players. I got reimbursed for most of them.

'I just like helping the club. In April 1967, Billy Bonds visited Fratton Park with Charlton Athletic and broke his nose in their 2–1 win, so I drove him to the old Royal Portsmouth Hospital, which is now Sainsbury's in Commercial Road. I've always been involved in helping with the kit, though, and the dressing room is busier than it has ever been with the amount of staff these days.

'It used to be a sacred place and, during the early 1950s, when Jimmy Stewart was kit man and I was the mascot, I would sit near Len Phillips in the dressing room and he once told me: "What you hear in this place, son, don't tell your parents." I even met Field Marshal Montgomery in there, introduced by the manager, Eddie Lever.

'I'm still living the dream. Standing on the Wembley pitch with the FA Cup in your hand, you don't get much better than that, do you?

'Sue is my second wife. We married in 1998 and she understands what Pompey means to me; she doesn't interfere. She has no interest in football, which I don't think is a bad thing. The last time she went to a game was against AC Milan in November 2008, when I had a spare ticket.

'When I get home from an away game on a Saturday night, she asks what the trip was like and already knows the score having looked out for it on the TV, but that's as far as it goes. I don't mind that. The first night I took her out, I told her: "If you can put up with my football, you can put up with me." It has never been a problem.'

Pride of place on the landing at Harris' Southsea home hangs a framed letter congratulating him on 65 years' service at Fratton Park. It is signed by Sir Alex Ferguson. Printed on headed paper from the legendary former Manchester United manager's company, ACF Sports Promotions, it reads: 'What an achievement. I was always aware of your presence every time we played you, sometimes to my annoyance! I hope you have a very enjoyable evening to celebrate your anniversary and outstanding commitment to the club!'

On the occasion of his 60th anniversary in 2012, a shocked Harris received a midday phone call at home from Ferguson, wishing him all the best. A gesture of immense respect towards the multitasking Fareham lad who is approaching Pompey involvement during an eighth different decade. Similarly, Harris possesses reverence of his own towards a figure closer to home – McCormack.

He added: 'Kev's a friend. I think you have to know how to handle him, but his bark is worse than his bite.

'In the Leasing.com Trophy match at Oxford United the other night, we gave a debut to Harvey Rew, a seventeen-year-old from Gosport. He came off at half-time, but hadn't brought his coat.

"You're going to get cold, aren't you," said Kev. "I gave you a coat at the beginning of the season and you should have brought it with you." Then Kev went into his bag and gave him another coat.

'Kev's family remain in Wales and his dad, Liam, is a lovely person. That's where Kev gets it from – his dad is the life and soul of the pub. Kev doesn't unwind enough though; he never has time, but he's very hard-working. You don't get the youth team helping with jobs any more, they're not allowed to.

'He's got a big heart and when I broke my left ankle in a hit-and-run in October 2007, he was the first person to come and see me that evening in hospital. He then returned the next day, this time bringing Pompey midfielder Sean Davis.

'Last year on Sue's birthday, we were going to the Golden Lion in Southwick and Kev insisted we didn't get a taxi; instead he would drive us there himself. He's like that; if he can help, he will.

'He shouts at me, but I don't take any notice; it goes over my head. The other day Brandon Haunstrup told him off: "You should show some respect, Kev. You shouldn't speak to Baz like that." I don't mind, you're in football. Gordon Neave was worse than him.

'In the late 1970s we had Keith James, a pal of Alan Knight and an England under-18 international whose hair was grown long. It was always straggly, prompting the manager, Frank Burrows, demanding he got it cut.

'He didn't and one day at training at Fratton Park, Gordy reminded Keith of the request and he was a bit lippy back. So Gordy grabbed hold of him, took him around the back of the Fratton End to where there used to be a little workshop, and put his hair in a vice. Then left him there for 30 minutes – he got his hair cut after that!

'Kev and I have a lot of fun and I give it back sometimes. I have no problem with how he treats me. We travel together and share a room together. He likes to play music before he goes to sleep, but it doesn't bother me. I can go to sleep in no time, but get up early. There's a lot of good in him and he expects everyone to put in the same effort he does.'

Certainly McCormack is known at Fratton Park for his high work ethic – and generosity.

England international Mason Mount may be a Premier League player for Chelsea, but he remains an avid Pompey supporter who once idolised Andres D'Alessandro, a mercurial Argentine winger who spent six months on loan with the Blues. McCormack's friendship with Mount's dad, Tony, led to the youngster being presented with a shirt signed by his hero, a touching gesture, the gift still hanging up in the twenty-year-old's Cobham home. McCormack also assisted in fundraising to enable terminally ill sixteen-year-old Beth Tiller to spend time away with her family. The Denmead schoolgirl, who had been diagnosed with non-Hodgkin's lymphoma, passed away in April 2018.

Yet the time to focus on looking after himself is approaching as he contemplates a future without Pompey – and possible retirement in 2024 around his 25th anniversary.

'My wife tells the story of how she once drove past Fratton Park with my son, then aged six, also in the car. He pointed to the ground and said: "Daddy lives there."

'I've missed much of my kids growing up, which is hard, but you do it for a reason, to give them a better life, the same as everybody in work. Would I change anything? Yes, I suppose I would – to spend more time with them.

'Obviously you are not going to get that back now but I can't knock the job I've done because it has been a big part of my life. Football is important, but life is more important. Family is more important. We must work to live, but you have to enjoy it – and I love my job.

'It's either dedication or just stupidity, but that's my work ethic. I won't put things off and I just like to do things properly. My dad taught me that – there's no point going back over it, do it properly the first time.

'My wife, Sarah, has been understanding and I'd be lost without her to be fair. As big as I am, she wears the trousers.

'I don't want to be carried out in a box. In three or so years' time I would like to say to the club: "I'll still work for you, but I don't want to travel." It will be time for a younger person to come in and carry it on – 25 years in the role would be a long time.

'I've made some friends and have probably annoyed some as well, but not intentionally. The trouble with me is I'll say what I think. If I'm wrong, I will apologise, but if I'm not, then I won't; it's the way I've been brought up. Say it as it is, especially when working – I'm old school like that.

'When you are working with people 24/7 you aren't going to get on with them all the time. You have your oppos in the Marines who are your best buddies, although you aren't going to get on with them every day, but you have to go into battle with them so you trust them with your life.

'I am a great believer in being honest. If you don't like someone, don't talk behind their backs, speak to their face. That's how I was brought up and my father was the same; he gave me good values.

'The secret to being a kit man is patience, making sure you look after the players well because they are important. They can be labelled overpaid stars, but that's not their fault, that's what they are good at.

'As a boxer, if I felt good and looked good then I performed well. That's what I attempt to do for these players to the best of my ability.

'I cannot say this job has been easy, it hasn't; it has been hard, very hard, but I wouldn't change it. I wouldn't change it for the world.'

GARETH EVANS

21 October 2019

The nineteen-year-old arrived to discover his footballing fate filled with expectation. Crewe Alexandra boss Dario Gradi had assured the talented apprentice that a two-year deal would be tabled, a heartening pledge delivered several months earlier to sweep away intensifying nerves. Instead, Gareth Evans was told that he would never make it as a professional footballer and ushered through the exit. Academy manager Steve Holland tossed crumbs of consolation to the youngster, citing a trial at Nantwich Town and a contract with Alsager Town as bright alternatives. Their non-league statuses brutally reflected the destiny now plotted for the attacking midfielder.

Since being discarded by the then-League One club in April 2007, Evans has amassed 529 appearances and netted 91 goals as a Football League performer. His list of honours consists of a League Two title, League Two play-off triumph, the Checkatrade Trophy and a Wembley man-of-the-match award. Holland is now employed as England's assistant manager, having initially established himself as Gareth Southgate's trusted lieutenant at under-21 international level, and the teenager he foresaw having a future in the Northern Premier League Division One South has just racked up his 200th Pompey outing in a League One trip to AFC Wimbledon.

'The other day I was talking with my dad about my impending 200th appearance and he said: "Not bad for somebody deemed not good enough for professional football!"' grinned Evans.

'I had served my two-year scholarship at Crewe and was expecting a pro deal. I'd heard a couple of other lads had been given contracts and, in my mind, felt I was better than them. Besides, in the February, Dario Gradi told me they were going to give me two years: "Don't worry about it, everything is in place." Then, at the end of the 2006–07 season, Gradi became technical director, with Holland appointed first-team coach and Academy director.

'With us youth-team lads being called into the office one by one to discuss our futures, Holland told me: "You are never, ever going to be good enough to play professional football, unfortunately. But I've set you up with a trial at Nantwich Town and you've got a contract at Alsager Town if you want to sign for them."

'I sat there in complete shock – I hadn't been expecting that. I just told him: "Fuck off, you're wrong," and walked out.

'Even though you've been released, you're supposed to go in and finish all your educational duties, which were A levels in history and French, and a BTEC in Sports Science, but I ended up doing them from home. I never went back.

'Obviously Academy coaches don't get every decision right. I don't hate Steve Holland because of it – it's what he thought at the time – but don't let anyone tell you that you're not good enough. You have to believe – and prove it.

'That's football, it's a game of opinions. Dario obviously thought I was good enough and that hopefully I could break into his first team the following season, but Steve didn't.

'I've seen him since. He was Chelsea's assistant manager at the time and I was having food with friends at Alderley Edge. He came over and said: "Hello." It was very awkward!

'I'd been kicking a ball since the age of two or three, so for someone to turn around and say I was not good enough at nineteen was tough to take. I can appreciate that probably the most difficult part of being a coach is telling lads that their dreams aren't going to be realised, but I used it to motivate me, to prove people wrong.

'Each summer the League Football Education hold Assessment Trials involving all apprentices released at the end of the season, which included me in 2007. Back then it involved a 90-minute match and, because there are so many players, you might only have fifteen minutes in front of a stand full of Football League scouts with their clipboards.

'It was roll-on, roll-off subs, so you could be put on for fifteen minutes and the ball may not even come to you, then you're substituted and that's it.

'Luckily, I started that game and within ten minutes had scored twice. I thought I had done all right considering I played the entire game, while everyone else was on and off! I netted four or so times in total and, without wanting to sound big-headed, I knew I was better than the players there.

'Port Vale spotted me and their manager, Martin Foyle, took me on trial all pre-season and let me attend their tour to the Five Lakes Resort in Colchester. I did really well, scoring three or four goals during friendlies, but the club had massive financial problems.

'They wanted to sign me but couldn't even afford £100 a week – so Martin contacted his good friend Ian Brightwell, the manager at Macclesfield Town, incidentally my home-town club. Funnily enough, seven or eight lads at Crewe who signed professional contracts that summer didn't get game time during the 2007–08 campaign, whereas I was playing week in, week out in League Two, making 45 appearances and scoring seven times in my debut first-team season – it had worked out better.

'My best mate at Crewe was James Bailey and still is to this day. He went on to break into Derby County's first team, although he doesn't play now; he's a personal trainer these days. Luke Murphy, who was in the year below but in my scholarship intake, went to Leeds United, Burton Albion and this season appeared as a Bolton Wanderers substitute against us. Apart from them, no one else came through.

'It's fair to say I took a difficult route and ended up having a reasonable career. To make 529 appearances so far is quite an achievement.'

In reaching his 200th game for Pompey, Evans joined Matt Taylor and Linvoy Primus as the only players to reach that landmark in the 21st century – and only the tenth to do so in the last 27 years. The journey that eventually brought him to Fratton Park in July 2015 is testament to a steely single-mindedness which saw him quit Manchester United on his own terms when aged fourteen. The Red Devils recruited him for an undisclosed fee from Crewe at the age of ten, having identified him as a central midfielder of immense potential. Evans' age group notably consisted of Jonny Evans, Danny Simpson, Ryan Shawcross, Fraizer Campbell and Kieran Lee, peers who ultimately would progress into a first team still under the tutelage of Sir Alex Ferguson.

An Old Trafford season-ticket holder who had accompanied dad Steve to Inter Milan and Barcelona en route to Champions League glory in 1999, Evans treasured his footballing education at The Cliff and Carrington. Then, in the summer of 2002, he elected to walk out in order to return to Crewe, a destination he believed offered a greater first-team pathway.

He added: 'Believe it or not, I decided to leave. I had a great time at Manchester United, travelling the world, but they had bought Ruud van Nistelrooy for £18.5m, then the following summer Juan Sebastián Verón arrived for £28.1m.

'They were no longer dipping into the youth team, and as such, progress had become pretty much non-existent. Whenever they required a player they would spend millions instead of promoting a youngster. I didn't see a way through. In comparison, Crewe had produced the likes of Dean Ashton, Rob Hulse, Robbie Savage – they had a conveyor belt of talent and, I felt, were a better option for my professional football career.

'My dad informed Paul McGuinness, the head coach of Manchester United's Academy, that it wasn't really working out, and that I favoured Crewe. They were understanding but quite angry that I wanted to leave, because they believed no one was better than Manchester United, which was true to a point.

'I'm a massive United fan and, even after leaving, would go back to watch the first team. I had been a season-ticket holder in Old

Trafford's family stand since the age of two, before moving to the second tier of the North Stand.

'Growing up, Eric Cantona was this mythical figure, with his collar up, scoring wonder goals and flicking the ball around the corner, a genius. I liked David Beckham for a while, but that wore off. Ryan Giggs is my all-time favourite United player.

'We would see the first team all the time, but as a twelve-year-old, I was scared to death of walking past Roy Keane. He just didn't want to acknowledge you whatsoever and had that piercing glare. You didn't say a word in case he told you off!

'I would see Beckham arguing with Ferguson all the time. Beckham would have driven up from London in his red Ferrari and the manager wasn't happy with it. I can remember one argument which involved Beckham taking off his gloves and throwing them on the ground.

'With hindsight, my career would obviously have been totally different if I'd stayed at United. You see players coming through now and, aged about 21 or 22, earning really decent money. Then, should they go anywhere, it's to a Championship club on a two-year deal, whereas if you're out of contract at Crewe, you're looking from League Two downwards.

'It was a gamble, and ultimately it didn't really work out at Crewe, so maybe if I had remained at Old Trafford my career would have mapped out differently. When I left, another central midfielder joined my age group – Danny Rose. Years later we would win the League Two title together at Pompey!'

Deployed as a striker for Macclesfield, Evans spent two seasons successfully fighting relegation before earning a move to fellow League Two club Bradford City for an undisclosed fee, where he was converted by manager Peter Taylor into a winger. The tour of the north continued with a free transfer to Rotherham United in June 2011, back in the Football League's bottom division. Evans marked his full debut with two goals in a 4–1 win at a Plymouth Argyle side containing future Premier League performer Conor Hourihane, while Lewis Grabban and Adam Le Fondre lined up for Rotherham. However, a frank midgame exchange with his second Millers boss, Steve Evans, drove his exit to Fleetwood Town in January 2013.

He said: 'Andy Scott recruited me for Rotherham, then in March of that first season was replaced by Steve Evans who gave me a new contract in the summer and told me I would never play for him again in the November!

'I was in and out of the team. Basically he wanted his own players and then, with the right winger injured, I was back in, working on shape and set pieces on the Friday ahead of a trip to Dagenham & Redbridge.

'We turned up at the ground and, upon entering our changing room, noticed some lad wearing his own stuff. It turned out to be Luke Rooney, on loan from Swindon, and he was starting on the right ring, with me on the bench! Evans hadn't said a word about the change of plan. I had been told I was playing.

'At half-time we were 2–0 down and he substituted Rooney, bringing me on at left-back and pushing the left-back, Josh Morris, on to the right flank. Anyhow, around the hour mark, one of their players went down injured so I passed the ball out for him to receive treatment, prompting Evans to go mad at me by the side of the pitch.

'I tried to calm it by saying: "Right, okay," and he continued ranting in front of the whole Dagenham stand, going on and on until I finally snapped: "Shut up you fat c*nt." He said: "What?" and I replied: "Relax," and walked off. He didn't say anything to anyone for the rest of the game.

'We ended up losing 5–0 and I knew I was getting it in the dressing room afterwards. The scoreline wasn't my fault, but he didn't say a word to anyone else, shouting at me for 30 minutes solid. I was told to report to his office at 8am the next day, bringing my tracksuit, club suit, everything – I was out.

'I still trained, albeit by the side of the pitch while my team-mates worked on set pieces and featured in eleven v elevens. If Evans turned round and saw I had slowed down, he'd shout at me. I played once more, as a half-time substitute against Wycombe

Wanderers ten days later because of injuries, but that was it. When the January transfer window reopened, my contract was cancelled by mutual consent and I joined Fleetwood Town on the same money.

'When Gillingham visited Fratton Park this month for a goalless draw, he was present as their manager and said: "All right, Evo, how are you?" I walked past him without saying a word; I had no interest. I'm not going to be your mate after you treated me like that.'

By the summer of 2015, Evans felt unfulfilled by his footballing journey to date, craving heightened challenges, an aspiration that saw the out-of-contract midfielder reject a new two-year Fleetwood deal as a consequence.

Following a maiden League One season in which he amassed 46 appearances and four goals, for the first time in eight summers the midfielder was content to be marooned without a club in pursuit of other employment. As a free agent, the 27-year-old was uninhibited by the necessity of a transfer fee to secure his services, which turned out to be a deciding factor. Newly appointed Pompey boss Paul Cook had already recruited Kyle Bennett, Kal Naismith, Enda Stevens, Gary Roberts, Christian Burgess and Michael Doyle. Next on his list was Evans.

'In June 2015, I went on holiday with my girlfriend, Hazel, and my parents and lay on a beach in Lagos, Portugal, thinking I didn't want to go back to Fleetwood,' said Evans.

'I'd had enough. My time was spent there and I didn't really enjoy it that much any more. I needed a new challenge.

'People have different aspirations when they join a club. Some want to earn £50,000 a week to ensure that when they get to the end of their careers they don't need to work again. The motivation for others, such as me, is to have good memories of scoring big goals, playing in front of large crowds.

'During my time at Pompey, I've had the opportunity to go back up north and earn more money. But do I really want to sacrifice everything I've got down here, everything I've always wanted in my career, to move up north for an extra few hundred quid a week?

'Pompey have filled a void and ultimately the gamble has paid off. I put my future on the line by coming on trial here – if it hadn't worked out, I'd completely burnt my bridges elsewhere and we were now into the season.

'My agent, David Threlfall, had started putting my name out and there were offers coming in, but they were mediocre League One clubs that were only ever going to play at that level, which is the main reason why I left Fleetwood.

'Then Paul Cook got in touch, wanting to look at me for a couple of days in order to assess my fitness. Well, I hadn't been training, just running, going to the gym, generally trying to keep myself ticking over.

'On my first day on the south coast, the players were instructed to run along Southsea seafront – and I finished five minutes ahead of everyone else; it wasn't even close. Cookie was on a bike, keeping up with the leaders and shouting, which in this instance was me and Michael Doyle. With twenty minutes to go, I was aware I still had a bit left in my tank and pulled further and further away from Doyley. To this day, he reminds me of that and says: "I can't believe you did that to me. I have never seen anyone run like that!"

'I knew I was doing well because Cookie was struggling to keep up on his bike, and he ended up following Doyley because I had gone! As my time at Pompey continued, Cook would drive down the esplanade in his car instead, winding his window down to shout!

'My trial was a lot longer than it was supposed to have been. I scored in a friendly against Coventry City and nothing was mentioned about a contract. I netted the opener and crossed for the other in a 2–0 friendly win at Woking and he didn't say a word to me about a deal.

'I didn't want to push the issue and scouts were turning up to watch me on trial. Concrete offers arrived from the likes of Gillingham and Walsall.

'It came to the point where I nearly had to leave. There were deals coming in from elsewhere and I couldn't go another month without pay. Then, approaching the final week of pre-season, I told Cookie I needed to know where I stood. He said they would put in an offer that afternoon and it was sorted, a twelve-month contract with an option.

'I think he was toying with me. He wanted the lure of a contract to get the best out of me rather than resting on my laurels. I suppose he didn't really know me as a character at that point.

'During my trial, I stayed at the Royal Beach Hotel in Southsea. Once I received my contract, I was told if I hadn't been taken on then the club would have paid the bill but as I had signed, I had to cough up.

'Anyhow, after putting pen to paper, I returned to the hotel and their staff had packed up my stuff and put it behind the reception desk – they had basically booted me out of the room!

'The bill was £2,200, with a club discount, which also included food I had put on it. Well, I needed to eat! There were quite a few lads staying there – Kyle Bennett, Michael Doyle, Ben Davies – everyone was booted out of their room and had to pay for it. To be fair, I had just got a contract. At least I was getting money, so what's a hotel bill? Just pay it.'

Evans netted on his Pompey debut in the season's opener against Dagenham & Redbridge in August 2015, scoring the first goal in a 3–0 win with a far-post header from Bennett's left-wing corner. A fixture on the right of the attacking three in Cook's favoured 4-2-3-1 formation, he was an integral member of the team that reached the League Two play-off semi-finals, before falling to a stoppage-time 3–2 aggregate defeat at Plymouth.

The next season, following the departure of right-back Ben Davies and the arrival of right-winger Carl Baker, Evans was pushed into an unfamiliar full-back role, albeit armed with attacking tendencies. Pompey won the League Two title after a 6–1 Fratton Park victory over Cheltenham Town on the last day of the 2016–17 campaign. They occupied the table's summit for the final 32 minutes of the season and an Evans penalty was among the goals.

'Paul Cook wouldn't let you get away with many things. For instance, if he found out lads were going out drinking too much he would clamp down on it, but there was a balance,' said Evans.

'In March 2016, we drew 1–1 at Mansfield Town, the week after a 3–0 home defeat to Newport County. He recognised that the whole place was gone, everyone was down and automatic promotion was effectively over, so he decided to pick us up by injecting a bit of enjoyment.

'We were given a couple of crates of beer to drink on the bus on the way back which, on paper, wasn't professional, but it brought the lads together. A few beers, a few home truths, move on – and we reached the play-offs.

'He had this ability to sense when the lads were a bit low and would be spontaneous to generate a lift. He wouldn't keep repeating the same training session day after day, there would be random stuff to keep it fresh, such as playing head tennis instead of analysing a game, competing at water polo in the Roko pool or swimming in the sea.

'On one occasion, he got the lads together and told us to drive to Southsea – for another six-mile run, we thought. Instead he marched us to a cafe, ordered 30 bacon butties and 30 coffees and we sat talking football and about the weekend's game.

'Then there was the register we had to sign each day, which demonstrated his more regimented side. You had to be in by 9am and, with the register by his office, he always knew when somebody was late. There were times when he would drag you into his room when signing it.

'It was a massive surprise when Cookie quit in May 2017 so soon after winning the League Two title. Being out of contract that summer, I was on the phone to him every day, although it was actually Leam Richardson as you could never ring Paul Cook! He would go mad and fine you, even though you had his number. It was a case of "Don't ring me!" I once got a rollicking for texting him.

'Everything had to go through Leam, so I had him ringing saying: "Have you signed anything? Don't sign anything," with Cookie chipping in in the background. I did wonder why he took such an approach. Surely he wanted me to sign? He and Leam wouldn't say much, it was basically: "We are desperate to have you, but don't sign."

'Eventually the club offered the two-year contract I felt I was worth and I signed. I hadn't spoken to Cookie or Leam for two or three days, they were away in Portugal. Besides, he'd told me many times he wanted to keep me. Encouragingly, Kyle Bennett had also penned a new three-year deal two days earlier.

'Then, within fourteen days, the manager was gone. He didn't say a word. We'd finished the season and everyone had gone back to where they were from, so there's no way he could have got the lads together and thanked us. Some may have spoken to him, but I didn't even receive a text.

'Nick Meace, who was our physio before following Cookie to Wigan, has since told me they didn't want me to sign a new Pompey deal because they were keen on me going with them. I don't know, it's stuff you hear.

'We didn't have a clue he was leaving and I was devastated. We had a great group of lads who had just been to Marbella together, and if we could have added another three or four players we could have aimed for the Championship, potentially. But he decided to leave us for a club not as good as Pompey.'

While Cheltenham ranks as Evans' favourite Pompey moment from his first 200 appearances, the Checkatrade Trophy final success over Sunderland in March 2019 edges it out at the finishing line. More than 40,000 Blues fans were present at Wembley for the highest attendance in the competition's 36-year history, totalling 85,021. Evans, reeling after being dropped by Kenny Jackett for the occasion, climbed off the bench to replace Ronan Curtis on the left wing in the 56th minute, with the Blues trailing to Aiden McGeady's opener. He turned in a man-of-the-match display, crossing for Nathan Thompson's first ever Pompey goal which served as an 82nd-minute equaliser. Then, with the scores level at 2–2 after extra-time, Evans was among the successful penalty-takers in a 5–4 shoot-out victory.

'The day before that final against Sunderland, I checked the team sheet on the noticeboard outside the gym and saw I wasn't in the starting XI. I was devastated.' Evans added.

'I felt I had made a massive contribution towards Pompey playing at Wembley, appearing in almost every round and I was captain at Bury for the semi-final, scoring the opener from a free-kick and also involved in the second goal in a 3–0 win.

'Ahead of Wembley, I wasn't playing badly in League One and had scored twelve goals, while Ronan had trapped his finger in a door two and a half weeks earlier and trained only once in the build-up.

'The day before the game we worked on shape, and I wasn't involved but Ronan was. My only other time at Wembley was with Fleetwood for the 2014 League Two play-off final – we won 1–0 but, as an unused substitute, I didn't set foot on the turf. Now I was back with Pompey and thought I would again miss out.

'I was desperate to lead Pompey out at Wembley. Instead I was sitting on the bench wearing a yellow bib, watching the lads in the starting line-up come out of the tunnel in front of all those flags from the Pompey end. I was in the squad but I didn't feel like I was experiencing it.

'When I came off the bench, introduced on the left for Ronan, I wanted to prove a point – which is what I did.

'Everything worked out in the end, but even after the celebrations and heading back to the team hotel, I was still upset about not starting. I set up the equaliser and scored a penalty in the shoot-out, yet instead of 10/10 buzzing I was 8/10, despite the fact we had won. Still, I was delighted for everyone associated with the club.'

This season marks Evans' fifth at Fratton Park, the same length of first-team service as Christian Burgess and bettered only by Academy graduates Jack Whatmough and Ben Close. The campaign has so far been a source of immense frustration for the Fratton faithful, with their side lagging behind early promotion pacesetters Ipswich Town and Wycombe. For Evans, there was the ignominy of appearing as a substitute in August's hard-earned 1–1 draw at Blackpool – only to be hauled off after 25 minutes to be replaced by Ellis Harrison in the same right-sided position. Around 36 hours later, the vice-captaincy held since Jackett arrived at the club two years earlier was removed, with Brett Pitman's reign as captain also at an end. Tom Naylor and Lee Brown were their replacements. Both decisions understandably rankled with Evans.

He said: 'I don't really like drama. I would rather plod along. I don't want to be associated with negativity, but there was nothing positive about it.

'What happened at Blackpool had never occurred before in my career, and I never expected it. I still don't know to this day what really went on. Marcus Harness pulled up with his sore thigh and the manager turned round to the bench and said I was going on, which was fine. We were 1–0 up and needed to see out the last five minutes of that half. I think I touched the ball twice, but mainly helped out defensively.

'When you're leading away from home, the hosts will come out and have a go at the start of the second half. We were under the cosh a little, they equalised and then the board went up. I couldn't believe it.

'In my mind there were lads not playing well who weren't considered for substitution. I felt humiliated.

'As I came off the pitch, the manager said it was tactical, so I sat down and thought: "Now keep your mouth shut." I was fuming.

'I'm an honest person, but I couldn't sit there and say: "I have been absolutely atrocious and fully deserve to be subbed." Maybe I should have got to a few balls a bit quicker, but I think that every game.

'In the dressing room afterwards, the manager apologised to me, stressing he felt the need to make a change and reiterating that it was tactical. When I came in on the Monday afterwards, the vice-captaincy was removed, although, in fairness, I don't think the incidents were connected.

'It's not like I had called him names or been disrespectful, because I do respect him and everything he has achieved in his career.

'That morning, Brett and I were the only ones in the changing room and he told me he was no longer captain. Then Joe Gallen came in and said the gaffer wanted to see me straight away. I knew it was either about Blackpool or the vice-captaincy.

'I was told we were moving in a different direction. The manager believed the captain and vice-captain had to be regulars and I wasn't going to be a regular. I was actually more bothered about the captaincy. I had worn the armband on occasions and now knew I would never skipper Pompey again under this manager. It took a few days to get over, but you have to train as hard as you can and work as hard as you can.

'As a 31-year-old, with more than 500 games in my career, you don't expect to be brought on and taken off in the same game. It hurt at the time, but you have to move on.

'It was actually a week and a half of being really annoyed and frustrated. Days later we hosted Crawley in the Leasing.com Trophy and I was forced off at half-time with concussion. When I returned a week later, in my first training session back, Sean Raggett completely wiped me out, leaving me with two dead legs. He was on my side as well!'

Evans' cherished 200th game petered out into a forgettable occasion, a stoppage-time defeat ensuring Pompey retreated to the Kingsmeadow dressing room pursued by chants of "We want Jackett out" from irate Blues fans positioned behind the away dugout. The visitors would have been disappointed with a goalless draw, such was their encouraging display. As it was, central defender Terell Thomas headed home Max Sanders' free-kick three minutes into time added on to claim a 1–0 victory for the hosts. That galling outcome left Pompey languishing seventeenth in League One by mid-October, while ramping up the clamour for Jackett's removal.

As for Evans, off the pitch, he and wife Hazel are expecting their first child, a boy, on 12 March 2020, anticipated to be born in Portsmouth. In August, he gained a 2:1 BA (Hons) degree in Sports Writing and Broadcasting, a two-year fast-track course affiliated with Staffordshire University and funded by the Professional Footballers' Association, with Derby's Curtis Davies and former Arsenal and Eastleigh keeper Graham Stack among his classmates. Now aged 31, he continues to revel in the life he has carved out on the south coast.

'It was a massive moment playing 200 games for Pompey, especially having been told I would not be good enough to perform as a professional footballer,' added Evans.

'It's tough to reach that landmark at a club like Pompey. You don't just turn up on a Saturday, you have to remain fit, be good enough to get into the team, stay in a manager's plans and avoid injury. That's 200 matches pretty much over four years, averaging not far off 50 appearances a season, which is difficult; you have to make yourself available and put your body on the line.

'If you were a Shrewsbury Town player, I have no doubt it would be a whole lot easier to reach 200 games than it is for Pompey. At Fratton Park you are under much more scrutiny and greater stress. It's a tough club to play for and more of an achievement here than the likes of Shrewsbury or Crawley Town.

'It means a lot to me and, speaking to Christian Burgess, who also looks like he is going to reach the landmark this season, other people treasure the accomplishment as well. If Burge had done it at his last club, Peterborough United, he wouldn't be anywhere near as bothered as doing it for Pompey.

'Losing to Wimbledon, and in those circumstances, taints my 200th game a little. It would have been great to win. Hopefully, I can toast victory when my 250th Pompey game comes around!'

10

MICHAEL APPLETON
23 October 2019

The opportunity was sufficiently enchanting to lure Michael Appleton away from the Premier League. No longer satisfied with his role as Roy Hodgson's right-hand man at West Bromwich Albion, the ambitious 35-year-old craved a managerial position of his own. Pompey had tabled a tantalising offer, a licence to restructure a Championship club with aspirations of a top-flight return, bankrolled by a wealthy Russian businessman.

In November 2011, Appleton was unveiled as the Blues' boss. Within fourteen days, chairman Vladimir Antonov had been arrested in connection with a multi-million-pound bank fraud. Before the month's end, owners Convers Sports Initiatives (CSI) were in administration, with the football club dragged into the descent towards financial oblivion. A bold blueprint had enticed the ex-Manchester United midfielder to Fratton Park, yet reality sentenced him to the toughest managerial stretch in Portsmouth Football Club's 119-year history.

'I remember having a chat with Sir Alex Ferguson a few months after I left Pompey and he told me such experiences during my first job would shape me,' said Appleton.

'According to him, I had probably gone through more in twelve months than most managers would in 25 years. He was right, of course. I will never, never come across such issues again. It doesn't matter what type of pressure I am under, losing streaks, whatever, it won't come close to what happened during that year at Pompey. I had to deal with chaos.

'The lifespan of a manager is not great, but it's part and parcel of what we do; we are going to get sacked at some point. There aren't many bosses who go their whole career without being dismissed once or twice.

'However, when you are put into situations where a member of staff loses their job and there's the possibility of losing their house off the back of it, it's a different story.

'There were periods when we weren't being paid and I had to give staff time off, either a day or afternoon, to enable them to meet their banks, some attempting to reschedule mortgages. Probably five or six members of my staff had to remortgage or delay payments. It was incredibly sad.

'I would seek Sir Alex's advice in my early days at Fratton Park but, if I am being honest, probably one of the mistakes I made at the time was that I tried to take everything on my shoulders and deal with it myself. That's what you learn, that there are people out there to help you, but I took the burden, keeping it away from other staff and players. I was the manager after all.

'We had good staff who kept me pumped and motivated, but there were details I had to keep away from them. If they had really known the severity of the situation, their morale would have suffered. It was very lonely, and it was tough. I was living in Winchester on my own, returning from the training ground around 7pm as I attempted to get my head around what was going on. I would arrive back to an empty flat, fend for myself and then wait to wake up the next morning. Here we go again, it's Groundhog Day!

'I look at my time at Pompey and, as difficult as it was, I view it as a success because a lot of what I experienced improved me as a person, a leader and a manager. I'd be surprised if anybody who worked with me at the time thinks anything different.'

The man who appointed Appleton was jailed for two and a half years by a St Petersburg court in March 2019, having pleaded guilty to bank fraud. Vladimir Antonov, formerly Pompey chairman and CSI majority owner, had obtained a 150 million ruble (£1.75m) loan from Sovetsky Bank to a front company, in the knowledge it would not be repaid. London's High Court had previously ruled in May 2016 that he owed a collapsed Latvian bank £65m after committing financial fraud. However, Antonov was convicted *in absentia*, having fled England the previous year while on conditional bail as he faced extradition to Lithuania to answer charges of stripping £412m of assets and funds from Snoras Bank. Appleton met the disgraced banker just once, during his second interview for the Fratton Park job at the London offices of Snoras. The aspirations of Antonov and CSI's joint owner, Roman Dubov, convinced him to take the plunge and quit West Brom.

He added: 'I know this is going to sound absolutely crazy, but here was an opportunity for my first managerial job under owners who seemed reasonably stable and possessed a lot of money.

'I was 35 and this huge club with a great fan base and ambitions of returning to the Premier League offered an exciting pathway. The remit was basically to get the club promoted within five seasons with the owners eager to build upon each campaign. Then there was the construction of a new training ground, as at the time we were based in Southampton, which I couldn't get my head around to be honest.

'Finally, I was told of potentially a new stadium, whether that was on the site of Fratton Park or elsewhere I am not too sure, I can't quite remember. I actually advised them not to touch Fratton Park at that stage. It made sense to wait until a Premier League return, simply because it could play a massive part in getting the club back into the top flight.

'As for the training ground, I was happy to talk about designs. I can recall speaking to David Moyes before Finch Farm was built for Everton in 2007, a project he helped plan and put into place. There wasn't a massive discussion about the youth side of it, although they were obviously aware of my background of working in West Brom's youth set-up, with a record of producing players. I have no doubt that was one of the reasons why I got the job after they spoke to twelve or thirteen candidates. Overall, this presented the opportunity for me to oversee Pompey's reconstruction from top to bottom, which really appealed.

'I met Vladimir Antonov once. The first interview was conducted with Roman Dubov and Pompey chief executive David Lampitt at offices somewhere in London. Antonov was there for the second meeting, along with Roman, at CSI's offices in London. It was a similar sort of process to the first interview: lots of questions, lots of answers, but I wasn't asked to present anything.

'It was quite relaxed. As a young coach enjoying working with Roy Hodgson at West Brom at the time, I hadn't gone in there thinking: "I need to get this job." If it didn't happen at least I'd be able to go back to The Hawthorns.

'Antonov asked a few questions about the type of players I would bring to the club, the style of play, the usual generic stuff you would probably get in any football manager interview process. It was the first and only time I met him and it lasted about an hour.

'After nineteen days of being manager, CSI went into administration, although at that point we were unaware of how much it would affect Pompey. You try to concentrate on the football side, relaying the message to the players that, irrespective of what was happening with the owners and the business, let's focus on trying to win matches.

'Then it became obvious there was a chance we may go into administration and be docked ten points.'

With debts of £58m, in February 2012 Pompey entered administration for the second time in 24 months, accompanied by a ten-point deduction implemented by the Football League. CSI entered administration two and a half months earlier, with the ownership reverting back to Portpin by default as a creditor, with the familiar figure of Andrew Andronikou also re-emerging. Andronikou, of UHY Hacker Young, had overseen the Blues' last administration and the subsequent sale of the club – to Portpin. However, following a High Court hearing in which HMRC successfully argued that Andronikou possessed a conflict of interest given his previous involvement, PKF's Trevor Birch (the former Chelsea chief executive) was instead appointed to the position. With the club preparing for administration, Appleton had already been operating under severe financial constraints, a challenging scenario which would snowball.

'The first meeting I had with administrators was a different group, led by Andrew Andronikou,' he said.

'They announced that seven members of my first-team staff, almost all of them, had to leave to keep the club running which to me wasn't an option and I told them so. I now had to find another way of keeping them.

'The players had already taken a pay deferral of 20–25 per cent, but received assurances that they were pretty much protected by the Football Creditors Rule, whereas staff weren't. We may get our pay back over time, but we weren't 100 per cent protected.

'I pulled the team into the training ground's dressing room, the staff among them, consisting of physios, masseurs, sports scientists, the kit man; everyone was there. I then asked the players how important those guys were to them. Did they require them on a day-to-day basis?

'I wanted to stress the staff's importance and the necessity of keeping them around – with the only solution being the players offering to take a little more of a financial hit.

'It was a little bit naughty and I was taking a risk. I didn't want to embarrass people and I had no intention of confronting the players; it wasn't about challenging them or threatening them, there was none of that.

'The message was: "If you don't need them and think you can prepare for games without them, then the reality is they will lose their jobs." It was very tongue in cheek and, at the same time, very serious.

'I closed by telling them that they had half an hour to think about it before training and asked the captain, Liam Lawrence, to come to my office when their decision had been made.

'I couldn't have been sitting down for more than ten seconds before Liam knocked on my door and said: "Whatever it takes to keep them in their jobs, we'll do it." The players subsequently donated an extra five per cent of their wages to keep seven staff members in their jobs until January at least.

'I know some of the players took a bit of stick, and one or two of them probably deserved it, but the majority were good lads and good people. We had an incredible spirit within the camp and, despite everything that was going on, we never let it get us too down. We tried to stay positive and there was an incredible togetherness within the group.

'We endured all sorts of ridiculous situations, such as coming into training one day and Kev McCormack telling me: "I'm not sure if we are going to be able to train – we have no equipment."

'The issue was that the locks had been changed on the container which housed our equipment as those renting it to us were owed money. As far as I was aware, they had also emptied it. So we had to think on our feet, instead spending the day at the David Lloyd Club in Port Solent. The company were soon paid and we trained as normal the next day.

'Then there were scenarios where players were injured, but you didn't know how badly because we couldn't afford to get a scan! That happened a few times. I remember Liam Lawrence was one of the first. He needed a scan on his injured calf and we couldn't do it, so he funded it himself.

'Then there was not being able to order food for the canteen, so we chipped in to pay for the chefs to get the ingredients in. Sometimes it was easier bringing in your own packed lunch, or to grab a sandwich and can of Coca-Cola from the service station down the road, but you had to do it, it was the only way to keep up your energy and stay fresh.

'There was equipment constantly being sold, like bits of printers, computers, laptops – they had to find money from anywhere. It seemed every single day I was coming in and being presented with another issue. You can't tell the players everything. You can't even tell your own staff as you need to protect them. I would like to think that 85–90 per cent of the time I was as honest as I could possibly be and, if there was stuff I kept back and didn't tell them the truth, it was for their own benefit rather than mine.

'We even had a transfer embargo which I hadn't been told about. I don't know whether that information was withheld for my own benefit, but the message from above was constantly: "We'll be fine, don't worry about it, we'll be able to do what we need to do."

'However, I ended up having a massive row on the phone with the Football League and probably lost my cool. At the time I'd like to think I kept a lid on my temper, maintained my humility and tried to represent the football club as well as I possibly could – but that day I went berserk!

'We had a one-in, one-out policy, a crippling injury list and needed to loan players out to raise money, yet remained under embargo and was only allowed to bring in a couple of loans at a time. As we had youngsters Adam Webster and Ashley Harris with three first-team appearances between them, I was told they counted as senior players, which meant I was permitted to sign fewer loanees as a result.

'We were on loudspeaker – our chief executive David Lampitt on one side of the table and me on the other – and I got my views across. It didn't necessarily help the situation, but they weren't going to change their minds. They weren't doing all they could to help us – they told me that they were there to help, but not in the way we wanted. I was trying to get the best for the football club to give us an opportunity to find a way out of the mess.

'Through the restrictions they imposed, it felt as though they were making it as difficult as they could for us to stay in the Championship; that is the best way I can put it. The embargo was one thing, obviously difficult to deal with, but the biggest kick in the teeth was, from February 2012, coping with losing players loaned out to bring money into the club – Liam Lawrence, Erik Huseklepp, Stephen Henderson and Hayden Mullins.

'In the case of Lawrence, we were deprived of our captain and a massive presence in the dressing room. Mullins was very experienced, Henderson was on fire at the time and Huseklepp was chipping in with goals and creating them. I understood the situation, that we were trying to keep the club alive and it needed to be done, but we had to replace them with kids.

'I was also concerned that young players performing really well, such as Jason Pearce and Joel Ward, would also depart. I told Trevor Birch: "Look, come on, they can't all go, surely? I need to put a team out. Just cut me some slack!" I needn't have worried because they were lower earners at the time, so it didn't happen.

'Still, from January we reduced our wage bill by a ridiculous amount. From memory, it dropped from around £13m to £3m.'

Before the formality of administration and a ten-point deduction, Pompey were eighteenth in the Championship, riding ten points clear of the relegation zone with a game in hand. Meanwhile, off the pitch, within six days of PKF's appointment, 30 staff redundancies were announced, among them chief executive Lampitt, chief financial officer John Redgate and fellow director Nick Byrom. Some of the remaining staff members were asked to reduce their hours to part-time status, while players were asked to defer more wages. Appleton soon lost first-team coach Stuart Gray, an analyst and two scouts as the campaign culminated in tumbling out of the Championship, a fate sealed in their penultimate game, a 2–1 Fratton Park defeat to Derby County. It meant two relegations in three seasons for the 2010 FA Cup finalists.

Appleton said: 'Trevor came in and very, very quickly the board were let go. So I had my first job in football as a manager and all of a sudden there was no chief executive and no finance director! My relationship with David Lampitt was fine. We had only worked together for three months and, with there now being no board, I reported straight to the administrators.

'To be fair, Trevor was to the point and honest about things, which I respected. I would rather have bad news quickly than a slow maybe. At times during that season there was the challenge of having to deal with players not getting paid. As Bury and Bolton Wanderers recently found out, it's very difficult motivating people when they are not receiving wages. I understand that's life, it's what it is, but finding a way to keep players motivated is key.

'I would tap into them as people rather than footballers, stressing the point that somewhere along the line they once played the game for enjoyment, not money. So if I could promise they would eventually receive that money, in the meantime, perhaps they could cope without it and play football as they did aged twelve or thirteen for the local team on a Sunday while wearing a smile. That was our approach and it worked.

'In my case, the supporters provided the motivation. They spurred me on at times and my relationship with them definitely helped. We were going through a troubled period, yet there was still a lot of goodwill from them. They recognised that we were attempting to play good football, trying to win games and striving to stay in the division. That inspired me, it kept me going and gave me energy. I remember being in the media room after one game and being told I had to go back out to speak to the fans as they wouldn't leave the stadium unless I did – this happened three or four times!

'When you leave a football club, you don't get to tell your story and give an insight, which is why I agreed to do this interview. If people actually knew the truth, they would probably have a better understanding of the reasons why I eventually looked to move on.

'I have absolutely no doubt whatsoever that if we hadn't gone into administration and suffered the subsequent points deduction that season, we would have remained in the Championship. Even then, it took until the penultimate game to be relegated – considering we got that far, I still think it's one of my best achievements.'

By the summer of 2012, the need to slash the player wage bill had reached crisis point and, following a close-season fire sale of prized assets and compromise agreements with others, eight senior footballers remained. Joint administrator Birch warned that unless Dave Kitson, Liam Lawrence, David Norris, Tal Ben Haim, Luke Varney, Erik Huseklepp, Greg Halford and Kanu all left Fratton Park, the club would be liquidated. That prompted supporter group SOS Pompey to reconvene and, in July 2012, congregate outside the Blues' Wellington Sports Ground, Eastleigh, to put pressure on those concerned – in their own inimitable manner.

At the time, Appleton was located in Benahavís, Marbella, accompanying a now youthful squad supplemented by triallists on a ten-day pre-season tour. An intermediary kept him in touch with SOS Pompey's plans, while Pompey's boss collaborated with coach Guy Whittingham, left behind in England to oversee the senior players' fitness and to ensure they were at the training ground that day rather than the David Lloyd Club. Appleton believes that fan demonstration in sight of the remaining players had an impact. Just four days before the 2012–13 campaign kicked off, all had departed, including the much-criticised pair Dave Kitson and Tal Ben Haim.

Appleton added: 'It wasn't only the fans getting messed about. I was being messed about too, and you can only take so much before saying: "Hold on a minute, something needs to be done." I was right behind the supporters and what they were doing. I wanted the players to realise how severe the situation was – and after SOS Pompey paid a visit, I think they did.

'I actually got on really well with Tal Ben Haim, honest to God. It was a terribly difficult situation for everybody as they signed contracts in good faith, and whoever offered those deals are the ones who should answer the questions, not the players.

'Having said that, we found ourselves in a difficult situation which required reasoning and understanding in order to come to an agreement. Some players came to an agreement quickly, some didn't. Tal was slightly misunderstood, if I am honest.

'He didn't help himself at times, don't get me wrong, but he was definitely misunderstood. There were certain other players at the club, whom I am not going to name, but who I felt were an absolute disgrace. Maybe one day I will dig them out and let people know exactly what they were about. There was one in particular, but, ultimately, someone like Tal bore the brunt of it.

'Personally, I don't think Tal was a disgrace, he was misunderstood and difficult at times, but there were certain other players who were far more difficult to reason with than him. Don't get me wrong, he wasn't an angel, but there were at least three or four others who were worse and should have got a lot more stick.

'If you had a pop at Tal and said something disrespectful, because of his mentality and nature he would have a go back and end up saying something stupid or wrong. Rather than processing it and thinking: "You are wrong. I'm going to respond this way and these are the reasons," he would react as he is fiery. I would speak to him around that period as I knew he was getting a lot of stick, but I understood both sides, and I was the middle man.

'With others, however, there was no understanding. It was black and white, whereas the reality of the situation was grey. Yes, they signed contracts in good faith, but the club had gone into administration and something needed to give. Everybody had lost; there were no winners – not the club, the staff or the players. Plenty of creditors had to accept X-amount in the pound but certain players wanted every single penny.

'Tal never walked away with everything he was owed, I can assure you of that, it was nowhere near. Meanwhile certain team-mates of his, who continued to train, got to the stage where there was no point them being there because it was detrimental to the group. The talented young players who departed that summer were the killer for me, with Jason Pearce, Stephen Henderson and Joel Ward the first sold, all remaining at Championship level.

'We had built such a good relationship over a difficult period at the club. I'd like to think that still helped from a development point of view, not just on the pitch but off it, and it's great to see them go on and have such good careers.

'As a young coach and manager at the time, it was devastating, but there was nothing you could do about it – and you couldn't replace them because we didn't have the money to do it. As Oxford United boss, I lost my two best players every year, then had an opportunity to replace them. That is part and parcel of football if you are at a club which has to sell. At Pompey, we just didn't have the money to do that.'

While Birch was reducing the wage bill to ensure Pompey could continue existing through administration, Portpin resurfaced as potential owners once more. Despite the emergence of Pompey Supporters' Trust as rivals to take over the club, Balram Chainrai and Levi Kushnir retained pole position and, as they neared completion in the summer of 2012, Appleton was invited to meet them in London. Following discussions about how they would fund the team, the duo settled on the £4m playing budget suggested by the Blues boss, a sum he believed could make the club competitive in their fresh League One surroundings, potentially securing an instant return to the Championship. A fortnight later, ahead of the start of pre-season, there was a substantial shift in mood – the budget was now, inexplicably, set at £1.5m. Suddenly Appleton was challenged to recruit a new squad on a shoestring, condemned to offering month-to-month contracts to players as the club continued to exist on an unstable footing.

'I was recruiting players you wouldn't normally have signed for a club the size of Pompey, a club with ambitions of reaching where they should be which is the Championship, minimum,' said Appleton.

'It was hard for me, thinking: "I'm going to have to sign this player, it's all I can do." We should have been looking at bigger and better players, yet financially we couldn't manage it.

'Earlier that summer, Balram Chainrai and Levi Kushnir had asked me to treat everything as a clean sheet. Here was a blank piece of paper – what would I need to get us back into the Championship?

'It was a difficult question to answer. For instance, if I requested a £4m budget to achieve promotion, that would sound like a lot of money at that level, yet a hell of a lot of clubs have spent more in recent times and struggled to get out of the league. Within that you have to meet wages for a squad of 22–25 players, plus transfer fees.

'They were very direct and straight to the point. It wasn't a warm meeting in any way, shape or form. They weren't disrespectful, but their approach was: "Right, okay, let's deal in facts. Where are we? What can we do? How can we do it?"

'Still, when I left that meeting I was under the impression that whatever I needed – within reason – I could bring the players in, good players, to allow us to fight at the top end of League One and win promotion.

'Almost two weeks later, I received a phone call from Trevor Birch informing me that the budget would be a third of what was discussed with Portpin. I had to forget about signing players on six- or twelve-month deals; the club would be run on a month-to-month basis – and, when the money ran out, there would be no Pompey.

'There were loads of players lined up, with probably at least nine or ten ready to attend our pre-season tour in Spain. I had better not divulge names, as it's not fair on them, but they were free agents and good players, and now I had to be dead straight – I couldn't guarantee them contracts.

'To be fair, when I first met Chainrai and Kushnir, it was going to be fine, a proper budget. They were reluctant owners. They were thinking: "We have something we don't particularly want, but if we back it a bit, we might actually have something worth something again." Then the landscape changed completely.

'I was pretty angry, and I tried to ring Chainrai three or four times, but they weren't interested. I haven't got issues with them not wanting to speak to me. It was more a matter of if they'd told me what I was up against from day one, at least I would know what I was dealing with.

'Instead I had wasted a lot of my time and effort over that summer, speaking to agents and players, getting into my car and travelling two to three hours to secure what I thought was going to be a great signing that could give everyone a lift. All of a sudden, I couldn't do that. To this day, I have no idea why they changed their mind. Still, we had to plough ahead with our recruitment plans, despite the reduced budget, and immediately needed other players for Spain, which was to consist of friendlies against Gibraltar and Brighton & Hove Albion.

'The idea of that pre-season tour was to take people into a nice, welcoming environment and persuade them to sign before we returned to Portsmouth. You could argue I was misleading people, and I suppose I was to a degree, but you always felt something was going to happen, an oligarch from somewhere coming along and saying: "Right, there you go, crack on and go for the league." Everyone has hope and I was no different.

'I wanted to sign players so I had to come up with some kind of attraction to get them to come to Pompey, even though I was aware that only month-to-month contracts would be on offer.

'I didn't want to spend the summer at the training ground not doing anything, not knowing if that training ground was even going to be there because it was closing down so many times, so we approached a couple of wealthy Pompey fans.

'We created a package where we said it'll cost X-amount to go to Spain for ten days, in a decent resort. We'll play a couple of sides and, if you fund it, in return we'll allow you to come on a couple of away trips with us during the season, spend time at the camp in Spain, be part of a couple of team meetings, all that type of stuff – but we can't afford the trip without you.

'A local businessman called Dave Ellis helped out, which gave me the green light to push my hand a little with agents and players and say: "Look, this is the situation. We are in a bit of a bother, but we are off to Spain and it will be great to get your player involved as there's a nice hotel and good pitches to train on."

'By the time we got them back to England, we could hopefully work on them, be positive, and get them signed by the end of the month. That was the tactic – and loads of them stayed, so it worked.'

Pompey's financial constraints and the Football League's ongoing stance dictated that Appleton was prohibited from signing any player ahead of the 2012–13 campaign. A Capital One Cup clash at Plymouth Argyle marked the season's curtain-raiser, with the Blues naming nine teenagers in their starting XI. In addition, they were granted special dispensation to field goalkeeper Simon Eastwood on non-contract terms, while assistant manager Ashley Westwood completed the line-up for a 3–0 defeat. Desperately requiring additions ahead of their opening League One fixture against Paul Groves' Bournemouth days later, Pompey signed twelve players in 48 hours before the Fratton Park encounter. The dozen made their bows in the 1–1 draw which began the campaign in promising fashion, with Izale McLeod netting a debut goal.

Appleton added: 'We actually came close to being unable to fulfil that Bournemouth game, but signed a hell of a lot of players very late on. Among the substitutes was Adam Webster, whom I had given a debut to against West Ham United the previous season at the age of seventeen. I always knew he would be a centre-back but he was comfortable at right or left full-back, so I tried to take a little pressure off him and play him in those roles initially.

'He was a young defender and, considering some of the teams we were up against, with West Ham getting promoted through the play-offs that season, I was more than happy playing him. However, I wanted to take a bit of the sting out of the situation and hand him a little freedom to express himself.

'We had seen the talent day in, day out, in training, and Webbo was performing at a level that belied his age. If at that time you had asked what standard he was, I would have said top Championship, bottom Premier League, which is how it has panned out as he's now at Brighton.

'Another Academy youngster I handed a debut to in the 2011–12 season was Ashley Harris, obviously very different to Webbo and a forward. I saw him as more of an impact player, to be honest, but ended up having to play him quite regularly. He was a small lad who had the ability to get away from people, but if he took an extra touch or tried carrying the ball, people could get back at him. He had that burst for two or three yards, then they got back, and we were aware of that.

'Ash had a good spell around the side at the time, scoring two league goals, one of which came in a 3–0 win at Crawley Town in September 2012, when Webbo crossed it in for him. I liked bringing Ash off the bench to give the crowd a bit of a lift if we needed it. With young players, it just shows it can go one way or the other; there's such a fine line between success and failure.

'I was always aware of Jack Whatmough, who was younger than the others. If I had stayed, Jed Wallace would have ended up playing a lot of football. The troubles at the football club probably benefited a few players because it presented them with more of an opportunity than they probably expected.

'I decided to sell Sam Magri to QPR because I felt it was good business for the club, rather than something we needed to do. I just felt he was short, if I am being honest, which is why I allowed the sale to go through.

'That's a football opinion. I didn't think he was at the level that a couple of other people felt he was – and it represented a good deal for the club. It had nothing to do with needing to sell him at that time.'

Still entrenched in administration by October 2012, there were developments, however, with the Football League declaring they were not satisfied with Portpin's tabled offer for the club. It prompted the Trust to be declared as preferred bidders by administrators PKF, the door suddenly swinging open for the prospect of fan ownership. However, the following month, Appleton walked out on Fratton Park for Blackpool. A mere three days short of his one-year anniversary, the manager tendered his resignation following a 1–0 home defeat to Brentford which signified a fourth straight loss.

At the time, the Blues were seventeenth in League One and had been eliminated at the first-round stage of the FA Cup by Notts County the previous weekend. Blackpool's interest was already public knowledge and, within 24 hours of the loss to Brentford, he was unveiled alongside assistant Ashley Westwood at Bloomfield Road.

'As difficult as my time was at Pompey, I absolutely loved it, but the final six weeks of the job took its toll on me. I had stopped enjoying it,' explained Appleton.

'My routine was now taking training in the morning and driving to Fratton Park in the afternoon to hold meetings with the administrators or potential new owners. I did that almost every single day for six weeks – that's not football management. I wanted to work with my players and staff, preparing for matches and analysing the opposition, but instead had to spend two to three hours in the boardroom.

'I found myself doing things that were not within my remit, such as speaking to different groups who wanted to buy Pompey.

There were two or three groups from Asia, one from America, and I was expected to be in attendance to talk football, the squad, plans for the future if the finances were right, pretty much everything I mentioned in the interview with Vladimir and Roman at the very beginning of my time at the club.

'There would also be meetings with Trevor and the administrators, discussing how we could keep the club running for an extra couple of weeks. I wasn't just a coach or a football manager. I was a board member, except there was no board, just me and Trevor.

'Don't get me wrong, you can argue that was what the role required at that time but, having since spoken to other managers who have been in similar situations, their roles were pretty much to coach the team and try to win games of football, regardless of what was going on in the background.

'My departure for Blackpool was very sudden and could have been dealt with better, but my enjoyment of the role had gone completely. I was at my absolute lowest point after losing to Brentford. I went home that evening and my energy levels were not where they should be.

'I was aware that everything occurring off the field was getting on top of me and affecting me. It was definitely starting to impact upon my mindset during the matches. My mood in between games changed and I was struggling to stay positive because I didn't have anyone to lean on. When you are put into that situation and have to continue motivating people while feeling awful, it becomes difficult. For my own sanity, I had to do something different.

'At various stages, three clubs at Championship level came in for me. Trevor Birch was very open about it in the press, yet I was hoping it would get better at Pompey. Eventually you reach the point where you ask whether it actually is going to improve. Will I at some point be the scapegoat for all this?

'In addition, I was going through a few personal issues. My kids were living up north, and it was a difficult time and got on top of me. When the opportunity arose to join Blackpool, it meant being closer to them. I don't think people realised what was going on for me to arrive at that decision. I had to leave Pompey.'

Appleton's Bloomfield Road stay spanned 67 days, before quitting to join Blackburn Rovers. His time at Ewood Park was equally short, sacked after winning four of his fifteen matches at the helm. He would rebuild his reputation at Oxford United, winning promotion to League One and taking them to Wembley in the Football League Trophy in successive campaigns. Following spells at Leicester City as assistant manager and at West Brom, where he served as first-team coach before taking charge of the under-23s, Appleton was appointed Lincoln City manager in September 2019, after Danny Cowley's departure for Huddersfield Town.

For his fifth League One match in charge, he was reunited with Fratton Park, an encounter which yielded a 1–0 victory for his former employers, through John Marquis' first-half goal. It represented a first win in three league games for Kenny Jackett's men, lifting them into sixteenth place following their erratic start to the campaign. As for Appleton, seven years after walking out of the Blues, unfinished business remains on his mind.

He added: 'I am 43 now and would be absolutely gutted if I never managed Pompey again.

'Regardless of everything, I had such a good time in my year at Fratton Park and, I'm sure the fans would agree, as difficult as it was, we had our moments and tried to enjoy it as best as we possibly could.

'At some point in my career, I would love to have the opportunity to manage there in different circumstances. It's a fantastic club.'

CRAIG MACGILLIVRAY

13 November 2019

The bedroom was different, yet reassuringly familiar; comforting surrounds for the prodigal son ahead of a homecoming complete with local media fanfare and a crowd numbering 3,408. It had been five and a half years since Craig MacGillivray departed Knaresborough, quitting a teaching job and bidding farewell to his family to chase a long-coveted footballing fortune. He returned in November 2019, boasting international recognition with Scotland, a Wembley winner's medal and League One residency as Pompey's first-choice keeper. The FA Cup's first round proper had lured the 26-year-old back to North Yorkshire for a match-up with Harrogate Town, the club he represented with such distinction, earning that cherished Football League breakthrough with a transfer to Walsall in June 2014. MacGillivray also featured for local rivals Harrogate Railway Athletic while serving as a sports teacher at a number of neighbouring schools, including the town's Burnt Yates School.

Following Pompey's 2–1 win on that rain-ravaged Monday evening, he slept in his old bed, having made the nostalgic three-mile drive from Wetherby Road to the family home. Poignant reminders for MacGillivray, who has savoured his remarkable rise since starting out as a flying right winger and student at Leeds Metropolitan University.

He said: 'The team flew up on the morning of the game, but while they were staying at a hotel that night ahead of travelling back on the coach the next day, I was due to link up with Scotland. I had to catch a train to Edinburgh the following morning and it was easier doing that from Harrogate station. So, I went back to my parents' house after the match, literally five minutes away from Town's ground. It was like driving back from a game all those years earlier: the same house, the same journey; I was living my life from five and a half years ago! I was back in my old room; that was weird. It's very plain in there now, literally a bed and a TV on a little bench. I pulled the blind up in the morning and it was a real flashback. I used to do this all the time.

'It's amazing hearing footballers' backgrounds. I love doing that as it's a natural way of getting to know people, and with my own journey there's a lot of stuff people would probably never realise. I have never taken this for granted – and never will. A football career is very short and, as a goalkeeper, if you are fortunate enough to play until your late thirties that is brilliant, but then that's it. An outfield player might get to his early thirties, as that's how short a football career tends to be, so you simply can't take it for granted. Yes, football is a very emotional sport, full of ups and downs, but when you actually strip it right back it comes down to a short career.

'At the season's start, I was probably sitting there fuming after games because we hadn't won, but you have to step away and remember we are all living, we're all breathing, and thankfully we are all fit and healthy. There are a lot of people out there who aren't and would give anything to swap with me, understandably so, because I am fit, healthy and doing something I love. I hurt after games and sometimes I am fuming. Should I make a mistake, I'm not happy about it, but it has gone, done, you can't change it, it's happened, so you try to put the next one right. Thankfully, we are now picking up results and it's good. There is no denying that when you are winning, of course the dressing room is a lot happier; that's how football works, but strip it right back.

'I wasn't in a club's academy. I went to school, did four A levels, went to uni and quit that for footballing opportunities, before ending up at Harrogate Town and then in the Football League.

Any kid that ever asks about being a professional footballer, look at me. I was 21 when I entered the Football League. I didn't break into a first team properly until I came to Pompey at the age of 25. Okay, perhaps that's young for a goalkeeper, but I still didn't get a regular opportunity until reaching my mid-twenties. You see clubs all the time bringing people in from non-league and, in the same summer I joined Pompey in 2018, Blackpool recruited centre-half Michael Nottingham from Salford City at the age of 29. Finally, he had his chance. We had Louis Dennis here last season, who had arrived from Bromley at the age of 25 and was as frustrated as anything at Fratton Park. It was a case of "I'm never going to get my chance, I'll never be picked to play" but you will eventually; it all comes back around. If you work hard enough, you make your own luck.

'When I arrived at Pompey, how many people thought I was ready to be a back-up keeper? It would have been: "He hasn't played many games; who the hell is this? Where has he come from? Why are we taking him?" There are a lot of players out there and just because they haven't played at this level doesn't mean they can't.'

Born in Perth, Scotland, and initially raised on a remote farm in Glenshee, the MacGillivray family moved home six times with dad Donald's work for the Scottish Borders Ambulance Service often dictating their location, switching between Scotland and North Yorkshire. They would finally settle in Knaresborough, with fourteen-year-old MacGillivray enrolling in Boroughbridge High School, which would provide his education up to the completion of four A levels. As a promising winger in his youth, he featured for Wetherby-based Kirk Deighton Rangers, earning a six-month trial at Leeds United before switching to the role of goalkeeper at the age of sixteen and joining Knaresborough Celtic. Soon he was on the books of Harrogate Railway's youth set-up, alerting Leeds to his footballing potential once more – this time as a keeper.

'During my second year of A levels, Leeds invited me for a week-long trial after spotting me playing for Railway in an FA Youth Cup game, which was fantastic, although the trial lasted a year! At the end of the initial week, Neil Redfearn, the under-18s Academy coach, said: "Look, I know you are doing your A levels, but we have Alex Cairns as a keeper and no one else, so we want you here to see how you develop."

'What an opportunity that was. I suppose many people would have gone after a couple of months, especially when you weren't being paid, a case of "If you are not going to give me anything then see you later." However, I wanted to do well and show willing, even if nothing came of it in the end. Still, on my day off on a Wednesday, I would go into school, while after training I studied for A levels with the other Leeds lads working on BTECs and it was carnage, absolute carnage.

'For me, it was incredibly hard to combine the two commitments. Some of that Leeds age group didn't think they needed the BTECs they were studying – then I was around when they were told of the decision to release them; it was heartbreaking. Only two of that twenty-man squad were retained – Alex Cairns and Ross Killock, although the following year there were quite a few, such as Charlie Taylor and Sam Byram. As for me, I had nothing to show for that season. Nonetheless, I had a year's worth of coaching. If I look back now, I honestly think it was already decided that Alex would get pro terms, but they wanted me around just in case he got injured. Now we're both regulars in League One, with Alex in his fourth season at Fleetwood Town.

'Having passed my A levels, I was now without a club, so returned to Harrogate Railway and went to Leeds Metropolitan University, now called Leeds Beckett University, to study a sports coaching degree at their Carnegie Campus. Then, in October 2011, I quit university after a few months to join Stalybridge Celtic, who had spotted me in a reserve game against them. As a full-time club in the Blue Square North, they offered me peanuts, literally just expenses, but it represented a chance to do something I had always dreamed of, so I deferred my course for a year.

'During the 2011–12 campaign, I made four first-team appearances, but decided to leave at the season's end. I could drive, but had no car, so travelling from Harrogate to Manchester was a two-and-a-half-hour train ride each way and also required one of the lads to pick me up from the station or catching a taxi. It was an unbelievable opportunity, I loved it, but I could no longer physically do the travelling, I had to get something closer to home – which was Harrogate Town.

'Meanwhile, my parents sat me down and told me that while I was playing part-time football, I shouldn't be moping around the house doing nothing, and had to get another job, which became teaching.'

Spotting an advert for Sports Xtra, MacGillivray joined a company supplying sports teachers and teaching assistants to six schools around the Harrogate and Knaresborough area, primarily dealing with children aged four to eleven. Gaining qualifications alongside the job, he combined a career in education with turning out for Harrogate Town in the Blue Square North, the sixth tier of the English pyramid.

'Harrogate Town once had a home match and my pupils from Burnt Yates School came along. It was a planned school trip outside of school hours, and they were at the game with a massive banner saying "Mr MacGillivray". Little things like that touch you. In those days, and I don't know whether it is still the case, there was a shortage of male teachers in primary schools. Certainly, I never saw any when I entered the six schools I worked in and my sister, Eilidh, teaches at a Wetherby primary school where there are also none. That's a shame, especially for the boys in terms of lacking male role models. As soon as you walk into the building, honestly you are a god. It was a case of "A man is actually teaching us now"; it's amazing, those things I'd never really thought about before.

'There are kids who don't necessarily like PE, so we had to adapt sessions and lessons to ensure that everyone could join in. We've all been there: you try to do something, some can do it, some can't, and there is the potential to feel embarrassment. So, you must try to put on a lesson that everyone wants to participate in. It might be a case of putting four or five hoops in a row and asking them to hop from hoop to hoop on alternate feet.

'The government were placing a lot of emphasis on the importance of being active when I started teaching in schools, but the issue remains that a lot of kids these days would rather play computer games than take part in daft little things like hopping on alternate feet or catching the ball in your other hand. As a kid, when Wimbledon was taking place everyone wanted to play tennis for two weeks. If it was rugby, let's play rugby, and the same with football and the World Cup. I remember ten or eleven of us playing the playground game 'Wembley', but instead of the usual pairs you were a team from the World Cup. These days, one of the first questions kids ask is do you play FIFA, Fortnite or Call of Duty? What do you do in your spare time – computer games, watch TV or watch films?

'Regardless, in life there will be times when you need to be coordinated; it doesn't matter what you do. So, you go into a primary school and for the next twelve years those kids are going to be taking part in PE lessons, so why not learn? I actually discovered that with a lot of primary school teachers I worked with, as soon as they got an opportunity to drop their PE lessons, they would jump at it. I sympathise with them, having so much marking and preparation to carry out, so if someone like me was willing to take one of your lessons you would bite at it. The same for extra-curricular activities. At one school, which had 30 kids in total, there were no teams or clubs, and they had never taken part in school competitions. We managed to organise a football tournament involving the whole district, with 24 schools invited. We had gone from nothing to hosting this event – I was proud of that.

'Sometimes, when a teacher was ill or had to attend a meeting, I had to stand in for them in class, following instructions to teach them maths – and I am not great at maths, especially algebra! Initially the kids called me Mr MacGillivray, but it's not the easiest thing to pronounce for five- or six year-olds, and some were really struggling with it, so I told them to call me Craig. If ever I had to take anything outside of PE, they had to call me Mr MacGillivray though, as it was effectively someone else's lesson. I really enjoyed teaching, then five years later I saved a penalty at Wembley in front of 85,000 people. How weird is that!'

To contrast with that Checkatrade Trophy experience against Sunderland, a crowd of 194 were present to witness MacGillivray's Harrogate Town debut against West Auckland in the FA Cup second qualifying round in September 2012. By that stage of the 2012–13 campaign, the keeper had already turned out for Harrogate Railway in the Evo-Stik League First Division North, taking advantage of dual registration to gain regular football elsewhere within the town. His manager at Town was Simon Weaver, who would oversee all of MacGillivray's 90 appearances during a successful two-season stay, culminating in his move into the Football League with Walsall in June 2014. Upon his return with Pompey almost five and a half years later, remarkably Weaver was still in charge of a Sulphurites side which nowadays inhabits the National League.

> MacGillivray said: 'Town played at Guiseley on a Tuesday night and the first-choice keeper, José Veiga, was knocked out and stretchered off. The following match was against West Auckland and from that point I became a regular. After five appearances, Simon Weaver handed me a two-year contract and at the end of the season Newcastle United and Doncaster Rovers were in for me. There was also interest during the following season, 2013–14, and, in January, Bradford City's goalkeeping coach Lee Butler came to watch and wanted me but Town insisted on a serious fee which stood in my way.
>
> 'At the end of the day, if the club see you as an asset why should they let you go? Of course they won't. However, they were asking ridiculous numbers, more than £100,000 up front for a twenty-year-old kid playing Blue Square North football.
>
> 'I was sitting there in front of Simon Weaver saying: "Come on, you ain't getting that much for me. It's never going to happen." Still, I was regarded as an asset. I understood that and carried on what I was doing. If I were in their position, I would have done exactly the same thing. Then that summer I finally reached the

Football League, with a move to Walsall who paid compensation as I was out of contract.

'In the five and a half years since I've been gone, Wetherby Road has changed massively. The club have been given planning permission for new stands, with a number of temporary stands currently in use and the Main Stand being the sole remaining one from when I played. Then there is the artificial playing surface, which was installed two years after I left, and there is no getting away from it – that gives them an advantage. The whole reason they changed it was because of the state of the pitch during my time at the club. There used to be an awful slope in the bottom corner, so they attempted to level it out, but unfortunately there was a bad summer in terms of rain, so it didn't seed properly and churned up. During my two seasons, the pitch was horrendous. It would cut up terribly and we had so many games called off, ensuring a big fixture backlog that got ridiculous. So they brought in 3G (third generation artificial turf technology), which earns more in revenue for pitch hire and matches always go ahead.

'The ground is still as dark as ever though, even when the floodlights are working! One thing I do not miss is how dark it is. When the ball comes into that box, you see it and then it has gone as the lights are so bright among the darkness. It's like flashing a camera in your eyes – you can't see. During the Pompey game, there was a corner delivered which I followed, but, before you knew it, it had gone, so I punched blind. You cannot see a thing and, chatting to their keeper, James Belshaw, he said the same – midweek evening games are still a nightmare for keepers.'

MacGillivray arrived at Fratton Park on a free transfer from Shrewsbury Town in June 2018, among ten summer signings as Kenny Jackett overhauled a squad that had finished eighth in League One. Aged 25, the keeper had amassed just 33 appearances in four seasons in the Football League since his Harrogate Town departure. He was challenged with overhauling Luke McGee as the Blues' number one, a former Tottenham Hotspur stopper who registered 50 outings during the 2017–18 campaign, his first at the club having been recruited for an undisclosed fee.

MacGillivray, a perennial back-up at Walsall and Shrewsbury, quickly established himself as Jackett's first choice, becoming an ever-present in a League One season culminating in play-off semi-final elimination at the hands of Sunderland. They had, however, overcome the same opposition in the Checkatrade Trophy final just seven weeks earlier, with the Scot saving Lee Cattermole's spot-kick during a 5–4 penalty shoot-out triumph. Then, in November 2019, he was back at the club that had facilitated his ascent into the Football League. MacGillivray almost missed his emotional Harrogate return following a training ground injury to his right quad, an issue which ruled him out of the previous match in the form of a League One encounter with Southend United.

'As much as I wanted to play against the team where I started my career, for the sake of one match I couldn't put myself in jeopardy and risk six to eight weeks out. You have to see the bigger picture; that must take priority. Thankfully, I passed my fitness test the day before the game and was back at Wetherby Road.

'I know Harrogate like the back of my hand, as I spent plenty of time in and around the area. I've still got mates there, including the club's analyst Jon Lally, while midfielder Jack Emmett, who came on after 31 minutes, is a friend and was a youth-team player often training with the first team during my time.

'It wasn't a nice game of football, in horrible wet and windy conditions, and it was about whoever dealt with it better on the night. You can see why upsets happen. You are on a hiding to nothing as you're expected to win, but if you do, no one bats an eyelid. If you lose, you get absolutely slated, although at one point we thought the game wouldn't happen when the lights went out twice before kick-off. The referee had told us that if they went off once more, that would be it. As it was the match began 55 minutes late.

'In terms of the pitch, I had played a competitive match on 3G once before, for Walsall at Sutton Coldfield Town in a Birmingham Senior Cup game. You know you're not going to get any bobbles, but it's more slippery because there's no traction from grass. We had a couple of training sessions on the University of Portsmouth's artificial pitches at Furze Lane in the build-up, more for footwear reasons, getting used to your feet not sticking as firmly as on a normal pitch.

'As you aren't allowed to wear metal studs on an artificial pitch which are my usual footwear, I had to buy moulded boots for the game – Nike Tiempos – although I'll probably never wear them again. When you're used to being on a certain surface, these little differences become big, when actually they aren't really. Of course, it's going to feel like a massive difference, but at the end of the day you have to deal with it. If not, there's going to be an upset in front of the TV cameras.

'I've been on the other side of that situation, playing for Town against League Two Torquay United in the FA Cup first round in November 2012. We beat them 1–0 on their patch. The amount of luck we had that day was ridiculous; upsets can happen.'

Indeed, after two pre-match power cuts that plunged Wetherby Road into lengthy darkness and forced supporters to remain outside in the rain while Northern Power's technicians intervened, it took seven minutes for Mark Beck to stir up BT Sport's hopes of witnessing an FA Cup shock. However, ten minutes later, Brandon Haunstrup levelled with a maiden Pompey goal on his 50th outing. The collector's item arrived from the unfamiliar position of right-back, the left-sided full-back selected ahead of James Bolton, while Ross McCrorie was sidelined with a hamstring strain. Then, four minutes before half-time, the match-winner arrived, Ronan Curtis settling the tie 2–1 in favour of Jackett's men with a stunning right-footed shot from 25-yards.

After the final whistle, MacGillivray's fan club gathered round the keeper. Among the estimated 20–30 family and friends were his ex-Boroughbridge High School PE teacher and former sixth-form mentor. Pompey's infuriating start to the campaign had left them thirteenth in League One at the time of their Harrogate trip, yet their keeper's own campaign had been brightened by his first international call-up in August. The next day he travelled from North Yorkshire to meet up with Steve Clarke's Scotland squad for their Euro 2020 qualifiers against Cyprus and Kazakhstan. MacGillivray still awaits his debut, having served as one of two goalkeepers on the bench behind Wigan's David Marshall.

He said: 'You cannot go any higher than representing your country, even if you're a Premier League player. It is the highest point of a footballer's career and, if just over a year ago you would have said I'd get that opportunity, I probably would have laughed. For a start, people thought I was English! A member of Scotland's staff once said to me: "So what's your pathway into Scotland?" It's me, it's me! Some think it was my parents. My dad's Scottish but I was also born there.

'As I grew up in Yorkshire, that's the accent I have. When I open my mouth I don't sound Scottish, yet if you look at videos of me aged four or five I had a broad Scottish accent, and my dad still does and lives in Aberdeen. There are a few players in the national squad not born in Scotland. Liam Cooper is from Hull and qualifies through his grandfather, while Oli McBurnie was born in Leeds but his dad is Glaswegian and a massive Rangers fan. There are probably more, but it happens quite a lot. At Pompey we have Ronan Curtis, who was born in Croydon, south London, but moved over to Derry at the age of ten because his mum is from there and he now represents the Republic of Ireland.

'I've really been welcomed. Andy Robertson is the nicest guy in the world. There are some top, top players there and you wouldn't know it off the pitch. Everyone is pulling in the right direction, nobody is hiding in their room and they are sitting downstairs having a laugh and a giggle. Scottish football for a long time has been quite negative as we haven't qualified for a major tournament in 21 years, and, as I understand it, in recent times a lot of lads didn't want to be there, but now they do because this is a good group. This squad should be doing a lot better than it is and, fingers crossed, come March the country will reach a major tournament again because the squad is miles better than in the previous few years, that's for sure.'

MacGillivray has effortlessly settled on the south coast, although mum, Sue, was born in Hayling Island and his aunties reside in Hedge End so his roots in the area run deep. The 26-year-old lives in Liphook with girlfriend Lally, whose dad is a staunch Pompey supporter and former North Stand season-ticket holder who gets his match tickets from an alternative source these days. It has proven to be a remarkable eighteen months in the life of the former PE teacher.

'There is no such thing as a timescale. If you work hard enough you will get an opportunity – and when you get an opportunity, it's up to you to take it. Life is what it is; everyone's timescales are different and everyone's opportunity comes along at different times. When it does come along, you have to give it your best shot. If you don't then only you can have that regret. That's something I told Louis Dennis when he went to Leyton Orient in August. "It may not have worked out here, and you decided to take a different option, but only you can grasp that opportunity at Leyton Orient. If you don't, you can't sit there and say *Oh, I wasn't given the chance again.* It is up to you."

'Admittedly, I used to be a bit of an Eeyore, grumbling about how things weren't working, but you get older and adjust to the fact that you need to look at the bigger picture. You can have your negatives, but finish that thought with a positive.

'The human brain is a magical thing: if you think negatively, you'll be negative – if you think positively, you'll be positive. I believe if I sat in a room with anyone, even if they were the most negative person in the world, I could flip them just by talking because positivity is infectious. Negative mindsets and body language are infectious, and they can rub off on people and make them negative, so be as happy and positive as you can. When I was younger, my dad would always give a positive and then add a "but", to finish on a negative. I'm always going to remember the negative, unfortunately. It's human nature; the negative stays there and festers. It's the same when you receive a bit of criticism – you remember the criticism, but why? I find it fascinating. When I was at Walsall, it was so frustrating. It used to grind my gears that on occasions I'd get a first-team opportunity, did nothing wrong and then was dropped straight out of the team.

'I've reassured Alex Bass here at Pompey that I know how it works. He came in and had a worldie against Oxford United in the Leasing.com Trophy, then didn't have a lot to do against Gillingham but earned a League One clean sheet, only to drop out of the side when I was back from international duty. I had that for four years. It's not nice, but you have to make sure you do everything possible so when told you are losing your place, you can ask why. There's nothing better than putting someone on the back foot.

'Since joining Pompey, I've experienced the best moments of my football career, and it has been a fantastic club for me so far. When you watch play-off finals and cup finals, you sometimes see penalty shoot-outs and think the keeper must be on cloud nine after saving one at Wembley and winning. So, to sample that feeling myself was incredible. It was also my first win at the home of football, following three previous defeats in which I had remained on the bench for Walsall and Shrewsbury.

'My three most memorable moments in football have been coming to Pompey and getting the chance to play games, the Checkatrade Trophy final and receiving the maiden call-up for my country. Hopefully there will be a fourth in the shape of promotion to the Championship.'

John Jenkins

Ian and Abby Chiverton

*Jack Whatmough with partner
Demi and their daughter*

John Westwood

Sam Matterface

Lee Smith

Kev McCormack and Barry Harris

Gareth and Hazel Evans with their son

Debbie Knight and Ashleigh Emberson

John Jenkins and Milan Mandarić

Bob Beech with Balram the python

Carl and Ellie Paddon

Basher and David Benfield

Paul Banks

Mark Kelly

Benjani Mwaruwari

Milan Mandarić, Ashleigh Emberson and Debbie Knight

16 November 2019

The birthday party was no surprise but a shock attendee prompted tears from an overwhelmed John Jenkins. More than nine years had passed since Milan Mandarić last visited Fratton Park, consecutive footballing ventures keeping him away from the club he regards as his sporting soulmate. The Pompey family were gathering in The Legends Lounge to commemorate the improbably sprightly Jenkins' 100th birthday after Fleetwood Town's League One visit.

Arrangements were revised when Cod Army boss Joey Barton inconveniently declared an adjournment nine days before the date, exercising the option to postpone the match after his squad was weakened by three international call-ups. Notably it was the fourth Saturday of the season without a Blues fixture by mid-November. Nonetheless, the core of the 100th birthday celebrations remained unaffected, as did Mandarić's pledge to be present for his friend.

Journeying from Zagreb, Croatia, for the occasion, he booked in for a breathless 48-hour homecoming at the club he owned for more than seven years before bidding farewell in September 2006. Many still revere the charismatic figure who brought Premier League football to the south coast, ending a top-flight absence of sixteen years and overseeing the induction of the likes of Harry Redknapp, Robert Prosinečki, Paul Merson and Linvoy Primus into Fratton folklore. In 2003, he was awarded the Freedom of the City in recognition of his sporting contribution to Portsmouth. Now aged 81, he had been lured back through an immense sense of respect for the ex-boardroom steward and D-Day veteran Jenkins.

'You can see John is a special man; everyone loves and adores the guy. He deserves that recognition, and his personality and approach is so positive,' said Mandarić.

'When I arrived at Pompey, on the very first day I remember how nice John was. He behaved like he had known me forever and was instantly my friend. I had come into a different world and this man was a constant friendly face.

'I couldn't miss his 100th birthday. I've been waiting for this for a year; it was in my diary. Not many knew I would be attending, but my secretary Ros organised everything and I am so happy to see all these wonderful people again.

'John couldn't believe it when I arrived. He told me a few times it was great to see me, but this was his day. He is such a special man with so much positive energy, and he talks to people with real warmth.

'These people love him; it's incredible. I said: "John, during this evening look at yourself in the mirror and you will see a very happy man with so many friends." These people aren't here by accident. They came to pay their respects to his personality and what he has achieved in life.

'I don't go to many functions these days, but this was a special one and one I will cherish. I fondly remember the time I was here with these supporters, helping me to get where we wanted.

'Not one man can do it without support – we achieved it together. I was here for seven years, and during that time we were promoted to the Premier League and remained there; it was a lot of fun and there were many great times.

'Of all the clubs I have owned, people ask why I like Pompey so much. Why do I love them more than any other club? It is simple: this is a family and the family care for their club.

'I told supporters at the time that I wasn't an owner but rather a caretaker. They owned this club a hundred years before me and would do so after me. I promised that, during my time here, I would do my best for them – that is exactly what we did together.'

The party brought five generations of Jenkins' family together inside one room. Among them were daughter Diane, who turns 80 next year, granddaughter Ali aged 56, and the youngest, two-year-old Arlo. Joining Mandarić on the guest list were club Hall of Fame inductees Alan Knight and Andy Awford, ex-Pompey, Ipswich and England striker Ray Crawford and former Havant & Waterlooville manager Mick Jenkins.

In addition, ex-Blues chairman Iain McInnes, now Gosport Borough owner, negotiated a 55-mile dash from Wimborne Town tbe present, having attended his side's 2–1 BetVictor Southern League Premier South success that afternoon. Pompey's first-team squad and club staff paid for Jenkins' cake and balloons, while the club donated a signed shirt, framed by Eric Coleborn through his Glass & Mirror Centre business. There was even the present of a Gillingham shirt with 'Jenkins 100' emblazoned across the back, a touching gesture from Paul Scally, the chairman of Pompey's League One rivals.

Fratton Park receptionist Debbie Knight helped orchestrate the event alongside Ashleigh Emberson, Keri Clark and Malcolm Drew. Hailing from Fareham, she is now in her 22nd year working at the club, surviving three crippling administrations, yet her sunny nature and distinctive laugh cannot help but lift club visitors, while she jokes of her role as one of Jenkins' many 'girlfriends'.

Knight said: 'John is such a lovely man, genuinely a lovely man. Everyone adores him and he is so knowledgeable about everything. I learnt more from John Jenkins about D-Day than I did at school.

'A while ago he had pneumonia and went into hospital. We were really worried about him, then all of a sudden he popped back up and everything is fine again.

'The lovely thing is he still wants to come to the club, not just to watch the football, which is definitely part of it, but to catch up with everyone – and everyone loves seeing him.

'He goes to the Good Companion pub most days for lunch and they know what he wants – he has his own place reserved – and when he was poorly they offered to deliver his dinner. Paula, the landlady, went to Tesco to get a card made for him. When they found out who it was for, they told her: "Oh no, you're not paying for that. We will."

'John mentioned to us how the other week he caught a bus to Baffins and, on his way back, a man who had been across the road in the laundrette came over and said: "John, I hope you don't mind, but we saw you come off the bus and ordered you a taxi and have paid for it." Everyone loves him because he is so genuinely lovely.

'Milan coming to his party was a big secret. You think of how many staff and associates have come and gone throughout Milan's life and all the clubs he has owned over the world – yet he made the effort to be there for John's big day.

'We sat John down and, when Milan arrived shortly afterwards, we led him over and he said: "John, do you remember me?" He replied: "Milan," and started crying.

'Milan is Milan and he doesn't change – such a nice guy. As receptionist, I immediately knew his mood for the day every time he walked through the door! A bad mood and he would go straight up the stairs, a good mood and he would come over and speak. It's like a little community. We are a family, and even when you leave you don't lose that connection.

'I am the oldest office junior in the world. I make the tea, tidy up, put the dishwasher on, but wouldn't change it for the world. I love it, absolutely love it, and the people are fantastic.'

The club also coordinated a touching nine-minute video consisting of warm messages delivered from present and past Fratton Park managers Kenny Jackett, Avram Grant, Harry Redknapp, Michael Appleton, Tony Adams, Steve Cotterill and Paul Cook. There were also contributions from fan favourites Linvoy Primus, Pedro Mendes, Svetoslav Todorov, Tom Naylor, Ricardo Rocha, Ben Close, Lee Bradbury, Gary O'Neil and Johnny Ertl. Others included chairman Michael Eisner, ex-chief executive Peter Storrie, former first-team coaches Leam Richardson and Ian Foster, television presenter and broadcaster Fred Dinenage and legendary football commentator John Motson.

The montage was the brainchild of Ashleigh Emberson, who personally contacted all those featured, utilising the technical skills of the talented Ollie Marsh from the club's media team to create the finished product. Emberson, from North End, has been an invaluable presence at Fratton Park since March 2003, hired as an office junior before rising to become personal assistant to a number of managers and owners over the years. Her present role, PA to Executive Management and Player Liaison Executive, consists of working for Mark Catlin and Kenny Jackett, a responsibility befitting the faultless efficiency and organisational skills admired by all those who have worked alongside her.

'You could see the shock on John's face when Milan came in, and similarly when Iain McInnes arrived late on,' said Emberson.

'Not everybody could attend the party, we knew that. People have busy lives, so I texted some to ask about the possibility of recording a video message – everybody we contacted came back with one.

'Give Harry Redknapp his due. He phoned back and said: "I'll do it," and within half an hour I received it. John Motson called and mentioned: "You do know I'm not good with phones!" so got his son to film, sending it the following day.

'We actually only used half of Tony Adams' video. It was the longest we had and there was an inappropriate word used which had to be cut out!

'The last one we received was from Johnny Ertl, which made me cry, as did Tony's and Fred Dinenage's – they were saying such lovely things about John, it choked me.

'The managers all know him. His routine was to enter the manager's room after a game and pour them a glass of wine or serve beer, often being invited to share a drink himself, sometimes with chairmen present.

'That stopped about a year ago. If John was able he would still go down, but the stairs make it difficult for him these days.

'Looking back, we've had some horrendous moments at the club over the years, but you have to pull together; we're a family, after all.

'I remember watching work colleagues – friends – called into a room to see the administrators and told that they no longer had a job. They came out crying while we remained at our desks.

'Me and Debs were summoned together to see UHY Hacker Young administrators Terri Mulgrew and Michael Kiely in the boardroom at our former Rodney Road offices and were grateful to learn we were staying.

'Through both administrations I've seen, some months you would queue up to be paid and were handed money in bank coin bags, a mixture of notes and coins, which you then needed to pay into your own bank.

'At one stage we were informed by Trevor Birch that the club may be over. I was pregnant, approaching maternity leave, and cried on the shoulder of Guy Whittingham, sitting next to me, who did his best to reassure.

'Having said that, Trevor must be the only administrator in the world that can still come into an office years later and everyone runs up to give him a hug. He was so lovely, a people person, and very approachable.

'When he left, he took us out, as well as his own staff who had worked alongside us day to day. We went for drinks at the Duke of Buckingham in Old Portsmouth, and then across the road to the Good Fortune Chinese restaurant. He paid for it all.'

Emberson was appointed during Mandarić's seven and a half years at the club, a period which also saw Pompey's owner plough through eight managers, among them two stints with Harry Redknapp at the helm. Alan Ball was already in charge upon the Serb's June 1999 arrival, with Tony Pulis, Steve Claridge, Graham Rix, Velimir Zajec and Alain Perrin all serving as manager before being shown the door when the chairman's oft-fragile patience ruptured. Then there was Redknapp, the pair possessing a curious relationship, often combustible, occasionally toxic, yet essentially a close companionship that has evolved into a lifelong association.

Redknapp was also the only manager to escape Mandarić's bloodied axe, walking out on Fratton Park before later returning to outlast the chairman and subsequently claim the 2008 FA Cup and a maiden excursion into European competition. In November 2004, Pompey's manager sensationally quit the club he had steered into the Premier League before retaining their top-flight presence in the following campaign. He was replaced by newly installed executive director Velimir Zajec. In little more than a fortnight's time, Redknapp and assistant Jim Smith were unveiled as the new management team at arch rivals Southampton. Just 379 days later, with the St Mary's club having been relegated and dropping to twelfth in the Championship, Redknapp returned to the Fratton Park hot seat.

Mandarić said: 'I cannot tolerate failures. Maybe I have been accused by a lot of people of constantly changing managers, but when you are at the top you are responsible. You are responsible for your supporters and responsible for getting those results to move the club upwards.

'When I was running big factories and big manufacturing businesses, I always believed that if something works then you give support to them. If it doesn't work, you should try to correct it – if you cannot correct it, you must change it. It's as simple as that. It is no different in football; it's just another professional business.

'Harry is the best manager I've ever worked with, but we had moved apart at the end of his first spell with us. In that period I wanted to do something different, change a few little pieces, but there were no serious arguments. Nobody did anything right or wrong, but for some reason we weren't as close.

'Then one day he told me: "Milan, I think I want to go and have some rest. I need time off football." I was pissed at him – he said he was going to take a vacation somewhere and then, all of a sudden, fifteen days later he was at a press conference over there! I had no idea.

'We all make mistakes, but you have to face it, correct it and move on. Nobody is bigger than the club. No player, no coach, no chairman, and when the chairman makes mistakes, you must recognise it. If I make mistakes then we are going to correct it – and we did.

'Bringing in Velimir Zajec was a mistake as he didn't have any experience or the personality required. You have to be hard and disciplined, and he didn't have it. I recognised that quickly and made a change there.

'Then we struggled with his replacement Perrin and I needed something serious to bring to the club, something different so people would say: "Wow, wait a moment, what is this now?" Harry coming back was the answer.

'So many were unsure over my decision, while a lot of people thought it was the right move later on. The time was perfect to bring him back.

'Harry was ready. He was watching what was happening and knew he had made a mistake in leaving. At one match I spoke in the boardroom to his brother-in-law, Frank Lampard Sr., and mentioned that I was thinking of making changes and bringing Harry back.

'He responded: "If you approached Harry, he would walk to be with you." That's how it started.

'I called him and he came very late at night to my apartment in Port Solent, so no one could see him. We sat down, talked and shared a bottle of wine – we made up. Life was never boring with Harry!'

With Pompey languishing third from bottom in the Premier League in December 2005, three points adrift from safety, Mandarić recalled his former manager to replace Frenchman Perrin following an unsuccessful seven and a half months. Redknapp's spending power in the January transfer window was bolstered by the Blues' owner selling 50 per cent of his stake to businessman Sacha Gaydamak, whose father, Arcadi, was later convicted by a French court for tax offences and money laundering. Boosted by the January 2006 arrivals of Benjani Mwaruwari, Pedro Mendes, Sean Davis, Dean Kiely, Noe Pamarot and Andres D'Alessandro, Pompey embarked upon 'The Great Escape', earning a remarkable 20 points from a possible 27 from March onwards to avoid relegation with a game to spare. Redknapp's return, undeniably divisive among the Fratton faithful, had been a triumph.

Mandarić added: 'We had personalities that fitted each other and knew one another very well, so it was no problem having him back. Harry has that charisma and knows football.

'I remember when building the team to be promoted, he was bringing in all these old players, such as Shaka Hislop, Paul Merson, Tim Sherwood and Arjan de Zeeuw. I said: "Harry, our team is too old, we are never going to make it," and he replied: "Don't worry, we'll do it."

'Every day he told me he needed two more players and eventually I was pissed at him and said: "When are you going to say you need just one player?" He would always insist his squad was down to the bones – what bone was he talking about?

'I appointed him because of his personality and how he could get the best out of the players. He had the talent to be able to connect with both experienced players and youngsters, which a lot of managers have difficulty in doing, but he handled it without a problem.

'I still love Harry and we are good friends. I talked to him last night and he told me: "My God, I would love to be there with you at John's birthday." He's a good man. Although my favourite Pompey memory was when we destroyed Southampton 4–1 in April 2005, when Harry was their manager!

'I went to visit Lomana LuaLua in the hospital who had malaria, and he told me: "Mr Chairman, not too many people come," and I said: "No problem, Lua, I am here to see you; you will be okay." He then made me a promise: "I'll get back and will repay you Mr Chairman because you visited me and everybody else is scared." I responded: "You already have paid me with that Southampton game!" Well, in that match he scored two goals, did his stupid backflip and got himself injured after 28 minutes!'

In July 2006, two and a half months after completing The Great Escape, Mandarić sold his remaining 50 per cent stake in Pompey to Gaydamak for around £32m, staying on as non-executive chairman. With the Serb keen for a swift return to football club ownership, he identified Championship side Leicester as a target and, in September 2006, relinquished his Fratton Park role to pursue challenges elsewhere. The visit of Bolton Wanderers represented his farewell, with a win promising to send the Blues to the top of the Premier League after six matches. Instead, Kevin Nolan's first-half winner settled the match 1–0 in favour of Sam Allardyce's team as Redknapp's side conceded their first league goal of the campaign. Nonetheless, the Fratton faithful chanted the name of the departing Mandarić on an emotionally charged Monday evening under the lights.

'I later went to Leicester City and Sheffield Wednesday. I respect those clubs. They are good clubs with good supporters whom I had a good relationship with,' added Mandarić.

'I really have to say, though, deep within my heart there is one club and it's Pompey.

'The one thing I regret is that while Leicester and Sheffield Wednesday benefited from being left in the right hands, that didn't happen at Pompey. Gaydamak did all right, he did okay, but then sold the club to some other people.

'I thought it was my time to leave Fratton Park. When I lived in Monaco and owned Nice, we had just won the Coupe de France and my friend, George Best, was telling me: "You've got to come to England; that's the country for you."'

'I took over Pompey and thought I would stay two or three years but, with the love and respect of these people, I felt this was my home and that I had to achieve something here. I committed myself, put some money in, not a lot of money compared to today's football, but money to improve the team and infrastructure.

'After seven years, though, my time was done. I had delivered everything I promised and wanted to leave on good terms, on a high, and to be able to go away and think about my time with fondness, which I do. I cherish that time very much.

'I love challenges, and football gives you a lot of challenges. Leicester were in trouble when I went there. They had owners who didn't want to do anything with the club any more, but then I went to Sheffield Wednesday and it was the same thing. These clubs were in trouble and I tried to get them back.

'Sometimes you make sacrifices in your life when owning a football club, and it was my time to leave Pompey and let somebody else continue. I didn't have any problem with that. I loved the club when I left – and still love it today.'

Mandarić's legacy also consisted of a 'present to the fans', namely the implausible acquirement of Robert Prosinečki. With previous residencies at Barcelona and Real Madrid to his name, the Croatian international was lured to the south coast in August 2001 through his close friendship with Pompey's owner. The mercurial talent proceeded to register nine goals in 35 appearances during the 2001–02 campaign under Graham Rix, including three goals against Barnsley in February 2002, the sole hat-trick in an illustrious playing career. A furious Prosinečki later refused the offer of the match ball after the Fratton Park encounter finished 4–4, the Blues letting slip a 4–2 advantage, with the chain-smoking midfielder later reasoning that he wasn't comfortable acknowledging the feat having drawn rather than won. At the season's end, aged 33, he joined Slovenian side Olimpija Ljubljana (now owned by Mandarić) to be closer to his ill father in Zagreb, Croatia. To many, Prosinečki remains one of Portsmouth's greatest players of the post-war era.

Mandarić said: 'Robbie is boss of Bosnia & Herzegovina. I am very much in touch with him, and if I stay with my club and decide to make many changes, he will be my next manager.

'We first met in Monaco when I was owner of Nice and became friends. After I took over at Pompey I told him: "Robbie, I need your help, I need you to get involved," so he came in, no problem. He shook my hand and was never interested in a contract. I just said what I would do for him and I did. That was it.

'Of course he had to sign a contract to be registered for the club, but money-wise it wasn't a concern. He said: "I know you will take care of me and let me do the job." That's the type of guy he is; we are good friends.

'He played for Barcelona and Real Madrid and on the training ground you would see Robbie take the guys on and sometimes, when he lost the ball, the assistant, Jim Duffy, would yell: "You've got to tackle; you've got to get into the game."

'When I told that to Harry Redknapp, he said: "That's stupid, you give the ball to Robert Prosinečki; he's not going to tackle anyone, just give him the ball!"

'What a special player – he was my present to the fans. He's a good person too, as solid as a rock, someone you can rely on. He is also a very sensitive guy and he needs to have support; he also needs to be loved, like all of us, then he can perform. If he feels he's just there because of his name, that makes him unhappy. I can promise you, he loved it at Pompey.'

Mandarić spent almost three and a half years as Leicester owner before selling in July 2010 to Thai billionaire Vichai Srivaddhanaprabha who, in a remarkable feat, would later claim the 2015–16 Premier League title. The Serb then completed a takeover of League One Sheffield Wednesday, a residency which spanned four years, before departing in January 2015 after the club was purchased by a Thai consortium led by businessman Dejphon Chansiri. He is currently in his fifth season as owner of Slovenian top-flight club Olimpija Ljubljana, winning the title twice, while dividing his time between the club, Dubrovnik and San Francisco. Then came a special occasion to lure him back to England.

Mandarić added: 'Watching those fantastic video messages to John, I saw Gary O'Neil on there. When I became owner, Alan Ball told me there was a young player I had to look at and took me to a Pompey youth game. I saw Gary, such a talent and one of the many good players we had here during my time.

'I loved Paul Merson and after training had finished he would stay and shoot the ball, practising in small goals, the same thing George Best did with me at San Jose Earthquakes all those years before.

'After Monday evening training, the San Jose coaching staff and a couple of the players would stay behind for a 4 v 4 match with small goals and afterwards go out for a beer and pizza. On one occasion, there were only six of us and George had the idea of me and him playing against the other four.

'I said: "George, you are crazy." He replied: "Don't worry, just go over there and I'll give you the ball so you just have to put it into the net." Sure enough, he took all the guys on, then gave it to me to score! He was my biggest ally when I came to England and helped me a lot.

'I had so many memorable moments at Pompey. Every day I walked down the street or entered a restaurant and supporters wanted to talk to me about football – and I enjoyed that. I was always open with them and they liked that. It's about communication, being honest, not beating around the bush – that's the way I am.

'During my time at Pompey, I only asked the fans for two things – trust and support. Give me those and I will give you everything I have and make it happen for you.

'I wasn't an owner at Pompey. I told fans: "You, your dad and your grandad came before me – and your children and grandchildren will be after me." I've always had an unbelievable relationship with these fantastic supporters.

'Fans love their clubs, of course they do; this is a special place, though. It's not a club – it's a family.'

BOB BEECH AND CARL PADDON
2 December 2019

The carpet python's agitation was fading, a hearty breakfast of defrosted rat tempering his morning mood. Bob Beech has harboured more than 50 snakes at his Milton home over the years, but this is the only resident to have warranted the honour of a name. Recruited as a hatchling from a reptile show at Havant Leisure Centre, the arrival of the household's newest addition coincided with a chance email which subsequently sparked inspiration – Balram had been christened.

The dark humour exemplifies the rabble-rousing ringleader of the supporter movement known as SOS Pompey, agents provocateurs in the protracted conflict which once raged around their beloved Pompey. The group operated as the militant wing of the Portsmouth Supporters' Trust, adopting unorthodox and often surreptitious methods, while their brothers-in-arms maintained a more diplomatic demeanour in order to negotiate triumph on the battlefields.

Chief antagonist was Balram Chainrai, multiple-time owner of the Blues through his Hong Kong-based investment vehicle Portpin and complicit in putting the club into administration twice within 24 months. SOS Pompey orchestrated the uprising, protest marches and demonstrations, screaming defiance to adversaries underestimating the might of a unified fan base. Gatecrashing news agendas of international media, their passionate rhetoric persuaded the Premier League to grant them an audience, becoming the first supporter group invited into the Gloucester Place headquarters, entertained by chief executive Richard Scudamore as football chiefs scrambled to reach a resolution.

And while Chainrai was ultimately vanquished at the High Court in April 2013 as fan ownership seized control, his yellow and olive-tinged namesake continues to consume rats at the home of SOS Pompey's chieftain.

'I suppose Balram would have the hump if he knew who he was named after, but the truth is very few of our animals have names. If they have a name it's because they have earned one,' Beech said with a smile.

'For instance, we had a monitor lizard called Freddy. Well, he wasn't called anything until the day he escaped. We couldn't find him in our contained reptile room and wondered whether he had wandered outside, with it being summer. So we asked our neighbours whether they had spotted this thing which was tip to tail about six to seven feet long, had huge claws and great teeth, but friendly.

'My wife, Linda, then said: "If you see him, give him a shout. His name's Freddy." That was news to me, so when we returned inside, I asked how long that had been the case.

'She replied: "I thought if I gave him a name he would seem more friendly!" I'm sure Mrs Krueger also believed that about her son.

'We've also had Horrible Horace, an Argentine black and white tegu, a beautiful lizard called Diablo and, of course, Balram. The day we bought him, we came home and I sat down and started opening up emails – correspondence about the ongoing situation at Pompey. One of them said: "Have you seen what that snake Balram has done now?" Well, that tickled me – and his name stuck. Those who know find it amusing, but most people don't get the connection.

'Being a python, he likes rats, a couple a week. You can't feed them every day, they'll grow too big. I suppose it's quite apt – strike when prey is vulnerable and then squeeze the life out of it. Snakes are not affectionate either, although will give you a good cuddle. Still, during the SOS Pompey stuff, I found spending time with my reptiles quite therapeutic. You could switch off from the battle for a couple of hours, whether feeding or cleaning them out. It was something I needed as it was an intense period.

'What the Pompey Supporters' Trust did was above and beyond the call of duty. Guys like Mick Williams, Mark Trapani and Ashley Brown put their lives and businesses on hold to save our club, though I maintain the Trust couldn't have achieved what they did without SOS Pompey's antics. I've joked with Ashley a couple of times about this. If you deemed this the Second World War, then basically the Trust were the USA, letting us fight it out and then coming in at the end to take the glory! As fans of our football club, we have a debt to those guys, but it wouldn't have happened without SOS Pompey.

'We brought the situation to the attention of supporters across the country, and we captured the interest of the world's media. Once we started to make a nuisance of ourselves, the goings-on at Fratton Park could no longer be ignored. At its peak, purely because we were a Premier League club, I once had media from fifteen countries contact me in a day wanting to talk Pompey. Hong Kong, the USA, Canada, Australia, New Zealand, Spain, Scandinavian countries, it was mad.

'At that particular time, and with respect to the Trust and other supporter bodies, they were doing nothing. So we decided to roll up our sleeves and get stuck in.

'Days after the owners went into administration in November 2011, there was a fans' conference at Fratton Park on the morning of our match with Coventry City – it was the last one I ever attended. We were sitting around a big table and the two topics on the agenda were the hot water in the South Stand and which coach company we should use for away travel! I was the Chicken Licken of the piece: "The sky is falling in, guys."

'Somebody said: "Well, they've told us it won't affect the club." I explained the club was going, and they needed to get their heads around it, but they weren't interested. The sky is falling in, that's the expression I used, the sky is falling in. Yet they were talking about hot water in the South Stand and which coach company we should use. It doesn't matter because there won't be a South Stand and there won't be any away games.

'I got up and said: "If we are not going to discuss the only thing that matters at this football club right now then there's no point me being here" – and I left. My friend, Carl Paddon, was waiting outside and asked how it went. My response was: "We are stuffed. We need to mobilise now more than we have ever done because there's a storm coming and this club is about to go."

'We sat in my front room and plotted. For a laugh, we called it Operation Armageddon and vowed that, should Chainrai get the club again, not one single game would ever kick off at Fratton Park. Back in 1969–70, there was a South Africa Rugby Union tour of Britain and Ireland amid massive anti-apartheid protests. Among the things they did was claim that they had spread glass on the Twickenham pitch so the game couldn't go ahead. Were they telling the truth? The authorities couldn't risk it.

'We wanted to become a nuisance, to superglue all the locks around Fratton Park on a Saturday morning, write SOS Pompey on the pitch using weedkiller before a televised game. Another suggestion was invading the pitch during the match, or in the warm-up handcuffing ourselves to the goalposts. I know they'd have got the bolt cutters out, but it would have been enough to delay things and cause a problem, getting the message out. Thankfully, because of the efforts of Ashley Brown, Mick Williams, Mark Trapani and lots of others, it wouldn't come to that, but all these things were lined up. I'm a student of history and sometimes you just have to say: What is it worth to you? We were prepared to cross the line.'

It was in Fratton's Shepherds Crook pub where a group of disenchanted supporters conceived of SOS Pompey in September 2009. A 1–0 home defeat to Everton signalled a fourth successive Fratton Park loss from the start of the 2009–10 campaign. Matters off the pitch would also deteriorate significantly. The following month heralded a third owner since the start of the season as the club began to unravel with wages not paid on time, a winding-up petition presented by HMRC and a transfer embargo slammed into place.

By January 2010, with Pompey having sat bottom of the Premier League since the opening week of the campaign, SOS Pompey decided to launch their first demonstration of strength against those overseeing their club's dismantling.

Beech added: 'We were sitting in the Shepherds Crook and a couple of fans were saying: "Someone needs to do something, someone needs to do something." Hang on a minute, why has *someone* got to do something? Why not you? So I said: "Okay, *I'll* do something!" Just like that, SOS Pompey was born.

'Although we were protesting about a very serious issue, we also wanted to conduct ourselves with a smile, to have a bit of a laugh, definitely not taking ourselves too seriously. We worked closely with the Trust, this good cop, bad cop partnership. If there was any message they needed to get out, I told them to leave it to us, we'd sort it. I called it "plausible deniability".

'We decided to launch our first demonstration as the club was in a mess. We didn't know who owned us, who was pulling the strings, and why was this Premier League club suddenly in financial peril, especially following a summer of pocketing millions from selling players. One owner, Sulaiman Al-Fahim, wanted the game halted so he could walk onto the pitch and wave at us. He asked for the summer transfer window to be extended especially for Pompey – and we were thinking: "What's going on?" He was here for five minutes and replaced by Ali Al Faraj, who was late paying the wages for each for his opening three months in charge.

'A large-scale protest was scheduled to take place before a Premier League game against Birmingham City. It was advertised, so the police got in touch requesting information, while Portsmouth City Council requested the standard seven days' notice to hold a protest. Still, I wanted everything done by the book, to prevent criticism from those in authority. Then the match was called off, waterlogged pitch apparently. Call me an old conspiracy theorist, but you had to wonder whether it was anything to do with the 2,000 Herberts about to march down Frogmore Road. Let's be honest, it wouldn't have been the worst thing those owners did at Fratton Park.

'Anyhow, on the morning that Birmingham game was scheduled to be played, I received a call from the police. It was mentioned if we postponed the protest as well, they would have no objection with it taking place on another date. Definitely a case of you scratch our backs and we'll scratch yours. For us, that was agreeable, especially with a match-day protest likely to make a far better impact – and the following Saturday was a home FA Cup fixture against Sunderland.

'So it was rearranged for seven days later, although meeting at Guildhall Square was like having a birthday party. The booze and the buffet were laid out and you're hoping somebody turns up. Still, we were encouraged at the 500 present, then, once the walk to Fratton Park started, we collected others.

'There was one moment which really touched me and I'm gutted I never got their names. We reached Fratton Bridge down Goldsmith Avenue and I noticed an elderly couple standing there, so I said something along the lines of: "Are you okay? We won't get in the way."

'To which they replied: "No, no, we couldn't manage the walk from Guildhall Square, so we've been waiting here for you," and joined the protest! They walked quite happily, hand in hand, with somebody giving the lady one of the posters, which she willingly held up.

'At one point down Goldsmith Avenue, everyone suddenly sat down in the middle of the road – it was a spontaneous thing. The chief inspector walking alongside me didn't know what was going on – and neither did I!

'Then we arrived at the club, and I can picture the image now, standing on a small wall outside the ground's entrance and looking up Frogmore Road. It was packed, and everyone appeared to be holding up a question mark poster and there were banners too. Somebody needed to give a speech, which fell to me, before Micah Hall's son and daughter – Lawrence and Paige – and Joyce Tynan, representing support across the ages, handed over a letter to the chief executive, Peter Storrie.

'The reaction of Pompey's fans was beyond our expectations and, the following Monday, I received a phone call from Sky Sports News asking to do a piece to camera outside Fratton Park about the protest. During the interview, they enquired what we were going to do next and, I have to be honest, none of us had actually thought that far ahead! On the spur of the moment, I announced that, as we were soon to play at Fulham, we would take our protest to the Premier League's headquarters earlier that day. No one had thought about it, but, upon reflection, it occurred to us it was actually a good idea. The last thing the Premier League needed was us turning up – and within days I received a call from them offering to meet us if we cancelled the protest. That's how SOS Pompey became the first fan group to be invited to meet them. Suddenly we had credibility.'

The June 2011 takeover headed by Convers Sports Initiatives (CSI) signalled a new Fratton Park era, prompting SOS Pompey to stand down, although they continued to scrutinise. Six months later, following chairman Vladimir Antonov's arrest in connection with bank fraud, CSI entered administration. Pompey followed suit in February 2012, reverting back to the ownership of Chainrai by default as a creditor.

With debts of £58m, PKF were appointed administrators of the then-Championship club, headed by former Chelsea chief executive Trevor Birch. By the summer, the necessity to slash an unmanageable player wage bill had reached crisis point and, following a close-season fire sale of prized assets and reaching compromise agreements with others to depart, eight senior footballers remained. Joint administrator Birch warned that unless Dave Kitson, Liam Lawrence, David Norris, Tal Ben Haim, Luke Varney, Erik Huseklepp, Greg Halford and Kanu left Fratton Park, the club would be liquidated. That prompted SOS Pompey to reconvene and, in July 2012, they gathered at the Blues' Wellington Sports Ground in Eastleigh to put pressure on those concerned – in their own inimitable manner.

'On the morning of the demonstration, we put out an announcement calling for supporters to meet us at the training ground. The attendance was brilliant,' said Beech.

'The truth was, one or two people within the club hierarchy knew we were going to do something. Michael Appleton, who was in Spain for Pompey's pre-season, was consulted and gave us the wink, although he wasn't involved in the organisation. First-team coach Guy Whittingham ensured the players would be there for training rather than at the David Lloyd Club, and Trevor Birch was aware we were up to something. There were phone calls going backwards and forwards the day and night before – and it worked perfectly.

'Instructions came from the Trust. The message was basically: "The club will die unless these players agree to cancel their contracts, and we need your help in approaching them." To this day, I still maintain that, whether you like those players or not, each one of them had signed a contract with Portsmouth Football Club in good faith and deserved to be paid every single penny due. All we were asking was could a deal be reached?

'The idea was to hand each player an open letter which simply stated that while they were owed money – and we agreed they should get it – if a deal couldn't be reached then the club would die and nobody would receive a penny. One training ground gate was locked shut and the other ajar so, as the players turned up, they had to stop and wait for the guy inside to open it, by which time we could approach them and hand over the letter.

'Some were as good as gold, the likes of David Norris and Liam Lawrence, who insisted the last thing they wanted was for the club to die and were keen for the situation to be resolved. Ben Haim didn't want to talk to anybody, he wasn't interested; he didn't even wind his window down, instead looking straight ahead. As for Dave Kitson, he glanced at the letter then tossed it back at us – but we weren't finished with him.

'When the players were inside the training ground and all accounted for, the gates were shut. However, Trevor Birch called me and Carl into the complex, just in time to see Kitson standing in the car park, and wasn't his face a picture – "All right, Dave?!"

'Funnily enough, his attitude changed. He claimed he thought we were press and that was the reason he didn't want to talk to us, although the fact that all of these people were standing around in Pompey shirts, it must have been obvious we didn't work for the *Daily Mail*.

'Now Carl was getting quite shirty. It was he who handed Kitson the letter in the first place, and he enquired: "What are you going to say to me now?" The striker mumbled something and we again gave him the letter, this time reading it in full in front of us, before saying: "Well, I haven't been offered a deal." One moment, Dave. I called Trevor over and explained what Kitson had said, before adding: "Somebody is now lying, and I'm not quite sure who it is."

'Trevor responded: "I can assure you that every player has been spoken to. Whether it be to them or their representative, every player has been offered a way out." Kitson subsequently said he'd have to look into it, or something along those lines, and scurried off.

'I'm sure he believed he was dealing with a couple of stupid football fans who knew nothing, but we'd been around the block by that stage.

'We still had other work to do, however, and Birch informed us: "We need a deal in place by 10 August; if not then I'm going to close this club." When I asked whether it was on the record, he confirmed it was – quite clearly he wanted the message out.

'So I texted Mark McAdam from Sky Sports News with the words: "I'm coming out with something big, you may want to go out live." And they did, breaking news. Portsmouth Football Club will cease to be on 10 August – boom! The blue touchpaper had been lit.

'The demonstration was an absolute success and eighteen days later all those players had left, so the club could continue.'

Carl Paddon's Pompey devotion was ingrained through Christmas packages, a cherished VHS cassette traditionally among the seasonal contents that crossed the Irish Sea to his Belfast home. Dad, Neil, a soldier in the Army and based hundreds of miles away in Portsmouth, was keen on distance learning, a formative footballing education responsible for his son parading a Blues shirt among the customary Liverpool and Manchester United strips on the school playing field. The arrival of a video depicting a clash between Oxford United and Pompey in November 1992 proved particularly captivating to a beguiled youngster. A remarkable 5–5 draw for Jim Smith's side was replayed repeatedly. Paddon was entranced by a Manor Ground crowd euphoric at a monsoon of goals.

In the summer of 1993, a south-coast visit from Northern Ireland comprised of a maiden Fratton Park trip for a pre-season friendly with Real Sociedad, Lee Chapman's double and a Mark Blake goal delivering a winning introduction. At the age of eighteen, he booked himself in for a four-week stay in the city where his father and grandparents lived. Today he is 35 – and remains a Portsmouth resident. Paddon's Pompey grounding began on Shankill Road, west Belfast, and the Irishman would establish himself as one of the leading figures during SOS Pompey's fight to keep the club in existence.

'I would have gone to jail to save my club,' he said. 'I was so focused, I was blinkered, and consequences didn't occur to me. I would have done anything; nothing could be ruled out. At that time, hand on heart, I would have done anything, absolutely anything. The only real thing I had in my life was Pompey – and it was being abused. I have changed over time, as other things have become more of a priority within my life, but back then Pompey was the sole reason I was pumped. It was being abused in front of my eyes. I was witnessing it, and I was prepared to stop it. I was like a kid with reins on, with Bob [Beech] my parent. That was our relationship: he was the calculating one and I was the one who wanted to cause as much damage as possible – and I was prepared to do anything. Going to jail really wouldn't have mattered.

'At one of the hearings at the High Court, in December 2012, Levi Kushnir and Deepak Chainrai were present, and they must have felt our anger when looking at them sitting there. When you look people in the face whom you have been fighting against for so long, you kind of lose any rationale. After it was adjourned, I wanted to kidnap Deepak Chainrai. We had a big flag, and I was saying we should wrap him up in it and take him round the corner. We chased them down the road and they got away in a black cab.

'That's what we did; there are no ifs, buts and maybes. That's what people have to understand. Forget heading to work or going out in the evening with your girlfriend, you are prioritising fighting these people. When the pressure cooker has been boiling away for years and finally it releases, there is no rationale. I was blinded by it, blinded by the anger, blinded by the hurt. The love I had for the football club was overriding. At that time, if you were siding with Balram Chainrai's team you were an enemy. We saw you as an enemy, and we would seek you out and destroy you. Simple. That's the mentality we had. You needed to be destroyed.

'The first time I actually got involved with SOS Pompey was when I saw a Facebook post from Brendon Bone saying there was going to be a protest. Being from Belfast and hearing about protests I was "Yeah, I'm all over this!" We met at the Shepherds Crook and I can remember the day quite vividly. I had never met Bob before. He was standing outside and I asked if he was leading this protest. In my mad Belfast mentality, I asked if we would be making petrol bombs and all that kind of stuff! I wasn't even joking. I have one way of protesting. At the time I was thinking: "Forget this, something needs to be done" – and then I saw that Facebook post calling for people to meet up at the Crook. I was up for that. Unfortunately for those that tried to ruin the club, Bob and I clicked that first day we met; it was a case of: "Let's cause a bit of trouble here."'

In one instance, SOS Pompey's call to arms involved a social media appeal to bombard the Football League with protest phone calls and emails of complaint about their handling of the club's ongoing ownership issues. Such was the response, it crashed the league chiefs' server and phone lines. Paddon was at the forefront of militant approach but his Pompey devotion also extended to involvement in charities such as Pompey's 12th Man, while he orchestrated syndicates through SOS Pompey to purchase fourteen Trust shares in the club.

He added: 'I don't think people realise how close we came to going into non-league. There was a Plan B drawn up and we owe huge thanks to a lot of people. Pompey is in the heart and soul of the community and we'd all had enough. That's the difference with what has gone on at Bolton Wanderers and Bury. Yes, those fans are hurting, but I don't see what they have tried to do about the situation. I can understand why supporters won't get involved because it can take over your life. It took over mine, and it took over Bob's; it became the sole priority. Whether that was right or wrong, there was no other way to approach it. You had to be committed 100 per cent, and there were those of us who were. It seemed everything we did was effective.

'Bob was the wise bull and I was the young, mad bull. He always had to keep me on the reins because I just wanted to cause a lot of collateral damage and didn't think of the consequences. Bob was the sensible head. We could do things no one else could as we had access to certain people in the national media. No other fan groups have had that, apart from the Blackpool guys, who had a lot of similarities with ourselves; they were also up for the fight.

'It will happen again to clubs, I am under no illusions. When you have every Premier League club wanting to pay £250,000 to Richard Scudamore because he is stepping down from a £2.5m-a-year job as executive chairman but aren't willing to save a club twenty miles down the road, it will never change.

'The day the club were taken over by the fans, I received a message from Ian Peach telling me we had been saved and I started crying. It was a relief as it was unhealthy what we were doing; there was a lot of stress involved, and then suddenly it was over. I had just dropped my daughter, Ellie, off for her first day at nursery and her mum thought I was getting emotional at that! We have since split up, and I don't think I ever told her what it was really about.

'SOS Pompey haven't officially retired; we have never once said that's us done. I still have access to the Twitter account! When I see something I'm not happy about, I will voice my opinion, as that's the type of person I am. I hope it never happens again and that's not just my football club but anyone else's and I really feel for Bury.

There needs to be a safeguarding procedure because nothing has changed.

'The outcome justified the commitment, so I don't feel it was wasted. We didn't want to do it for any credit, we did it because we cared; we did it because we cared for our football club. I have an eight-year-old daughter, and she is the most important thing in my life now, yet for a good three or four years, Pompey was everything. It wasn't just about going to football, it took priority over my job, my relationship, it was everything. At that point, saving the club was the greatest achievement in my life and something I can look back on with fond memories. We did it, and everyone involved knows who did what and I was part of that and, yes, I'm proud. The number one intention of those people was to kill our football club. We took them head-on – and we won.'

The magnitude of that supporter-driven accomplishment was revisited in August 2019 as Bury and Bolton battled to avoid liquidation. Bolton's survival was secured through new owners Football Ventures, signalling their emergence from administration, but Bury became the first club to be expelled from the Football League since Maidstone in 1992. Having failed to fulfil their opening six fixtures of the campaign, the 134-year-old Gigg Lane-based club, which last season were promoted from League Two, were liquidated. Pompey supporters prevented such a lamentable fate six and a half years earlier – and the plight of their League One companions inevitably stirred memories.

'During our troubles, I actually approached the Football Supporters' Federation and called for a mass fan protest aimed at those running the game,' said Beech.

'For 90 minutes of a football match, I am all for supporters giving each other stick, chanting: "Who nicked my stereo?" and "Clear off back to Guildford," to me; that is fair game. For the rest of the time, however, we should be united, even with Southampton, because the Football Association, Premier League and Football League are quite happy for us to be divided. If we're divided, there is nothing we can do – but come together and we can establish an immovable force, football fans across the country standing as one.

'So how about, one Saturday, let's not attend a match, instead tens of thousands of football fans across the country uniting, marching together, wearing their club colours? You would soon see some action from the football authorities. We called the idea: "Can we have our football back?" The FSF didn't quite get it, they were a bit establishment. That was that.

'The truth is, fans of other clubs aren't interested until it's them. And when it is, they've had it worse than anyone else. I don't want to see any single club go out of business through bad ownership, but I cannot actually bring myself to have a go at the Football League for expelling Bury, purely because you had enough chances. After going into administration for the second time under Chainrai, if the Football League had told us: "We're going to relegate you now," you couldn't really argue because there comes a time.

'If we are demanding that the football authorities do something about bad ownership, when they actually do something about bad ownership, you cannot moan: "Oh no, that's not fair." Bury are saying it's unfair to expel them from the Football League because of what the owners did. Yes, possibly, but you were quite happy when last season you won promotion from League Two under the same bad owner. You cannot have it both ways.

'But the truth is, the football authorities don't care about ownership and finances all the time it is going well. We stepped up and did something, although, I have to say, some supporters from other clubs did back us. The pre-season friendly at Aldershot in August 2012 was a great one, and their fantastic fans joined in by singing: "Get out of their club." We stayed behind afterwards to protest – it was a spontaneous thing.

'Our Fit And Proper banner was passed around Anfield's Kop before kick-off while they sang 'You'll Never Walk Alone" during our March 2010 visit, thanks to the help of the Spirit of Shankly guys. Similarly, we held joint protests outside Old Trafford, whose Independent Manchester United Supporters Association, or IMUSA, were complaining against the [American] Glazer family's ownership. I kept on pointing out that it was ironic they were called *"I'm USA"*. I think that wore thin after a while! Still, they also passed around our flag inside the ground during the game.

'There were even people in Hong Kong getting our message across. We created T-shirts bearing the SOS Pompey symbol – a pitchfork and torch – with the message "No matter how bad things get, at least I'm not a Scummer", and they sold by the bucketload. On one occasion, I got chatting to somebody travelling to Hong Kong on a business trip and he wanted a dozen of these T-shirts for a "jolly wheeze up my sleeve". It turned out he persuaded some of those he was doing business with to wear the T-shirts and join him visiting Chainrai's offices. They knocked on the door and asked: "Can we speak to Mr Chainrai, please?" The response was that he wasn't there. "Yes he is, he's over there – hello Mr Chainrai." They were soon ushered out of the offices!

'The last thing the Football League needed was for fans to own Portsmouth Football Club. They are quite happy patronising little AFC Wimbledon, patting them on the head, but they couldn't stand the idea of fans owning a club the size of Pompey – and owning it successfully.'

Tony Goodall, the leading figure in Pompey Independent Supporters Association, passed away suddenly in March 2012, his memory preserved through the regular fans' conference adopting his name. The previous month, Jim Riordan had also been taken from the PISA collective, a respected activist who claimed to be the first Briton to play for a Russian professional football team and had named one of his two cats 'Pompey'. For Beech, there was personal cost during the lengthy fight, a sacrifice he was prepared to make.

He said: 'Success was against all odds and there are quite a few who don't understand what we did. I'm also well aware of others bigging themselves up for the part they played. I know who did what and I also know those who did nothing. I've consequently had arguments with some who have said to me: "You just wanted to be on television and in the papers" – and I have not as politely pointed out that I was self-employed, so how much do you think that cost me? Well, I had to declare myself bankrupt. I was a taxi driver not working, spending all my time trying to save my club. This isn't a woe-is-me story, don't get me wrong; it was my choice to do it, but I was devoting more time to doing Pompey stuff than earning a living. Nobody knows that because I didn't want them to as it's a bit embarrassing, but I made my bed and had to lie on it. Such is life, I'm still breathing.

'I'm lucky, though, I have a fantastic wife, Linda, who supported me through all of it. During the height of the fight, I actually asked her why she had never moaned, as she certainly would have been justified in doing so. She replied that it was the first time I had been positive and focused since losing our daughter, Charlotte, through an asthma attack in 2009. She encouraged me to do what I had to.

'On one occasion, I received a text from Linda. We literally hadn't seen each other for days and she sent a message which read: "I know you are alive, I've just seen you on the telly." Then there was the day when I was at the High Court. Proceedings had been adjourned and there were rows of TV cameras, with me switching from one to the next for interviews. Then my phone rang, it was Linda, and with it being a windy day, I bent down, put my finger in an ear and attempted to talk to her. She had called to let me know she was off shopping and was there anything I needed, that was all. During our conversation, I looked up and all these microphones and cameras were pointing at me. I told Linda: "I have to go, babes," and turned around, which immediately prompted the question from those journalists near me: "What's the latest?" "We are out of brown sauce apparently!" They thought it was an important phone conversation – well, it was kind of important.

'Linda is more than my wife, she's my everything, and one of the unsung heroes of SOS Pompey. We couldn't have achieved what we did without SOS Pompey – and I couldn't have succeeded with SOS Pompey without her support. She's an important part of the Pompey story, just as much as anything we did.'

The date with destiny was fixed for April 2013 at the Rolls Building of the High Court, the backdrop for a final showdown between Portpin and Pompey supporters. Beech was not present in the public gallery, asked to watch from afar. Portpin accepted an out-of-court settlement with administrators BDO (formerly PKF) to release their charge on Fratton Park, thwarting liquidation and thrusting the Blues into fan ownership.

The Trust were handed a 51 per cent stake in the club, the remainder owned by high net worth investors of a Pompey persuasion. The supporters had their football club back. That evening, Beech returned to the Shepherds Crook, alongside trusty lieutenant Paddon, to toast victory at the venue where SOS Pompey was born.

The 53-year-old added: 'In August 2012, Chainrai announced that he was out. He had pulled his latest bid for ownership of Pompey. Then I saw my friend Kate Osterholm with her mum, Jane, across the road, and she was carrying a bottle of champagne.

'I shouted not to open it. "Why? We've won," she replied.

"We've won nothing," I told her.

'I explained it was like the end of the film *Carrie*. When you put your guard down, the hand will suddenly rise up from the ground and grab you. Chainrai was always going to come back. I took no pleasure in being proven right – he restated his interest seven days later.

'Fast forward to almost eight months on, when Chainrai had to concede defeat at the High Court. Kate and I would often joke about this bottle of champagne still chilling in her fridge, so when I heard the news, I texted: "Open your champers."

'Seconds after, the phone rang, and it was Kate: "Does that mean what I think it means?" she asked. "Yes," I replied. "We've done it."

'She had a little cry on the phone – and I shed a tear too.'

BASHER BENFIELD
AND PAUL BANKS

22 December 2019

A distressing fall the previous evening forced Basher Benfield to abort plans for an eagerly anticipated pre-Christmas drink with friends at the Newcome Arms. Not that failing health permits sizeable alcoholic consumption these days; his favourite tipple is nothing more intoxicating than lime cordial.

The doctor paid a 1am visit to the Copnor home in which the Pompey fanatic resides alone, the house call booked following a slip which saw him crash against a living-room chair, sustaining an excruciating injury to his left side. Born with mild spina bifida, his body now rapidly deteriorating, Benfield has come to rely on a wheelchair to aid mobility in recent years, a cruel destiny accepted without a hint of self-pity. Having suffered a stroke and undergone a kidney transplant early in life, doctors had not expected him to live beyond the age of 40. Remarkably, next month marks his 56th birthday. Regardless, it is estimated that he has been absent from fewer than twenty Blues fixtures since the 1980s, including friendlies. The rare blemishes on his proud record were brought about by his ongoing ill health, save for the two friendlies he missed following the passing of his mum in the summer of 2006.

On the morning of the Ipswich Town encounter at Fratton Park, Benfield is forced to reluctantly cancel his Newcome Arms commitment, the pain from the fall refusing to abate, visibly wincing on occasions during conversation. Missing the League One fixture that afternoon is, however, inconceivable. Not under any circumstances.

It is set to be an emotional day for the Pompey family, with the city in mourning following the passing of John Jenkins earlier in the week, just 32 days after celebrating his 100th birthday. His passing represents a third blow within a fortnight, with revered former manager Jim Smith and Ron Saunders, the third-highest scorer in club history, also departing. An emotional pre-match tribute is to be held, culminating in a minute's applause. Benfield is determined to be in attendance, present from his usual vantage point in the South Stand lower, despite obvious discomfort.

He said: 'Around six years ago I was in Queen Alexandra Hospital with a kidney infection, being drip-fed intravenously following treatment, but Pompey were playing at Bristol Rovers. I persuaded them to let me out for the afternoon before returning – unfortunately we lost 2–0. There have been times when I've attended Fratton Park games wearing my hospital wristband after popping out for a few hours. It's like going outside for a cigarette, except I'm off to football, but I'm always back by 6pm. I hate missing games and I get really grumpy if I'm not watching Pompey. Following them has been part of my life for so long, but sometimes I have to be sensible and consider my health.

'Last night I had a fall. I slipped and stumbled, catching my side on a chair. I rang the emergency number and the locum doctor visited. He told me it was bruising so we'll have to wait and see the full extent of the damage. I've got to take it a bit easy. I'm no longer going to the Newcome today as sitting in a pub for a couple of hours will be difficult. It won't stop me from going to the game, though; absolutely no way. My body is packing up – it is what it is – but at least I'm still here.

'I should have been dead around 40 – I saw the file in hospital as somebody had left it out. I wasn't supposed to know what was contained within it, but it was quite interesting, and that's also how I discovered some of the details behind where my new kidney had come from. There had been a road traffic accident in the West Country involving a female and the kidney was a near-perfect match. You don't get names, just the briefest of information, and it was very hard deciding whether to write and thank the parents, potentially bringing back bad memories for the family. I decided against it. I couldn't be certain how they would react and I didn't want to intrude on their grief, but I am so thankful for their kindness.

'That was nearly twenty years ago and I am still here, so every Pompey match I can attend is a bonus for somebody lucky to be alive. It's a struggle sometimes, in this weather especially. My legs seize up through the rheumatism and there are days when I don't want to climb out of bed. I know I have to, so I force myself. I could just lie there, but it doesn't achieve anything. My condition has become worse and worse over recent years. At first I started walking with a stick, then a crutch, now it's either a walking frame, a wheelchair or a motorised scooter. It's a downward spiral, but there is nothing I can do to stop it.

'I'm thankful to be alive, though. I'm lucky as it could have been a lot worse, and you have to laugh. Whenever I visit the pub they ask: "Are you still alive?" I reply: "Yes, I'm still here!" It's just banter, gallows humour; they know me, I'm not going to change. To me that's life, and every day is a bonus. That's why I keep myself active. I sit here a lot in my chair at home and try to go out in the scooter when I can. Sometimes I am at the club near enough every day, attending various supporter meetings – I like to keep involved.

'I was born with a mild form of spina bifida, so always walked with a bit of a limp – I knew it was coming eventually. Then in Gibraltar on a Pompey tour in July 2012, I was walking down the road and the next thing I knew I was lagging miles behind everyone else and I couldn't catch up. I was shattered and my back was killing me. That was the first sign.

'I used to enjoy going round cathedrals and old churches, but I can't really do that now as they're not always accessible to wheelchair users. Having said that, they can't build a lift at Fratton Park, which was constructed in 1899, but the Colosseum in Rome is almost 2,000 years old and has one! I wish someone would explain to me why!

'It won't stop me from attending matches, though. My dad, David, pushes the wheelchair for home matches. He is aged 83 and my carer, which is the wrong way round I suppose, but it's good to spend time together. As well as meeting up at the Newcome, I was meant to be watching Pompey Women at Crawley Wasps tomorrow, but my body is not going to be able to do two matches in two days; it's saying "no" after that fall. I have to consider my health. I need a couple of days off really, so I'm going to play safe and just watch today's match against Ipswich. We have four away matches in a row coming up, three of which will involve travelling there and back in a day while Fleetwood Town in the FA Cup will be an overnight stay.'

Howard Benfield was born in Gladys Avenue, North End, although there's uncertainty over the precise location, setting one foot into this world at his grandparents' home before birth complications saw him rushed to hospital. Similarly, the point of origin of his 'Basher' moniker is indeterminable, handed to him as a baby for reasons he would never discover. Only his late mother and two aunties referred to him by the birth name Howard.

At least he can identify the dawning of his Pompey affiliation, the landmark event coming on 18 March 1972, when he accompanied his father to Fratton Park for a Second Division encounter with Norwich City. A Ray Hiron double ensured a winning introduction for the eight-year-old who savoured a 2–1 Blues triumph in a crowd of 13,902. Benfield estimates that he has since watched at least 2,000 Pompey league matches. Factor in cup competitions, friendlies and games involving the reserves and the youth team, and the tally swells to more than 3,000.

'I once sat down with Alan Knight and we worked out I had seen 794 of his 801 Pompey appearances,' added Benfield. 'I have never kept records, unlike other Pompey fans I know. I was married in the early 1980s, but football takes over your life. Due to illness, I was unable to have children. I suppose if I had, it would have affected my chances of going to matches!

'Travelling abroad in pre-season is hysterical. I returned from a tour to Ireland in the summer of 1998 to discover that my kidneys were failing. Even before that I was feeling rough. I couldn't shake this bug and in the mornings I was expelling at both ends so visited a doctor, who took a blood test and later told me I should be in a coma. My creatinine level was 1,200, but a normal person should be about 200. I was poisoning myself without realising.

'Dialysis followed which involved visiting St Mary's Hospital three days a week and being connected to a big machine that cleans the blood for up to three and a half hours. I worked for Raymarine on the Eastern Road, a yachting company, but had to retire at the age of 34 as the treatment left me exhausted. When I had my kidney transplant in August 2000, my legs packed up temporarily for six months; it turned out I was allergic to the drugs. I also missed Grimsby Town, Cambridge United in the Worthington Cup and then Gillingham away on the Friday night – I was absolutely gutted. I hadn't missed a home game in years! The Gillingham match was actually televised, so my friend recorded it and brought it into my ward at St Mary's for me to watch ten minutes after the final whistle, I had purposely avoided the score.

'In the 2014–15 season, I had to miss successive away trips to Morecambe and Carlisle United because of medical advice, the doctors banning me from travelling due to ill health! Even before any of this happened, I had a stroke in 1990 and missed Middlesbrough away. Living in Leigh Park at the time, I sat on the settee and suddenly wanted a cigarette, though I had never smoked in my life! Your mind goes, and I was obsessed with lime jelly for some reason, but I was lucky as I only lost a bit of my memory for five days before it returned, while the stroke left a little bit of a weakness in my right finger.'

Benfield's belief in fan representation previously saw him serve as activity organiser for non-football events with the Pompey Supporters'

Club (Central Branch), while he is current chairman of Portsmouth Disabled Supporters' Association, a responsibility which allows him to attend the regular gatherings of the Tony Goodall Fans' Conference. During the Portsmouth Supporters' Trust's successful battle to seize control of their club, he financially contributed to two syndicates raising funds to meet the £1,000 valuation of shares.

It was through his close involvement with the Blues that he got to know the late John Jenkins, the long-time steward of Fratton Park's boardroom and such a distinctive presence around the club for 91 years. Pompey dedicated the front page of their programme against Ipswich to the cherished 100-year-old, whose death became national news as media outlets revisited his speech in front of the Queen at the D-Day 75 commemorations in June 2019. Meanwhile, Jenkins' long-standing seat in the directors' box was adorned by a bouquet of white roses, chrysanthemums and lilies in tribute to his passing, with an emotional video shown on the large screen before kick-off. Similarly, there was also public recognition of the immense Blues contributions of Jim Smith, who led them to the 1992 FA Cup semi-final against Liverpool, and Ron Saunders, a striker with a remarkable record of 162 goals in 261 appearances.

Benfield said: 'John Jenkins was a lovely man who didn't live far from me and would always stop to chat; I had known him for a long time. The respect the city had for him was amazing. As for Jim Smith, he was a tremendous manager and his first season in 1991– 92 was incredible. He brought through talented young players and produced a really good, entertaining team. Boy could he drink! I remember sitting with him at breakfast during a 1994 pre-season tour to Greece, with Howard Kendall also present – and he could drink too! Kendall was manager of Xanthi at the time and had three bottles of wine lined up in front of him, and it was only 8am!

'Looking at other bosses, Judas was a great man-manager, but had to have money. That's what I call Harry Redknapp, 'Judas'. I hate him with a passion; I cannot stand that man. You should never, ever go to Scum. I was with Nigel Tresidder when he asked Judas whether he would be joining Southampton after quitting

Pompey – he assured us he wouldn't. Well, fifteen days later he was appointed as their manager. I actually heard him deny it, so I have no respect for the man – and I don't feel like that about many people. When he came back to Pompey a year later, I never sang his name, and I wouldn't have done so even if he'd won the FA Cup twenty years in a row. There are those of us who have no time for that man and what he did.

'Of the others, Alan Ball was great if he had no money, but present him with a transfer kitty and it was pointless, as we saw the second time round as boss. Milan Mandarić gave him the finances and he recruited the likes of Rory Allen and Jason Cundy, some awful players. Terry Fenwick's coaching was fine but as a manager he was an idiot. John Gregory with all that whistling to players in a match was absolutely useless, Richie Barker was a bad mistake, Ian St John was an appalling boss and Jimmy Dickinson wasn't really a manager. I did like Jim Smith, though!'

Benfield's unflagging devotion to the Pompey cause has, over decades, seen him follow his club to the USA, Nigeria, Hong Kong, Spain, Gibraltar, Germany, Scotland, Portugal, Northern Ireland, Italy, Norway, France, the Republic of Ireland and Greece, usually in the company of Paul Banks. Banks, from Fratton, has coordinated Pompey supporters' coaches since 1985, the brand of 'Banksy's Bus' now synonymous with Blues away travel. When Sky declared a 12.30pm kick-off for the August 2019 trip to Sunderland, it had brutal ramifications for those Pompey supporters negotiating a 669-mile round trip scheduled to total eleven and a half hours by car. A Banksy's Bus departure time of 2am ahead of a gruelling 21-hour day did not prove as appetising as conventional kick-off times. As a result, just 27 places were accounted for on the Wheelers Travel 57-seater coach overseen by Banks. Run in conjunction with the Pompey Supporters' Club (Central Branch), the fixture tinkering represented £700 in lost revenue.

Still, Banks has orchestrated fan travel across the globe and, along with Benfield and John Westwood, numbered among the eleven doughty Pompey fans present in Abuja, Nigeria, for a pre-season tour in July 2008. The schedule consisted of three matches, including the Blues' encounter with Manchester United which erupted into a riot outside the National Stadium as disgruntled locals were priced out of buying tickets.

Banks, a courier driver for Hampshire County Council, said: 'Anything in pre-season, we are there. We love watching Pompey – and it's handy to have a nice holiday as well! Nigeria was a nightmare, though. When we turned up at the team hotel, Kev McCormack, the kit man, told us we must be mad – I think he was right! We arrived in Africa with no idea where our hotel was. 'The Golden Gate' it was called, and there were drivers at the airport arguing who was having our fare. When we finally reached our accommodation, there were armed guards standing outside!

'I took with me about 50 Pompey shirts from different seasons to hand out to locals, which regularly meant hundreds of kids running up to us most days asking for more, long after we had run out. They followed us everywhere, especially when I had my Kanu top on – they absolutely love him. One day Westwood was walking around in his football match gear, and the way he moves is exactly like Captain Jack Sparrow from *The Pirates of the Caribbean*. Anyhow, the locals thought he was some kind of witch doctor!

'Where we stayed, we had a taxi driver called Austin who travelled with us wherever we went. He never left our side, even wandering to the local market with us. He was brilliant. There was also a guy attached to the hotel who acted as our minder; he was named Johnny and insisted he could get us anything we wanted. He was especially handy in the first game of the trip against Kano Pillars when he managed to stop a 'Pompey Supporters' Club Central Branch' banner being lifted. However, we still had two big flags stolen inside the ground when we dropped our guard. Years later, I found one of them on eBay! I'm 100 per cent sure it was mine because it had the same embroidering of 'Pompey'. I've no idea how the seller got it – they wanted £50 too – but I'm not buying back our own flag!

'We were treated very well in Abuja and were invited by the British High Commission to attend a barbecue one day. Pompey were also there, with Harry Redknapp arriving at the same time as us and coming over for a chat. It was a gated place, with armed guards, and we didn't have to pay a penny.'

Banksy's Bar is open for business. It's difficult not to be considering it also serves as the front room in his Newcome Road home. The salubrious saloon is equipped with a pump serving Carling Extra Cold, three fridges, an electronic dart scorer, three televisions displaying Sky Sports while Pompey-themed memorabilia swallows up the surrounds.

As part of a family syndicate that triumphed on the New York Lottery, Banks and his wife, Sarah, utilised their share of the £400,000 windfall to create the distinctive bar within their terraced house. Married since 1988, the couple are season-ticket holders in the North Stand, and along with daughter, Kirstie, their lives devoted as much to Pompey as to each other. Bubbly Sarah's rambunctious laugh inhabits every sentence as she expands on her husband's anecdotes, having joined him on the majority of his travels.

With its blue-painted frontage and Pompey curtains, their home is recognisable to passers-by who are often encouraged to sample the Banksy's Bar hospitality, including supporters from the likes of Blackpool and Oldham Athletic. Visitors are encouraged to make a voluntary contribution of £10. The roaring trade of a match day once saw 32 supporters occupying the house for a pre-match pint before the visit of Liverpool, their number stretching into the lounge and garden. For those regulars no longer able to sit at the bar, memorials are in place, among them Dave Barclay, Nigel Tresidder, Alan Price and Mick Spencer, ensuring their spirit is an eternal presence.

'Those who have passed away remain at the bar. Sadly we have lost some right characters over the years, but you make so many friends from following Pompey,' added Banks.

'We travelled to Real Betis in Spain to watch Pompey in August 2011 and, on the final night, John Westwood had run out of cash. He was paying for everything on a credit card and a bit worse for wear, swapping drinks for fags. I was hungry so left him to it. In the morning we had to catch our flight to the airport, but it turned out

Westie hadn't slept in his room. He had fallen asleep in the hotel lift and been travelling up and down in it all night!

'We got him to the airport where he fell asleep at the check-in desk, and, while I was getting a paper, I then heard a clang and clash and it turned out he had fallen over. Airport staff didn't want to allow him to fly, so I volunteered to take responsibility and sat next to him. I did warn him: "You have to be quiet – and no drink." He wouldn't shut up though and he was so loud, so in the end I gave him a whack in the face. Well, he was going to sleep anyway, so I just helped get him there! When he woke up, he asked: "Did you hit me?"

'In this country, we once had a midweek game at Hartlepool in February 2013 and ended up using four coaches by the time we got home! The first, which was actually Northampton Town's team bus, crawled into Victoria Park, then we received a message during the game saying it had now broken down, so Vision Travel sent out another one. That was fine, but it was agreed we would change coaches at Northampton services for a third, which would then finish the journey to the south coast. That was okay until it caught alight outside Legoland and the fire brigade were called. We finally got home at 7.45am – on our fourth coach of the trip!

'On another occasion, at Newcastle United, I didn't even return home on our coach as I had to stay behind to be assessed in hospital! We were being escorted away from the ground by police and this idiot cut us up, so the coach braked sharply and I flew back, banging my head on the floor, which knocked me out. Apparently, somebody shouted: "I don't think he's breathing." An ambulance took me to the nearest hospital and, funnily enough, one of the ambulance men knew Guy Whittingham as he went to school with him. The X-ray didn't show any damage and I had to find my own way back with Sarah.'

Despite Pompey's unconvincing start to the League One campaign, they had risen to tenth ahead of Ipswich's south-coast visit. A run of one defeat in their last eleven fixtures in all competitions had lifted Jackett's side to within three points of the play-offs with one match in hand. The second-placed Tractor Boys sat eight points ahead, with their Fratton Park visit pinpointed as an opportunity for the Blues to reduce the arrears even further in the hunt for promotion. Yet Pompey's 4–1 loss at Accrington Stanley the previous weekend represented their biggest Football League defeat for almost six years and was stirring up more displeasure towards their manager.

For the Crown Ground encounter, Jackett had been forced to field a new-look back four, with Christian Burgess suspended, Lee Brown and Brandon Haunstrup injured and Oli Hawkins absent after partner Aimee had given birth to son Jett. With the January transfer window just days away, the Blues entered a pivotal period – both in terms of promotion ambition and the manager's standing among supporters, although one fan was adamant that Pompey's boss should continue to be backed.

Benfield said: 'We must keep Jackett until the end of the season. In his first campaign we consolidated, finishing eighth, and were only five points from the League One play-offs, while last season we won the Checkatrade Trophy and reached the play-offs. Any other year we would have gone up with 88 points. I don't believe there are any good teams in League One this season. If we win today against Ipswich and then on Boxing Day against Wycombe Wanderers, we will have clawed back six points on the top two – then it will start to get interesting.

'I can understand the criticism of the manager, but unfortunately some of the youngsters are expecting Premier League players and those days are gone. We are a League One club for a reason and we haven't got the players to achieve the miracles they expect. I'm not on Twitter, simply because of the absolute rubbish posted on there by these keyboard warriors, sixteen-year-olds who know nothing and start rumours. They don't understand football.

'When I was a teenager, I would watch reserve games in the company of a well-known local supporter called Ted Burridge. We talked so much football and I learned. Kids now play computer games, whereas when we grew up we actually went outside and played football. Still, Pompey have had an average start to the season and the manager has made some strange decisions, but we are still in touch with the play-offs and should be good enough to finish in at least sixth place.

'We have a slightly better team this term, more of a cohesive unit, although they are playing in the wrong positions at the minute – we can all see it. You don't buy John Marquis, a striker who has scored 26 times in two of his last three seasons, and then play him in the number ten role, while Oli Hawkins, for all the will in the world, will never be a centre-half. He's a striker – the positional change does not work.

'So far, the January transfer windows in Jackett's hands have been awful, absolutely dire, and we probably need four or five signings to help us challenge for automatic promotion. We require a third keeper if Luke McGee goes and probably need another central defender. Hopefully Jack Whatmough will soon be back to take that spot, but if his left knee goes again then that's it, and you are taking a gamble on him being match-fit soon.

'Up front, we already have Marquis and Ellis Harrison. Brett Pitman can come off the bench, and the wingers are okay. My dad and I call Ryan Williams 'half an hour late'. Have you ever noticed him – he is always just missing the tackle, half an hour late.

'The full-backs have been atrocious. Jackett signed James Bolton to be right-back and then plays the left-footed Brandon Haunstrup there, which says a lot. I fail to see what Bolton brings to the team at the moment; he's meant to be an attacking full-back.

'Finally, changing captains was not done the right way, even if the appointment of Tom Naylor was the correct decision. It should have been implemented in the summer, not during the second month of the season. I would have kept Gareth Evans as vice-captain though; there was no point in changing that. Having said that, January is ahead of us and I believe we can sneak into the play-offs and win promotion back to the Championship.'

The Fratton faithful earned the result they craved against Ipswich, toasting a 1–0 success that lifted them into ninth spot. The rejuvenated Ronan Curtis, dropped for poor form ten weeks earlier, registered his seventh goal in ten matches to inspire a heartening outcome against a Paul Lambert side that had been early League One pacesetters. The scoreline should have been more emphatic, such was Pompey's dominance, with the visitors losing skipper Luke Chambers to a second bookable offence in the 88th minute. And, irrespective of his bruising fall the previous evening, Benfield was present to witness a crucial triumph.

'My right hand is clawed now, so it's pretty much useless; it's like a chocolate teapot, although I can just about hold a pen. There are barely any muscles in my left arm as they took them out more than twenty years ago when it became infected in hospital during dialysis. At least I can still use it, but it's weak. Then there's my frozen shoulder – I've been waiting six months for that to be looked at – while my legs and knees are getting weaker and weaker.

'I rely on my friends – Steve Tovey or Dave Clarke – to push my wheelchair at away matches, while Dad and my girlfriend, Sue, help me with Fratton Park games. I can't change the way I am. I won't be getting a new body overnight, but it won't stop me watching Pompey. Nothing will.'

MARK KELLY AND THE ACADEMY

17 January 2020

Burdened by lofty comparisons and unrealistic expectations, Mark Kelly represents a playing career unfulfilled. Proclaimed the next George Best by England World Cup-winning deities Alan Ball and Jack Charlton, the slight left winger was empowered by a Republic of Ireland debut at the age of eighteen, eleven days before his maiden Pompey start.

By the age of 23 it was over for the youth-team graduate, his right knee devastated. Tim Breacker's challenge against a knee locked on the rigid surface of Luton Town's unforgiving artificial pitch snapped medial collateral ligaments during the final minutes of a reserve game in January 1991. There were comebacks, but no more Pompey first-team appearances. After four Republic of Ireland caps, 56 Blues appearances and one month on loan to Tottenham Hotspur, Kelly retired in 1994.

An alternative path emerged: reinvention through youth coaching driven by misgivings over his own handling as a youngster, the result of a lack of information rather than malicious intent. During the past decade, Fratton Park's prolific youth set-up has seen 44 players progress to Pompey's first team, totalling 1,048 matches and 94 goals. Four of these players have gone on to achieve full international honours. Now in his second spell as Academy head, Kelly has played a pivotal role in these remarkable results.

He said: 'Alan Ball was the first to throw around the George Best comparison, then Jack Charlton said it in a Republic of Ireland press conference: "I haven't seen ability like that since George Best." It was one of those things; not really a help, kind of a hindrance. Suddenly everyone is lining up to kill you and I was eating grass for the next six months! Jack followed it up in an article claiming one of his biggest regrets was that I didn't play in any World Cup, so there are some nice accolades. That's the frustrating thing – I didn't fulfil what I should have done considering my ability.

'I can look at it now and understand it. I was within a system that had a major flaw. I was probably eight stone five pounds wringing wet, far too light in a time where contact was contact. Let's be honest; at times you almost had to get done for assault to receive a yellow card. I was a left winger, dropping the shoulder, driving in, driving out, encouraging kicks because it drew fouls, but despite playing in that manner, my physicality was never addressed. I was small, sly and quick, but when you're repeatedly taking power knocks you need to be able to take some impact. We were often instructed to go on six-mile seafront runs, which was great for me. I'd put my trainers on and shoot off; however, what I actually should have done was build myself up in the gym.

'These days, everybody has their individual programme and there are a lot more areas of development, whereas back then it was a case of here's the ball, there's the pitch, let nature take its course. There wasn't enough planning. One season, at the age of eighteen, I played 78 matches, consisting of international fixtures as well as club matches. Even the structure around the protection of a young lad coming through was poor. There was far too much volume and not enough structured process.

'Today everything is planned a lot better. We have games, as many as two or three in a week, but not to the extent of what I was put through; that was far too much. You have to protect talent.'

Kelly returned as Academy boss in June 2014, following four and a half years away, replacing Andy Awford after he was elevated to the position of Pompey first-team manager. Kelly's influence on Kenny Jackett's current promotion-chasing side is obvious, with current squad regulars Ben Close, Alex Bass, Brandon Haunstrup and Ryan Williams having emerged during his time at the helm. In addition, Leasing.com Trophy progress has this term presented prized opportunities for teenage talents Leon Maloney, Joe Hancott, Josh Flint, Eoin Teggart, Bradley Lethbridge, Harvey Rew and Haji Mnoga.

'We have a massive reputation because, let's be honest, the list is long – and the production line keeps churning,' added Kelly.

'At meetings with academy managers, they often ask how we do it, how does it happen, what do you do that's different? I don't give too much away; they need to work that out for themselves. We'll keep hold of that, thank you very much!

'It's not all about throwing money at it, because I know of some clubs spending millions and not producing a single player. There are actually quite a few of those around, and if my name was on that list I wouldn't be too happy. I want that step progression to keep happening, I want kids to have opportunities and it's my job to ensure that still happens. You hear a lot of things from the outside such as: "Kids are disappearing; other clubs are taking them from us." No they're not. The kids who want to be here are here. If you wish to move to another club, try it there. We know what we are; we're trying to give people an opportunity.

'If you analyse clubs throughout the Professional Development Phase, which covers the ages of 18 to 23, some have 60 to 70 players in that area alone, so how can you produce anything when you have those kinds of numbers? A club not far away from us has 32 kids in their development group. How are they going to develop? Where are they going? What is the next step progression? Their first-team squad will have 40 players, so that's 72 players spread across two teams – and they're spending fortunes on it.

'We prefer to operate with small groups. Presently I have fifteen scholars, which is a small group. Additionally, there's the next stage, the third-year scholars, who are Lethbridge, Hancott, Flint and Maloney. That's nineteen players in total. At most clubs you'd have 45 players between those two areas.

'There are clubs that hoard them, promise all sorts and exploit the attraction of being a professional footballer, but the opportunity has to be provided and there must be a pathway. We regularly receive the released lists of clubs and one of them, from London, sent me the names of eight lads and not one of them had made as many as five appearances throughout the entirety of their two-year scholarship. Here, small numbers work, and we try to push them on, expose them to football, give them a pathway, and when we had our financial troubles, the kids stayed.

'During the early days of fan ownership, there were discussions about scrapping the Academy. They had to look at figures and how to balance things. The question was raised: Is the youth set-up needed? Scrap the Academy and you would lose a generation of kids, and you can't pick it up later. It takes a minute to make the decision, but it takes ten years to put it back together again.

'Youth development is about long-term planning. There is a lot of step progression throughout. Should you make that split decision to rip it up to save money, to get it back you have to go back to the beginning and start again. To be fair, our chief executive Mark Catlin and chief operating officer Tony Brown always backed retaining it. We knew that within the system there were some boys who would probably help keep the club alive through sales and sell-ons, while others would give value through performances.'

The Academy toasted another triumph earlier this month when graduate Close reached 150 appearances for Pompey's first team upon his introduction from the bench at Fleetwood Town in a 2–1 FA Cup win. It represented the first time in 39 years that the landmark had been reached by a Portsmouth-born player, last accomplished by left-back Keith Viney in January 1981 under Frank Burrows.

There was also a start for second-year scholar Haji Mnoga in the previous week's Leasing.com Trophy fixture at Walsall, lining up at right-back in a 2–1 victory in his first outing of the campaign and the fourth of his Blues career. The seventeen-year-old from Somerstown's season had endured misfortune in August when he broke the fifth metatarsal in his left foot, a curious occurrence passed off by Kenny Jackett as the consequence of falling off a kerb while walking to Southsea's Victorious Festival. Still, after returning to action last month, Mnoga was handed his first professional contract, securing him until the summer of 2021.

Meanwhile, there was the heartening sight of another Academy product, Jack Whatmough, on the bench in the 2–1 League One win over AFC Wimbledon which lifted Jackett's men into seventh, their highest placing of the season so far. It signalled the end of an absence spanning more than eleven months as the centre-half's latest gutsy battle back to fitness edges him towards a place in the first team.

Kelly said: 'Another one of our lads that has come through, Ben Close, is a great kid, quietly going about his business and is now starting to score more goals. We would see it all the time through his youth-team years, 25-yarders into top corners, into bottom corners; he is developing nicely and is a fantastic ambassador for the Academy. His physicality and strengthening needed to come, although technically he was always proficient, but people play in different ways. He's not a central midfielder who flies in, he's one of those that gets on the ball and tries to feed it, to use it a little more than others.

'Ben has really started to understand where his strengths lie and is now delivering. He might have been a bit quiet on the goal front in the early first-team days, but now I'm seeing some great strikes in matches. With Jack, injuries are frustrating, but we have all seen enough of him to know that if he can get past this he will be a massive asset to the club and, going forward, will have a great career.

'Over the years he's really had to improve his heading. He went through a process of working extremely hard to develop that, putting in a shift, and the outcome is what you see today. Attacking the ball, that aggression, the lovely timing – he worked hard at that as it didn't come naturally. Jack will put in a shift behind the scenes to get to where he wants through development. He has an amazing attitude and is prepared to push himself to develop.

'Moving onto Haji, it was great to see him play this week. It's a first step, but now he has to get into the process of really trying to develop himself to stay in the first-team squad. There's still a lot of work to do in different areas, he knows that, because as a kid of seventeen there are things to look at. He's a strong boy and can play technically as well. He can handle the ball, whereas psychologically he needs to do a bit of work on patience and consistency. He's a good kid, quite shy, reserved in himself, but ambitious in the things he wants to achieve.

'Mind you, if you had seen Haji at fourteen you wouldn't have signed him! He was all over the place, like a car crash, and his feet went from size six to size eleven. He couldn't even stand up at one stage. However, he worked through it. I am sure at other clubs Haji would have been out of the door at the age of fourteen, but it's about time, consistency and patience; you have to see what blossoms at some stage. I believe we have been really, really good at that, knowing those little key elements of what to look for and what to ask for.

'Paul Hardyman and I watched Adam Webster as a twelve- or thirteen-year-old and said: "This boy's a Rolls-Royce." Seriously, we knew. The problem is, you hit growth spurts at different times and this is what people from the outside don't see. Kit Symons and I grew up together in Basingstoke and we were very close, like brothers really. I was in the first team and Kit was breaking through, but he really struggled with growth spurts at that point and would often be left crying and frustrated, regularly saying: "I don't know what's wrong with me; I'm all over the place."

'Growth spurts can hit. Webbo had one at the age of nineteen. One morning he came in and had to crouch down to go through the door – he must have shot up three inches. Then there's the effect that has on your body's system. He was playing right-back in the first team and a bit gangly, slipping over at times, yet a year earlier was representing England under-18s, gliding across the pitch. Then that stupid growth spurt hits, but you've got to come through that and be patient. We still know where you're headed.'

Webster's regard had soared by the time he left Fratton Park in June 2016 following 81 appearances across three divisions. He was sold to Ipswich Town in a deal that saw Pompey receive £750,000 plus Matt Clarke in part exchange, a player who himself would later be sold for a significant figure. Last summer, Webster arrived at top-flight Brighton & Hove Albion, via Bristol City, for a club record £20m, and has registered seventeen Premier League starts during the campaign so far, netting at Aston Villa, Arsenal and Tottenham Hotspur. Elsewhere in the top flight, the Blues' Academy is represented by Matt Ritchie (Newcastle United), Joel Ward (Crystal Palace) and Asmir Begović (Bournemouth), while Conor Chaplin was this week named the Sky Bet Championship Player of the Month following nine goals in his last twelve appearances for Barnsley.

'Conor was a left-winger at the age of fifteen and, being an old winger myself, I said to him: "No you're not, you're a centre-forward," added Kelly.

'He wasn't a natural wide player. If you're drifting inside that much you might as well play straight down the middle. Then scoring hat-trick after hat-trick convinced him! Just by talking to him it was clear he knew the game. We had a youth-team match at Plymouth Argyle and, having played a lot around that time, I put him on the bench, but he was pestering me during the game, saying: "Kells, put me on, put me on."

'When I asked why, he replied: "The centre-half is so weak on his left-hand side it's embarrassing." So, I brought him on and, honestly, with his first touch he faced the kid up, dropped him to his left, making sure he was nowhere to be seen, and then buried a shot into the top corner. Conor turned to me and mouthed, "Weak on his left-hand side!"

'We had Matt Ritchie, who was always very highly technical. He wasn't the paciest player in the world, but he had a lovely gait and feel for the ball; it was just physically he needed to catch up. That left foot, you always knew it was there, but sometimes you go through a process aged fourteen, fifteen or sixteen when your physicality lets you down a little, so you can get caught in areas and overpowered. We have always delivered the message that you must put yourself in there anyway and Matt certainly had the mindset and the tenacity to do just that.

'In the same youth team was Joel Ward, a late developer. One pre-season we took the lads to Thorney Island, West Sussex, for three days with the Royal Marines, who would drill them and get them to do different tasks. Joel won everything: swimming, canoeing, bike riding, climbing ropes, jumping off things. He always had to be first; that was his mindset – he had to win. The Marines even said to me afterwards: "If he hasn't got a career in football give us a shout because you don't find these kids very often!" Mentally he is that strong, which is his major strength. Physically Joel is great, always in superb shape, but technically he had to work on it. We would shout at him to not overcomplicate things. Don't attempt 50-yard passes, just keep it short, keep it moving, then use your other attributes to get to where you need to go. He developed so well and has gone and made the most out of what he had; it's that mental attitude, that determination to succeed.

'Another was Asmir Begović, who, as a fifteen year-old, couldn't kick the ball out of the box very well so one of the full-backs had to take goal kicks instead. They could get a lot more distance, so he had to develop that side of his game. When Asmir scored with a clearance against Southampton in November 2013, I sent him a text saying: "Oh my God, things have changed, mate!" He was always technically proficient, clean hands, a great shot stopper – elements that gave him something to work with – while he was very, very single-minded and incredibly driven, setting a pathway for himself all the time. You wouldn't meet a nicer lad, but he had to develop. You don't get everything naturally; you have to work on your ability.'

The necessity to identify talent outside the conventional catchment area has led to the club advertising for a new head of youth recruitment. An appointment is pressing, having lost the services of Neil Sillett at the turn of the year, tempted away by Premier League Brighton. The 56-year-old's Fratton Park appointment in February 2019 had represented a return to his spiritual home, having previously served as physio for eight years during the 1990s.

Retaining the family home in Purbrook through subsequent roles with Derby County, Crystal Palace, Costa Rica, Puerto Rico, Aston Villa and the Scottish FA, Sillett was reunited with a club he truly understood. Soon, he was exposed to the challenges facing academies outside of the top flight.

'Pompey are a Category Three academy and find themselves on an icy slope,' said Sillett.

'Category One academies can offer better facilities and everything is a little nicer when the kids turn up, but I don't think that is bad for Pompey. If you want to play for Pompey you have to understand what the people are, what the city is and what the club is. The club is protective of its players, but not as protective as it should be. Now that's not Pompey's fault, it's down to the Elite Player Performance Plan, and I find that scary. Clubs can identify a player and tell him not to sign his scholarship, allowing them to recruit him for about £70,000 in compensation. They can also promise a two-year scholarship and, once they reach the age of seventeen, it turns into a two-year professional deal on £2,000 a week, sometimes £10,000, yet that player may never feature for the first team.

'Chelsea are the best model at the moment. They spend fortunes on their academy but receive fortunes as well, selling players for millions who have never been in their first team. While I was global senior scout at Villa a few years ago, I picked out two promising Chelsea teenagers who weren't in the first team and were available for loan – their names were Mason Mount and Callum Hudson-Odoi.

'I reported back to our manager, Steve Bruce, with my recommendations, but there was a problem. They were earning more than every Villa player apart from John Terry and a loanee from West Ham United, Robert Snodgrass. You have to be pragmatic, look elsewhere, and we have been proactive in other avenues to find talent.

'Ireland is one area Pompey are looking at and the north-east of England is another, through a partnership with Wallsend Boys Club in North Tyneside. During my time there, we also adopted an approach to monitor the under-16 teams of all London's Category One clubs, compiling dossiers for each. You may pick up one or two released players but are behind the likes of Fulham, Derby, Nottingham Forest and other Category Two clubs in the pecking order. A player let go by Arsenal may prefer Watford or Charlton Athletic to Pompey, I'm afraid.

'Another source is the inner-city academies around the London area, which contain kids who have dropped out of club set-ups for whatever reason. There are five or six of these academies which operate as second-chance places, getting kids off the street, providing training and life skills. There are a bunch of youngsters starting to emerge from these academies and we are working closely with them, including organising trial games near the M25, where they are invited to play against our under-16s. They are raw, uncoached in a lot of ways and often have a bit of work to do behaviourally, but there's potential.'

As a schoolboy centre-forward associated with Watford, Sillett played with future Pompey boss Kenny Jackett, who was operating as a left-sided central defender at the time. Sillett would go on to secure apprenticeship terms at Coventry City, before being joined by his dad, John, after taking over as manager from Don Mackay in 1986. By the time the Sky Blues won the FA Cup against Spurs in May 1987, Sillett Junior had retired through injury, occupying the Wembley bench in his capacity as assistant physio. In 1989, he ventured back to Hampshire, the county of his birth, to take up a role in Pompey's medical team during John Gregory's tenure as boss, the first of five managers he worked alongside during the next eight years.

The late Jim Smith was his favourite, later tempting the physio to join him at Derby in the Premier League. Sillett fondly recollects the circumstances behind a youthful team selection for the curtain-raiser of the 1991–92 First Division campaign; a trip to Blackburn Rovers which has entered into Fratton folklore. That season yielded an FA Cup semi-final appearance against Liverpool and marked the breakthrough for a crop of prodigiously talented home-grown youngsters, including Darren Anderton, Kit Symons, Andy Awford and Darryl Powell.

Sillett added: 'That team at Blackburn came about through circumstance, with Jim actually playing a completely different side during shape work in our final session before travelling to Lancashire. He had fallen out with a few senior players, so changed his mind.

'His week was pretty routine, with an eleven v eleven or eleven v seven on Thursdays, involving the first eleven against kids or whoever else. That afternoon after training, he turned to me and said: "The kids did better than the first team today, what do you reckon?" We spoke about it for ages.

'Jim didn't trust those senior players to perform as he wanted. He trusted them as people, but not their performance levels over 90 minutes. He would rather go with the hunger and desire of the kids he had seen play against them that Thursday. It was the making of that semi-final side. The original line-up contained Graeme Hogg, Kenny Black and Steve Wigley. Certainly four or five who featured in the training game were not included at Ewood Park two days later.

'Jim taught me that when you go with youth they can be up and down, so you must be the one who picks them up when needed, help them through what could be a tough baptism and all the while handling expectations of fans and the board, because that needs doing as well. If you put in four or five youngsters today and lose five matches on the trot, with those players making mistakes, how would the Fratton Park fans react? Yet Jim's call was: "I can handle it, this is my policy and I'm going to brave it out. I believe they are good enough."'

Sillett's latest Fratton Park stint spanned eleven months, before becoming the third member of Pompey Academy staff to be lured to Brighton in little more than two years. Installed as the Seagulls' national scout coordinator, the change of scenery offers the opportunity to recruit talent from Category Two and Three set-ups, rather than focusing on released lists. Certainly Sillett is proud of his contribution to maintaining Pompey's bountiful production line.

He said: 'During my time at Pompey, we didn't sign anyone for money as such. Gerard Storey and Harry Anderson arrived from Portadown in the Northern Ireland Football League Championship, but no money was paid up front. Instead, should they get into the first team or move on, there are bits we have to pay to their former club. Ireland is a hotbed and the signings of Storey and Anderson have, in turn, seen a positive change in Eoin Teggart, who arrived from Cliftonville the previous year. I think he demonstrated that in his Leasing.com Trophy appearance against Norwich under-21s in September. Teggart has something about him, but last season struggled a little being away from home. Since the arrival of the other Irish lads, we have noticed a big improvement. He has come out of his shell a bit, and he's livelier around the group and more confident.

'It was while watching Teggy play for Northern Ireland under-17s against Greece in February that I spotted Storey, a player who made his debut for Portadown at the age of sixteen. So, I went to see him feature in a domestic game and built a relationship with the club. We had him over for a week and he signed after impressing a lot of people. Storey has an awfully long way to go, but you take raw potential and he has plenty of that, while physically he is good.

'Anderson is also from Portadown and even more raw. He played four first-team games for them while still at school, scoring twice, so I watched him on video and then went over to see him with my own eyes. We also signed him after a week's trial, with both Irish lads arriving in May 2019. He actually played rugby until he was twelve and needs to make up for the time he hasn't spent in academy football. Sometimes when you find these raw gems, you do wonder what they would have been like with eight years of academy training – or what they are going to be like in two years' time following full training.

'I look for kids who have something special and I believe that I have an eye that can spot that. I remember the story of how Brian

Clough wore a false moustache and hat to watch Garry Birtles at Long Eaton United. The Nottingham Forest manager saw him make one turn and turned to Peter Taylor and said: "That's enough, let's go," then went home. The point is, sometimes you will see a player do something that other players just can't do.

'There is a first-year scholar at Pompey, who I won't name, and he can do things others can't. He hits these wonderful passes and it's no fluke – he does it all the time. I didn't recruit him, but the first time I saw him here I thought: "Oh, my days."

'I watched Chelsea under-19s play their Ajax counterparts in November at Cobham. It was a brilliant game, a 1–1 draw, and Chelsea's right-back was the quickest thing I have ever seen. Technically he's a little short of being a Chelsea player, but he will play at the top level because he runs like no one else. He was called Tariq Lamptey and I was blown away. Even if he misses an opponent three times in the tackle, he will still catch them because he's that quick. He's already an England under-20 international. I had flagged him up as a possible loan for Pompey.

'I worked with Steve McClaren at Derby County and, while maybe I didn't always see eye to eye with him, he did teach me that to be a Premier League player you must be exceptional at something and that's what I look for in kids.'

Progressing through Kelly's Academy set-up is a famous footballing name of particular significance to the Pompey faithful – Benjani Mwaruwari. Zimbabwe international striker Mwaruwari established himself as a cult figure, registering twenty goals in 94 appearances over two spells with the club, including a pivotal role in the fabled Great Escape of 2005–06. Yet while that playing link was severed in the summer of 2012, his son, Benjani Junior, has maintained the family's Blues association. A promising forward attached to Shaun North's under-15 and under-16 sides, it's a comfortable fit for a name entrenched in Fratton folklore.

'When my son was eight he was spotted by Pompey – but they didn't know who his dad was!' said Benjani, who featured in the

Premier League with Manchester City, Sunderland and Blackburn Rovers between Pompey spells.

'He was playing for Ringwood, a local team, just for fun, and a Pompey scout saw him and approached my wife and asked: "We want that boy. Does he play for a club?" Then they asked his name and discovered it was Benjani; they had no idea! "Oh my God," they said. "We liked his dad, we'll sign him." They saw his ability, and it was nothing to do with me; I was not involved, which I like.

'Sometimes you don't talk about your son, as you don't want him to hear your praise; you want others to judge whether he is a good player. Before that, when I was at Manchester City and living in Manchester, my wife took him to a local team to see if he could play, to see his courage. It was too young to judge, so we just let him enjoy his football.

'Eventually, a coach called Richie came up to me and said: "You need to come and watch your son. You do know he's a good player?" Richie offered to take him for extra training, so I told him to go ahead if he felt the talent was there. Then we came back down south following my return to Pompey and he was signed by the club in 2012 to play in their under-8s. When I had my testimonial in Harare, Zimbabwe, in May 2012, my son came on for me to play in the second half. He was aged eight and some of his moves made people say: "Wow, I want to see him when he's older!"'

This is the youngster's second season back at Pompey since accompanying his family on a two-year sabbatical in South Africa. Upon their return to England, Benjani approached Kelly about re-enrolling his son in the Pompey Academy, a set-up he regards highly. The request was inevitably granted.

The ex-Zimbabwe captain added: 'I don't pressurise my son. If he manages to come through, it's all up to him. For me it is not about pushing him. I want him to discover and see and love the game without me pushing. Going back to South Africa slowed him down. Training over there is not the same as working in this country with a club like Pompey. Before we left he was unbelievable, and since coming back it is clear he needs time, but he is getting towards his old days.

'There are lots more opportunities for all my children in England. My two girls are into gymnastics and take part in a lot of stuff. In Africa they didn't always have the chance to explore what they enjoy doing. Now we are back, all of my children can explore, and they have the opportunity to choose.

'My son is a bit different to me as a player. He also dribbles a lot and scores goals, but if you want to make the most out of the game, you need to have a bit of hard work. That's what I'm trying to teach him. I've told him you don't have to look at me, just play the game and make sure you're playing it right and fight and fight every time you train and play – the rest will follow.

'He's quiet, like me, but is clever, he's a clever boy, and I am pleased he's back with Pompey, who have some good coaches, many still there from when I was around. Mark Kelly and Shaun North are good people. We'll see how it goes, but I don't want to put pressure on my son; just let him play and enjoy it. He's with some good players here.'

This week Kelly has overseen the departure of Josh Flint, an attacking midfielder from Waterlooville who netted on his Pompey first-team debut against Norwich under-21s in September. That represented one of two Leasing.com Trophy appearances for the nineteen-year-old, who has been released at the end of a six-month deal as a third-year scholar. Having trialled at Walsall, the former Fratton Park season-ticket holder has now linked up with Isthmian League Premier Division side Bognor Regis Town, whom he has already successfully represented this season. For Kelly, it's farewell to another young charge now seeking to go it alone.

'I look back and try to make some sense of how my life has formed,' the 50-year-old added.

'From that young player representing Pompey and starting matches for the Republic of Ireland, into dark times of injury and the unknown, to spending the next 22 years involved in youth development. It's about having a real understanding of what players will go through, both highs and lows, trying to give people your time. Listening is the key.

'Why am I still doing this job? Someone has to be fighting for the kids, I suppose.'

16

CONOR CHAPLIN AND BEN CLOSE

26 January 2020

Conor Chaplin's exit from Fratton Park requires little vindication. The diminutive striker's career has galloped forward at remarkable pace, outstripping the club that served as home to him for fifteen years to settle in the Championship. Severing the apron strings in August 2018, Chaplin left for Coventry City in search of regular first-team involvement.

Almost seventeen months after his heart-wrenching separation from Pompey and with another change of club to his name, the forward boasts nine goals and six assists for new team Barnsley in this season's Championship, a level previously uncharted by the 22-year-old. A return of five goals from six matches during December, including a first senior hat-trick which came in a 5–3 win over QPR, subsequently earned him the Sky Bet Championship Player of the Month award. With impeccable timing and at the peak of his powers, Chaplin is earmarked for a Fratton Park return in the FA Cup fourth round, pitching an emotional reconnection with his spiritual home. He can also look forward to a reunion with Ben Close, the former roommate who accompanied Chaplin during his rise through Pompey's Academy, the pair having remained friends despite the distance.

'I still look at videos of when we won the League Two title, and those times were the happiest of my life,' said Chaplin.

'I worry I won't be able to experience that again in my whole career. That was my home. I had won promotion with my club, and I just worry I'm never going to top that feeling, which is quite scary. I'd like to think I've got many years left of my career, but even if I manage to get promoted elsewhere, I don't know whether it will be as special. It was being at my club, with that fantastic bunch of players, and finally ending ten years of shit. That meant a hell of a lot to me and I was part of a group that started the rise.

'When Pompey are back in the Championship after however many years, I'll know for a fact that I contributed towards that. Even though I am no longer there, I'll have played my part. Do you know what? That makes me proud and it makes me so incredibly happy. It's my club. At school I was "Conor who plays for Pompey". It's the club where I spent 80 per cent of my life, which is frightening when you think about it.

'Leaving was the worst thing in the world, but it was a decision I had to make and don't regret it. I'm now playing in the Championship and I was never going to get that opportunity under the current Pompey manager – and that's nothing against Kenny. He wanted me to stay and he tried everything he could to get me to remain, but the decision I made was solely for my career. I needed to leave and play football. I'd speak to friends and family about my worries. I was so scared of ending up as one of those kids with such big potential yet never fulfilling it. That was one of my worst fears, and I hated that. There's always going to be hype around young lads who break into the first team early and score goals, and I understand that, but I was determined not to be that kid who had a great start only to never play, eventually vanishing from the game.

'Ashley Harris is one I can think of. I used to speak to Adam Webster about him all the time because I was so intrigued about what happened. He used to tell me Ash was the best player in training every single day and the first-team players could not believe how good he was. Then he suffered an injury, a new manager came in and Ash eventually fell out of the game. It scared the life out of me, and it still does. That's probably a big reason why I try to be so professional and dedicate everything to being as good as I can be, working as hard as I can.

'Pompey is an unbelievable club, an absolutely unbelievable club. I would have loved to have continued there, but that wasn't to be. There are no regrets about leaving and it has turned out to be the right decision.'

Chaplin came to Pompey's attention as a six-year-old playing football in a Worthing Dynamos open day in Durrington, West Sussex. Upon returning home, an answerphone message awaited him, scout Steve Martin enquiring whether the youngster would be willing to attend a Blues development centre, based in Chichester.

Chaplin joined the club's Academy under-9s once age permitted, with first-team midfielder Gary O'Neil in attendance at his signing, posing for photographs. Initially regarded as a left-winger, Chaplin occupied the same age group as another future Pompey first-teamer, Brandon Haunstrup, before being converted into a free-scoring centre-forward at under-18 level by Academy boss Mark Kelly and coach Mikey Harris.

A first-team debut awaited Chaplin in December 2014, aged seventeen, appearing off the bench in a 3–2 home defeat to Accrington Stanley. He would go on to feature 122 times and score 25 goals for the Blues, before departing for Coventry in August 2018.

'I loved playing under Paul Cook, but didn't like him as much as I do now!' Chaplin laughs.

'For a young lad, I would knock on his door all the time wanting to know when I would get a chance and he was amazing. On some occasions he would bollock me, other times he'd tell me to clear off, but he managed me really well to be fair to him. I didn't appreciate that at the time, but, looking back, now I do.

'Cookie would respond with: "You are the only person I hate coming into my office because I have nothing to say to you and everything you say is right." He would actually admit that his dad was absolutely hammering him for not playing me! Honestly, every time it was: "You have every reason to come in here and tell me you should be playing and I can't explain why you shouldn't." How do you respond to that?

'Sometimes his reasoning was that if I didn't score, I wouldn't affect the match enough for the team, which was probably true at the time. Fair enough, I was younger, less experienced and didn't know the game. Mind you, he's the manager who has scared me the most. I was petrified of him, especially having to knock on that office door, but also knew he loved me.

'I remember being left out of the squad alongside Kal Naismith at Morecambe in August 2016 and, while sitting in the stands, I noticed a fan had contacted me on Twitter asking whether I was injured. I was contemplating replying and, to be fair, Naisy killed me a bit by egging me on to tweet something back! So, I sent "No mate" along with a thumbs up, before deleting it at half-time, but the damage was done.

'Outside Cookie's office at the training ground was a register which we had to sign whenever we arrived or left. There was this AstroTurf leading up to the building, which we named 'The Green Mile', and the lads hated that daily walk. If we'd lost, he'd be in the worst mood ever.

'Following that Morecambe match, a 2–0 defeat, I went in to sign and noticed the coaches and other staff around a table chatting, so I kept my head down, signed the sheet and started to leave when I heard the shout "Where do you think you're going?" He got me into his office, clearly aware of that tweet, and screamed at me. I was very, very apologetic. We then carried out training as usual and afterwards his assistant, Leam Richardson, pulled me aside and told me to see Cookie again. Apparently, he had calmed down. So I did and he was fine with me. His intention was to scare me, to make me realise that I shouldn't get involved in things like that. He was right, of course. Cookie had been very clever in how he dealt with it and I learnt. I want to be a manager when I stop playing and will reference a lot of the things I saw from him!'

Chaplin netted eight times during the 2016–17 League Two title-winning campaign. Primarily a substitute, he started the final two matches as Cook's men swept their way to top spot following ten victories in the last twelve fixtures. In the summer preceding that memorable season, Chaplin and Close were among the Pompey contingent that travelled to Dublin in July 2016 for a six-day stay at the Johnstown House Hotel, with two pre-season friendlies arranged.

Cook's 'work hard, play hard' mantra was designed to engender team spirit and, following a 3–3 draw with Sligo Rovers, the management and most of the squad opted to miss the team coach back to the hotel, preferring to perform karaoke at a nearby pub. Chaplin was among a handful of players who dutifully decided to forgo the late-night revelry in order to meet the departure time. However, he would later incur his manager's wrath following another night out during the trip.

'We played Bohemians on the final day of the tour, winning 2–0, and afterwards went out for a meal,' said Chaplin.

'There was an early flight home the next day, but that didn't stop a few of the lads deciding to stay out for a few drinks – Gary Roberts, Enda Stevens, Kyle Bennett and myself. These were three senior big hitters who assured this nineteen-year-old, "Come with us, we'll look after you."

'Well, I got in all sorts of bother. I was finished at 2am so Enda put me into a taxi and sent me back, only for me to return to the wrong hotel and have no idea where I was. I eventually got back to the right place. Enda and Robbo managed to make it to breakfast, having returned about 30 minutes earlier, with Cookie laughing and joking with them, obviously aware what had gone on. For our first training session back in England at Roko, we were instructed to run three four-minute laps around two pitches. Now I was a kid, not as fit as the other boys, at the time rubbish at running, rubbish. I didn't know what I had to do to get myself fit.

'When Cookie announced the groups, I was alongside Enda, Robbo, Michael Doyle, Carl Baker and Gaz Evans. They were the best five runners in the squad and I was thinking, "Oh my God, there is no way I can run with these; I'll be so far behind."

'The gaffer read my face and could see I was worried and asked what was wrong. "Nothing," I told him.

'Then he said, "Look, if you want to drink with the big boys, you can run with the big boys." He had known all along and never said anything! On that run I was getting lapped and all sorts. I was in a whole world of trouble; it was horrible.

'We would never have gone up if we didn't have that togetherness in the squad. There were times during that season when it was coaches against players, a lot of rifts, a lot of arguments, and many times the gaffer was so emotional he'd tell the players to "Fuck off home."

'Cookie knew that to get the best out of that squad he had to really piss them off, to get them incredibly angry with him, and he was right. A lot of players worked so hard to shut him up; it was so clever, and he knew that. In the last two months of that promotion campaign it was coaches against players that got us over the line; that togetherness as a group of footballers made us unbeatable.

'When Michael Doyle held that meeting after the Crewe Alexandra defeat, it was, "We will show them all. This is us versus them." Cookie engineered that – he meant it. There was a divide between the coaches and the players. Some coaches weren't allowed to talk to us; it was so, so clever.'

Surveying the wind and rain-ravaged artificial pitch at Miltoncross Academy on a blustery south-coast evening, the coach of Moneyfields' under-16s was heartened by the number of players in attendance. The grey woolly hat impeded recognition but, having helped train the youngsters for the past two and a half years, the presence of Ben Close no longer warrants a second glance. The Pompey first-teamer maintains a family connection with the Portsmouth Youth Football League A Division side, his brother, Harry, playing in the centre of midfield, while dad, Malcolm, serves as manager.

Harry was not in attendance on that Tuesday night, instead training with Pompey's under-16s, overseen by Shaun North and Close's team-mate Christian Burgess, although he's not under consideration for a permanent place. Still, there was a new face at Moneyfields' latest session, triallist Harvey Brown, a talented goalkeeper highly recommended by Petersfield under-16s.

The necessity for his arrival was prompted by regular keeper Dan Barrett breaking two fingers on his right hand during the previous match, although he still appeared for training, permitted to play out on the pitch with team-mates under strict instructions to avoid contact.

Close thought he recognised the dad of fifteen-year-old Brown who scrutinised the hour-long session from the sidelines. The familiarity wasn't misplaced. It was Ashley Brown, who had spent four years on Pompey's board, spanning community ownership, including the point at which Close made his Blues bow in September 2014.

Close said: 'A few of the lads thought it was a one-off having a Pompey player coaching, but they're probably bored of it now! My brother most likely gets fed up with somebody shouting at him. I expect high standards from him so imagine he gets a bit annoyed. He's a central midfielder and getting better all the time, and I'm excited to see how he does in the next few years. I initially started helping out with the team because Harry plays for them and it has gone from there. Coaching the lads is something I really enjoy.

'Football is a short career and I want to stay in it, and the idea of taking a team, putting my ideas across and watching them learn really appeals. It's something I believe is for me in the future. They play on Sundays and I stand on the sidelines, looking for signs that they've taken my sessions on board and have applied them to their game. When that comes off, it's really enjoyable.

'Over the years, I've learnt so much from my dad and Pompey coaches, picking up useful things I'm now trying to pass on to these lads. There have been several great coaches I've played under, the most influential being Paul Hardyman and Alan McLoughlin, but I also learnt a lot from John Perkins and Ian Whyte.

'There are some really good boys here and a great set of parents, with a lot of them coming to watch, which you can't say about many teams of this age. Mind you, sometimes the parents want to talk about Pompey more than the kids do!'

The Close family are firmly established in local football, their association with Moneyfields all-encompassing. Dad Malcolm is treasurer of the club's youth set-up, which consists of eleven teams, while mum Kat serves as secretary, her admirable dedication also extending to the upkeep of Moneyfields' Copnor home. Their weekly voluntary duties include maintaining the playing surface, putting up nets and cleaning the changing rooms, while the pair have been known to assist with the installation of advertising hoardings and the painting of doors and frames at the ground.

Born in Newcastle, Malcolm arrived on the south coast to serve in the Royal Navy, based largely within the local area at HMS *Collingwood*, HMS *Excellence* and HMS *Sultan*, while he was also drafted to British aircraft carrier HMS *Hermes*. Kat's mum was landlady at The Leopold Tavern in Albert Road, the pub where she met the man who would later become her husband, before settling as a family, first in Eastney and then Haslemere Road, Southsea.

First-born Ben began his footballing journey with Wimbledon Park Tigers under-6s, based at Craneswater Junior School. Managed by Malcolm, their fixtures regularly involved encounters with Jack Whatmough's club, Gosport Falcons. The promising youngster joined the Blues at under-10 level following a successful trial, having initially caught the eye of Pompey in the Community coach Paul Hardyman during holiday sessions. So began the journey which would lead to 152 appearances and sixteen goals, in addition to establishing a firm friendship with Chaplin.

Close added: 'We're really close and text each other in the build-up to games, chatting about the opposition and how we think we'll do. Then, either on a Saturday night or the Sunday, we'll speak on the phone about how it went. I think we'll always be like that. He's a good lad, funny, great company, and we have similar interests. Mind you, Conor tries to make friends with everyone. Whoever we played against, he would talk to one of the opposition players on the pitch at any given point; it's quite funny. Brandon Haunstrup and I noticed it several times. "How the hell does Conor know him?" There's no link there, he's just initiated a conversation!

'When he scored his first Pompey goal at Morecambe in April 2015, I was on the bench and buzzing for him, but he couldn't really celebrate as we had lost 3–1! I peeked to see Conor in the changing room afterwards and he had a glum face because he didn't want people to misread his happiness.

'We both made our debuts in that 2014–15 season under Andy Awford, but I am forever in the debt of Gary Waddock for ensuring it wasn't my last season at Pompey. Adam Webster, Bradley Tarbuck and I were all out of contract that summer and I'm pretty sure I would have been released if I hadn't started the final three matches.

'Waddock had stepped up from assistant manager to serve as caretaker manager when Awfs left by mutual consent. Straightaway he put Webbo in at centre-half for the trip to Stevenage and he had the game of his life. Then he selected me to join him in the team against Bury, Mansfield Town and York City. I played pretty well in those games and it turned out incoming manager Paul Cook had his scouts watching. I received a new deal and Cookie later admitted to me that I had impressed at Mansfield, while Webbo also stayed. Tarbuck, who only appeared as a late substitute in the last game, was released.

'You need a lot of luck in football. If I hadn't played in those three matches, I might not have made it as a professional footballer in the Football League.'

Close made fourteen appearances, including six league starts, during Cook's first Pompey campaign in 2015–16. However, despite that heartening breakthrough, he watched from afar during the following campaign as Portsmouth clinched the League Two title, having been sent to non-league Eastleigh for regular first-team football.

'Paul Cook probably came a year or two early for me in terms of where I was in my development,' said Close.

'I was still young, not mentally ready to play 30 games a season, and definitely wasn't prepared physically, which showed in his second season when I kept picking up injuries because my hamstrings weren't strong enough.

'At least I got a taste of the dressing room, which contained big characters such as Michael Doyle, Gary Roberts and Kyle Bennett.

Everyone remembers their first bollocking from Michael Doyle and for a lot of us it was in his first Pompey training session! He was on my team and the first time I gave the ball away the abuse came, prompting me to think: "Bloody hell, I'm not doing that again!" Then, shortly after, I received the ball and did it again. I knew what was coming, and he was shouting once more. "Who is this?" I thought. "I don't like playing with him."

'That's just the way Doyler was. At the time I didn't realise how much he wanted to win, even in training, and it was a tremendous learning experience for me. He had incredibly high standards, and there was never a day off with him, never a session where you could take it easy and relax as he would be on to you straight away. The longer I knew Doyler, the more you came round to him. Off the pitch, if you needed help or advice, he would be fantastic, but on the pitch he was a different man. Once he crossed the white line, he wasn't your friend, he was your team-mate, and not afraid to let you know what he thought.

'At the time, there's no doubt I was afraid of making mistakes when playing alongside Doyler, but for the long term it was a good thing. I can deal with that now, and it wouldn't bother me whatsoever if I had someone hurling abuse at me for giving the ball away. He just wanted the best. He's probably the scariest player I have encountered here. David Connolly liked me, to be fair, but I've heard some pretty horrible stories in terms of him and young lads such as Nick Awford and George Branford!'

Close grew up idolising Pompey favourites Lomana LuaLua, Niko Kranjcar, Lassana Diarra and David Norris, while he attended the 2008 FA Cup final victory with his dad and other family members. Unbeknown to him, eleven years later he would be part of the Blues side that lifted the Checkatrade Trophy following a 5–4 penalty shoot-out success over Sunderland in March 2019.

The 23-year-old added: 'The Checkatrade Trophy final was the best day of my career, and it will be hard to ever top it. I know some say the competition isn't that important, but to win at Wembley in front of more than 40,000 Pompey fans was wonderful. I can still picture half the stadium being blue and then that feeling when climbing the stairs to collect the trophy.

'We got a bit of a battering in the first half and fell 1–0 behind, but at the interval we regrouped. We couldn't walk off that pitch thinking: "I wish I had done this and that, but lacked the bravery." After the break, we started passing the ball, the crowd lifted and Gaz Evans came off the bench to change the game. We were the better team in extra-time, but Sunderland nicked an equaliser out of absolutely nowhere. I had already been substituted after cramping in just about every muscle in the lower part of my body. I was slumped in my seat watching it thinking: "How have they stolen that?" But then we won on penalties.'

Chaplin was present for that Wembley final, attending with three of his friends, located among the Fratton faithful. Since leaving the Blues with 36 starts and 86 substitute appearances to his name, the striker has finally achieved the regular first-team football he craved, firstly at Coventry and then, following a July 2019 switch, with the Tykes at Championship level. Upon his Fratton Park return, Chaplin was named in Barnsley's starting line-up, while Close earned a timely recall to Pompey's midfield, with loanee Cameron McGeehan unable to face his parent club.

It was Close who opened the scoring on 37 minutes, with a low right-footed drive from the edge of the area for his sixth goal of the season. By the time Chaplin also etched his name on the scoresheet in stoppage time, it represented nothing more than a consolation in a 4–2 defeat for the visitors. John Marquis, Ronan Curtis and Christian Burgess also netted for Kenny Jackett's side as they conjured up their finest display of the season to book a place in the fifth round against Arsenal on home territory.

With spirits inevitably high during the comprehensive win, the Fratton End revelled in a spot of nostalgia late on in the game, reprising Chaplin's 'He's one of our own' song, followed by 'He should have stayed here', sung to the same tune. The 22-year-old refused to celebrate his last-gasp strike, having pounced inside the box after Alex Bass had initially saved well from Jacob Brown. Instead, he simply retrieved the ball and returned it to the centre spot, his face devoid of emotion.

That evening, Chaplin reunited with fellow Academy graduates Adam Webster, Nick Awford, Jack Maloney, Elliot Wheeler and George Branford for a meal in Gunwharf. Yet, as he hurried away from Fratton Park to attend the gathering, he encountered Kenny Jackett on the touchline, with Pompey's manager stopping to congratulate the Worthing youngster on his Championship form.

'It was horrible how it ended at Pompey,' admitted Chaplin. 'Football is so political, but you don't know that as a kid, and at the time I had to be someone I wasn't in order to get out and play for the sake of my career. I had to let the coaches know that I didn't want to be there. It was hard because I loved all the boys, but they knew I had to leave.

'I wasn't going to play and didn't believe Kenny was going to get the best out of me. I was proven right. I'm now in the Championship but imagine if I'd stayed and struggled on loan in League Two; where do you go from there?

'Kenny didn't want me to go, Mark Catlin didn't want me to go, but they'd been made aware of my desire at the end of the previous season. That summer I was in Kenny's office every morning asking to leave, I promise you. When he agreed, I was still in his office every morning asking for updates. I knew offers were there and they were concrete; otherwise I wouldn't have put myself in that situation. I was told I couldn't leave until a replacement was found, which I completely understood, and that was the reason for the delay in getting my move to Coventry, with Barnsley also interested.

'At the start of that final season, I appeared once in the opening five matches, with a trip to Doncaster Rovers next up. Kenny asked if I wanted to be involved, which put me in a quandary. Considering I was determined to leave, I didn't want to pull on a Pompey shirt and not give everything. I'd rather not go to the Keepmoat Stadium. I explained my thoughts to Kenny and he understood; he was good about it. Any other club and I would have played, gone through the motions. I've seen that happen at Pompey before, and you see it everywhere. However, I didn't want to be that person at my club, a club I have such an emotional attachment with. I didn't want to pull on the Pompey shirt and not give 100 per cent. It wouldn't have been fair to the club or the fans to not try my hardest. Besides, if I had played and scored, that may have persuaded Kenny not to let me depart after all.

'I didn't travel with the squad and then, six days later, the evening before transfer deadline day, Kenny rang and said: "Look, I've got people coming in tomorrow; get yourself up to Coventry and sort yourself out." Coventry were Pompey's preference because they felt Barnsley were going to be a direct competitor, which they turned out to be as they won promotion that season by finishing second.

'This summer I was trying to give advice to Jamal Lowe on his situation. It was tough for him, and you have to do what's best for your family, but clubs make it hard as well. It's nearly impossible if they don't want to sell. I explained that you have to be honest with the manager and club. I never lied to Kenny and never lied to the club. Kenny was the same towards me and that's why I respect him so much. He was nothing but honest with me, which I really appreciated.

'He could have easily lied to me, feeding me words to keep me beyond the transfer window, then I would have been stuck there until January. As it was, leaving was scary. I was so comfortable at Pompey as I knew every single person at the club and I got on so well with them all. Then you arrive somewhere completely new. For the first time in my life I was moving away from home. I'll be back at some point, though – I know I will. In my eyes it's the best club ever, such a good club and such good people.'

MICHAEL DOYLE
AND CARL BAKER

2 February 2020

King's Lynn Town have looked imperious at the summit of the Vanarama National League North. With only one automatic promotion place on offer, Ian Culverhouse's side are ominously positioned entering February, with play-off scraps on offer to the closest six clubs that trail.

Watching from below is Carl Baker whose swansong at Brackley Town is gathering pace, his footballing farewell due to take place at the season's end. The fifth-placed side represent a last shot at glory for the 37-year-old whose footballing portfolio already includes three promotions. Now in his second season with the Northamptonshire outfit, the attacking midfielder is hoping for a final flourish before accepting retirement and pursuing his coaching ambition.

For a player that spent three and a half seasons in the Championship and won the League Two title with Pompey as recently as May 2017, there is no hint of disdain over seeing out footballing days in non-league surrounds. After all, as a seventeen-year-old, Baker played in Liverpool's Sunday League, while working full-time in Knowsley Borough Council's planning department. A mainstay of Paul Cook's promotion-winning Blues side, these days he earns £600 a week but the tantalising lure of last-gasp career glory motivates him most.

He said: 'I've had a few good years in the Championship and two Football League promotions, but still don't feel like I've ever really been a professional footballer. I've always felt a little embarrassed when people ask for an autograph or a photo. They should be asking Premier League players, not me!

'Football has come full circle. After being released by Liverpool and then Tranmere Rovers, I started off in Sunday League at the age of seventeen, working my way up to National League North and onwards. Now I've come back down. Last season was going to be my final one before retiring. I joined Brackley to win promotion, but we lost on penalties in the National League North play-off semi-finals. Suddenly I had unfinished business. I didn't want to bow out of football like that. Now I have a last chance to experience what I had at MK Dons and Pompey, albeit on a totally different scale.

'I still have great memories of being promoted from the Conference North with Southport in 2005. The manager at the time, Liam Watson, is one of my best mates and, whenever we catch up, we still talk about that day. Whatever level it's at, these are tremendous memories that'll stay with me for the next 50 years of my life.

'After last season, the Brackley gaffer wanted me to sign for another year, so I've given it one last go. Hopefully we can win promotion and I can experience that feeling once more. If we don't, at least I'll know I tried. I attend a lot of functions at Coventry City nowadays and they always ask about my best memories in football. They probably want me to say Coventry stuff, but I mention the promotion with Pompey and my time at MK Dons. They were the favourite years of my career, arriving towards the end. I had to wait a long time.

'You actually get a bit jealous when watching other clubs earn promotion. I'd see those players celebrating and would be envious. How I would have loved to be in those changing rooms, spraying champagne, jumping up and down with the lads, in a stadium with the fans on the pitch. I thought it was never going to happen but it did. Now when I see teams achieving that, it doesn't bother me at all. I've already accomplished it and instead it takes me back to happy memories. That's what you play football for, moments like that. As a footballer, obviously you have a nice life, financially it's good, but for me money is irrelevant compared to those memories. I just want to experience that feeling one more time.'

Hailing from Prescot, Merseyside, Liverpool fan Baker spent six years on the Reds' books before being released at the age of sixteen, his class of 1998 including Neil Mellor, Darren Potter and Jon Otsemobor, while Steven Gerrard and Jamie Carragher thrived two years above. Despite that devastating setback, he went on to enjoy an eleven-year Football League career totalling 357 appearances, 64 goals and two promotions.

Baker said: 'After next being released by Tranmere, I worked full-time in the planning department of Knowsley Borough Council for three years. It was shirt and tie, Monday to Friday, nine to five. During my first year, I turned out with my brother and his mates in a Sunday League team called The Carrs Hotel, which was based in Prescot and competed in the I Zingari League. It was adult football and I was a skinny seventeen-year-old boy who would get absolutely smashed by twenty-stone fellas, volleying me everywhere. I played on the wings, out of the way, trying not to get kicked. Back then I didn't dribble anywhere near as much because the pitches wouldn't allow it and you had to pass to avoid being booted.

'Our home ground was Holt Playing Fields in Rainhill, commonly known as 'Dog Shit Park', consisting of a tin hut to get changed in and four or five pitches. We'd have to put the goalposts out before the game – big wooden ones, not metal – requiring three people to carry them. The dressing rooms were basically one big room, with the teams getting changed at opposite ends. There was no divide, so you could hear team talks, while you'd get fellas smoking as they were changing and wrapping crepe bandages around their knees. We'd head to the chippy after the match and then it was back to the pub, where we'd have a few pints, watch the

Premier League game being shown on the television, and then go home.

'I'd left Liverpool some twelve months earlier following eight years with their youth set-up. Ahead of my departure, Academy Director Steve Heighway reassured me that they would send off letters to all 92 league clubs and see what came back. I thought I would get at least 40 responses. I got three; Tranmere, Crewe Alexandra and Preston North End. I trained with Crewe before joining nearby Tranmere, who were managed by John Aldridge.

'Sometimes there's a better way of making it in football. You get young lads at an academy being sold a story and a life that's probably not going to be there for them, then they fall away from it. Some of our team played on Saturdays for Prescot Cables, getting paid £40 a game, so I ended up turning out for them one day and The Carrs Hotel the next. Then I scored twice against Southport in a Liverpool Senior Cup game and they signed me, which took me into the Conference North. That's where I am now, seventeen years later. Some of the stuff I see in the dressing room can be frustrating. You see lads eating a Mars bar or coming in with a bottle of Pepsi, but you have to accept the level you are playing at.

'Not everyone is going to be super-fit or willing to spend their money on protein shakes after the game – it is what it is. I'm playing at this level for a reason. I am not different to a lad working full-time and stopping at a chippy on the Friday. In our dressing room there are a couple of personal trainers, our central midfielder is a builder, the left-back is a schoolteacher and another lad runs a company helping disabled children. We're all playing at the same level.'

With Pompey having lost in the League Two play-off semi-finals against Plymouth Argyle in his first season, manager Paul Cook sought to strengthen in the summer of 2016. Having managed Baker at Southport nine years earlier, he turned to the MK Dons midfielder, a free agent having turned down a fresh twelve-month deal. Then aged 33, he represented a third close-season recruit, following Danny Rose and the permanent signing of Matt Clarke. It turned out to be a promotion-winning campaign, with Baker missing just one league match, ruled out with a hamstring problem at Hartlepool United, as he scored nine goals in 46 appearances in all competitions. Crucially, he netted in two of the Blues' final three matches to ensure his team, already promoted, would maintain their momentum to claim the League Two title on a dramatic last day.

Baker said: 'I was around the swimming pool on a family holiday in Cyprus and Ian Foster, a former coach at Coventry, rang to ask if I would be interested in joining Pompey. It was a club I had always wanted to sign for.

'Previously, in September 2014, I was a free agent after leaving Coventry and was invited into a corporate box for Pompey's game at Burton Albion, where I met chairman Iain McInnes, Mark Catlin and his wife, Elaine. However, I ended up joining MK Dons because they competed in League One, a division higher. Then, in the summer of 2016, through Fozzie, they declared an interest in me once again, only for it to go a little quiet, so I ended up training at Barnsley before taking a medical ahead of a scheduled signing the following day. I was handed a kit and put up in a hotel that evening, but then the chief executive, Ben Manford, who used to be my agent, called to say the lads had now been given the day off, asking me to instead stay in the hotel for an extra night before joining up for the rearranged training session. Well, I had already been there for one night, and I wasn't keen on staying for another, hanging around with nothing to do all day. I wanted to sign and get it done. For whatever reason, they were dragging their heels, so the chief executive agreed that I could drive home and then come back the next day – but I never did return. I received a phone call from Pompey offering me a deal, met Paul Cook, Leam Richardson and Robbie Blake for a meal at Casa Brasil in Port Solent and felt like they wanted me more, so I signed for them two days later. I still have the Barnsley training kit at home – my lad sometimes wears it around the house!

'My debut came on the opening day of the 2016–17 season, which I marked by scoring in a 1–1 draw with Carlisle United at Fratton Park. How it finished level, I will never, ever know.

258 ✳ POMPEY

They were down to ten men for most of it but their keeper, Mark Gillespie, was unbelievable. It was the most one-sided match I have ever been involved in. Despite the result, after that game I knew we were going to have a great season. There was absolutely no way we weren't going to be challenging playing like that – we were class that day.'

Upon his Pompey arrival, Baker found a trusty travel companion in former Coventry team-mate Michael Doyle, the pair sharing car duties to negotiate the twice-weekly commute from the Midlands. Doyle, Pompey's skipper, was a powerful presence around Fratton Park, voted *The News* and *Sports Mail*'s Player of the Season by supporters in his first season. The combative midfielder also left his mark on team-mate Christian Burgess during a half-time dressing room altercation, with fans realising something was amiss when neither player reappeared for the second half of that November 2016 visit of Stevenage.

'I used to love wearing the number seven shirt, but that was the only time I wished I wasn't!' smiled Baker.

'Burge was number six and Doyler was number eight. I was sitting next to them, and that's how it was the whole season. At half-time against Stevenage they started arguing. Then, when they started going for each other, I was trying to hold them off! It was passion, heat of the moment stuff, probably lasting five seconds. It was blown out of proportion.

'Doyler was giving Burge a bollocking and he stood up for himself, so the skipper went for him and grabbed his head. Burge then picked him up and threw him and, as Doyler fell back, his foot struck him in the head, cutting it. He didn't kick out, it was just momentum. They're both good lads. They shook hands and were fine with it. If anything, it probably brought them a little closer.

'They were both instantly substituted, which surprised me. Cookie was tough and streetwise, and I thought he would love that happening in the dressing room, because it does happen often. I can understand that you don't want the players fighting, but it's passion and it shows people care, rather than lads sitting there and not saying anything. They could have both been sent out for the second half, fired up and competitive. Instead, Cookie brought the pair of them off. Doyler was fuming, charging around and kicking off. The way to piss him off was to substitute or not play him – that's how you got to him.

'It was goalless against Stevenage at the interval. Not having those two on the pitch for the next 45 minutes affected us massively; we ended up losing 2–1. Cookie made it clear that their behaviour was unacceptable, sending out a strong message to the dressing room. I can see his point, but, in terms of the game, it cost us. Not only that, he also cancelled the players' Christmas party, which was meant to be a trip to London, all booked and paid for. However, considering we all had passes from our wives and girlfriends, we decided to go out for a few beers in Southampton on the Saturday night instead!

'Initially it was maybe three or four of the lads keen to make a night of it, then others got wind and wanted to join them. In the end, we agreed that either we all went, or nobody did, so nearly everyone turned up. The players stuck together. The next time we trained, the gaffer had everyone running non-stop, doing laps of the pitches – it felt like ten hours. Somehow, he had found out. We later discovered that the four or five lads staying in digs near Fratton Park were a bit loud when they returned home at 4am. I'm not sure of the exact story, but I was told that their neighbours, big Pompey fans, got in touch with the gaffer to complain! Looking back, there are different ways of dealing with things – the initial incident could have been settled within a minute, a shaking of hands and then going out to play the second half. The fact both Burge and Doyler were subbed, we lost and then the gaffer mentioned it in his post-match interviews, ensured that it suddenly became a big issue.

'When Doyler left for Coventry, Brett Pitman arrived to take over as skipper and there was a big, big gap in terms of how they carried out the job, even though there is no right or wrong way. With Doyler, we would sit there watching him, knowing he'd lose his head over something as silly as making a cup of tea wrong because he wanted to keep us on our toes. That's what got us through at times. In contrast, Brett would say very little. He was quiet, a really nice lad, but kept himself to himself a bit. He came in, got changed and didn't say much. You'd be there sometimes and not know if Brett was in. With Doyler or Gary Roberts, you definitely knew they were there!'

Michael Doyle's desire for a last hurrah has similarly seen him drop into non-league, albeit through a sense of duty, refusing to walk out on Notts County in their time of need. Now aged 38, he was the Magpies' skipper upon their relegation from the Football League on the final day of the 2018–19 campaign, following a 3–1 defeat at Swindon Town.

In previous seasons, Doyle had secured successive League Two promotions, first with Pompey and then with Coventry, before being recruited mid-season by County boss Neal Ardley to aid their battle to remain in the division. Relegation proved to be unavoidable, however, condemning the Irishman to non-league football for the first time in his career, with the Magpies currently sixth in the National League.

Doyle said: 'It didn't bother me, dropping into non-league. I probably could have stayed in the Football League, not being arrogant or anything. It was in my contract that if the club were relegated, I could leave, but I'm not that type of person. I have always been committed to success.

'It would have been easy to come here for a few months before running away, but that's not me; I want to achieve something. I came to help the club stay in the league although I didn't manage that, but I want to be part of taking it back. I've had longevity at every club I've been at; I've bought into them. This is no different. I'm 38 and at the stage of my life where I am contemplating what to do next. I've had an unbelievable run, being fortunate enough to play to this age, but now I'm eyeing my next move, that step into coaching or scouting, wherever you can find that foot on the ladder.

'At the same time, I will never forget that final day against Swindon. I said to myself I wanted to be a part of this club coming back, which is something I achieved at Pompey and Coventry. Notts County were eight points from safety when I arrived, but we managed to take it to the final match. There was so much stuff going on behind the scenes on a weekly basis, and it was hard.

'This is a big club and I would love to be part of it getting back into the Football League because everything is there. It would be great to finish my career with a bit of success. Non-league football is what it is. If you come into it with the wrong mentality, moaning about how everything is different, the smaller crowds or the 4G surface, you are going to struggle. This is the level you are playing at so get on with it. If you go through the motions it won't be great. I see everything as an experience, so try to do the best you can. Ideally you don't want to play in the National League, but I'm enjoying being part of something, it's a new project here and I'm no quitter.'

Doyle made 97 appearances and scored three times during two seasons at Fratton Park, culminating in a League Two title win. That achievement was clinched with a 6–1 success over Cheltenham Town, his final Blues match before returning to former club Coventry six days later as a free agent. After leading the Sky Blues to League Two play-off final success over Exeter City at Wembley the following season, he moved to struggling Notts County in January 2019. Under owner Alan Hardy, the turmoil devastating the famous old club gradually became apparent, as staff went without pay in May and June, while a winding-up petition was served over an unpaid tax bill worth reportedly £250,000. In July, Danish brothers Christoffer and Alexander Reedtz completed a takeover to put the Magpies back on a firmer footing, albeit in non-league surroundings for the first time in their history.

Doyle added: 'There has been a lot of upheaval. I signed on January deadline day and, by the end of February, was told I wasn't going to get paid and the club might be going into administration! I thought, "Bloody hell, what's going on here?" Unfortunately we then went two months without getting paid, which was tough. It was the first time in my career I'd experienced that, but we had great support from the fans; they were right behind us.

'As players, we're covered through the PFA, but staff at the club aren't. What it highlighted was how important the club is to a lot of people, with the fans rallying to raise more than £2,400 for staff, which was fantastic. Kion Etete was sold to Tottenham Hotspur in June, which ended up paying the wages for that month.

'Following relegation, there was a high turnover of players which wasn't necessarily a bad thing but, with the club under a transfer embargo, we returned for pre-season with only six or seven senior players. To be fair to the manager and his assistant Neil Cox, they gave us a great pre-season and kept us strong, but the uncertainty remained. We didn't know what was going to happen.

'We held a lot of player meetings and the one thing we stressed was the importance of training and getting what we needed out of pre-season. Then, a week before the season started, we were taken over, which was great and meant that the signing of players could begin. I'm sure 90 per cent of the manager's targets had gone by then, but we managed to sign some good players. Now things are quiet behind the scenes, which is great, believe me.'

The Pompey associations at Meadow Lane are not merely restricted to their former title-winning skipper. Former Fratton Park loanees Damien McCrory and Wes Thomas are first-team regulars, as is midfielder Richard Brindley, who spent time on trial with the Blues last summer, before his Notts County switch. Former St John's College pupil Christian Oxlade-Chamberlain, who left Pompey for the Magpies in August 2018, is also on their books.

Doyle said: 'I feel fit, am still playing regularly and not missing games through injuries, but if I don't retire this year I certainly will next year. I don't want to look too far ahead, so let's just see what happens and evaluate it at the end of the season. You do look at the next stage of your life and I have been considering that for a long time but every year I've managed to play 40-odd games. Normally, when you're coming to the end of your career, you play ten to fifteen games and your body starts to let you down. I have been very fortunate. I've always felt good and I've managed to play quite a lot of games, so you don't even consider it. I'll just look at things in the summer.

'My UEFA A licence will be completed by the end of the season in preparation for the next stage of life. I'd love to stay involved in the game through coaching, but have also looked at scouting – anything to get a foot on the ladder when you've finished playing. The game doesn't owe anybody anything, so you have to keep busy and grab each opportunity with both hands.

'Football is my life. It's part of my family and I want to stay involved in the game. But firstly I want to bring a bit of success back to Notts County. It's a big club, a sleeping giant in a sense, and hopefully I can play a part in bringing it back up.'

Within 26 days of capturing the League Two title, Cook walked out on Pompey to join Wigan Athletic, a club newly relegated from the Championship. Managerial replacement Kenny Jackett swiftly decided that Gary Roberts and striker Michael Smith were surplus to requirements, but he did hand Baker a pre-season opportunity as a holding midfielder. He lined up in the unfamiliar role alongside Danny Rose in a July 2017 friendly defeat to Bournemouth at Fratton Park, retaining his place for the League One opener against Rochdale. Before August had ended, Baker had made his 50th and final appearance for the Blues.

'I was a little disappointed because central midfield was never my position,' said Baker.

'We won 2–0 in that opening match against Rochdale, but I wasn't great on the ball and felt I'd had a poor game. That was the end of it for me, and I played just three more times for Pompey. I had never featured in that role during my entire career – usually it was on either wing, or as the number ten. The previous season I did quite well on the right wing for Cookie, playing most games and scoring a few goals, so I felt hard done by.

'Kenny Jackett never saw me play in my favourite position. I would have liked to have stayed that season as I was still contracted, but when I knew he wasn't going to select me, I wanted to leave.

I liked his honesty. That's what I always ask from managers, to be transparent. I was told that I wasn't part of his plans, he was looking to bring players in, and, while he was happy for me to stay, I wasn't going to be a regular. I had played the majority of matches the previous season and didn't want to take a step back and not feature. Gary Roberts was sent to train with the kids; you see it all the time in football. When a new manager comes in, he brings his own people, his own players. It was time for me to move on.'

Baker's contract was cancelled by mutual consent in August 2017 on transfer deadline day, allowing him to pursue a return to Coventry, but he never again played in the Football League. The emergence of an alternative offer with Indian Super League club ATK prompted a late change of heart, although an Achilles injury sustained during pre-season ruled him out of the entire campaign. Baker returned on a pay-as-you-play deal with Coventry and was in line for a second debut, only to tear his calf in training the Thursday before, denying him a final chance to feature in the Football League. Keen to maintain a playing career, he dropped into the National League North with Nuneaton Town in August 2018, before switching to divisional rivals and promotion contenders Brackley halfway through the season. The Saints finished third that campaign, losing to Spennymoor Town on a penalty shoot-out in the play-off semi-finals.

Aside from continuing to represent Kevin Wilkins' side, the Solihull-based footballer has also established the Carl Baker Football Academy, catering for more than 150 children aged between four and fifteen, while also offering a BTEC diploma football and education programme for sixteen to eighteen-year-olds, competing in the English Colleges League.

The 37-year-old added: 'My first away game with Brackley was at Alfreton Town. I walked on to the coach and noticed it was full of older people, so I said my apologies and climbed back off. I thought it was the fans' coach, but it turned out it really was the team coach – the supporters travel with the players!

'In the Football League you would only travel with the first-team players and staff. You could lie across four seats if you wished. Sky Sports was on the television, there were tables to play cards and a little kitchen to serve food during the journey. Now it's like getting on a Ryanair flight!

'I still love it, because if you didn't you would call it a day. I'll happily sit and chat with a fan sitting next to me. In a year or two, I know I'd do anything to sit on a coach for four hours for a game of football or to drive to Pompey for a training session. By then it will have gone – you've lost it and you can't do anything about it. I will miss playing. I'll probably still be kicking a ball around with my mates in a Powerleague five-a-side, just for the love of it. There's no better feeling, whether you're in the Championship on £7,000 a week or with your mates, paying a fiver to play. You're still playing football, having a laugh and competing. What a game.'

ROG MCFARLANE
AND MICK HOGAN

7 February 2020

With chicken breast heading the shopping list, Pompey goal-keeping coach John Keeley placed an order with his supplier. For fifteen years Roger McFarlane has been employed as Pompey's training ground steward, offering a selfless service that exceeds his remit. The job specification does not detail the selling of five-kilo boxes of poultry at £23 a time to coaches, nor the sourcing of smoky bacon ribs to satisfy Paul Cook during his Blues tenancy. Nonetheless, having been involved in the butcher trade for more than half a century before retirement, McFarlane possesses impeccable taste and meat industry contacts to satisfy the appetites of colleagues at the club's Copnor Road training base.

The 76-year-old's versatility has long rendered him an invaluable presence at the club, an association stretching back to the Premier League era. During Pompey's top-fight heyday, five training ground stewards patrolled the former premises at Wellington Sports Ground. Today there is only McFarlane, still faithfully at the service of players and staff, no matter how bizarre the request.

'It's not like working, is it? It's a hobby. I see the players as normal people – you hear their problems when they're down, and some you get quite close to, such as Hermann Hreidarsson and David Nugent, but others you don't. They may be footballers, but they're human beings too. I don't care how much talent you've got – you're no better than me, mate, and I am no better than you. We are equal; that's how I view it. Mind you, the things they ask you to do. They think you're a magician when I'm actually a retired butcher who works at a training ground! At least I can help with meat orders, although I've argued with Christian Burgess and Danny Rose on many occasions. As vegans, I've told them they'll end up with rickets and bandy legs without it in their diet!

'In the Premier League years, players would come to us to fix their cars, not that I know anything about being a mechanic. I remember Glen Johnson arriving one day and asking us to jump-start his black BMW, which had been left at the Concorde Club across the road. Why on earth he didn't just ring BMW I don't know, but instead he threw the keys to me and my colleague, Keith Stretton, and disappeared. So, we went over to see what could be done and discovered that there was hardly enough power in the key to even lift the boot! Still, inside was a box within a box, which contained the car's battery floating in water. God knows how it got like that. Once drained, the car worked fine, and I drove up and down the M27 to make sure!

'Papa Bouba Diop owned a Chrysler and once turned up to training asking if we could fix a puncture. So, I made a few phone calls and was quoted £175 for two new tyres, but they wanted me to pay up front, so I put the cost on my credit card. Papa settled up with me the next time he was in. He also gave me a bottle of champagne as gratitude.

'Another time Peter Crouch arrived with a pigeon trapped in his car. It had jammed in the front air vent of his black 4 x 4 and he was trying to get it out. Apparently, it had been wedged in there for three days, but it had taken him a while to realise. Crouchy had wondered what his dog kept barking at! Well, Hermann being Hermann thought he could put his hand in there to pull this pigeon out, but couldn't, of course. In the end, the RAC man was called out, who reached the grill through the bonnet and managed to remove the bird. We put it on top of Crouchy's car, then it rocked back, dazed, before flying off without a care in the world.

'I used to argue with David James all day long about saving the planet. He owned a car powered by rapeseed oil and one day it broke down, so I asked whether he wanted us to get the fuel from Tesco or the garage! Another duty we had was walking Younès Kaboul's Jack Russell, which came with a pink lead. He would bring it into training every Tuesday as he was heading to London afterwards for his day off. So, either Keith or I would walk it around the car park while Younès was busy playing football.

'They could be kind, though. Players had to be there at 9.30am, ready to train for 10am, and one of them, I can't remember who, once asked me for the time. I explained that my watch was broken and thought no more about it. Come lunchtime, when they were beginning to leave, this guy handed me a magazine produced for Premier League players and said, "There are some decent watches in there, you know." On the first page was one for £5,000 and he helpfully added, "Let me know. I can order you one if you're interested." Blimey, the only thing wrong with my watch was the wristband had snapped!'

McFarlane's initial involvement with the club he supports was as stadium security, a two-hour shift which saw him tasked with locking up and setting the Fratton Park alarms each evening. Then, in 2005, he relocated to the Eastleigh-based training ground of the then-Premier League club in a full-time stewarding role. It was a glorious period that saw the Blues register their highest top-flight league placing in more than half a century, as well as competing in European competition and reaching two FA Cup finals.

When financial constraints led to the sacrifice of their fixed training-ground base, a nomadic existence beckoned, spending almost two years flitting between pitches at Eastney Barracks, South Downs College, Furze Lane, St John's College and Fratton Park. McFarlane's services were no longer required, but he returned upon the unveiling of their new Hilsea training ground in December 2014, this time on a voluntary four-day-a-week basis following retirement.

He added: 'Players are buggers sometimes. One day I heard this clinking. It sounded like aluminium on aluminium, but I couldn't work out where it was coming from. The mystery was solved when I spotted Matt Taylor and Sean Davis on top of a six-foot high gantry used for filming and analysis – they were having a sword fight with poles!

'On another occasion, a ball smashed through a canteen window, with the chief executive, Peter Storrie, among those sitting eating at the time. There was glass everywhere. Luckily no one got hurt and we soon discovered that Davis was the culprit. The players had been having a bet on who could shoot through an open window and he was off target. They'd get bored very easily and once, Jermain Defoe, while waiting for his cousin to pick him up, noticed his team-mates' black BMWs were parked in a line, so he sprayed a fire extinguisher over them. One belonged to Sulley Muntari. When he came out, he turned to me and said, "Sir, my car is covered in white." He always called me 'Sir', and I reassured him, "Yes, it has blown in on the wind. The car will be all right in a minute."

'Talking of cars, the first day Carl Dickinson arrived on loan from Stoke City he turned up in a white BMW, so the players decided to turn it into a Mr Whippy ice-cream van. When that died down, he would come in a red BMW, which they transformed into a fire chief's car, with an upside-down blue bucket on the roof and stickers. The best prank they pulled was dressing his vehicle like a police car and arranging for a policeman to tell him off. The policeman, a friend of the players' liaison officer, was in on the joke. He warned Dickinson that he was in trouble for impersonating the police. You should have heard Dickinson pleading his innocence!

'I liked Lomana LuaLua and he once told me a car would be arriving at midday with a delivery of takeaway food. It had been paid for, and all I had to do was to receive it and store it somewhere safe. Well, within ten minutes of them arriving, LuaLua came out and hid behind vehicles in the car park, handing out the takeaways to a number of the African players, such as Benjani Mwaruwari.

Understandably, they were keen to ensure that Harry Redknapp didn't find out.

'Kanu and John Utaka were always late for training. Kanu's brother drove him in a people carrier which had a mattress in the back so the Nigerian international could sleep during the journey, and nine times out of ten they arrived late from North London. Utaka was the same, never on time, and it was always the fault of the traffic lights or something, yet Lauren was driven from London every day and never late.

'The biggest joker was Luke Varney; he was a nightmare. He drove Liam Lawrence mad to the point where Liam would ask me to guard his washbag whenever he was in the canteen. "Don't let the little lunatic near it," he'd say. One day Varney found a cricket ball in Kev McCormack's kit room and shouted to Benjani to pick up a plank of wood and face him: "Benji, it's England v Zimbabwe." He declined and Varney instead bowled it down this corridor like Fred Trueman, as fast as he could, and it smashed through a partition! Crackers, but as funny as you like.

'If somebody couldn't find their boots, they would usually be up a tree and you could guarantee that on Fridays the Jacuzzi would be full of bubbles. They would go everywhere. You can guess who emptied the bottle of Fairy Liquid into it. The tricks he would play on people; you never knew what was going to happen. He was the type of character we just don't seem to have these days.'

McFarlane was forced to take time away from his training ground post in November after suffering a stroke while collecting his grandson, Oakley. He had been in rude health ever since undergoing pioneering heart surgery 26 years ago, ditching smoking and alcohol to refine his lifestyle. Then the pensioner was hit by a stroke, but, within two weeks of being admitted to Queen Alexandra Hospital, he had returned to training-ground duty, shrugging off the setback.

McFarlane said: 'When I lived in Yorkshire, I suffered a heart attack. Then, while at Barnsley Hospital, had a cardiac arrest in the lift as they were moving me to the coronary care unit. I'm told it took three goes to bring me back. They required ten volunteers to carry out a new procedure in heart treatment, involving the use of shockwaves to bombard the artery's blockage. I became the first person in the world to undergo the treatment, making the local and national news as a result.

'I'd been absolutely fine until, in November, I arrived to collect my grandson from his mum's home in Fareham to take him training with Pompey's under-11s and tried to say, "Oakley, are you ready? Get into the car," and it came out jumbled. My daughter, Paige, looked at me and said, "Dad, your face." Apparently, the left-hand side had dropped, so an ambulance was called. I couldn't speak and was unable to write properly. I'd left my shopping in the boot of my car – oven-ready bangers and mash and some doughnuts which I'd bought from McColl's for dinner – and was trying to tell my family they were there, but it was like a game of charades, and they couldn't work it out!

'I'd suffered a stroke, but fortunately it all ties in with the heart attack from decades before. Having been on aspirin all these years, my blood was thin, while the open-heart surgery had left my arteries totally clear. It thankfully meant the blood clot had nowhere to stop, which saved me, along with the help of my healthy lifestyle.

'In the early hours of the following morning at QA Hospital, I woke up desperate for the toilet and was told by the nurse that if I could say 'baby hippopotamus' then she would take me. Well, I could! I was speaking again! Then, at around 8.30am, my daughter called wanting to know how I was. I was in the mood to wind her up and said, "Paige, what are you doing ringing me and waking me up? I was in a deep sleep!" She replied "Dad, you can speak!"

'My stroke was a mild one, there was no brain damage, and after three days I was allowed home, but instructed to take a few weeks off work and not to drive for a month. After a fortnight, I asked Bev, who lives in the next road and also works at the training ground, to drive me in every day. You just get on with it. It happens, and it can happen to anybody.'

✳ ☽ ✳

The affable Mick Hogan chuckles at his own jokes. For more than 30 years, the taxi-driver-turned-Fratton-Park-press-room-steward has inflicted his off-kilter comic timing upon match-day media visitors. Laughter never strays beyond politeness from newcomers, while regulars are used to rolling with the punchlines. Nonetheless, home fixtures are considerably livened by the cheery Hogan, one of Pompey's biggest characters, whose hospitality includes a supply of home-made cake for visitors. Seasoned press box inhabitants have become accustomed to witnessing the cracking of that warm smile amid the seriousness of football matches.

'Me and BBC Radio Solent's Guy Whittingham have a thing where, should I get a bit noisy, he jokily turns around and shushes me,' grinned Hogan.

'When Laurence Herdman worked for them, many a time he would give me a right filthy look because of the noise I was making! Some stewards look for a bit of extra money in their pocket; they're not interested in football. It's a job to them but it's more than that to me. Admittedly, I can be vociferous, and many times media manager Neil Weld has told me to calm down, that I shouldn't be saying this or that, but it's a football game, and you can't hold back your passion. It doesn't get easier to control with age either, I'm 66 now and just can't help myself. I love my job, absolutely love it. I get to watch games at Fratton Park and am paid to do so.

'When the fourth official signals time added on, I head down to the tunnel area ready to watch the teams return to the changing rooms, which always gives me a little buzz. You're a bit awestruck – it doesn't matter your age. It's a chance to take it all in, to watch players' reactions, sometimes seeing a door taken down or a foot put through the plasterboard wall. You get a few frayed tempers down there! The referee takes a lot of stick, usually from the visiting manager or coaches, who wait at the top of the stairs as the match officials have to walk past them to reach their own dressing room. They get quite het up, but I've never seen Kenny get involved; he's not like that.

'As a fan and a steward, I have seen this club go through an awful lot, up and down the league twice, plus three administrations. To see us win the League Two title on the final day of the 2016–17 season was pretty emotional. There were tears in my eyes, but that's the passion. You watch the struggles, then that happens, with all those supporters celebrating on the pitch.

'The 2008 FA Cup final was the highlight of my time at Pompey, and I was in the dressing room celebrating with the players. There were a few drops of bubbly spilled on me and I managed to get an empty bottle which Kanu signed the neck of for me. It's in my lounge at home, my pride and joy. That's the unique position I have. Considering I work only on a match-day basis you've got that link with the team, and one of my duties is to get the players to interviews. My son Mark and I were under instruction to grab the players on the Wembley pitch and take them to the TV interviews, but we got a bit carried away, cheering, shouting and celebrating with the players. The TV reporters had to get the players for themselves as they walked past!

'I returned from Egypt to attend that final, cutting into my holiday. It was booked before the quarter-final against Manchester United and I didn't give a thought to us getting past them, but we kept winning. There was me, my partner and two friends, all scheduled to go from Wednesday to Wednesday, but there was absolutely no way I was missing the final; it just wasn't going to happen. I didn't care if I needed to swim back. So, I flew back to Heathrow Airport on the Friday, attended the game, celebrated winning the FA Cup, and then returned to Egypt on the Sunday! The flights probably cost as much as the entire holiday.'

Hogan's Blues association began in the 1987–88 campaign, when Alan Ball was manager. Initially recruited as a South Stand steward, he was soon relocated to the press room. Born in the city, his family moved to Weymouth when Hogan was aged five, but after leaving school he returned to work in a variety of jobs including his brother's Southsea newsagents, refitting ships in the dockyard, and then for British Gas as a meter reader and coin collector. However, it was his ten years spent as a taxi driver that provided him with the greatest insight into the individuals who presided over Pompey's demise and near-extinction. Having seen service with Streamline Taxis, City Wide Taxis and then Aqua Cars, Hogan was utilised by the Blues on a voluntary basis to transport high-profile figures. Among regular passengers was Sulaiman Al-Fahim, the purported Dubai-based billionaire who endured a disastrous 41-day spell as Pompey owner in 2009, hastening the club's descent towards financial meltdown.

'At the time there was a club car, a brown BMW 7 Series, which was available when somebody of substance required it,' added Hogan.

'As a taxi driver, I did a lot of running around for the club and they asked if I could start driving Al-Fahim around. I'd pick him up from Heathrow Airport, where he would land on his trips from Dubai, and take him to his hotel, although on one occasion drove him straight to Fratton Park for a match against Bolton Wanderers, which we lost 3–2. Sometimes I would use an S-Class Mercedes from the Eastern Road dealership, but Al-Fahim always moaned: "I tell the club all the time that I want to be picked up in a C-Class." When they actually managed to get a C-Class, he said: "At last, they have listened to me."

'On one occasion, he'd been to a match at Fratton Park and was staying at the Solent Hotel & Spa in Whiteley, scheduled for a 5.30am pick-up the following day to fly home from Heathrow Terminal Five. However, there was a bit of drama. The car was kept at the club and, the previous evening, Pete Giles, husband of our then ticket office manager Elaine, had used it for another job. He had also taken the only set of keys home with him and I didn't have a contact number. So, I had to use my seven-seater Hackney cab to collect Al-Fahim.

'When I arrived at the hotel, he was with three other people and, bearing in mind the bloke had a flight to catch, he told me: "Yeah, yeah, we won't be long," and they went and had breakfast. I tried warning him there was now a chance he could miss his plane but he didn't listen. Once they had finished eating, he came out and caught sight of his taxi, a grey Peugeot, Portsmouth-licensed seven-seater cab with a 'For Hire' sign fixed on top. He was really pissed off at that, a man of his standing who demanded a C-Class Mercedes!

'So, there we were, heading to Heathrow, hitting traffic, and he was going off on one. It was a traumatic journey and it didn't matter which way you went – you would be stuck in traffic. I tried to explain, but you have to be polite and realise who he is and that you are just a driver. Of the four travellers, he was the only one with a flight to catch, so, when we arrived at the airport, he ran in and I followed behind with a suitcase in each hand, both of which had dodgy wheels, heading to the check-in desk where we discovered that the gate had shut. It was too late. Al-Fahim was frantic. He said something about getting back to Dubai for a football tournament he was organising, but it was no good. Out of curiosity, the guy behind the desk asked him for his name. Then, after checking his computer, looked up: "Your flight is tomorrow, sir. Not today."

'Honestly, you could have heard a pin drop. Al-Fahim was very embarrassed. I ended up taking all of them back to the hotel he stayed in near Harrods and he caught another cab to the airport the next day! Al-Fahim wasn't a great talker and never gave me a tip; in fact, none of them ever did. Don't get me wrong, he wasn't aloof or snotty, he just wasn't a great communicator. His suitcases told you everything about him and his supposed wealth. They were battered and well-worn, with dents. I remember thinking: "Christ, look at the state of them. He's meant to be a billionaire!"

'The last time I saw him was after he had sold the club. He would turn up for the occasional game, which in this instance was a midweek match at Crystal Palace. I'd gone to a grubby burger van before the game and was heading towards the ground when I saw a bloke go up to Al-Fahim and punch him fully in the face. He must have had a couple of good shiners after that!

'I drove another owner, Balram Chainrai, on one occasion. It was in the BMW and Daniel Azougy and two other men were with him, heading to a hotel in Regent's Park, London. We left the club and had just joined Velder Avenue when he spoke to me from the back, his exact words being: "How much are the club paying you, then?" To which I replied: "Actually, I'm doing it for nothing, I'm doing it for the club." They were the only words he said to me the entire trip and I didn't receive a tip!'

When Pompey became the first Premier League side to enter administration in February 2010, Hogan was among the creditors, owed a £30 taxi fare by the club, and the sum was written off during the CVA process. He retired from the taxi trade in August 2015 to help with his son's new venture, the Parade Tea Rooms, in Southsea.

Mark Hogan himself had served in Pompey's press room as a steward since the age of eleven, later dividing his time between working as a commis chef, leading to his employment at Buckingham Palace, Windsor Castle, Balmoral Castle and Holyrood Castle, with his responsibilities including making the royal breakfast and preparing the vegetables for dinner. He eventually quit his Fratton Park responsibilities after nineteen years to focus on his Southsea business. The replacement was Annie Davies, Hogan's next-door neighbour in Highland Road and a South Stand regular whose ten-year-old granddaughter, Peaches, is a Pompey fanatic.

Hogan added: 'When Mark left, the club didn't want to pay anyone else, but there are certain match-day duties when you need another person. Annie jumped at the chance. The pay is irrelevant. She loves doing the job and is brilliant at it; everyone loves her. For the Checkatrade Trophy final against Sunderland, she was given a press pass and allowed pitchside, enabling her to walk around Wembley before the game. She was so made up. Things like that make someone's day, if not their year.

'The way I see it, the press room represents my home and you have to look after your guests. Everyone who visits is there to work, so when they travel a long distance to see us it's nice to give them something. There's tea, coffee and sausage rolls, which the club supply, but we also give them cake, which Mark makes at his own cost in the Parade Tea Rooms, while Annie and myself give out biscuits and sweets, along with the plates and cutlery. We don't mind. I can't let people come here and get nothing, especially from faraway places. I like people enjoying themselves, especially if they laugh at my jokes!'

Away from his training-ground commitments, McFarlane can also be found keeping vigil in Pompey's Anson Road club shop on match days, before relocating to The Legends Lounge after kick-off. Fratton Park has been his home since September 1956, when a twelve-year-old from North End caught his first glimpse of Pompey for the visit of Arsenal, sparking a passion that would last a lifetime.

McFarlane smiled: 'Hermann Hreidarsson was an amazing guy, and very funny. He would go past a team-mate and smack them on the back of the neck to wind them up; it didn't bother him. He would regularly playfully beat people up. He gave another steward, Keith, a horrible time, throttling or rugby-tackling him. He didn't do it to me, thankfully, because of my age! He wasn't the most fashionable and one day, when out training, some of the players took his clothes, put a broom through the arms like a scarecrow and hung it from the ceiling.

'On another occasion, he arrived at the training ground and I said: "Hermann, you stink. What have you done?" Well, apparently dried fish is a delicacy in Iceland, and he had a bag of it which stunk the place out. It smelt vile and he was popping them into his mouth like sweets.

'Hermann's family are lovely and came to the training ground quite a lot. His wife was a former footballer and his two daughters were massively into netball. There was an instance when he had about twenty footballs lined up to autograph, so his daughters asked if they could sign them on his behalf and he agreed. He was at the centre of the Reliant Robin antics, which involved the players having to customise the car when their chosen team were eliminated from the Champions League. The first one to do it was David Nugent, who had it chromed. Sean Davis sprayed it red and another player transformed it into the A-Team van. There was even a loudspeaker installed to sound like a fire engine and farmyard cockerel at one stage.

'In the end, it was decided that they would auction it off to raise money, but it didn't sell on eBay. David James then suggested getting Sky Sports to come down and blow it up, selling tickets for people to come and watch. Hermann stepped in, though, and bought it, exporting it home. Apparently, it's the only three-wheeler in the whole of Iceland.

'He's a brilliant guy and invited me and my sons to visit him over there, giving us the address of the most beautiful house with a lake beside it where we could stay. He offered to meet us at the airport and we wouldn't have to spend any money; he would look after us. I never went in the end, and I really should have. As training ground stewards, we wore gold ties and I asked him to sign mine as a souvenir. I still have it. It reads: "To my mate, Roger," with a happy smiley face. I've worked with some fantastic people.'

MARIE AND DAVE CURTIS

10 February 2020

A mother's love is unconditional and without reservation, yet not blind to footballing fallibilities.

'When Ronan returned home from that Bolton Wanderers match at Fratton Park, I told him: "You played absolutely shit today. What was wrong with you?"' said Marie Curtis, mother of Pompey's thirteen-goal top scorer.

'We say that to every single one of our boys when talking football. That honesty is important – you give them the good and give them the bad. Other times it's: "You had a fantastic game today, son; we're really proud of you." Ronan took a bit of stick from the fans that day, but supporters pay their money and are entitled to their opinion. If he's not playing well, obviously they're going to give him crap. He's going to have to pull his socks up. We always, always, tell our boys to give 100 per cent – then we can't ask for any more. As I say to Ronan, there are always better players, so he needs to be on top of his game at all times.'

The decisive moment of Ronan Curtis' burgeoning season can be pinpointed to September and his 62nd-minute withdrawal against rock-bottom Bolton. With the left-winger below par, sarcastic cheers greeted the announcement of his substitution, an inevitable departure from the field of play for the Irishman as his determination to rediscover his touch gave way to frustration. The 23-year-old's sputtering early-season form had been an ongoing source of concern as doubts began to multiply over whether he could match his eye-catching exploits from the previous campaign. Subsequently, a tight hamstring and selection preference deprived him of a starting spot in Pompey's next five matches.

Since being restored for the trip to Bristol Rovers at the end of October, Curtis has scored eleven goals and registered five assists in nineteen appearances to establish himself as an early contender for the accolade of the Blues' player of the season.

Dad Dave said: 'What happened with the fans against Bolton is football; you accept that. We attend games and naturally people say Ronan is this, Ronan is that, but, as a parent, you can't take any notice. You can't turn round and say: "Oi, that's my son." You just have to listen to it. By the same token, during one match, John Marquis' wife, mother, brother and his two children were sitting near us in the South Stand and there was a bloke in front with a lanyard around his neck saying all sorts. It was embarrassing. It was, "That bloody Marquis is useless," and all the time his family were sitting behind, hearing every word. I quietly pointed out to him that Marquis' relations were there, but he just gave me a look.

'The way we see it is, if you've got to the stage where you're offended by people's remarks then you should no longer attend. The fans pay their money and you can't say anything back; just get used to it and let it go. Although, in fairness, Ronan doesn't receive a lot of stick. What people didn't know was around the time of that Bolton game he was in a bad relationship and had so much on his mind, while we'd gone back home to the Republic of Ireland. That affected him on the pitch.

'Ronan is very, very close to us and we stay with him whenever we're in Portsmouth. He'll return to his house, go upstairs and if we aren't there will be on the phone asking: "Where are you, Mum?" His mother treats him like a baby – she does all the washing, all the ironing, all the stuff in the house. He'll ring her on his way back from training and say: "Mum, can you change the bedsheets for me today?" and she'll say: "They are already changed, son!" She even takes his designer clothes to the dry cleaners.

'There's an argument that Ronan is playing so well because we are back in England at the moment. Kenny Jackett has also noticed the difference in his game. He has actually told Marie: "I know when you two are over here, because he plays excellently. When you go home, he doesn't perform as well. Make sure you stay until the end of the season!" We're a very close family and the last time we returned to Ireland was during that bad run of form. He rang and said: "Why aren't you coming back?" I told him: "To give you peace." He replied: "I don't want peace!" We're now staying until the season's end.'

Curtis, the youngest of eleven children – six boys and five sisters – has settled into a rented two-storey house situated in the heart of Old Portsmouth and remains surrounded by his family. His parents are allocated their own room, older brother Blain is also currently booked in as a guest, while the Christmas Day gathering saw Marie cater for sixteen members of her sizeable brood.

Curtis was born in Croydon, south London, before moving to Donegal, in the Republic of Ireland, at the age of six, although Marie grew up opposite the Brandywell Stadium, home of Derry City in Northern Ireland. Her brother Pius often helped her over the wall to get into matches for free, before paying for his own entry. Dave, whose friendship with former Welsh international and Crystal Palace defender Chris Coleman would later see him become Ronan's godfather, was born in Croydon, though his parents hailed from Cork and Donegal.

Ronan was rendered eligible to represent either Northern Ireland or the Republic of Ireland, choosing the latter and featuring at every level from the under-15s upwards. Then, in November 2018, the League One performer marked his senior international debut as a second-half substitute for Mick McCarthy's side in a goalless draw against Denmark in the Nations League. To date, the lad from south London has appeared three times for the Republic of Ireland.

Marie said: 'We would go along to games to watch his older brother, David, and Ronan could be found kicking a ball around on the sidelines. Once, when he was aged five, to keep him happy I kicked a ball to him and he passed it straight along the line to me which caught the attention of two scouts, from Millwall and Charlton, standing nearby. One of them came across and asked Ronan to do it again. Sure enough, he kicked it straight to the feet of this man, in a perfectly straight line. The scout was impressed and said: "Would he mind joining our Academy when he becomes six?" I said: "Sorry, he's a little boy just enjoying himself." Besides, we weren't going to be around because we were moving to Ireland.

'His brother, David, was a very good striker. When he was aged ten he was chosen for the FA's School of Excellence in Lilleshall but, being dyslexic, was worried about the academic side of things so didn't end up going. He played for Croydon district alongside Steve Sidwell and both were chosen to represent Surrey. David also played in the youth set-ups at Wimbledon, Crystal Palace and Millwall, but never made it into the Football League.

'Before Ronan was born, I managed a men's football team in the late 1980s, which David played for. We were called Waddon Wanderers and competed in the Croydon Saturday League. There was a big, big green and we would go over and watch players, recruiting boys from there to play for the team. I'd take them twice a week for training and then turn up on a Saturday for the game and give them instructions. If they weren't playing well, I would take them off. It didn't bother me – I was the manager.

'That team included Tony Wilkinson, whose son Conor would later play for Bolton and had a loan spell at Pompey. On one occasion, Tony wasn't playing well so I hauled him off. He pulled off his shirt and threw it at my feet. I said: "Go, and don't come back." In the middle of the week, he came knocking on my door wanting to return. I told him: "No, you can't. I won't have anybody disrespecting me on the sidelines. I am not having it." He was very apologetic, but I continued: "You didn't let me down, you let your team-mates down. When I took you off I did it for a reason. You weren't playing well, so I put somebody else on and we won 2–0." I told him to apologise to the boys in the changing room and then warned the rest of them. It never happened again; I was very strict! I ran the team for three years before we moved to Ireland, winning the league twice in that time.'

When Ronan was born in March 1996, the choice of Chris Coleman as godparent was an obvious one. The Curtis family had formed a strong bond with Crystal Palace's players of the era, with David on their books and Marie working as head housekeeper at the Hilton Hotel in Croydon, where the club's players would regularly use the gym facilities. Dave and Marie socialised with a group that included Coleman, Richard Shaw, Marc Edworthy and the future manager of England, Gareth Southgate.

'We were close to Chris Coleman and his then-wife Belinda, while our eldest daughter Siobhan would babysit their eldest child, Sonny,' said Dave. 'We held dinner parties at our house, sometimes putting up a big marquee in the back garden, with the Palace players coming round. On occasion, Marie would get the Hilton's head chef to make dinner in our kitchen.

'Gareth was one of the nicest people you could ever meet, but didn't really mix with the other players and ended up marrying a local girl, Alison, from the council estate in Addington. His personality used to come out when he was with Palace keeper Andy Woodman – nice fellas, and they would sometimes watch kids' matches, including when David played for Selsdon Juniors. Gareth always knew that Marie had tea and sandwiches with her and would come over to talk and help himself to his fair share!'

Ronan's sole footballing involvement during his Croydon upbringing was in the school team at Regina Coeli Catholic Primary School. His true formative football years took place in Donegal, before eventually making his name at Derry City, the only Northern Irish club in the Republic of Ireland-based League of Ireland. His senior bow arrived in May 2015, one month after his nineteenth birthday, and the winger progressed to earn under-21 honours while affiliated with the Candystripes, where the brother of Stoke City's James McClean, Patrick, was among his team-mates.

Dave added: 'Funnily enough, Ronan is a really common name in Ireland. Once the manager came over and asked: "Can we call him Curtis? I have three Ronans out there!" So, he has always been known as Curtis – some people thought that was his Christian name!

'He was always highly regarded. His brothers Blain and Declan are a lot older and played for Finn Harps in the League of Ireland, then managed by Felix Healy, whom I would often have a chat with about football. When Ronan was aged nine or ten, Felix was adamant that he would go on to be a better player than the other two. He originally played for Kildrum Tigers, before moving to Swilly Rovers in Rathmelton, County Donegal. He scored goals for fun, with a hat-trick almost every week and, at the age of fifteen, they wanted to promote him into the senior side, to play against men's teams.

'He was very small and I was concerned about somebody of that age facing 33-year-olds, particularly in Ireland where they don't hold back and the referees don't protect you. So, I told them that Ronan would only be allowed to step up if he played in the position I wanted him to, on the wing, so he could only get hit by one player. They agreed.

'Ronan loved it at Swilly – it was like a family but it couldn't go any further as it wasn't a big enough club. Then Derry City spotted him and wanted him in their academy, so he moved there. The first time he was selected for the Republic of Ireland under-21s they were at a training camp in Malaga, Spain, and we were invited to go out there with him. The manager, Noel King, came over to me and said: "Can I just say thanks for letting Ronan come along. I've been after Ronan for years now and this is the first time I've managed to get him."

'Apparently, they had been chasing him for the under-19s, but had never received a reply. It turned out that Derry's manager, Kenny Shiels, would have liked Ronan to play for Northern Ireland instead. There were times when Ronan was asked to play for Northern Ireland but declined because he was already training and doing well for the Republic. That's his country.'

Curtis was Kenny Jackett's first recruit ahead of the 2018–19 campaign, arriving in May 2018 for an undisclosed fee from Derry. Challenged with adapting to the Football League, he was perceived as a gamble, earmarked for regular bench action to ease him in. Yet an encouraging pre-season resulted in the then 22-year-old being handed a starting spot in the opening match against Luton Town as a strike partner for Brett Pitman in a 1–0 victory.

For the remainder of the campaign, Curtis operated on the left of the attacking three in Jackett's preferred 4-2-3-1 system, racking up twelve goals in 49 appearances, earning his manager's vote as the club's Young Player of the Season. Inevitably, the Curtis family turned up in numbers for the Fratton Park gala dinner event, filling a table for ten. However, a freak injury involving the front door of his Old Portsmouth home almost lost him a finger on his left hand during that first campaign and came perilously close to denying him a place in the 2019 Checkatrade Trophy final against Sunderland.

Marie said: 'Ronan came back too early from that injury; he wasn't himself at Wembley. They told him he would be out for six weeks but he was back playing in fifteen days. The team were travelling to Walsall for a midweek League One game; he was in a rush and he hates being late. As he pulled the front door shut, the wind caught it and trapped his finger, leaving the top of it hanging off. I was in bed and heard him shouting: "Mum!" I went downstairs in my dressing gown to see what was going on. Straight away I put the injured finger under a cold tap. He went mad because it stung.

'We didn't know any hospitals in the area, so I rang Kenny Jackett and told him not to hold the coach, explaining that Ronan needed to get medical help. They sent Jack Hughes, one of Pompey's physios, to meet us in the reception at Queen Alexandra Hospital. Ronan was warned that he might lose part of that finger and we were in hospital from 8.30am until 4pm, but thankfully they saved it. The surgeon said: "It's nice and pink at the minute, and if it stays pink you will be fine. If it doesn't, we'll have to cut it off."

'A couple of months earlier, his brother, Declan, did the same thing, but lost the top of his finger past the nail. He owns a valeting business in Derry and, when a woman began reversing her car back, he shut a car door and trapped his finger. When he opened the door, it fell out, but he didn't have the sense to pick it up and take it with him, leaving it behind. Ronan's wasn't as bad as that and he wanted to play in the following game against Scunthorpe United, but the concern was there may be an infection should sweat or grass get into the cut, possibly leading to him losing the finger. He was determined to make it back as quickly as possible and returned to start against Sunderland in the final.'

With January's transfer window shut, Curtis last week signed a new three-and-a-half year Pompey deal, a reflection of the pivotal role he has played during a run of two defeats in 23 matches in all competitions to lift the side into sixth place. He was among nine players whose deals were set to expire in the summer, although, in the case of the Irishman, the club possessed a twelve-month option.

Since September, Pompey have held off from opening contract negotiations, preferring their players to focus on hauling their team up the League One table, avoiding potential distraction. Those affected are Christian Burgess, Lee Brown, Brett Pitman, Luke McGee, Oli Hawkins, Brandon Haunstrup, Adam May and Matt Casey. However, they made an exception for the in-form Curtis, previously one of the lowest earners at Fratton Park.

'The media were saying this club has come in for him and that club has come in for him, but Ronan said all along that he wanted to stay at Pompey and get them up,' said Dave. 'They offered him a few quid more at the beginning of the season, which was later bumped up to agree to a new deal. We accept that Pompey, in this league, can pay only so much, but you have to earn enough money to live, and he was struggling a bit. Honestly, as true as I am sitting here, Ronan never wanted to leave. It never, ever entered his head.

'When it became clear that he was leaving Derry, we wanted him to come to Pompey; it was always going to be the best place for him. That summer, even before Pompey came in, there was interest from Cork and Dundalk. Ronan wasn't interested. He didn't want to play against his Derry team-mates, which would have been three times a season in the League of Ireland. They would have paid more than his original Pompey contract, but he couldn't do it to his friends. By the time Reading came in, he had already told Pompey he would join them and wouldn't be changing his mind. Reading's manager, Paul Clement, was offering a lot more, but Ronan had decided on coming here. Besides, wages are nothing but hearsay until an offer is put on the table.

'Ronan could have gone to Swedish top-flight club Östersunds FK in September 2017, where Graham Potter was manager before going to Brighton & Hove Albion. We took three flights to get there and the club was lovely, but he had been told a pack of lies over the contract so it didn't happen. He loves it at Pompey and he gets on with everybody. Andy Cannon is his closest friend and usually his roommate. Andy eats and sleeps here sometimes. Ronan was never going to leave in January.'

In the build-up to the Tranmere Rovers trip, it emerged that Brett Pitman was training with Bournemouth under-23s to maintain fitness. The striker's increasingly fractious relationship with Kenny Jackett resulted in sporadic appearances around Pompey, with the club explaining that he was training at home with a heart-rate monitor. With 42 goals in 99 appearances since his Fratton Park arrival from Ipswich Town in July 2017, Pitman initially proved to be a recruit of real quality.

However, following the end of the January transfer window, during which Swindon Town and Plymouth Argyle showed interest without receiving any encouragement in response, Pitman was cast further adrift. Having been omitted from the previous seven Blues squads, it was suggested that he might train with his former club, whose development side is managed by friend and former Cherries team-mate Shaun Cooper.

Marie Curtis herself invoked the ire of the former Blues skipper following a tweet after Pompey's 3–0 win at Rochdale in November. Pitman came off the bench to set up Ryan Williams for the third goal at Spotland, prompting Curtis' mum to post: 'Has Pitts put weight on or is it just TV?' During the aftermath, her son instructed her to come off Twitter. The absence lasted four days.

> Marie said: 'It wasn't meant nastily. We hadn't seen Brett for a while and then he came on the telly and I looked at Dave, he looked at me, and I said: "Has Brett put a lot of weight on, or is it just the telly?" He looked massive, but the tweet wasn't meant to imply he actually was fat.
>
> 'Ronan told me off for that Pitman tweet. He came straight into the house and said: "Mum, what are you doing?" I told him it wasn't meant nastily and showed him what I had said, but he responded: "It looks bad, and you can't put it up on Twitter." I wasn't going to delete it, though. Why should I? It's out there, so what's the point of deleting it?'
>
> 'I later spoke to Brett and told him: "That wasn't meant nastily. Can I just apologise if you took it the wrong way." He wasn't happy about it, though. When he scored the winner against Altrincham in the FA Cup, he ran towards the South Stand, looking straight at where I was sitting, and did a shushing signal, putting a finger to his lips. I knew it was directed at me. I never bothered asking him about it; I wouldn't give him the satisfaction. If he wants to do it, fine; it's only a bit of banter.
>
> 'I came off Twitter for a bit, but not long; you won't keep me off there! I mainly put things on there to encourage the lads, or to get people to vote for the players. For instance, we had four Pompey players in the FA Cup team of the round after beating Barnsley.'

Marie and Dave's November return to Portsmouth may have coincided with an upsurge in their son's form, yet they credit the introduction of a new pre-match routine for the improvement: bingo. Joined by brother Blain and occasionally team-mate Andy Cannon, Ronan and his parents are regulars at Cosham's Crown Bingo on evenings before a game, considered a means of relaxation for the 23-year-old ahead of Pompey duty. He has emerged as an integral figure during Pompey's drive towards a club record nine consecutive wins in all competitions, sealed with a 2–0 win away at Tranmere. Curtis' parents were unable to be present at Prenton Park to witness the historic feat, with Dave confined to his house with the flu while Marie instead travelled to Nottingham with terminally ill grandson, Brae, to attend a hospital appointment.

Curtis was not on the scoresheet on this occasion, though he weighed in with two assists. The first was a thirteenth-minute free-kick delivered from the left which bounced before being headed home by Sean Raggett from six yards out, his first goal for the Blues. Then, on 51 minutes, the lead was extended when Curtis unselfishly squared to Ryan Williams, who took two touches before drilling in a low left-footed shot from the edge of the area. It meant that, for the first time in Pompey's arrival in the Football League in 1920, they had established nine consecutive victories, in the process lifting them into fifth spot, their highest position of the campaign so far.

Dave added: 'I think we'll get automatic promotion. As long as we continue playing as we have been and, touch wood, don't get any injuries, I really believe we can do it. I have always said that, even when we were losing earlier on. Half a season is nothing. It can be turned around; there's plenty of time. The manager has now got his squad back as the majority of the injuries have cleared up. There's only Andy Cannon, who missed Tranmere and is expected to be back in a week. Ronan's doing really well at the moment. People may think he is a cocky little sod at times, but he does it to wind up the opposition players. He has always been like that, and it comes from playing against his older brothers growing up.

'We enjoy it down here. Marie and I walk from the house in Old Portsmouth to South Parade Pier and back every day, and we normally attend the nearby Cathedral of St John the Evangelist on a Saturday evening. The people are really nice, and that's why Ronan chose this area to live in. He's not going to be pestered by people knocking on the door or nightclubs with customers falling out drunk. The worst noise you get here is the chiming of the cathedral! Our family love living on the south coast.'

CHRISTIAN BURGESS

20 February 2020

Pompey's fourth-choice central defender, Christian Burgess, is questioning his Fratton Park future and attracting substantial transfer attention. By his own admission, just six weeks earlier he would have happily prolonged his south-coast stay, but his employers had since challenged the team to transform a disappointing league position before improved contracts would be handed out. His home since June 2015, last month the history degree graduate marked his 200th Blues outing by netting in a 2–0 win over promotion rivals Sunderland, another personal triumph during a resurgent campaign. Burgess' stock among the Fratton faithful has never soared as high, quite an accomplishment considering he was a mainstay in the sides that claimed the League Two title and Checkatrade Trophy.

Yet uncertainty persists. The 28-year-old's Pompey deal expires at the season's end, an increasingly precarious position given the club's decision to postpone contract talks. An exception was made for Ronan Curtis earlier this month, while home-grown prospects Alex Bass and Haji Mnoga were handed extended deals at the turn of the year. Now it's finally Burgess' turn at the negotiating table with the club announcing that they're ready to talk. Burgess' eyes have, however, been drawn elsewhere during the frustrating wait.

'You're not going to tell Ronan to wait on a contract, so the best thing to do is sign him up,' said Burgess. 'The same with Alex Bass, the same with Haji Mnoga. I don't have a problem with that – football is a business. What I don't agree with is the club's perception that if they give one person a contract then everyone will want one. That's not how football works.

'If a team-mate gets a contract, everyone says, "Well done," and that's their own business. Just because Ronan is given a new deal, doesn't mean I think I should as well. They are the correct decisions for the club. Tie Bassy down, he's a top young keeper; tie Ronan down, he's a top young talent – it makes business sense. I'm glad Pompey have done these things, and I don't think anyone would begrudge that. I was always comfortable with it.

'Bassy has the potential to be a top keeper – I am talking Premier League. I've seen enough to say I wouldn't be surprised one bit to see him there within five years. He has a good frame, comes for the ball well at corners, has a massive kick, is a good shot-stopper – basically he has everything. Sign him up as it's the best thing for the club.

'Now the club have finally come to me and said they'd like to offer a new deal. They've opened negotiations, but I find myself with decisions to make as to where I want my next chapter to be. We haven't gone into details, so I'm unsure of the terms and length of contract being offered, although I am told there is room to negotiate financially. However, there are other options on the table now as people have put things down and said they would like me at their clubs. I'm into my last six months and have a few offers, both in England and abroad, so there are things to think about.

'If Pompey had offered something at the beginning of January, then I probably would have snapped their hand off and signed it. Now they have come to me and I've seen what else is out there. There are clubs in League One and Belgium, not the top flight in Belgium but the division below. It's hard to gauge whether it's a similar level over there.

'Basically, there have been talks. I don't know what will happen but I have some decisions to make. I've left it with my agent to deal with as I don't particularly want to get involved; I just want to concentrate on playing football. The decision doesn't need to be now. Mark Catlin has been fine, telling me I can put it to bed for a little while and wait until the end of the season. I am still open to everything.'

Burgess' seamless integration with the city as an Old Portsmouth resident and willingness to be involved in community work has long been admired, establishing him as an immensely popular player. In January 2017, upon the cancellation of Pompey's trip to Crawley Town due to a frozen pitch, he asked his Twitter followers for suggestions as to how he should spend his Saturday afternoon. He subsequently turned up at Bransbury Park to lend coaching assistance to Will Chitty's Skilful Soccer Youth under-12s, with the story later picked up in the USA, Australia and China as well as the English media.

For the last two years, Burgess has served as a Trustee of Pompey in the Community, the award-winning independent charitable trust affiliated to the club. Earlier this month, he was present for the launch of proposals for a new £3.5m sports complex in Copnor, crowned the John Jenkins Stadium. The Blues defender has also held out his hand to the family of schoolgirl Beth Tiller, who passed away in April 2018 through non-Hodgkin's lymphoma. While the terminally ill youngster was in Southampton General Hospital, he and team-mate Kyle Bennett paid a visit and later organised a collection among Pompey's playing squad to fund a trip to London for Beth and her family to watch her favourite show, *The Lion King*, including an overnight hotel stay. Burgess was the last non-family visitor before she passed away at her Denmead home and would later attend the funeral and wake. In October, he joined the Tiller family at Barnard's Restaurant in Denmead to mark what would have been Beth's eighteenth birthday.

'I am massively settled and I love it here in Portsmouth; it has been unbelievable.' Burgess added: 'The America's Cup is back in the city in June. I was there in 2016 and have the photographs. The amount of experiences I have had down here is fantastic, while I've made great relationships with my neighbours.

'Last season I received criticism from some fans following a match against Doncaster Rovers in February 2019, not that I read too much press on it or looked at Twitter afterwards. However, a card was posted through my door from a neighbour, basically saying, *We are so proud to have you here at Pompey and love everything you have done for the city and the club, keep your head up.*

'I didn't know them well, but what a thoughtful thing to do; it meant so much and was what I needed. That reflects what Portsmouth is about. It's a tremendous community, especially in Old Portsmouth where everybody knows their neighbours and it's lovely being part of that. My next-door neighbour lives in a flat which used to be quite a popular fish restaurant. There is a bar underneath and he often hosts events, putting on some snacks and inviting us neighbours around for a drink. I was once locked out, without my keys and phone 30 minutes before training. I approached my neighbour across the road and she gave me a lift.

'These are the things which make me love being here. In the summer, I'm always down the beach. I know the owners of the coffee shops because I'm often there, having a drink, eating vegan food and chatting about Pompey. I've been here a long time and know people. What I have here comes into my thinking when deciding the future, especially when you weigh it up against moving to another club which could be situated somewhere less nice.

'Portsmouth is a massive club, and if I was ever to leave it would be a serious decision. I'm really settled here; I love it on the south coast. Even if I did go, I would 100 per cent come back, either to visit or to do other things.'

Following a strong second half to last term, as Burgess seized the initiative during the long-term sidelining of Jack Whatmough through injury, in the summer he found himself in a familiar position. Pre-season saw him overtaken by new central-defensive recruits Paul Downing and Sean Raggett, before slipping further behind when midfielder Tom Naylor was trialled in the role during the friendly schedule.

Burgess, however, has roared back into the first-team reckoning, establishing himself as an essential selection and strong player of the season candidate, such has been the consistent nature of his performances, while Pompey remain promotion challengers and have now booked a return trip to Wembley on 5 April in the EFL Trophy final. Yet last July, after his return to training had been delayed by two days following an illness he picked up on his summer travels to Nepal, Borneo and Indonesia, he was labelled third-choice centre-half during a conversation with Kenny Jackett.

He said: 'My illness meant that, by the time I attended my first pre-season training session, everybody else had been back for two days. We finished that afternoon with three runs. I performed fine in the first and second. On the way back during the third, however, I blew up. It was like running through treacle – my legs went numb and I couldn't move them. I'd hit the wall and the boys were laughing.

'The following day, I was called into the gaffer's office where he asked: "What are your thoughts? You are probably going to be third-choice centre-half this season behind Downing and Raggett." He knew the situation from the 2018–19 campaign, where I wasn't too happy about being third choice so tried to leave halfway through. I was never a problem – I am not that sort of person – but I wanted to go out and play games.

'In that January I had a few clubs interested in taking me on loan, while the gaffer was open to my departure as long as he could find a replacement and a club willing to cover my full wages. That ruled out Bristol Rovers, but Peterborough remained keen. I thought I was off there to play under my old boss Darren Ferguson, then the gaffer changed his mind and told me I was to stay as he felt that everything was happening a bit too late in the window. That was that and two days after deadline day I was back in the team against Doncaster following Jack's injury.

'The following summer I was again Pompey's third-choice central defender. The gaffer asked if I would be happy with that scenario. I told him I wanted to play football, intimating that I wanted to sort something out sooner rather than later to allow the club time to source a replacement. I spoke to my agent, Brian Howard, and we kept our eye out, with Hull City particularly interested. It came out of the blue and I got a little excited. This was the chance to play in the Championship, managed by Grant McCann, whom I played with at Peterborough United and then under him when he became assistant manager. We spoke briefly about the move and the financial stuff and I was interested, especially being third choice at Pompey. In the end they opted to sign former Posh defender Ryan Tafazolli on a free transfer after trialling with them during pre-season. That was that, although my agent said it would have been a miracle move – from third choice in League One to the Championship!

'At one point I became fourth choice at Pompey. The boys were making jokes in the dressing room, with Tom Naylor at centre-half ahead of me, along with Raggett and Downing. I had no hope! In pre-season, I didn't start at Stevenage and came on during the second half of a behind-closed-doors friendly at Brighton & Hove Albion. Naylor and Downing were the first-choice pairing. The way it's worked out is absolutely crazy; you just couldn't write it. I was even dropped after the fourth game of the season, when we lost 2–1 at Sunderland. Then I appeared as a substitute against Coventry City when we were 3–2 up against nine men and it ended 3–3, which didn't exactly help my situation! Out of nowhere, I returned for the next match at Blackpool as a right-back! It wasn't until mid-September at Wycombe Wanderers that I was switched to centre-half and became a regular.'

Burgess grew up in north-east London, firstly in Seven Kings before moving to Ilford. His dad, Tony, had been on the books of West Ham United until he was released at the age of fifteen, opting to travel the world, settling in New Zealand and Australia for a total of fifteen years before returning. Christian was spotted by Arsenal playing for Valence United in Dagenham, Essex, and was included in the Premier League club's youth set-up from under-7 level in a team also consisting of Jack Wilshere, Emmanuel Frimpong, Jonjo Shelvey and Luke Ayling. Following his release from the under-11s, he joined boyhood team West Ham, spending a season on their books before being let go, after being deemed to lack the necessary pace to be a central defender. Then park football offered him the chance to rebuild.

'I joined Harold Hill Youth, who played in the Echo Junior Football League and were managed by Ricky Shelvey, the dad of Jonjo Shelvey. I had played with Jonjo at Arsenal before he moved to West Ham. He sometimes trained with his dad's team, mainly practising taking free-kicks from the edge of the box for an hour. I enjoyed those days. It was a decent-enough standard with regular boys, less pressure and I was playing as a central midfielder, after deciding I no longer enjoyed it at centre-half.

'I earned a trial with Charlton Athletic. Jonjo was now there and his dad knew the coaches. The weirdest thing was I ended up on corner duty. They wanted somebody to take them so I volunteered. No one was going to do it. I hadn't taken one before, so thought I'd try whipping in a few. It went well there and they asked me back, but I suffered an ankle injury and didn't really want to return, so that was that. My confidence was low, having been rejected by Arsenal and West Ham. I didn't want to go back into the academy system, so there was an element of relief when I left Charlton.

'While studying A levels in sixth form at The Coopers Company and Coborn School in Upminster, Greater London, I played for youth teams at Harlow and then Bishop's Stortford, progressing into the latter's reserve side, before training with the first team who competed in the Conference South, but I wasn't involved on match days. Then, just before my eighteenth birthday, I was invited for a two-week trial with Tottenham Hotspur, whose academy was headed by John McDermott, with Alex Inglethorpe as coach.

'I can recall Harry Kane being in the dressing room one time. He was a year younger, although I didn't really know of him at the time, but what stuck in my head was the kitman asking what Under Armour he wanted and whether he preferred a shirt to be long-sleeved or short-sleeved. It turned out he was getting fitted, having been called up to the first-team squad for the first time, a 2–0 Carling Cup win over Everton, for which he was an unused substitute.

'The manager was Harry Redknapp, and I spotted Jonathan Woodgate and Ledley King in the treatment room. However, there was no reserve side at Spurs. Instead the development policy was to loan out players who had graduated from the academy. Of my age group, there was John Bostock, Ryan Fredericks and Nathan Byrne, but I wasn't taken on. They told me I wouldn't have been ready to head out on loan after just seven months with the club. They would keep an eye on me, though, and advised me to finish my A levels and go to university, which I did. I qualified with an A in history, an A in PE, a B in maths and a C in AS physics. Unfortunately, it wasn't enough to meet the University of Nottingham's conditional offer to study history. Instead I went to the University of Birmingham, which was a great city for a student and whose football team played in a higher British Universities league.'

Burgess possesses the curious distinction of playing football at Wembley and cricket at Lord's, albeit the latter in the MCC Indoor Cricket School situated at the back of the ground. This month's dramatic 3–2 win over Exeter City has ensured that he will return to the home of football for the Leasing.com Trophy final, as Pompey seek to retain the honour they secured the previous year. The Fratton Park encounter with their League Two opponents was made memorable on the basis of the final eleven minutes, plus time added, which proved so pivotal to the outcome. When Burgess' outstretched right leg steered Joel Randall's left-wing cross past team-mate Alex Bass for an unfortunate own goal, it handed the visitors a 2–1 advantage with one minute remaining.

There appeared to be no way back for the EFL Trophy holders, yet they staged a remarkable fightback during time added on to claim a stunning 3–2 victory. Firstly, Cameron McGeehan's left-footed lob from the edge of the area cleared goalkeeper Lewis Ward, with a little assistance from a deflection, to level in front of a delirious Fratton end. Then, six minutes into stoppage time, Ronan Curtis cleverly controlled Tom Naylor's diagonal lofted pass on his chest before driving in a left-footed cross which was headed home at the far post by John Marquis. On for the injured Ellis Harrison midway through the first half, it represented the striker's thirteenth goal of the season and capped an improbable result for the League One side who had largely struggled to shine for the occasion.

Some eight years earlier, Burgess was a member of the Walmley Cricket Club team that progressed to the ECB Indoor National

Club Championships at Lord's. While at Birmingham University, he represented the Sutton Coldfield-based cricket club, who several years earlier had supplied Chris Woakes to Warwickshire and, subsequently, England. As a talented batsman, Burgess opened for Walmley during their summer season and, when attention turned to the indoor cricket league, was part of the six-a-side team which in March 2012 ventured to Lord's. However, they slipped to a 36-run defeat, with Burgess removed by the second ball he faced, although he did claim two for 27 from three overs with the ball. Now he has the prospect of a second Wembley appearance to accompany that Lord's outing.

'While I played football for the university, I never featured for the cricket side as it was asking a lot to represent two different teams. I wanted to play proper league cricket in the summer before going home to turn out for Wanstead, although I did talk to the cricket boys, including Toby Tarrant, son of Chris Tarrant, who was also on my history course and is now a DJ on Radio X.

'I represented Walmley for two seasons and featured for their indoor team during the winter of my second year, playing our home games at Edgbaston's cricket centre. We reached the ECB Indoor National Club Championships, with the semi-finals and final staged at the MCC Indoor Cricket School. I was caught at mid-off trying to hit a six during our defeat, but we were still one of the best four teams in the country and I have a medal to show for it.

'I focused on football at university and Mark Burke, a former player with Aston Villa and Middlesbrough, was brought in to help our team, which contained loads of ex-academy players. He arranged a two-day trial for me with Middlesbrough and, when I was invited to return, I produced one of my best-ever games against Scunthorpe United reserves in front of the first-team manager, Tony Mowbray, who handed me a two-year deal. Having completed two years of my history course at Birmingham, I transferred to Teesside University. Considering my football commitments, the final year had to instead be spread over two years, consisting of a couple of evening lectures a week. I finished with a first.

'The season after I was turning out for the university, I made my Championship debut in front of 31,375 at Sheffield Wednesday. I was on the right of a back three which also contained Andre Bikey and Rhys Williams, the older brother of future Pompey team-mate Ryan.'

Following a maiden Peterborough season which consisted of 33 appearances and four goals, Burgess found himself transfer-listed in the summer of 2015, discovering the surprise development through the club's Twitter account. Then, while holidaying with friends in Hvar, Croatia, he received a phone call from the Posh's director of football, Barry Fry, informing him of Pompey's interest, with contact subsequently made by Paul Cook and then Mark Catlin as the potential move gathered pace.

With Peterborough having paid to recruit the defender from Middlesbrough twelve months earlier on a four-year deal, they required a fee, ruling out other suitors, such as Scunthorpe, but not the Blues. In June 2015, Burgess became new boss Cook's seventh recruit, joining the likes of Kyle Bennett, Kal Naismith, Enda Stevens and Gary Roberts, all of whom would be linchpins of the side that clinched the League Two title two seasons later. Yet during that glorious 2016–17 campaign came the flashpoint involving Burgess and skipper Michael Doyle in a half-time brawl during a match with Stevenage in November 2016. It resulted in the substitution of both – and the defender requiring ten stitches in a head wound as the Blues slipped to a 2–1 defeat at Fratton Park.

'While coming off the pitch for half-time, I remember David Forde shouting, but I didn't really know if it was directed at me, so ignored it,' admitted Burgess. 'The match was goalless at that point and I thought I'd done all right. Granted, we were not playing as well as we should, but were solid and not looking like conceding. I certainly couldn't think of anything I had done wrong. We returned to the dressing room and I took my usual place next to Doyler, only for Fordie to come in shouting at me, something about a backpass.

'I was trying to remember the incident and replied, "What are you talking about?" Now he has a bit of a temper and suddenly I was answering him back. Then Doyler piped up. As captain, he had something to say, while I considered myself a senior player, a regular in the team who led by example, so I had a bit to say too! From there it kicked off and ended up a bit bloody. After a few choice words between Doyler and myself, I shouted, "Come on then," leading to him grabbing my head. I'm picking him up, falling onto the bench, with the boys diving in to stop us. During the mayhem, his flailing foot caught me on the head, although the damage looked a lot worse than it was.

'My long hair had fallen over my face and I couldn't see anything during the ensuing melee but can remember feeling a little numb in my head and thinking, "What's that?" Then blood started coming down. I headed to the medical room, where the doctor applied ten stitches, but a quick bandage around the head and I would be fine to carry on. It all calmed down and Cookie popped in to see if I was okay, which I was. Then I heard the boys leaving for the second half and Leam Richardson came in to inform me that I wouldn't be going back out with them: "The gaffer says you and Doyler are both off."

'I was raging with a decision I didn't believe was necessary. The substitutes were outside on the pitch and were unaware of what had happened. Our coach Ian Foster had to go out and tell them they had two minutes to warm up!'

Further developments after the dressing-room incident escalated Cook's anger, yet succeeded in bonding the squad closer, including Burgess and Doyle. Following the Stevenage fracas, Pompey's boss ruled that the players' Christmas night out In Portsmouth, scheduled for that evening, was now cancelled. His team instead opted to go out in Southampton but the manager soon discovered their disobedience.

'The Christmas night out was pulled, along with travelling to Winter Wonderland in Hyde Park the following day, but we went out anyway,' added Burgess. 'In our group WhatsApp chat, the decision was made to start off at a pub near Whiteley, before moving into Southampton. So, there I was, at the start of the evening, sitting opposite Doyler, with a beer.

'He felt terrible about the incident. When the boys had gone back out for the match, he came into the medical room and apologised. For me it was nothing, one of those things. It happens in the changing room – I have seen it before and I have seen it since. We made up, had a hug, went out that night and shared a few beers with the boys; even Fordie was there with his soft drink. On the Sunday morning, we all received a text from Leam Richardson which read: "Listen, we've had a think about it, have Monday off, go out and enjoy yourselves on Sunday, you need to get together." We had already done it, of course. Happy days!

'With our London hotels still booked and table for a meal reserved for the Sunday, we headed there by train in dribs and drabs and met up for a great night of camaraderie and team spirit. It was tremendous fun, the best night I'd ever had with a football club. At one point, Enda Stevens requested the song 'All I Do Is Win' by DJ Khaled and from then on we sang it every time they brought drinks out. It became our dressing-room anthem whenever we beat someone, with a 1–0 win at Grimsby Town the following match its first airing.

'Anyhow, Cookie eventually found out about us drinking on the Saturday night, going against his wishes. He got us together on our return to training on the Tuesday and asked if anyone was not involved. The only one to put his hand up was Liam O'Brien. We gave him a look! The punishment was laps of the training ground all day, no footballs and no talking to the coaches, but we were all having a right laugh in our own bunches. If anything, it made our bond stronger and we became a really tight unit.

'There was still the matter of how Pompey would punish Doyler and me for what happened in the dressing room. For a time, the club were basically saying Doyler was done. Some of the hierarchy favoured getting rid of him and I was asked what I thought but I didn't want that to happen. As much as he has a fiery side to him, he would be a key part in trying to earn us promotion. We ended up winning League Two. Without him it could have been a lot different.

'When we returned to Portsmouth after winning promotion at Notts County, we went out celebrating and Doyler was the worse for wear. We headed to the Grosvenor Casino in Gunwharf late on and they wouldn't let him in – he didn't know where he was and was staring at the floor. I couldn't leave him outside in the street, so walked him back to mine, which was nearby, and let him stay there, before meeting back up with the lads for some more celebrating.

'I was very surprised when Paul Cook left that summer. We'd heard rumours, but he had just given Kyle Bennett a new three-year deal. The pair of them were close, regularly speaking on the phone. Benno was his player and told us that Cookie had assured him he wouldn't be going. Then Cookie left. I didn't begrudge him, that's football, and he knows more than me about why he arrived at that decision.'

With the end of February approaching, the Blues find themselves still involved in three competitions, ample motivation for Burgess as he contemplates the possibility of departing on a high. Pompey are embroiled in a gruelling schedule of sixteen matches in ten weeks, including the FA Cup visit of Arsenal and the Leasing.com Trophy trip to Wembley.

In terms of League One, they presently occupy sixth spot, four points adrift of leaders Rotherham United with a game in hand and scheduled to meet at the New York Stadium in April. With nine points separating the top eleven sides, the congested promotion race continues. Burgess is eyeing a glorious finale to the campaign and potentially his five-year Fratton Park love affair. Or maybe not.

He added: 'The longevity of my next contract is my priority. I am 29 in October; I don't really want to extend at Pompey for one year because then you're back in the same boat. A season passes quickly, suddenly it's January and once again you have six months remaining. You see older players getting one year here and there, and sometimes people just retire because they don't want that. You're like a franchise T20 player – you have no security, you can't settle anywhere and I'm not that old for a centre-half. I've received offers for three years, which is the longevity I want and will be a factor in my decision. In the meantime, I'm fully focused on trying to get Pompey promoted.

'I have been speaking to Gareth Evans, who has a year left from next summer and is currently out of the team. We've talked about how good it would be if we left having managed to achieve promotion. That's what we set out to do from the start: to take Pompey back to the Championship. I could leave a happy man, the happiest man in the world, I would be ecstatic. It would be a dream come true to accomplish what we said we'd do.

'Would I stay if we reached the Championship? Possibly, but there are other things to consider. Can Pompey then stay up? Is the funding going to be there for what is a tough league? Besides, if we go up, I might not be selected. Hypothetically speaking, players will need to be recruited and, while I may have played a big part in winning promotion, I could return to being fourth choice and not enjoying it. There are so many ifs and buts, and so much you have to consider. Let's just focus on playing football first.'

ANDY MOON AND GUY WHITTINGHAM

4 March 2020

Andy Moon's place in FA Cup history is assured, the soundtrack to Pompey's finest hour since their Wembley heyday. The BBC Radio Solent stalwart's passionate description of Andre Green's last-gasp winner earned *Match of the Day* billing and gushing commendation via social media as the city basked in its underdog achievement. It was January 2019 when substitute Green netted five minutes into time added on to beat Premier League-bound Norwich City at Carrow Road in one of the most eye-catching results of the FA Cup's third round. The commentary from Moon and trusted summariser Guy Whittingham indelibly captured that glorious moment which remains cherished, particularly by the pair themselves.

Now, another creative opportunity has arisen, with Arsenal scheduled for a Fratton Park visit in the fifth round of this year's competition. For the first time since departing the Premier League a decade earlier, Pompey host high-calibre opposition in the form of the Gunners, who are undergoing something of a rebuild following Mikel Arteta's mid-season appointment. Calling the occasion will be Moon, who first commentated on Pompey in the FA Cup during the wilderness years in the aftermath of their 2008 and 2010 Wembley appearances.

'Immediately upon reflection of that Norwich moment, I felt the commentary was probably okay; certainly I hoped I'd done Andre Green's strike justice. It never occurred to me that it would go viral,' said Moon. 'While you love commentating on 25-yarders smashed into the top corner, it's really nothing and then everything. The best kind of goal to commentate on are those which build from the back, so you can go through the gears before the moment culminates with a finish.

'On the way home from Carrow Road, Guy was driving, with me in the passenger seat, and at one point on the M25 both of our phones lit up with message after message. We had no idea what was going on until I scrolled through to realise our voices had been used on *Match of the Day*. Nobody had told us that would be happening!

'It was the perfect storm. With it being the late FA Cup game of the day, I don't think they had time to redub it with another commentator. Besides, they hadn't bothered to send anyone to the game. It was my first time at Carrow Road and the most notable moment in eight seasons of commentating on Pompey. You can't beat a last-minute winner against a club like Norwich in the FA Cup.

'I was shocked at the subsequent fan reaction; I didn't quite expect it. It's nice when a bit of your work receives recognition and reminds you of the privileges of the job. People have told me that they were jumping around their living rooms when they heard the goal being described, and it makes you realise just how special moments like that are to people. In my mind, I was very, very controlled the entire way through Green's goal, a belief I held until a few months ago. Then, for some reason, a work colleague played it back and I realised you could hear the emotion in my voice at the very end. It certainly wasn't as controlled as it felt at the time.

'You want a little emotion to come out. Sam Matterface's famous Pedro Mendes goal for Pompey against Manchester City was fantastic – that really was pure emotion of a moment – yet ideally you hope to maintain control in your voice. It's interesting; back in April 2012, I commentated on David Norris' dramatic Pompey equaliser at St Mary's. Tony Husband was originally meant to be calling the game but there was a late shuffle, so at the last moment I was brought into the Radio Solent team. Having listened back to it since, I was a novice commentator and by the end of the match my voice had basically gone. I just couldn't project the emotion. With experience, your voice becomes stronger, you learn how to look after it, but at that moment I wasn't able to generate the force I wanted.

'I don't like to rehearse things – just let it flow and some moments you will get brilliantly right. I did okay for the Green goal, but unfortunately didn't nail the Norris moment. That's life: you'll get some right and some wrong. I tried to speak to Andre Green about it a couple of times. He was such a quiet guy who didn't really chat too much, and within two weeks had returned to parent club Aston Villa from his loan. However, a few of his team-mates came up to make comments, while assistant manager Joe Gallen still jokes: "Without Andre Green, you still wouldn't have your moment." He's right!'

Born and bred on Hayling Island, with parents Colin and Frances still residing there, Moon has an affinity for the area. The 33-year-old attended Oaklands Catholic School in Waterlooville, an educational institution which boasts Southampton and England midfielder James Ward-Prowse among its alumni, although an association not entirely embraced by all pupils. Coincidentally, Pompey's long-serving media manager, Neil Weld, was in the same year as Moon's sister, Nicola, two years above. Long after all three had left Oaklands, Express FM's Pompey commentator Liam Howes also attended the school.

Moon graduated with a first in maths and computer science from Nottingham University, cutting his broadcasting teeth on university radio station URN, initially during an hour-and-a-half Wednesday evening sports show called 'The Score'. Then, following service as Radio Solent's non-league reporter, he was granted a first taste of Pompey action in October 2011, reporting on a 2–0 Fratton Park victory over

Barnsley, with Norris and Luke Varney the scorers. The following 2012–13 campaign saw the Blues inhabiting League One as Moon became the radio station's designated Pompey man.

He added: 'That first season was a real baptism of fire. From a football point of view, it wasn't amazing, and from a journalistic point of view I was probably way out of my depth. I was still working as a computer programmer for Xyratex, an offshoot of IBM, based in Langstone Technology Park, Havant, and I was sometimes required to visit factories in Malaysia and Japan.

'At the same time, I was trying to figure out what was going on at Pompey, which was a really good journalistic challenge, although I found myself behind the eight ball a fair few times. It wasn't until the arrival of Paul Cook as manager in May 2015 that things picked up for Pompey, although he was a challenge to deal with. He was far better for the written press than he was for me!

'He was in a constant rush to complete his post-match interviews, at times coming out of the dressing room shaking. He was either angry or buzzing following the result, and very emotional. You were always in danger of lighting the blue touchpaper and I did that a few times, in particular after an FA Cup victory against Macclesfield Town in November 2015 when I asked if he was happy with the performance. We ended up bickering for a minute. He was returning one-word answers and I recall thinking, "Just keep asking the question and keep going." Eventually he realised he had been a bit unfair and the interview carried on as normal, with Cook making jokes about it by the end.

'Pre-match press conferences on a Thursday afternoon were far different. Afterwards he'd speak off the record, often showing us statistics and the reasoning behind his decisions. From a journalistic point of view, it was fascinating to gain an insight into his thought process. I would enter those occasions with three dummy questions written on my piece of paper. Cook normally wanted to rant about something, whether it was Danny Murphy's opinions, football phone-ins or managers not receiving enough time in the job, so I carried two or three questions with the aim of drawing out that rant, before moving on to issues I felt were more significant. My interviews could last for seven minutes, but the first two responses would be deleted. You just had to move on from his bugbear of the week.

'As a manager, Cook really took everything quite personally. He was desperate to succeed. I think he underestimated how big a club Pompey was when he arrived at Fratton Park and he'll probably admit that himself. Yet there was always that unshakable faith in what he was doing. The reason he loved chatting after a pre-match press conference was because he wanted to emphasise that he wasn't just making arbitrary decisions; they were for good reason.

'That League Two title season was fantastic in many ways, but there were still incredibly low moments, such as the goalless Fratton Park draw with Hartlepool United, a 4–0 home win over Mansfield Town when supporters were booing him, while I missed the infamous Crewe Alexandra defeat as I was skiing. In the previous campaign, I remember Dagenham & Redbridge in April 2016, when it was toxic in the away end at half-time with the Blues losing 1–0, before Cook's side ran out 4–1 winners. Those final two months of the 2016–17 season were absolutely amazing, but even at that point I wasn't certain that Pompey were going to run away with League Two – you still thought the play-offs would happen again.

'I've always had a special bond with Meadow Lane: I did my first radio commentary there, it was the city where I went to university and I would watch Notts County. So, for Pompey to seal promotion to League One there meant a lot. After twenty minutes of driving home following that 3–1 win, our Radio Solent team stopped off for a beer and to breathe in what we had just witnessed. There was that adrenaline of the last hour. I had succeeded in climbing down onto the balcony where the players were celebrating in order to broadcast their views, while Kris Temple had managed to find Paul Cook's wife for an interview.

'The emotion struck afterwards, but you just needed to stop and realise what a special afternoon you had just experienced. I was extremely glad to have someone else driving the car home. I fell asleep, mentally drained, exhausted from it. That really was a likeable group of players and it was great to see them achieve the success the club had for so long been crying out for.'

Guy Whittingham wasn't occupying his customary position alongside Moon for Arsenal's FA Cup visit, instead preferring the company of Kolo Touré, Michael Carrick and Steve McClaren that Monday evening. As the Football Association's UEFA Pro Licence lead tutor since 2017, the 55-year-old is largely based at St George's Park, the national football centre situated in Burton upon Trent, Staffordshire. On the occasion of the Gunners' visit to Fratton Park for FA Cup action, Whittingham was overseeing a sixth of seven modules in the coaching course, with those present including Touré, Carrick, Exeter boss Matty Taylor, Bournemouth first-team coach Simon Weatherstone, Shaun Derry and former Mexico World Cup manager Juan Carlos Osorio. In addition, guest speakers included McClaren, Brighton & Hove Albion chief executive Paul Barber and Millwall boss Gary Rowett.

The stand-in among the three-strong Radio Solent coverage team for Arsenal was Danny Rose, a favourite from the 2016–17 League Two title-winning side and now seeing service at Swindon Town. The midfielder is on target for a remarkable fourth promotion from League Two, with the Robins presently three points clear of Crewe Alexandra with a game in hand. Whittingham has been a press box companion of Moon's since August 2014, the former striker renewing match-day radio duties just nine months after his dismissal as Pompey boss.

He is impeccably qualified for the role, as an inductee in the club's inaugural Hall of Fame following two goal-plundering spells, including 47 goals in the 1992–93 campaign. Later employed as Pompey's under-21s coach by Tony Adams, he progressed into the first-team set-up under Steve Cotterill, then, following Michael Appleton's decision to quit for Blackpool in November 2012, Whittingham was handed the longest caretaker boss tenancy in club history, totalling 29 matches.

'The administrator, Trevor Birch, asked whether I'd be prepared to be the caretaker manager for the foreseeable future. Within five days I was told that I needed to cut a million pounds from the wage bill by January!' smiled Whittingham.

'Izale McLeod was the biggest earner followed by Lee Williamson and, being on month-to-month deals, they had to leave, along with others. It was only fair the players were treated honestly. I didn't want to spring it on them in a few months that they'd no longer be needed. Besides, you wanted to give them a reasonable chance of being able to find somewhere else.

'McLeod wanted to get away, so was quite happy to leave immediately, mutually agreeing to end his month-long deal, and there certainly wasn't any animosity between us. Why would you want to keep playing for the club if you can arrange something else? He had a young family and was starting to build his own business, and we needed to save money on wages. Brian Howard's legs had gone and we needed energy in there. Darel Russell decided to join Toronto in the MLS, and as for Jon Harley, I see him every other week at Chelsea, where he is assistant coach in the development squad. We often chat about those times.

'Balancing the books didn't just involve the players, but also my staff, and, within a three-day spell, head of recruitment Luke Dowling, goalkeeping coach John Keeley and strength and conditioning coach Chris Neville had handed in their notices to join Michael Appleton at Blackburn. These were vital members of staff, so that's when the call to Alan Knight went in to help us out. We were having triallists in left, right and centre, including John Akinde's younger brother, Sam, while at one point Johnny Ertl worked out that we'd had 23 come into training over the course of two weeks. In total that season, we used 54 players in Pompey's first team. For a League Two trip to Scunthorpe United, we had just thirteen outfield players plus two goalkeepers. Fortunately, the Glanford Park pitch was frozen and failed an inspection the day before, otherwise we would have struggled.'

January 2013 was a tumultuous month for Pompey and their caretaker boss, signalling twelve playing departures, six arrivals, three backroom staff exits and a club in administration forced to slash employee wages by ten per cent. Whittingham's men lost all four of their fixtures, including a 5–0 New Year's Day humbling at Swindon Town, registering one goal across the entire month and having another two games postponed. They were also left without a training ground, unable to meet the rent at Wellington Sports Ground in Eastleigh, their home during those halcyon Premier League days.

Whittingham added: 'I suppose the caretaker boss is there to hold the team together until the club appoint a new manager. Considering the length of time I was in charge for and responsibilities such as finances and recruitment, I was acting like a proper manager. After being booted out of Wellington Sports Ground, there was the issue of where to train. Following my press conference ahead of a game against Notts County, we had to finish packing up, with the local media helping load the sofa we had just sat on into the back of a waiting van!

'At one stage we held talks with Hampshire County Cricket Club chairman Rod Bransgrove about whether we could create a sporting arena at The Rose Bowl, with training facilities catering for football, cricket and gymnastics. We actually had some really good gym equipment from the Premier League days which we loaned to them. However, the training link-up wasn't to be. It was felt that there lacked sufficient land for a football club. Instead we lived on a week-to-week existence, using playing surfaces at St John's College, Eastney Barracks, South Downs College, Furze Lane and, of course, Fratton Park.

'You only have to look at training grounds these days to understand how important the quality of the pitches are in terms of achieving success. Players need to feel comfortable and be able to do what is asked of them during practice. At Furze Lane, the contour of the pitch was like an ocean; you'd get seasick! Up and down those slopes, we picked up a couple of hamstring injuries and quite a few back problems, with Simon Ferry the major one. Obviously, AstroTurf is a more stable playing surface, but there are players with certain injuries that can be aggravated by it. Some of the older ones, plus Jack Whatmough with his knee history, couldn't use them. Instead players had to spend time in the gym, which meant you were unable to work on tactical play or even kick a ball around to maintain touch.'

With Pompey avoiding liquidation as supporters seized ownership in April 2013, they emerged from administration to appoint Whittingham on a one-year rolling contract as permanent boss. Despite relegation to League Two and a club record 23 games without victory, the Blues ended a wretched campaign on an optimistic footing, losing just three of their final twelve fixtures.

During the summer of 2013, Whittingham set about signing sixteen players to complement an existing crop of promising home-grown youngsters such as Jed Wallace and Adam Webster. There were returning quintet Patrick Agyemang, Phil Smith, Yassin Moutaouakil, David Connolly and Johnny Ertl, in addition to eleven fresh faces as the Blues scoured the free-transfer market to complete a massive squad overhaul.

Popular physio Steve Allen had been appointed as Whittingham's assistant manager, combining the roles, while retaining a pivotal presence in player recruitment, utilising an extensive contact list. The legendary Pompey striker would embark on fulfilling League Two promotion expectations armed with the lowest playing budget in modern Blues history by some distance, yet at a refreshed and rejuvenated club.

'We entered that 2013–14 season with a £1m playing budget, which was decent at that level, probably halfway up the league,' said Whittingham. 'I completely understood why. We had just been through two administrations and nobody wanted the club to return to such dark days. The most important thing was that Pompey had survived and continued to survive, and I was happy with that. The only thing we perhaps should have changed was to increase the player salary cap from £1,500 a week to £2,000. Had I been allowed that, we would have recruited one or two better footballers, and then it's up to me to fit people in using the remaining budget. To give you an idea, we had six players earning above the £1,500 mark during the previous season but that cap meant I couldn't go out and get us a striker.

'I tried to recruit a League Two striker, but a non-league club offered more than £1,500 a week. I was hoping the Pompey name would sway him, but it didn't. When you have conversations with people in charge, considering they are fans, they'll respond with, "Why would he go anywhere else? This is Pompey." Well, it's because they have a mortgage and a family to bring up and have been offered £250 a week more to go somewhere else. I am not blaming the club; that was the situation. They didn't want to enter into debt, so budgeted for what they believed crowds would be – they weren't to know. By the end of August, considering attendances were so good, I was informed I'd receive another £200,000 for my playing budget, which was great. The drawback was that I couldn't spend it until the transfer window opened in January and I had gone by then!

'We had to look at ways of recruiting and the physio, Steve Allen, was a big help. He knew Yassin Moutaouakil and David Connolly, while Romain Padovani was initially a triallist. On Padovani's first day of training, you're thinking, "Wow, he's a player," but we didn't have enough time to develop him. He was obviously a skilful footballer, but he needed to learn the English way a little. We got some recruitment wrong, definitely, but I've always said it takes several transfer windows to put together the team you want. Still, I thought we got some decent young players in, with a number going on to have decent careers at this level or above.

'As mentioned before, we lost out on lots of players, another one being Adebayo Akinfenwa early in the 2013–14 season. We went for him on loan from Gillingham and the striker wanted to come – we thought we had him too – then their manager, Peter Taylor, changed his mind. I have no idea of the reason; I still don't know why. The biggest setback was our first-choice goalkeeper Simon Eastwood joining Blackburn Rovers in May 2013. If I look back, that was the development which hurt the team the most. We really rated him following an impressive first season at Fratton Park and he was going to sign a new three-year deal, but changed his mind at the very last minute. His girlfriend was pregnant and wanted to move back up north, where they were from, plus our former goalkeeping coach John Keeley was at Ewood Park.

'I had to find another keeper, but who were we going to get? I phoned around to see who was out there and the name of John

Sullivan was put to me by his agent, Jamie Hart, the son of Paul Hart. Sully had done well at AFC Wimbledon the previous season, helping keep them in the Football League during a loan spell from Charlton Athletic, with manager Neal Ardley keen to sign him permanently. In terms of how it developed with him keeping goal for us, you have to look at yourself. Phil Smith was his back-up and then, following a couple of blunders, we changed them over, then swapped them again. Did I handle it properly? Probably not.

'Away at York City was Sully's seventh match and I don't believe I managed him well after a 4–2 defeat in which he made several costly errors. Footballers can be harsh and football is harsh – there is no soft way, no hiding place. Maybe he should have been able to cope with it better, but I was the one looking after him. As a manager, I was also learning at the time. The goalkeeping situation was not a good one during that time and demonstrated the importance of recruiting a number-one target, which should have been Eastwood.

'We also held high hopes for Simon Ferry, who I thought would have been a great player, but he never really got fit. He was a free agent and other clubs hadn't wanted him for some reason, although Matt Ritchie recommended him personally and his agent was a really good guy. Ferry had constant back problems though and I don't believe all the training ground stuff helped that injury. If granted time, we could have put a decent side together, but you know very well that football's about results. We weren't getting them.'

Whittingham was dismissed in November 2013, following a 2–1 home defeat to managerless Scunthorpe United, a fourth successive defeat in all competitions. Upon the final whistle there were boos among the 14,550 crowd, along with a distinctive Fratton End rendition of 'That was embarrassing.' Crucially, Pompey's seven-man board would take notice of that supporter reaction when gathering the following day to assess the future of a manager whose side had slipped concerningly to eighteenth in League Two. Whittingham was oblivious to such machinations, carrying out press commitments in Fratton Park's media room on the Monday afternoon ahead of a midweek home fixture with high-flying Southend United. The Blues boss had no inclination that, within two hours, his 21-game reign as permanent manager would be over, the first managerial casualty of fan ownership.

Whittingham said: 'I can recall thinking, "If I don't take this job now, am I going to get another chance?" Plus Iain McInnes had told a press conference that this wasn't a sacking club and that the manager would be present for the long term. You naturally believe what they are saying. The board actually wanted me to bring in an experienced head to assist and, looking back, I probably should have done. Perhaps that could have bought me a little more time, somebody to liaise with the hierarchy as maybe I didn't fulfil that aspect too well.

'Still, it doesn't matter how successful you have been in the past or how experienced you are, if you're not pleasing the crowd then they will let you know. Obviously, they were letting people know that they didn't believe I was good enough. Ultimately, the board agreed. That Monday, I had carried out my usual pre-match media duties, missing a call from Mark Catlin in the meantime, and was on the way to open a Petersfield old people's home for a friend of Iain McInnes. Then I received a call from the chairman. He asked if I could instead go round to his Warsash house for a chat. I had no inkling as to the reason behind it, as nothing had been mentioned on the phone. When I walked in, I saw Mark Catlin and Tony Brown and thought: "Okay, what's going on here then?" That's when I twigged.

'Just two weeks earlier, I had been told that we needed to be in the play-off positions by January, which was okay, no problem, and we were four points away. I backed myself as there were decent games coming up. Then a fortnight later I was gone. It's about results, I accept that, and they wanted to head in a different direction, fair enough, but it doesn't mean I liked it, though. They wanted to release a statement about my departure, saying that it was by mutual agreement, even though it clearly wasn't. I declined. I didn't want people thinking I had agreed to leave Pompey, as you still have to believe you are good enough.

'You could say that the decision to sack me was harsh considering two weeks earlier I'd been given an ultimatum to meet a target by January. However, that's football: they wanted results and those results weren't there. Ultimately, I wasn't good enough as Blues boss, but I gave it a go and when I see my name on that list of the club's managers, there's a lot of pride in there. I worked with some great people, the likes of Barry Harris, who would live and die for Pompey; it was a privilege.

'It took four managers until League Two promotion was achieved. The first person who took over was going to have a tough time, testing the water for everyone else. Having not been in such a position before, people make mistakes, even local businessmen in the boardroom, because football is totally different. I don't hold it against them because we were learning at the same time.'

In Whittingham's press-box absence, Arsenal inflicted a 2–0 defeat upon Pompey, eliminating them from the FA Cup. Nonetheless, it had been a heartening show from Kenny Jackett's side. The Blues boss surprisingly opted for six changes for the occasion: among those dropped were skipper Tom Naylor, star man Ronan Curtis, ever-improving centre-half Sean Raggett and fourteen-goal leading scorer John Marquis. What unfolded was a resolute display from the hosts, who had some fine attacking moments before Arsenal's Sokratis Papastathopoulos rifled home the breakthrough during first-half stoppage time. The Premier League club doubled their advantage six minutes after the interval through Eddie Nketiah to effectively settle the encounter, yet Pompey remained resilient, refusing to capitulate.

With the distraction of the FA Cup removed, Jackett's men still have a Wembley trip to look forward to in the form of next month's Leasing.com Trophy fixture with Salford City. Escaping League One remains the priority, however, with the third-placed Blues now three points short of Rotherham United in the second automatic promotion spot, with a game in hand.

Moon added: 'The turnaround under Kenny Jackett has been remarkable. Off the back of October's AFC Wimbledon defeat, there was the unmistakable feeling that the majority of fans wanted him out. I know he has always retained the complete backing of the owners, but losing two or three games in a row from that point would surely have forced a change in manager. You can always go on Twitter and find people wanting Pompey's manager to be sacked – even now – but around that period the voices were overwhelming. It was particularly noticeable during losses at Wycombe Wanderers and AFC Wimbledon, when some of those away supporters who pretty much see every Blues performance were calling for his head. The mood was definitely a little toxic.

'We are now in early March and I believe Pompey will finish in League One's top four. However, I'm fearful that their away form might cost them a place in the two automatic promotion slots. Looking at forthcoming away games, you feel they will beat an awful Southend, but there's also fellow promotion rivals Peterborough United, Oxford United and Rotherham. I can absolutely see them remaining unbeaten at Fratton Park and winning most of those home games, but if Jackett's side cannot pick up points on the road it will cost a place in the top two. I cannot see Pompey slipping out of the play-offs as they are too good at grinding out results. For quite a while I have estimated it's going to take 83–84 points to reach the top two. Jackett wears a poker face and he never gives anything away outwardly, but it must have hurt to hear fans from yards away at Kingsmeadow calling for his dismissal. To turn that round has been mightily impressive.'

Malcolm and Ben Close

Mick Hogan

Rog McFarlane

Marie and Dave Curtis

Christian Burgess

Andy Moon and Guy Whittingham

Ashley Brown

Mick Williams

Simon Colebrook

Iain McInnes

John Kimbell

Dom, Ellie-Mai and Sarah Merrix

Merrick
and Ian Burrell

Simon
and Ollie Milne

Johnny Moore

Abdul Khalique

Mark Catlin

ALAN KNIGHT
9 March 2020

F umbling around for an excuse, Alan Knight aborted his car journey and pulled into a pub at the Devil's Punch Bowl. He was supposed to be visiting his seriously ill mother, Joyce, in Chelsea's Royal Brompton Hospital, yet something more important had cropped up on that March 1989 evening: alcohol.

As a goalkeeper, he appeared 801 times for Pompey, representing the club in four different decades at all four levels of the Football League, sterling service recognised through the awarding of an MBE when his playing days had ended. Once alcoholism took hold, the man simply known as 'Legend' among Blues supporters was condemned to an existence of sleeping on the sofas of friends, while combating depression and suicidal thoughts.

Knight has now been dry for more than eleven years, has remarried and is employed as Pompey's club ambassador, a life transformation he credits to 28 days spent at the Sporting Chance Clinic, yet the memory of an evening seeking solace in a Surrey pub still gnaws.

He said: 'My mother had lung cancer and emphysema and I was on my way to see her in hospital. She wasn't going to get better but was supposed to be returning home to Balham the following day, with my father having gone back to set up the bedroom ready for her oxygen tanks.

'Halfway there, I stopped at a pub in the Devil's Punch Bowl and decided to have a drink. I needed to think up an excuse for why I could no longer go, a reason to stay there and continue drinking. I was going to use a bullshit story like the car had broken down and then drink and drink and drink. Alcohol was more important than seeing my dying mum – that's something I have to live with.

'I decided to call my parents' home and give my excuses, thinking my sister would be there to answer. Instead it was their next-door neighbour, who delivered a few home truths and told me to get my arse to the hospital. Thankfully, I listened. When I turned up, my mother was pretty pissed off with me. My whole demeanour and attitude at the time wasn't great. I was a bit of a big-time Charlie, focused on nobody but me. Being Pompey's number one had gone to my head and there I was trying to avoid seeing my seriously ill mother in hospital. As I left the hospital that evening, she told me: "You can love someone, but it doesn't mean you have to like them." They were the last words she said to me as she passed away that night.

'My light-bulb moment arrived while in residence at Sporting Chance almost twenty years later. I realised drink had taken over my life and all the shitty things I'd done revolved around putting alcohol ahead of more important things in life. Drink was more important to me than my parents. They were instrumental in my career, yet I wasn't very good to them towards the end of their lives.

'When Pompey hosted Southampton in April 2005, my dad, Ted, was admitted into Queen Alexandra Hospital with an abscess on his leg. He had gone in there kicking and screaming because he didn't want to leave his dog at home, moaning about how people never came out. I was Pompey's goalkeeping coach and, following that 4–1 win over Harry Redknapp's side, rang the hospital. I had planned to visit Dad after the game, but the lads were going out on the lash and I wanted to join them, any excuse. The ward sister told me he was currently sleeping but would be discharged the following day. Unfortunately, his leg developed sepsis and that evening he slipped into a coma. I never had the chance to speak to him again; he died 24 hours later. I could have at least given him half an hour after that game, but once again alcohol had a bearing.

'There was also the night my daughter, Rebekah, was born in 1992, when I was more concerned with going out in Havant to play snooker with the lads than being with my pregnant wife, Jennifer. I knew the birth was close, yet by the time I returned home I was pissed and couldn't drive and that evening she went into labour. I had previously been convicted of drink-driving in 1985 following a car crash, and any further transgression would have resulted in prison, so we ordered a taxi for St Mary's Hospital. That was me, being selfish rather than putting my family first. Drink was my God.'

Pressed into Pompey duty at the age of sixteen years and nine months, Knight marked his first-team entrance with a clean sheet during a 1–0 win at Rotherham United in April 1978. From that moment, the keeper from Balham, south-west London, established himself as a Fratton Park fixture. While Blues sides naturally evolved over the decades, Knight was the constant, a belligerent presence featuring in three promotions, a First Division play-off side and semi-finalists in the 1992 FA Cup. He was also a cornerstone of Alan Ball's iconic side of the mid-1980s, a hard-playing, hard-drinking outfit whose camaraderie was formed in the pub, creating riotous tales still rolled out with relish by supporters to this day. Knight's playing days spanned an era in which alcohol was a staple diet for the vast majority of footballers, who felt no intimidation when rubbing shoulders with supporters on a night out.

'I wouldn't drink 48 hours before a game – I had boundaries, rules around what I would do,' added Knight. 'Some may say I played as if I was pissed, but it wasn't true. Then, when I retired, those boundaries were no longer needed and I could drink when I liked. The wheels started falling off. I stopped going into work – I couldn't be bothered – and my routine involved sitting in the pub all day with people buying you drinks. People might think that sounds fantastic, but drinking wasn't fun at all; I hated it. Luckily Sporting Chance saved me. I could never see the point of just having one drink. If you're going to have a drink, then get smashed. There are those able to have the occasional drink – good for them – but I would have to get off my face.

'There was one occasion we had a drink the night before a game, certainly the only one I remember anyway, and that was away at Wolverhampton Wanderers for the final match of the 1990–91 campaign. Tony Barton was caretaker manager and there was nothing riding on the game. Normally we'd stay in a decent hotel, but this was more of a guest house. So, a few of us had some beers the night before. It wasn't mad, and it wasn't a case of go and get smashed, but we took liberties. I could try to make excuses, but we were out of order. I wasn't off my face and it didn't affect how we played, even if one or two others did go a little over the top, with the outcome being a 3–1 defeat.

'There was another occasion, during Frank Burrows' first spell as manager, when he dropped me for going out on New Year's Eve in 1979, despite not drinking. I was aged eighteen and, with a Fourth Division match against Aldershot the following day, sitting in my digs alone. Everyone else was out, so I decided to pop into the nearby Some Place Else Club in Palmerston Road at 11.50pm, just to see in the New Year – I wouldn't even have a drink. As soon as I walked in, the lads said, "What are you doing here?", so I left.

'I had a shocker against Aldershot the next day, done by three near-post corners in a 3–1 defeat, Alan Rogers netting our only goal for a last-minute consolation. In the dressing room afterwards, I saw the manager handed a piece of paper and, after reading it, he went berserk. Burrows pulled me aside and asked why, 48 hours before a game, I was seen in a place which served alcohol, breaking club rules. It also transpired Joe Laidlaw had partied that night and was another in big trouble with the gaffer. I hadn't drunk, but shouldn't have been there, lesson learned. As ever, it always gets back to the club; you think you're invisible, but everyone sees you. I was dropped after that incident and didn't play for the next thirteen matches, with Peter Mellor recalled. In fact, I played just twice more that season as we won promotion to the Third Division – although Joe Laidlaw remained in the side for the rest of the campaign!

'During Alan Ball's first reign, Wednesday was the night out for the boys and we always knew we'd get beasted by the manager on

Thursdays! The drinking culture was about building team spirit and, don't get me wrong, at the time it was fantastic – we were living the dream. However, the consequences weren't worth it. While I don't want to talk about other players' lives, looking back over the course of my time at Pompey and the lads I spent great times with, I have seen some of them go through living hell, while others have passed away. Was it worth it? At the time you think it is; there's nothing better, and you think you're indestructible, but that's not the case. As young men, you just don't think it's ever going to end.'

Knight's final appearance for his sole Football League club arrived in January 2000, featuring in a 2–1 First Division defeat at Norwich City, at the age of 38. Such distinguished service saw him named in the 2001 New Year's Honours List and invited to Buckingham Palace to receive his MBE from the Queen. It was a commemoration which warranted a congratulatory letter from Football Association chairman Geoff Thompson, albeit incorrectly sent care of The Dell with its accompanying Southampton address.

Keen to remain in the game upon retirement, he progressed into the role of the Blues' goalkeeping coach, helping nurture protégé and one-time goalkeeping rival Aaron Flahavan, a product of the club's youth system. Adjustment from playing was difficult, while, in August 2001, Flahavan died in a car accident outside Bournemouth having been three times over the legal limit. The goalkeeper was just 25 when he passed away, following 106 games in what appeared a richly promising career.

'There was the challenge of coming out of football, coping with that transition. I was never really comfortable leaving my playing days behind,' said Knight. 'The passing of Flav hit me hard, although I don't like to drag him in because that would be unfair, but that was a big loss for everyone, particularly myself. I was a goalkeeping coach with some fantastic keepers such as Flav, Shaka Hislop, Dave Beasant, Yoshi Kawaguchi and Pavel Srnicek, but it never replaced playing, and I probably didn't do myself any favours.

'Towards the end of my first spell as Pompey's goalkeeping coach, I wouldn't get out of bed, staying there all day, finding an excuse not to come into work – I was not in a good place. Then I went to America to work at FC Dallas in the MLS with my old Pompey team mate Colin Clarke and it was great for the opening six months, really good. I enjoyed the new culture and the team were doing well. Then my appendix burst and it became infected, causing an issue over a $100,000 medical bill, while on the pitch we were beaten in the play-offs by Colorado Rapids on penalties and Clarke was sacked. Coach Steve Morrow stepped up to be his replacement and asked me to stay, yet, despite the medical argument now being resolved, I missed my two daughters so came home in 2006. I probably should have stayed.

'I returned to England and everything had gone. I didn't have anything and slipped more and more into depression and the crutch of alcohol. There were suicidal thoughts; once I sat in a car contemplating getting a hosepipe. I'm not saying I would have gone through with it, but you think about scenarios involving the most painless way to achieve the end.'

The Sporting Chance Clinic would be Knight's salvation, agreeing to his pleas for admission in September 2008. The Liphook-based establishment provides support to current and retired sportsmen and women, offering residential care to treat individuals suffering from addictive disorders related to gambling, alcohol or drug abuse. Booked in for a 28-day programme with the PFA footing the bill, it changed Knight's life.

He said: 'It was around 7pm on a Saturday night and I was sitting in The Harvest Home, in Copnor, drinking with friends, when I burst into tears – enough was enough; something had to change. I was sofa surfing at the time as I didn't have a place to live, instead staying around the house of a friend, Paul Ridler. I had worn the same gear for three days running and earlier that afternoon walked past Fratton Park with a Pompey match about to be played. People were saying: "Knightsie, where has it all gone wrong?"

'I walked over Fratton Bridge back towards Copnor and could later be found standing outside Copnor Snooker Club having a fag with a pint in my hand. People would have noticed me. Then it was across the road to The Harvest Home for more beers. During the ensuing meltdown, my brother-in-law, Keith Viney, was called and took me back to his mother's, where I stayed overnight.

'The following morning, my daughters Jade and Rebekah came in and saw me, still the worse for wear. The look of concern and distress on their faces was the motivation I required, with calls soon made to Sporting Chance. I travelled there on the Thursday to be assessed, although I wasn't able to be included in the next intake for the 28-day course, which started on the Monday. I told them if I had to wait, I would be back on the beer. That night, they rang to say they had managed to juggle it, with two younger lads now prepared to share a room, which freed up space for me to stay. If it had been any longer it might have been a different story.

'Sporting Chance saved my life. I cannot speak any higher than that. When I entered, it consisted of two cottages around the back, with three main counsellors who were ex-users, including the late Peter Kay. It has since become more scientific, while courses can be tailored to suit those still employed. For instance, footballers who may be struggling are able to attend a five-day refresher, entering on a Sunday and coming out on a Friday to allow them to play a match at the weekend. Clubs prefer that approach to losing their player for 28 successive days.

'Going through the steps, you have to be brutally honest as there's no point in wasting your time. Some people enter rehab for a little breather, then get back on it again. I know it's a cliché, but you must hit rock bottom in order to provide the impetus and focus to not drink again. Some will attend to keep family members and employers happy, a motivation I would question. I have seen far too many people who have either been paid to go into rehab or instructed to by their loved ones. While that may be for the right reasons, in my experience it is more beneficial cutting them loose to find their own way, so they genuinely want to find a way through.

'My recovery was based around a holistic approach involving yoga, meditation, gym for fitness, and nutrition, in addition to the usual counselling sessions. One of my issues was being unable to sleep; it was terrible. I was sleeping on sofas at the time and my mind wouldn't shut off at night, with too many thoughts running through my head. I would worry about everything and anything. However, through medication and yoga I discovered I could switch off instead of fretting over who was going to buy the coffees in the morning and other scenarios driving you mad. These days I am proper grumpy if I don't have a good night's sleep. People often joke about me being in bed by 10pm, but it's what my body requires. I used to hate not being able to sleep, and the amount of people I talk to who struggle with sleep patterns is surprising. As part of our treatment, we would be taken to stables in Hindhead, blindfolded and encouraged to chat with horses, stroking them and leading them around, with the idea that horses can sense your fears. Well, horses scare me and I've not been anywhere near one since!

'I felt a little chucked back onto the street following my 28 days of treatment and it's a difficult adjustment. I was used to drinking and hanging around pubs, so suddenly my lifestyle had to change. I was asking myself, "Will I be dull if I don't have a drink? What am I going to do instead?" but it's up to the individual to replace the time you spend in a pub, normally through a pastime or hobby. To begin with, it was weird drinking Coca-Cola in pubs, which became a boring tipple of choice after a while, so then I tried lime and soda, and even non-alcoholic drinks such as Beck's Blue. Then I thought: "Why am I even bothering to have a beer if it's non-alcoholic?"

'I don't mind people drinking around me and I have no problem being around alcohol, although I can't stay very long in the company of drunk people as they bore me and normally get aggressive, which you don't need. My wife, Heather, will only have a couple of drinks on a night out. Should she want to stay, I'll leave and come back later to collect her. She probably enjoys herself better when I'm not there! Usually in a social situation, I can't deal with that goodbye crap, so normally I just go, without anyone noticing.

'I have lost friends since being sober. It's not that I've fallen out with them, but I just don't see certain people whose company I would have spent a lot of time in during the past. My mate Paul Ridler is a great lad who would do anything for you. He even let me sleep on his sofa, but it was bad for us to be together as we were two big drinkers. I could no longer be around him, which is nothing against Paul as that's not his fault, but it's important I do what I

have to do. I don't really see him any more, although now and again
I'll pop in or exchange texts, but life had to change.'

Following his time at the Sporting Chance Clinic, Knight rebuilt his
life, sharing a Waterlooville flat with friend John Hankey and gaining
employment with local company L. Jackson Groundworks Ltd. For one
of their contracts, he was required to dig holes at Heathrow Airport,
while during a snowy period he drove tractors with ploughs attached to
clear areas near runways.

Knight has served as Pompey's club ambassador since October
2013, having stepped down from a ten-month spell as goalkeeping
coach for Guy Whittingham's first team to fulfil the role which has
become a natural fit. Close attachment to Pompey in the Community
has seen him work on a number of health and rehabilitation
programmes with health trainer Paul Allen, in addition to a dementia
project. Knight is also patron of Age UK Portsmouth and has been an
unpaid presence on Express FM's Pompey match-day coverage over
the last six years, in addition to driving the club's media team to away
fixtures.

> He said: 'I have kept contact with Sporting Chance and, in the
> last few years, have returned to speak to residents about my life
> experiences, trying to help people get their lives back on track. No
> longer does it cater merely for footballers, golfers and jockeys. It
> has expanded into rugby and a whole host of other sports. I'm quite
> happy to share what I have learnt.
>
> 'The PFA are presently very interested in the mental health
> and wellbeing of footballers, which we are trying to introduce
> into the club in order to reach out to the professionals. Across the
> game, you hear of so many players struggling, young and old, with
> a number affected by mental health issues at different stages, so
> it's important to have safeguards in place. Everyone talks about
> injuries, such as breaks, sprains, pulls or ligaments, but the other
> big one is mental health.
>
> 'Pompey have been fantastic, appointing me as club ambassador
> more than six years ago and subsequently allowing me to construct

a role around it, working within the community and portraying a positive front, including attending funerals and supporting families. I also work with others within the club, such as new academy intakes. Part of the lads' induction involves me holding a talk educating them on wellbeing and mental health. My approach is to explain what has happened to me over 25 years, focusing on alcohol.

'When you go through it, you believe you're the only one. No one else has possibly experienced the same issues. You think nobody will take you seriously and that life is over. Then you speak to others and discover you're not alone after all. I've had dark thoughts, suicidal feelings, but there are people who understand and can help. The message is you don't have to suffer in silence.'

Knight has retained a hand in goalkeeping coaching this season, helping out with several academy age groups having answered former team-mate Mark Kelly's request for help during the club's ongoing search for a permanent employee. Having taken up the voluntary role two months before the end of last term, he has worked with a number of young keepers at the training ground including Leon Pitman, Petar Durin and triallist Taylor Seymour. The 58-year-old relinquished duties shortly before Christmas and can, of course, be found on match days circumnavigating Fratton Park's corporate lounges, chatting to supporters and observing Kenny Jackett's side's push for the Championship.

'I am a recovering alcoholic. It's there, you don't get cured – it's an ongoing process,' added Knight. 'Not having a drink shouldn't be regarded as an achievement as there are lots of people who don't consume alcohol. I am not saying I will never have a drink again – I don't think anyone can – but I'm unbelievably lucky. There are always reminders when addressing people at Sporting Chance and seeing friends going through the familiar problems.

'To be honest, I don't attend meetings focused on coping with alcoholism – it's not something I feel I need to help me. I have no qualms about them, and it's not something I find embarrassing.

I quite enjoy hearing some stories, some of which are uplifting, enlightening and funny. However others are harrowing and upsetting, which is probably why I don't want to attend. It brings me down a little hearing of people's relapses and their battle to start again – I sometimes find that difficult to listen to.

'It's nice when there's the passing of another anniversary of being free from alcohol, but I don't think too much about it. At this moment in time, remaining sober hasn't been difficult. I would love to say it has, but that's not the case. Smoking was probably tougher to give up, something I achieved eight years ago. During my playing days, a drinking session could see me smoke between 40 and 50 cigarettes a day, while I'd smoke around twenty a day normally.

'My wife, Heather, has been instrumental in conquering my addictions. We met at her ex-mother-in-law's funeral and were married within eighteen months, in July 2010. She's not a big drinker and hated me smoking. She's provided me with stability, love, support and belief which I never had. Then there's the extended family as a result, and three grandchildren – Amelia, Lily and Thomas – who have given me more focus. There are lots of people I need to thank for their help and patience during my recovery, but I would be here all day saying their names.

'In the past, everything was football, football, football, me, me, me. There's more than football. Your career can be overwhelming, rendering you blinkered, and sometimes imprisoning you within a bubble. There's more to your existence than your work. There's life.

Ashley Brown,
Mick Williams
and Simon Colebrook

13 March 2020

The phone call intruded upon a Friday evening at his South Hampshire home, yet, during such worrisome times, was accepted without hesitation by Ashley Brown. Hours earlier, the Premier League and Football League had postponed fixture programmes until 3 April as the coronavirus threat escalated. Overnight developments centring on Arsenal manager Mikel Arteta contracting the virus proved pivotal. Suddenly football was forced to initiate safety procedures. Pompey's players and staff that day were turned away from training and instructed to return home until testing kits could be obtained to assess their wellbeing, having come into contact with Arteta and his Gunners side during the FA Cup encounter eleven days earlier. As football's longest day turned into night, Brown was contacted by the National League's Michael Tattersall, with the chief executive eager to consult a trusted ally during unprecedented challenges.

As the Football Supporters' Association's head of governance, crisis club support and club liaison, Brown champions the rights of fans, in addition to pursuing football reform through lobbying the game's highest bodies. The softly spoken 50-year-old offers a richly respected insight, having been at the forefront of the Pompey Supporters' Trust's remarkable triumph, before residing on the Fratton Park board for the full duration of fan ownership. Now his leadership skills are required elsewhere.

Brown said: 'Last Sunday we got a whiff that games could soon either be suspended or potentially played behind closed doors, so, as a core group, we have been discussing our response and what we can do to support fan groups as well as clubs around the country. Today the Premier League and Football League programmes have been postponed. This scenario must be health-led – that is the most important thing here – but, as well as the health of people, there's going to be the health of clubs. This will be a very, very difficult time for them to survive.

'A lot operate purely on a hand-to-mouth basis and, should they lose match-day revenues, that's a big, big difference. It's not only your match-day tickets, but programmes, teas and coffees, bars, all gone. There isn't any other ongoing revenue. That's it, all dried up, yet that's what you rely on.

'In addition, a number of season tickets are bought on credit cards, and for some clubs that involves banks releasing the money on a game-by-game basis. In the absence of matches, this money will probably be withheld, so those clubs won't even have season-ticket money. In the meantime, you still have players and staff to pay and utilities costs, but no income. That may be okay for a week or two, but should it stretch into a month, two months or the rest of the season, that money is lost forever. There's a question fans must ask themselves, depending on what happens. If these games are not played or they are locked out, should supporters take a bit of a hit or argue that they want a refund? Those refunds could do permanent damage to a club.

'I have just taken a call from the chief executive of the National League updating me on their approach, which represents a slightly different stance. This weekend they are allowing clubs to take the decision whether or not they're going to play, which is understandable too. That initial response will then allow the National League more time to study evidence and consult before implementing their next move. There is the worry that if this goes on for a significant amount of time then more and more clubs will develop financial difficulties, from which they may never recover.

'Even before coronavirus, there were a number of clubs unable to pay the taxman, unable to pay players and staff, and that scenario will only worsen. Obviously, we don't want any club to disappear like Bury did earlier this season. I have been through it as a Pompey fan when we thought we were going to lose our club. I don't know how I would have felt if that had actually taken place, but luckily we survived. Macclesfield Town, Southend United, Oldham Athletic and Charlton Athletic are the ones probably taking up most of my time as far as crisis clubs are concerned. Oldham have been in court recently with the potential to be wound up, and Southend are rumoured to owe almost £700,000 to the taxman, let alone players.

'As for Charlton, what has cropped up this week seems to be repeating what happened to Bury, where people have managed to take over the club without providing all of the information to the Football League required to pass the fit and proper person's test. They are running at a significant loss and there doesn't appear anyone willing to prop them up with money. You also have an executive chairman in Matt Southall who has managed to pay himself a significant salary and award himself a flash apartment and a Range Rover SVR. As Pompey fans, we are familiar with these sorts of things and sadly they are still taking place.'

A blue plaque resides outside The Lady Hamilton pub, located in The Hard, to commemorate the founding fathers of the Pompey Supporters' Trust. On 29 October 2009, brothers Barry and Mark Dewing, Tony Foot, Micah Hall and Ken Malley gathered to discuss the creation of a football body to save the financially stricken club. Brown, a South Stand season-ticket holder, won election to the inaugural Trust board in the summer of 2010, later serving two spells as chairman, including during the period which would assure Pompey's continued existence at the High Court in April 2013. That represented a landmark occasion in Blues history, while Brown is convinced the supporters' successful fight also heralded essential change in the game's governance.

'I often say to the leagues or to MPs that fans are the best early-warning system, as was the case at Pompey. Knowledgeable supporters were the ones that first noticed the issues happening at the club and it's the same across the country,' added Brown. 'It's often fans who get in touch with us or the press to highlight issues and concerns at their club; they are a tremendous source of information. Anybody who writes off football supporters as individuals and says they can't run clubs is both naive and wrong. Every football club's attendance on a Saturday consists of a huge variety of skilled and knowledgeable people. Within those ranks are plenty willing to carry out the required research and investigation to uncover what is really going on.

'I believe football has learnt from what happened at Pompey, though. When we became the first Premier League club to enter administration, it prompted a whole set of rule changes and strengthening of governance. It really damaged the Premier League brand; they were embarrassed and didn't want it to ever happen again. When the Premier League does something, the Football League tends to follow, and there has undoubtedly been a bolstering of the rules, but it hasn't gone far enough, as we've seen recently.

'Things supposedly went quiet for a while, with the league boasting about not having seen a club enter administration for six years, then Bury and Bolton Wanderers showed that the cracks are still there. The likelihood is, if the coronavirus continues, we will see more clubs in massive trouble. The number of clubs that manage to survive tends to be down to luck. At any point, a series of clubs can easily collapse, which also applies to the Premier League. For instance, it was today reported that Southampton have made a £34m loss for the financial year ending June 2019.

'There are still benefactors operating in the Premier League and if they walk away then that can have a hugely damaging effect. Even if that happens, there is probably still going to be a billionaire willing to take you over; that's the reality. The Championship is actually where the biggest debts exist – it's just crazy. In the Annual Review of Football Finance 2019, twelve clubs reported operating losses of more than £10m for the 2017–18 season, with the league averaging £15m losses. More often than not, they're chasing the dream.'

Brown is steeped in Pompey history. His great uncle, Dennis Collett, served as chairman from 1966–73, the youngster occasionally travelling to matches in the Daimler of the local estate agent. Introduced to Fratton Park football at the age of eighteen months by mum Lesley, who remains a regular attendee, he once collected soup packets to help raise funds for SOS Pompey during an ever-familiar financial fight for survival around 1976. Then, with his club sounding a call to arms to join the battle for survival during the plummet towards administration in February 2010, the former IBM global asset manager stepped forward. When the fans seized control, he was among three Trust board members co-opted on to the club board, along with Mark Trapani and Mick Williams. Brown, however, retained his three season tickets, shared between himself and children Keeva and Harvey, and remains a fixture following his August 2017 boardroom departure after Tornante's takeover.

He said: 'All of football's modern-day problems began when the influx of wealth flooded into the Premier League, creating competition unlike any we had previously seen. Clubs have long wanted to win promotion to the top flight, but the culture of gambling in order to do so is relatively new. Football clubs were typically owned by a local businessman or collection of local businessmen who were fans of the club and known faces within the community. They didn't always run the club well, and there were still problems, as we have also seen at Pompey historically, but they were well intentioned and not gambling to the extent we are now witnessing.

'Don't get me wrong, there are plenty of good foreign owners and plenty of bad British owners, but that explosion of interest in English football around the world attracted a different type of owner. Some of them are just bonkers, absolute chancers, and others are crooks and want to come here to extract money, their whole purpose being to drain cash out of a club and move it into their own bank account.

'More often than not, you have an owner who is well intentioned but tempted into gambling on promotion, succumbing to the pressure created by fans. Even though they may be a self-made billionaire who has shown incredibly shrewd business sense throughout their career, at a football club they choose to blow it all away. Look at Ellis Short at Sunderland and Eddie Davies at Bolton, people who clearly made very sensible business decisions in their normal life, yet happily threw away £150–160m of their own personal fortune into football.

'There is another element, which is an important consideration. The FA's Rule 34 stated that "no member of a football club could draw a salary as a director" and any dividends were restricted to five per cent of the face value of any shares. That was abolished in 1983 when Irving Scholar's Tottenham Hotspur wanted to float on the stock market, signifying a change not merely in ownership style but the ability to take huge amounts of money out of clubs.

'Take Manchester United, a leveraged buyout by the Glazers. The club have subsequently paid hundreds of millions of pounds in interest on loans they took out to purchase it. In addition, those people instrumental in making that happen continue to pay themselves huge shareholder dividends each year. I'm not blaming the Premier League for this as they set out to bring money into football and have been extremely successful. What I would blame them for, however, is the trickle of money which finds its way down the pyramid and needs to be increased.

'The Premier League never intended to create or encourage dodgy owners to come here; you can't blame them for that. In fact, they have become stronger and stronger about who can be an owner. They don't control who can be an owner lower down the leagues though, and, should Pompey still be playing the Leasing.com Trophy final in three weeks, there's a question mark over opponents Salford City. The media will no doubt portray the dream return to Wembley of the Class of '92 and yes, it was lovely to see those guys originally going back to help their local club, picking it out of the gutter and pushing it forward. The reality is, though, Salford are also backed by Singaporean billionaire Peter Lim, who is the majority shareholder. Their climb out of non-league was achieved through paying over-inflated wages and creating the same issue in those leagues that we are currently observing in the gold rush of the Football League.'

Brown's counsel has been repeatedly called upon by the Sky Blue Trust in recent campaigns, a connection prompted by Coventry City's homelessness. They currently groundshare at St Andrew's, attracting average attendances of 6,677 as supporters boycott a second temporary residence in six seasons, despite leading the League One table by five points with a game in hand. Pompey underwent a similar skirmish when Portpin's fixed charge on Fratton Park threatened to separate the football club from its home of 120 years. Subsequently, in April 2013, administrator Trevor Birch took the argument to the High Court, seeking the charge to be released so the ground could be sold at the market rate of £3m to the supporters. Furthermore, the process was tied to a ten-acre site around Fratton Park which was purchased for approximately £3m by Trust ally, Stuart Robinson, after the land's owner, Miland Development 2004 Ltd, had entered administration. Today a Tesco Extra superstore stands on the area adjacent to the football club, yet the partnership with the Bishop's Waltham-based property developer also considerably benefited the Blues.

> Brown added: 'Balram Chainrai had a charge over Fratton Park, a questionable charge to be honest. He wanted £17.4m for Fratton Park, which he claimed he was owed, while we offered £2.75m based on multiple professional valuations. He then offered to rent it at £100,000 a month, that's £1.2m a year. Generally, a football club without a ground means you are nothing. No football fan wants to groundshare, not in this country. If you end up with your stadium in the wrong person's hands, they have you held to ransom.

'One of the earliest examples is Brighton, whose majority shareholder, Bill Archer, sold the Goldstone Ground for use as land to build a retail park. They had nowhere to go, groundsharing with Gillingham for two seasons before moving into the Withdean Stadium, which has got to be one of the worst Football League grounds you could ever visit. Their fortunes have turned around, but similar versions have happened repeatedly across the country, with people paying huge rents when clubs are separated from grounds.

'In terms of ourselves, I've seen people lambast Stuart Robinson and the money he made out of the Tesco deal, but the reality is, if it hadn't been for him, Pompey would have probably disappeared. Should we have managed to raise another £2–3m, we'd have bought that land and made money out of Tesco, like Stuart managed to, but we didn't. We spoke to a number of different property partners and concluded that most of them were there to rip us off, while, on the borrowing front, people weren't willing to lend us that kind of money at a sensible rate. We ended up with Stuart, who wasn't always the easiest person to work with, but without him the football club probably wouldn't be here. Instead, he lent us £1.5m along with £1.45m from the council. We had an issue paying up front for Fratton Park and the initial cash flow, so needed those two loans, otherwise we couldn't have finalised the deal.

'In the Pompey story, something not often talked about is the historic action of a Portsmouth City Council planner, who ensured land around the ground was protected. What that meant was when the club was in its dire administration, the one thing stopping a major developer coming in and building a bigger Tesco or hotel was that legislation. It fended off the vultures and a number of parties made enquiries to the council. It also meant that we received £3m from that Tesco deal, simply because somebody built a supermarket on land we didn't own. That's a pretty good deal in my mind.

'As part of the overall agreement, we had to confirm to the council that we were comfortable for the development to take place. We also received land behind the North Stand and an extra piece behind the Fratton End, which was calculated on the basis of how much space we required should we ever desire a cantilever second tier. We paid Stuart's loan back within a year, at a lower interest rate than the council's!'

Mick Williams has retained the email correspondence, the incredulity felt towards their brusque content refusing to diminish more than eight years later. A plumbing and heating merchant, he established himself as a central figure alongside Brown in the battle to seize ownership of Pompey, culminating in a place on the club's board once triumphant. He still bristles when reflecting on early beginnings, however, with recollections of sneering derision initially greeting the Trust's declaration of interest in a club left financially stricken following owners CSI's administration.

Such was the disdain, de facto administrators UHY Hacker Young demanded proof of funds for £100m to enable the Trust to be given credence. Williams subsequently felt compelled to write an email of complaint following that fractious December 2011 phone call with Peter Kubik. The documented response from the firm's assistant manager, Terri Mulgrew, confirmed the stance, albeit far more delicately. Nonetheless the eventual saviours had been laughed out of town.

'There was not a huge amount of support for the Trust in the early days. We were just a bunch of fans, apparently. We couldn't own a football club, not a chance,' said Williams. 'Following the collapse of CSI, the club itself hadn't yet entered administration, so I left three messages for Peter Kubik of UHY Hacker Young to call. In addition, I sent an email, which later showed a delivery receipt, so he'd read it. I eventually caught up with him by ringing his mobile phone and was told that, if we wanted to be considered, we had to show proof of funds for £100m, otherwise they wouldn't talk to us. That's the contempt we were treated with. He was not in the least bit interested in taking us seriously. The conversation started badly, deteriorated as it continued and almost ended in a row.

'PKF and Trevor Birch were eventually appointed by the High Court as Pompey's administrators ahead of Kubik and his partner, Andrew Andronikou, preventing them from returning for a second spell here. After losing out, Andronikou asked to meet the Trust, which represented a turnaround! It was held in one of Ashley Brown's offices at IBM, in North Harbour, but we weren't particularly interested in what he was communicating. I don't even know what he wanted to achieve; he was well out of the picture. After he'd gone we looked at each other wondering what the hell it was all about.

'On another occasion, Terri Mulgrew contacted me and we met in McDonald's near Fratton Park. She told me she was acting independently and, as she liked us, wanted to help. I think she was being genuine, but people were apprehensive of trusting her because she worked for Andronikou. I had a huge amount of time for Trevor Birch as he had a really difficult job and cared about it. As Trust momentum built and upon recognising that we were seeking financial help to buy the club, Trevor started to pass half the tyre-kickers on to us to sound out.

'One was Laurence Bassini, who had just sold Watford to Gino Pozzo, who still owns them. During a 30-minute phone call, he claimed, "I have £14m and can get you back into the Premier League." He didn't, however, want fan involvement, so I said we'd let him know, but never bothered. A few months later, Bassini was banned from involvement in a position of authority with any Football League club for three years, having been found guilty of misconduct and dishonesty over financial dealings at Watford.

'To be honest, I found him okay in that conversation. Admittedly full of bluster, but then if you've got lots of money you can be arrogant, can't you? He's since turned up trying to buy Bolton and now Oldham. Mark Trapani initially spoke to the Italian-American businessman Joseph Cala and it was my turn at a later date. He tried to convince me that the only way to build a business was "Revenue, revenue, revenue." I replied: "What about profit?" He responded: "No, revenue is the only way to do it." Cala was just a joke, so cocky, and it's no wonder he struggled at Morecambe and Gateshead years later. I have been in business for 30 years and there he was trying to tell me how to build a business.

The bloke is a nutcase; you must retain profit and expand, not focus on sales alone.

'Another was the financer Brett de Bank, whose wife I believe was a Pompey fan. We met in the offices at Snows BMW Portsmouth and he came across as genuine, but was another not keen on supporter involvement. As far as we were concerned, it was Trust or nothing because we were progressing quite nicely. Once we started getting a few of our own wealthy fans on board, everything began to take shape.'

At the age of 94, Harry Williams is no longer able to travel to Fratton Park. He introduced his son to Pompey in 1958 and the pair remained South Stand regulars until the recent intervention of ill health. Mick's devotion to the Blues soon stretched beyond match days, founding the club's first ladies team in 1968 along with the late Steve Keyte, while turning out for Fratton Sports as a midfielder, a supporters' side which competed in Sunday League, listing Barry Harris among team-mates.

Financial turmoil would prompt the launch of the SOS Pompey Appeal in September 1976, with owner John Deacon struggling to keep the club in business, a challenge which inevitably drew Williams' backing. Seeking to raise funds for the campaign, he contributed by setting a world record for playing football non-stop for over 41 hours, representing Portsmouth Junior Chamber against Pleasurama during the marathon match. Bernie Winters, who at the time was appearing in *Babes in the Wood* at the Kings Theatre with brother Mike, popped down to cheer on the footballers, although chairman Deacon didn't materialise. Unfortunately, the feat never had the chance to appear in the *Guinness Book of Records*, with two American teams beating their achievement within a few months, ahead of the book's next publication. Then, in August 2011, Williams was elected to the Pompey Supporters' Trust board, just four months before CSI entered administration, and was once more presented with the task of saving a club in crisis.

'Some people will say we started out trying to buy the club, but we didn't,' said Williams. 'Our aim was to be listened to by those running the club, maybe even achieving representation on the Pompey board, but as time went on it became apparent more was required, especially with Mr Chainrai in the background. On the night of Pompey chairman Vladimir Antonov's arrest for alleged bank fraud, I wrote an email to my new Trust board colleagues saying, "Oh, oh, this could be a problem." To which somebody – I'm not going to say who – responded to the group with, "Well that won't affect us, will it." I've since reminded him of that!

'Our bid to take the club out of administration reached the stage where I had to visit the offices of Portsmouth City Council to persuade them to loan us money. All three political groups needed to be won over and all gave me a tough time; it was an extremely stressful day. I had to come back another day to hear their decision. It was passed unanimously. I was gobsmacked and a bit emotional, to be honest. We couldn't have done it without the council's £1.45m loan.

'Another key moment in our attempts to save the club came in October 2012, when we were informed that Pompey would be liquidated that Friday as the administrators were running it at a loss. As a stipulation of the Trust being named preferred bidders, some of us were asked to put a minimum of £50,000 into escrow to cover expected losses for the coming week. I was the first to contribute, with ten of us eventually putting money in, enabling the administrators to continue dipping into the account over a number of months to meet debts and maintain the club's existence.

'The alternative was liquidation. Had we not managed to take over the club, we would have lost that money, with any new owner benefiting from us keeping Pompey alive. As it was, we received it back. That's why it's so laughable when people claim a white knight would have come along to save us. There was nobody else, so it was either we put in the money or it was gone, to be replaced by a phoenix club in non-league football. Anyone who insists otherwise really hasn't a clue.'

Williams resigned from the Trust board in March 2015, resulting in his departure from the club's board of directors. He retained links with the club's presidents, representing them on the Heritage & Advisory Board under the ownership of Tornante before he was required to step down after serving a mandatory two years. The 71-year-old also spent three years as the chairman of Pompey Women, before relinquishing his role in the summer of 2018, with the club stepping in to take Jay Sadler's team under their wing. He remains a Fratton Park season-ticket holder, along with wife Ann and children Charlotte and William.

'We proved without a shadow of a doubt that football supporters are capable of running a club effectively,' said Williams. 'We had a good guy as chief executive in Mark Catlin, who wasn't as superb as he is now. Initially he was quite inexperienced, while chief operating officer Tony Brown is ruthless but excellent at his job.

'Between us there were many, many years of business and managerial experience. We made mistakes and we had disagreements, but did a pretty good job, I feel. Right at the beginning we had a devil's own job to even get a bank account, let alone anything else. We were a bad risk, a toxic brand, and nobody would even give us a credit card, which you need in order to enter the FA Cup – you can't pay cash or send a cheque. Banks turned us away, and you can't blame them either, but Barclays came through for us.

'As for local businesses, some asked for personal guarantees and we were paying cash on delivery, but gradually it became easier as we won back trust. I was once walking behind the Fratton End and passed a bloke and a little boy. The boy said: "Look, Dad, there's the man that saved Pompey." I stopped and explained that I may have been in the paper a lot, but there were many, many people who helped save our football club, including him and his dad. When something like that happens, it makes you proud. The fans pulled off a fantastic achievement.'

At the height of their powers, the Trust represented the largest single shareholder in the club, possessing a 48.5 per cent stake. However, the emergence of Tornante as prospective owners subsequently captured the support of 81.4 per cent of the club's equity holding, following a charismatic pitch at Portsmouth Guildhall. The Americans' £5.67m takeover was completed in August 2017, with the Trust receiving £2.75m for their stake, valued at £1,000 for each of their 2,750 shares. During redistribution among Trust members, several worthy causes were also chosen to benefit, with £75,000 allocated to Pompey in the Community and £34,000 for the Pompey History Society.

Today, the Trust possess 2,200 members, with Simon Colebrook having served as chairman since replacing Brown at the helm in September 2017. The chartered accountant was elected to the Trust board two years earlier, following a number of departures, including Williams. Among those joining Colebrook on the new-look board in 2015 was Johnny Ertl, who had featured in Pompey's first team on seventeen occasions only months earlier. During its post-fan ownership existence, Colebrook has sought to evolve the Trust's influence within a club which once offered boardroom seats.

'I see our role as functioning in two parts, with the first serving as a critical friend to the club,' said the North Stand Lower season-ticket holder. 'Clearly, we support Pompey and, with three of our representatives on the Heritage & Advisory Board, form part of a consultation group which is provided with information on what's going on and the club's plans. Although we might not be part of the decision-making process, we are still there to give an opinion and are granted privileged access to people like Michael Eisner, Mark Catlin, Andy Redman and Eric Eisner. As critical friends, when things go right, we will say so. For instance, in terms of the coronavirus crisis, I genuinely believe Mark Catlin has handled it as well as he possibly could, keeping people informed but not creating fear and panic.

'The second part of our role is more community based. We have an opportunity to work with Pompey in the Community to mobilise more support for them through the public, as well as assist with funding for the John Jenkins Stadium project. Football League legislation states that every club should have a structured system for meeting their fan base four times a year. The bare minimum could consist of something as meaningless as hand-picking half a dozen fans, sitting them in a room and telling them some stuff.

'Our engagement with the club runs much deeper than that. There's actual dialogue and we're informed of matters in the concept phase rather than after the event. The Trust are presented with a fantastic opportunity to give feedback and help shape things. I sense genuine interest from Michael, Eric and Andy in what we have to say. Hopefully it will continue, and I see no reason why it shouldn't.'

With Tornante rejecting fan representation on the club board, the Heritage & Advisory Board was created to provide a consultation body between supporters and the Pompey boardroom, with meetings held four times a year. The most recent gathering occurred in February, when the Trust's three-strong delegation of Brown, Clare Martin and Phil Sandys met with directors Eric Eisner and Andy Redman at the Anson Road offices of Pompey in the Community. Colebrook served as the Trust's representative during the opening two years of the Heritage & Advisory Board but has since stepped down in the interests of rotation among the Trust's board.

He added: 'The club does listen. We raised the idea of Pompey promoting a responsible gambling awareness campaign, which Michael Eisner was immediately on board with, and in November it appeared on their official website. This season we also saw the implementation of our idea to provide free sanitary products to female supporters. Although these sorts of things may seem relatively small, it demonstrates the ability to pitch ideas to the club at a senior level.

'In January 2018, Leeds United released a cartoonish new club badge designed to mark their centenary, which didn't go down well with fans. The club emailed a copy to the Leeds United Supporters' Trust the day before it was launched and, in Leeds' eyes, that represented consultation!

'Around the same time, Tornante were in the process of rebranding Pompey's badge. In contrast, there was a detailed discussion of crest options, with supporters even shown six concepts to gauge opinion. We were allowed to provide input into a number of different designs, helping to steer it in the direction which has led to what we have now, which is a small change but enough to satisfy their needs for trademarking purposes.

'On occasions, the Heritage & Advisory Board are presented with financial details which wouldn't be shared in a wider forum, while there are day-to-day issues such as next year's season tickets and the new home shirts which enable us to give feedback. Pompey's stadium development represents the biggest issue associated with our future and that forum is probably the only place where all of the parties have the freedom to discuss ideas at a concept level, with fan input welcomed during that process. You obviously can't have an open consultation with 20,000 people. The Heritage & Advisory Board offers the opportunity to keep your finger on the pulse of how the club is running, while having the chance to ask pointed, critical questions face to face, and gauging people's reactions and answers.'

Aside from club matters, the Trust presently forms a pivotal role in proposals for a new £3.5m sports complex in Copnor, partnering Pompey in the Community and Moneyfields Football Club. Members have backed £250,000 of Trust funds to aid the ambitious project, utilising the remaining proceeds of share sale money which remains in club coffers with the potential to facilitate crucial work within the club and community.

Colebrook said: 'When the Trust formed more than ten years ago, it was during the initial stages of the club falling apart. We were attempting to get somebody to listen to the fans, and to make someone from the club sit down with us and hear supporter concerns. The Trust's current level of involvement may feel like a backwards step compared to four seasons of fan ownership, but it has actually returned to our original vision, operating within a structured, agreed forum at which the club and fans sit together and discuss the future of Pompey.'

MARK CATLIN, BASHER BENFIELD AND BARRY HARRIS

25 March 2020

Mark Catlin surveys his Gunwharf Quays surroundings through the window of his bedroom, the Spinnaker Tower a striking sight set against a blue-heaven backdrop on a glorious spring morning. The scene below remained dispiriting, however, with the usual steady stream of shoppers and workers halted during a government-driven lockdown in the battle to stifle the spread of coronavirus. Like others, Pompey's chief executive remains at home. Having officially shut down Fratton Park for business on Monday morning, the club's frontline business is presently orchestrated from his top floor apartment in the three-storey block located beside a picturesque Solent.

Over at Fratton Park, a security guard remains on patrol, while a maintenance man continues to oversee the stadium in its deserted state. Meanwhile, the turf, so impressively immaculate during the testing winter months, is to be preserved by a reduced groundstaff. Yet the Blues' 120-year-old home is out of bounds for other members of staff, forcing Catlin to conduct club matters from his bedroom, a workload which has escalated considerably during the ongoing pandemic.

Pompey's preference for transparency prompted the announcement that James Bolton, Andy Cannon, Sean Raggett and Haji Mnoga had tested positive for coronavirus. It soon emerged that Ross McCrorie was also implicated, taking the tally to five among their playing squad, with four having lined up against Fleetwood in the Blues' most recent fixture. The club has spent approximately £7,200 on the purchase of testing kits for 48 employees, including players, backroom staff and others likely to have come into contact at their Hilsea training ground. The subsequent outcome means Pompey are the club most affected by coronavirus within the English game, at least in terms of the public's consciousness. With all Premier League, Football League and grassroots matches presently postponed until 30 April, the infected quintet, said to be affected by mild cases, have indeterminable time to recover.

'It's our policy, generally, to be as open and honest as we can,' said Catlin, speaking during a phone call conducted from his bedroom. 'In this instance, a lot of our players have come into contact with people, via schools, commercial activities, when being asked for selfies while walking through a shopping centre. It was only right and fair that we dealt with this publicly. People need to know if they have come into contact with someone who has coronavirus.

'Fair play to Arsenal, who initiated that approach when revealing that Mikel Arteta had been infected. That was the watershed moment. Our thinking at that time was football would be allowed to continue, but behind closed doors. Then everything changed. With the greatest of respect, had it been a non-league manager I believe that weekend's games would have gone ahead, but this was Arteta, a high-profile figure. It was the straw which broke the camel's back.

'The decision to scrap the fixture list had been building anyway. There was quite a bit of pressure on the government and sporting bodies to shut things down. Initially the focus was on eliminating mass gatherings. We were working on the assumption that matches would soon be played behind closed doors, yet once it entered the footballing population, especially players and managers, other teams were not going to be happy about facing clubs whose staff had tested positive.

'On the Friday morning before our scheduled match against Accrington, their chairman, Andy Holt, stated: "There's no way I'm exposing my players; your players could potentially have it." We agreed with him. We actually had five footballers later test positive, but did they contract coronavirus before or after the game was set to take place? You just don't know.

'The figures of those infected within football are totally misleading. There are probably fewer than ten per cent of clubs that have had their players tested and, of those, some clubs are very reserved with giving information out publicly. In addition, I know managers who have requested testing for their players, only for it to be declined by those above, which I have sympathy for. I do ask the question, is there any relevance in taking the test when you're supposed to be self-isolating anyway? If you've tested positive and are not showing any symptoms, what are you doing? You're sitting at home playing PlayStation games. If you have bad symptoms, such as shortage of breath or a cough, then you go to hospital; it doesn't matter whether you've been tested.

'We have been honest and transparent, both in terms of testing and results, but why is football different to other businesses? Why are we the only ones testing? Why not supermarkets whose employees have continually come into contact with the public? Besides, it's only a snapshot of that particular day. You can take a test at 9am on a Tuesday, only to then pick up the virus from someone else after stopping off at the shop on the way home to get your milk. We have no idea how our players contracted the virus. Our first tests were taken fourteen days after coming into contact with Mikel Arteta, so everything should have been okay. It just shows how contagious this is.

'Of those players infected, four started our last match against Fleetwood. That may have had an impact on their performances, but they insist they felt okay, while I don't believe the statistics reflect an issue when you look at the distances run and high intensity. Fleetwood was a very hard-fought, competitive game, although it only takes players to be a little off to affect their displays.

'Most importantly, there is a danger of attaching a stigma to being infected. Should our players test positive, there's nothing wrong in saying that. It's not their fault. Of course, that would be different if something was avoidable, but it's not.'

The previous afternoon, League One chief executives came together via Microsoft Teams, with Catlin among their number. Dialogue has been maintained throughout the coronavirus crisis, with WhatsApp group chats and video calling employed as football club chiefs unite in the face of challenges unprecedented in the history of the game.

Financial concerns are high on the agenda as clubs battle to remain solvent after being stripped of their main sources of income, although the Football League have offered a temporary solution following the announcement of a £50m relief package for its member clubs. Each has been earmarked £252,200, in addition to a potential loan of up to £182,800. However, the cash injection represents the advancement of money Football League clubs are entitled to receive over the course of the current campaign, rather than a charitable act of generosity. Throughout the course of that afternoon meeting which overran to three hours, to Catlin it was clear some Football League companions could be forced into administration during the current brutal climate.

He added: 'Yesterday afternoon the chief executives got together to discuss this rapidly evolving situation. No one wants to put a date on when we might return to the fixture list; for 99 per cent of clubs the priority at present is how we get through the next couple of months with no money coming in. I don't want to point score, but since Pompey came under fan ownership and then Michael Eisner, we have run a self-sustaining model and tried to build up cash reserves for any future potential crisis, whatever that may be. As a result, we remain self-sustained and haven't yet asked for money from Michael during this period. There is an argument that owners should be free to put in money as and when they want and I sort of get that. I'm a capitalist. But what are these owners doing now? A lot of them are happy putting in a million pounds to buy a sexy player, but not to pay all the staff when there isn't any money coming in. I have long urged for self-sustainability and said that football clubs must be profitable; we need to change the whole culture. This must be that landmark moment.

'You cannot have clubs unable to pay staff after a week or two without a home match. We're now seeing a multitude of clubs asking people to take deferrals and pay cuts. There were lots of clubs on that call yesterday having the same conversation. I'm not knocking them for that because it's the right thing to get through this, but this crisis in football hasn't just happened this week – it has been building for years and years and years. A huge majority of clubs are relying on the next game or two to pay the wages at the month's end. Suddenly something completely unbudgeted has occurred, so that fragile economy has shattered.

'We have calculated the model and, suffice to say, can continue for quite a few months to come, even without going to Michael. That is down to living within our means and resisting fan pressure to gamble on the future of the club by signing players which you can't afford. I would be amazed if the Football League got through this without at least two or three clubs entering administration. If you are a typical League One club with, for example, fixed costs at £3m and an income of £4m, your playing budget should be £1m; it's not difficult. Then if you have a big player sale or a cup run, happy days, you've got more money to spend in the following year. Don't gamble on receiving it though, because that's where clubs are getting into difficulties. In that scenario, they are giving the manager £3m for his budget, so where are you going to get the other £2m from? That's right, it might be a player sale or it might be a cup run – it *might* be. You cannot operate like that.

'The Football League has forwarded money to us in the last week that is effectively a defibrillator. With no games, football clubs went into cardiac arrest and this defibrillator will get the heart pumping again. That's all it is. It will enable clubs to survive over the next month or six weeks, but I cannot see football coming back any time before May. Currently everything is on hold until 30 April. That is still more than a month away and, looking at the situation now with coronavirus deaths and cases rising, it seems a very long way off.

'In terms of potential Premier League assistance, the EFL already receive a substantial sum of money trickling down into the communities and the academies via solidarity payments. If they can help then great, but there are very few Premier League clubs making profits, so where is this money going to come from? This £1.5 billion which the Premier League supposedly has sitting in its bank account is an absolute fallacy; it is an urban myth. That was a snapshot of when they'd just received the TV rights payment, which was then distributed to the clubs. It passes through their hands – they don't sit on that money; it is all accounted for. They receive it, then it goes out via community trusts, academies, solidarity payments, parachute payments and payments to clubs.

'It's all right saying EFL clubs need help, but some in the Championship are paying more in wages than the Premier League. There will be Premier League clubs saying, "Hold on, we are running our clubs really well, so why should we help you out when you're losing £40–50m this year?" That's what capitalism is, isn't it? We don't live in a communist state. I'm not saying we shouldn't ask or seek help, but we cannot rely on that and think, "Don't worry, the Premier League are going to come riding over the hill like the cavalry and get us out of trouble." I am not saying we should turn money away, no one has said that. I am simply stating we shouldn't be relying on their help – there is a world of difference. We must become more self-sufficient.'

Identified among those at higher risk, Basher Benfield this morning received an NHS letter urging him to remain at home for a minimum of three months. A case of preaching to the converted for the pragmatic 56-year-old, who has already spent the previous week and a half in self-isolation, having undergone a farewell haircut in preparation for a long stint.

Benfield's ongoing health issues consist of mild spina bifida, while doctors estimated he would not live beyond the age of 40 following a kidney transplant, yet admirably his outlook is spared of self-pity. Living alone in his ground-floor Copnor flat, he has become reliant on FaceTime to see friends, while he communicates with girlfriend Sue through a closed porch door. As for following Pompey, Benfield is braced to be absent from fixtures should the current league campaign ever be allowed to resume.

He said: 'I'll have to accept missing Pompey games – it's either that or being dead. I cannot take the risk. I'll just sit indoors for twelve weeks, maybe longer, perhaps up to a year. Football returning on 30 April is pie in the sky, I'll tell you that now. I can't see Pompey finishing the league this side of Christmas. I would have gone had the Accrington match not been called off, but now I have no idea when I will next see them. What happens if coronavirus eases but doesn't disappear completely, then comes back? This could continue for at least a year and I have to accept probably not being able to see us play for that long because of my health. There's nothing I can do about it. I would obviously rather be out and about, but you just have to go through it. These idiots walking along the seafront at Southsea don't realise how serious it is.

'Being high risk, I've been isolating since the Wednesday before last. I'm limited to my nurse visiting on Mondays to change my nephrostomy bag, to take my blood pressure and temperature, and give me an Eprex injection to increase the number of red blood cells. My girlfriend, Sue, carries out the other twice-weekly injections from outside an open window. Sue's very good to me. She works in Fratton Asda, so delivers food to keep me stocked up. With the advice of my nurse, we've worked out a system where Sue knocks on my window and I remain in my bedroom while she comes in and puts the food away in the cupboards. I can then talk to her when she has returned outside.

'A TV engineer visited today, wearing what looked like a Darth Vader mask and gloves, but it's only right as he has to keep his distance for both of our sakes. It was a big white mask and you could only see his eyes. If he had said, "Luke, I'm your father," I would have been a bit worried! I've had transmitter problems, so haven't been able to watch Sky. I have my laptop so I'm not too bothered. There's nothing to watch anyway: no sport, not even Australian Rules football. I watch nature and history documentaries on my laptop. I don't like soaps and the last time I saw *Coronation Street* it had Ena Sharples in it; I would rather watch paint dry.'

A Queen Alexandra Hospital appointment has been scheduled for 27 May, representing Benfield's routine three-month examination, the check-up focusing on testing blood, urine and blood pressure. He's unsure whether he will be able to attend due to the necessity to remain confined to his house in the current situation. Other important hospital visits have already been shelved, including one to assess his problematic right shoulder, in addition to physiotherapy sessions, but he recognises medical needs elsewhere are presently more pressing.

He added: 'I've got a frozen shoulder which has been like that since the end of last year and is getting worse. I'm like the Hunchback of Notre Dame! I was meant to be going to hospital about it, but that's now well on the back burner. Quite rightly, the priority is to stop people dying. I see this as a three-month holiday and everyone has to get on with it; we must all stop indoors and do nothing.

'I'm fine at the moment because I've got two freezers full of food as I was ill over Christmas and lost my appetite, so that's still there, while my temperature was today checked at 35.8 degrees centigrade, which is fine. I've got my music to listen to, I do quizzes on my computer and keep in touch with everybody. Chris Gibbs phoned me last week and Steve Tovey called today. I recently spoke to my cousin Paul in Australia and finally got my dad to use FaceTime.

'To pass some of the time, I've been going to bed at 10pm and getting up at 10am, so that's twelve hours a day accounted for, which helps. Normally I'd have a shave and shower every day, but now I don't have to bother doing it so frequently as I'm not going out anywhere. The only time I can nip out is late at night to go around the square in my scooter, but is there any point? It might be a risk, so I would rather stay in and have the window open every now and again. What will be, will be, and there's nothing I can do. What's the point of worrying? Anybody can get coronavirus; they could be the carrier. We are nowhere near the peak of it yet.'

✳ ☽ ✳

Elsewhere across the city, a game of Monopoly remains unfinished, still spread across Barry Harris' dining-room table two days since its launch. Currently capturing the attention of the 76-year-old and wife Sue is Agatha Christie's *4.50 from Paddington* which is proving to be riveting television viewing. Separated from his beloved Pompey, Harris has been challenged to discover alternative means of keeping himself entertained, particularly following the necessity to self-isolate during the coronavirus outbreak.

Age dictates the Blues' long-serving boot man is perceived as highly vulnerable to the pandemic, despite being in rude health and remaining active through work responsibilities. Still, deprived of football and visits to regular drinking establishment Hole In The Wall, Harris finds himself fortified inside his Southsea townhouse, a fate which, as ever, is addressed in upbeat manner by the ever-cheery former Pompey mascot.

'I like to be out and about, but there are a lot of people worse off than me, like those on their own or currently ill, so you have to be positive,' said Harris. 'I feel all right and I'm doing okay. Sue has a bit of a cough, but neither of us has a fever. I think the word is "coping". I've been to the Co-op around the corner to get a paper and bread this morning, that's all. You've got to be careful as I'm not as young as I would like to be.

'Usually you look out of the window and see people around, but it's so quiet at the moment, although we have all got to be sensible. We're finding things to break up the monotony. We'll be playing Scrabble later to amuse ourselves, and we're happy enough. The other Saturday we started Monopoly and played it for two or three hours; it's still on the table now. The last time we played was a few Christmases ago when my son, Pete, and his wife cheated me after they'd had a few drinks. I went to the loo and came back to find they had nicked all my money – but I still won!

'Yesterday I went around the pub to get a takeaway: a jug of beer. John McThatcher, the landlord, is selling it off, but it's better than pouring it down the drain, isn't it? He was handing it out through the window at £3 a pint for my favourite ale, Goodens Gold. I don't like lager – it's the bubbles, you see. The Hole In The

Wall is Pompey's best pub by a mile. There's comradeship, banter and the price of the beer. Put it together and there's no better place to drink. I'm following messages on their Facebook page to see if there's going to be another sale soon.'

The Football League's request for all players to train in isolation until 30 April also grounds Harris' Pompey involvement, with the growing likelihood that the deadline will be extended well into the summer. The stalled League One table shows Pompey in fourth place, occupying a play-off position yet still harbouring legitimate automatic promotion ambition, placed just two points off second-placed Rotherham United. Kenny Jackett's men have nine league fixtures remaining, in addition to their Leasing.com Trophy final against Salford, whose original 5 April date has already been postponed, leaving the Wembley showpiece in limbo.

UEFA's decision to postpone Euro 2020 until the summer of 2021 has bought domestic leagues more time to fulfil their own competitions, a flexibility which fends off growing calls to void an incomplete 2019–20 campaign. Catlin, however, believes the argument to scrap the remaining league programme altogether is inhibited by the power Sky, BT Sport and other media partners continue to wield.

'Given my understanding of Sky's contracts with the Premier League and the EFL, failing to conclude this campaign is not an option,' said Pompey's chief executive. 'Although wiping this season and starting afresh would be the best thing to do in practical terms, financially it would be disastrous due to the television contracts with both entities. Quite simply, we have to finish the season, no matter when, even if it's in January 2021. I am not privy to the specifics of the Sky contract, yet, based on my limited knowledge of the subject, I believe there's a contractual obligation to complete this campaign.

'You have to balance everything up and, being pragmatic, should you take exterior media stakeholders out of the equation, then the logical thing would be to scrap this season. However, because we actually do have media stakeholders, ending it now would definitely not be the logical thing to do. Speaking hypothetically, I would end the campaign. In business, you cannot throw good money after bad; you must be pragmatic, no matter how much that's going to kill us as a club. For the greater good, it would be beneficial to have a degree of certainty when planning, whereas at this minute we just don't know. For example, contracted players need to be paid, yet it could be months before a match is next played. Then there are those whose deals expire on 30 June and may now be needed for selection beyond that date. It's a complete nightmare.

'We are presently in discussion with the PFA and what's being floated is extending the contracts of those whose agreements expire on 30 June, say, for another three months. However, my understanding is that the PFA will only agree if all of those out of contract are given longer deals; there can be no cherry-picking. Basically, it's all or nothing, which I believe is correct; after all, what are those players not offered a deal instead going to be doing during those three months? That would be unfair. There are no dates or timescales yet, because we just don't know, but extending players' contracts by default is currently on the agenda.

'In order to complete this season, I can see there being behind-closed-doors fixtures, even though the thought of that makes me feel sick. If that's what it takes to get this campaign finished so we can start again next year, then so be it. That's not very palatable to me, but, once again, you must be pragmatic during these times. Should mass gatherings continue to be banned but we can still fulfil games behind closed doors, that month could be key to enabling a lot of clubs to come through this crisis. As I've previously said, with media rights involved, it's not even on the agenda to scrap this season – you just can't do it. Should it happen, though, the tables would have to be wiped, along with all promotion and relegation. It wouldn't be fair on anyone because we're all in it together. A lot of the football fraternity I speak to would, if the media rights issue was removed, give it as long as they could to maintain integrity and finish the campaign, but there would need to be a line drawn in the sand. Whether that would be June, July or August, I'm not sure.

'I'm less concerned about the Leasing.com Trophy final. Being a one-off, that can be slotted in anywhere, even next season. The league remains the priority. Pompey are in a great position at this moment in time, and going up automatically is still very much within our control, so this season being scrapped would be tremendously disappointing. However, you must think of the greater good of football and obviously the health of fans and staff remains paramount.'

Pompey are to file accounts for the year ending 30 June 2019 next week, their encouraging content likely to prove crucial within the current bleak financial landscape for football clubs. The Blues have recorded a £2.05m profit, compared to the £1.36m loss from the previous campaign. Such figures have been bolstered by £3.33m earned through the player sales of Matt Clarke to Brighton & Hove Albion and Conor Chaplin to Coventry City. In addition, turnover has risen to £11.57m, an increase of £2.68m, primarily driven by their Checkatrade Trophy success and progress to the fourth round of the FA Cup, where Jackett's side were eliminated by QPR following a replay. The accounts, however, do not take into consideration Jamal Lowe's July sale to Wigan Athletic and the costly purchases of John Marquis and Marcus Harness around the same period. And Catlin believes Pompey are strongly positioned to cope with the financial challenges ahead.

'At this moment, most of our problems are from an operational view,' he added. 'Thankfully, we don't have that added pressure of worrying how we are going to pay the wages at the end of this month. I've been there before during my life in business, and it's not a great place to be. The reason we haven't got that is because, during the seven years since the scarring of administration, we've worked towards self-sustainability and maintaining a financial buffer. As an entity we are lean, fit, mean, all the different clichés, and it's at times like this that really comes to the fore.

'The coronavirus crisis could alter football. Being an optimist, I'm hoping that when we emerge on the other side, this game will be altered for the better. We live in footballing times when losing money is acceptable, when owners are deemed good because they pump money in. I just hope that culture changes.'

IAIN MCINNES AND
JOHN KIMBELL

29 March 2020

Iain McInnes was instrumental in saving one football club; now he's battling to keep another alive. Gosport Borough's campaign has ended prematurely, the ongoing coronavirus crisis prompting the Football Association's decision to scrap 91 divisions below National League level, with results expunged. Last week's directive also impacted the women's game, with National League South Premier Division among those affected, thereby calling time on a Pompey Women campaign decimated by fixture cancellations courtesy of persistent waterlogged pitches.

Having avoided relegation on the final day in each of his opening two seasons as Gosport owner, McInnes had armed rookie boss Lee Molyneaux with one of the five biggest playing budgets in BetVictor Southern Premier South. By the time the league was shelved, Borough's promotion aspirations were remote, placed eighth, still six points adrift of Tiverton Town in the final play-off position having played four games more. The gregarious McInnes had been a pivotal presence in preventing Pompey's liquidation, serving as chairman during the four seasons of fan ownership, culminating in that final-day League Two title triumph in May 2017.

Following Tornante's takeover, he sought a fresh challenge at Privett Park seven months later, striding forward to prevent the cash-starved non-league club from folding. However, with attendances averaging a disappointing 260 this term, he calculates that Gosport have lost £300,000, a deficit taken from his own pocket. Now deprived of league action since 14 March, he estimates another £80–90,000 will be required to keep the club alive through to August.

'As I speak to you now, Gosport Borough Football Club has not a single penny coming through the door: nothing, zilch,' said McInnes. 'We have overheads which we can't get away from, we have 30-day accounts for kit, coaches, supplies for the bar, heating, lighting and Sky television, all of which still have to be paid. However, at the moment, not one penny is coming through the door at Gosport and hasn't for the last two and a half weeks. There's no gate money and no clubhouse income. The only other way you generate income in this business is prize money. Well, there won't be any of that as the season didn't finish.

'Other streams include sponsorship income, which we're not seeing at the moment, while you can't bank advanced season-ticket sales for a campaign that you don't even know when it will start. There won't be one penny until the start of next season, whenever that is. The expectation is that the club carries on regardless, but if, this evening, I decide "Gosport Borough Football Club? Forget it, goodnight nurse, turn the lights out," then it has gone, most likely forever.

'I haven't had one call from a supporter, supplier, local business, sponsor or the local authorities. Not one asking if they could help, nobody. I'm not demoralised, I'm disappointed, because I have some really good people here. The league have declared this season 'expunged', but the players' contracts aren't necessarily expunged, they're all sitting there waiting for somebody to make a decision on whether they are going to be paid, which no club can afford to at this level, with no guidance or support from the league or FA.

'Next week we are launching a community scheme to help serve meals to care homes and people who can't go out or have no money. Our ground will be the storage centre, in conjunction with Gosport Voluntary Action and The Salvation Army, to deliver food to people's doors. We are putting ourselves out there to help our supporters and community at large. The cynic would say, "But what about us? Who is going to help us?" The answer today is no one.

'Since we have stopped playing, the club has needed £10,000 over the last three weeks just to stay in the game. I'm a big boy. I rescued Gosport and it's the most stable it has ever been financially. We did overcommit a little this year on the budget, but I could afford it. What I didn't take on – and what I am not going to take responsibility for alone – is to fight for a club when not enough people in the locality seem to care too much about what happens to it. I am not going to fight the tsunami that is the coronavirus at the same time. Why would I want to do that? It doesn't make sense. Things are desperate and there are clubs at this level who will not survive this – maybe Gosport will be one of them.

'The reality is sooner or later, somebody you know will have died from coronavirus, if that hasn't happened already. The best estimate is 20,000 people will be claimed by this pandemic, so how can we sit here and put pressure on the government to help clubs by saying, "What about the guys who play football on a Saturday afternoon, guv'nor?" As much as I would like some support, I'm not going to ask for it, and I don't think I'll get it anyway. The government didn't take on this responsibility, I did.'

McInnes represents a formidable character, exuding bonhomie and possessing an infectious nature, yet one born with a steely disposition perhaps underestimated by those crossing his path in either business or football. His forthright approach created conflict with other groups vying to seize ownership of a distressed Pompey during the 2012–13 campaign, with the club entrenched in administration and spiralling towards relegation to League Two. However, McInnes is not one to submit to intimidation, nor is the Paulsgrove lad prepared to back down in a confrontation.

'Whereas all my Warsash neighbours have gates and floodlights, I don't believe in it. Why would I want a gate to shut people out of my house? I quite like to welcome them,' added the 69-year-old. 'Anyhow, in the early throes of trying to take over Pompey, when we were beginning to get some traction, I returned home one afternoon and discovered all the front windows – upstairs and downstairs – were open. Well, that was really bizarre, as it wasn't a particularly warm day, while my wife, Jane, wasn't there and doesn't like fresh air anyway. Approaching the front door, I discovered it was actually on the latch and open. The previous week there were a couple of phone calls with a mystery voice saying: "We know your daughter's at Loughborough University and we know what nightclubs she goes to," before hanging up. I was told the administrator Trevor Birch experienced similar things, albeit not quite so clandestine, sometimes with people confronting him at his office or following him along the road.

'Well, it's not fun, is it? I called the police after the window incident. They asked what had been taken. Nothing. What harm had been done? Did anybody threaten you? Did you see any of them? It was a very professional job by our unwelcome house guests. At that point, Jane was concerned that our family's life was at risk. I'm not sure it was, but she moved to Port Solent for a while and I ended up going there to be with her. It wasn't just us she feared for, but our three children who, despite no longer living at home, would visit and stay at weekends, often with a number of friends. There were all kinds of weird and wonderful things going on with the outdoor swimming pool as well. My gardener found debris in there – rocks, stones and a few condoms – and asked if the children had hosted a party. There hadn't been any parties, of course.

'I wasn't really intimidated. Perhaps you should take it seriously, but I didn't. I suppose I was obsessed with making sure everything was going through with the Pompey deal. I ignored all that stuff; I couldn't let anything get in the way of saving our club.'

McInnes grew up watching his uncle, Phil Gunter, turn out for the Blues, the right-back registering 365 appearances during a thirteen-year Fratton Park stay. A home-grown player, Gunter notably succeeded in breaking into a team which seventeen months earlier had been crowned First Division champions for a second successive season. Gunter once rejected an England call-up on account of the fixture taking place on a Sunday and going against his religious beliefs. He was never given a second opportunity.

Initially living in Reginald Road, Southsea, above a hairdressers, McInnes' family moved to Bredenbury Crescent in Paulsgrove where he attended Hillside Infants School, befriending Bobby Stokes, who lived in neighbouring Leominster Road. The pair were footballing team-mates at the Grove Club where, on occasions, Pompey players Bobby Campbell and Tony Barton visited to train the youngsters, but Stokes was destined for bigger things, albeit with fierce rivals Southampton. The striker assured himself of an indelible presence in Saints folklore when his goal secured the FA Cup in 1976, their last major trophy. On the occasion of Stokes' April 1969 first-team debut against Burnley, McInnes offered moral support by accompanying his friend on the train from Portchester to the game, before cheering him on from The Dell's stands. Yet Fratton Park remained McInnes' home and, having sold his highly successful electronic component and distribution business, he answered Pompey's plea for financial assistance to enable the purchase of Mathias Svensson from Elfsborg in December 1996.

'When Terry Venables and Eddie Ashby turned up, Ashby cottoned on that I had a few quid, while I was suitably gullible about all things Pompey,' smiled McInnes. 'Eventually they needed to do some squad strengthening, but they had no money, so guess who received a call? It was from Ashby. It turned out Pompey were in desperate need of a centre-forward and he'd been told of a number of people who could potentially loan the club money to enable signings to be made. Among their targets was Svensson.

'I was told to expect a call from Venables, which never arrived, so I rang him at his nightclub. I was informed Svensson's Swedish club wanted £250,000, which was a lot of money to me. Anyhow, I agreed, and it was back to having Ashby on the phone to iron out the finer details. I actually found him okay as a person, and we definitely wouldn't have had the new Fratton End built in

1997 without him, and he deserves some credit in that regard. So, we agreed on £250,000, but on the proviso that I would deal with Elfsborg directly. I wanted to go straight to their chairman, Michael Ekberg, and transfer the money from my bank account to theirs. Ashby said he would get back to me. Within an hour he called to say: "You're not going to believe this, but we actually don't need £250,000; it's only £75,000." Great news. I asked the reason for this large reduction and was told: "I don't want to go into it over the phone; it's agents' cuts and agent deals. I've sorted it now, though." So, I phoned my bank manager at NatWest in Cosham, Malcolm Hargreaves, and the money was transferred. We had signed Svensson. He proved to be a good player too, scoring twelve goals in 51 games.

'A few months later, we played Chelsea at home in the FA Cup and I was contemplating how to promote Svensson being there and give the fans a bit of fun, so I bought a load of plastic Viking helmets. When Chelsea's chairman Ken Bates turned up in his big fur coat, I stuck a helmet on his head and asked him to wear it in the directors' box before the match. He told me, "I'll do better than that," and we both walked around the ground and in front of the Fratton End with these hats on before kick-off!'

Around seventeen years later, McInnes was at the forefront of supporter attempts to wrestle Pompey out of administration and claim control. He had initially declined an approach from the Pompey Supporters' Trust to join their fight, walking away unimpressed following a particularly fractious meeting designed to win his support. However, McInnes was persuaded to return to the table by Mark Trapani, a fellow future Pompey board member, and he emerged as one of the figureheads in the battle against Portpin to seize control. The electronics entrepreneur was also among a number of high net worth figures to put in money to prevent administrator Trevor Birch liquidating the club when it became insolvent.

He said: 'I never met Balram Chainrai face to face but spoke to him a number of times over the phone. The first occasion was not a good experience because he came on ranting and raving, and I couldn't understand him really. I replied: "I don't know where you've got my telephone number from, but I'm not talking to anybody who speaks to me like that," and put the phone down.

'That marked his card for me, as clearly this was somebody who was a bully. It was a pathetic attempt to try to invoke some kind of fear in me from day one, which didn't work, of course. I was quite relaxed about it – that's one of the great things about being a Paulsgrove lad. You respect all but fear nobody. After that, he came from another angle, believing I may actually be of use to him, so the next two or three conversations were along the lines of how he didn't want the club to go out of existence, but was keen not to lose his money, so what was the solution?

'Over the four or five phone calls we had, that reasonable approach became a common denominator, although we never had long conversations. However, I always suspected his business partner Levi Kushnir was really calling the shots. Now I love the Pompey fans to bits, but we didn't have a great deal of encouragement from them early on when trying to get the football club, with Chainrai becoming the de facto shoo-in to be owner.

'Avram Grant, a decent and honourable man, also kept calling me and I got the impression he had already been approached by Chainrai and was the go-to manager for when they took the club over, although nobody admitted that. The agent Pini Zahavi was also involved with that group at the time.'

Following the succession of fan ownership in April 2013, McInnes was installed as Pompey's chairman, with Guy Whittingham appointed permanent manager on a one-year rolling contract. The legendary Blues striker had overseen 29 matches as caretaker, a club record, yet was now entrusted by the board with the challenge of achieving instant promotion from League Two. However, within 48 hours of a 2–1 home defeat to managerless Scunthorpe United which left Pompey languishing eighteenth in the table, Whittingham was sacked. He was given the axe at McInnes' home in November 2013, following 21 games at the helm.

'I wouldn't say we appointed Guy as manager; I think we adopted him, although he deserved a real shot and to get the role permanently,' McInnes said. 'We had a really good relationship, too close with hindsight. It's impossible not to like and respect Guy, whereas Andy Awford is slightly more suited for that cut-throat role. We didn't live that far from each other and I'm always a great believer in getting to know the broader family. Guy's wife, Martha, is a lovely girl, as indeed are the rest of the family.

'I was conscious that Pompey were serving as a fan ownership blueprint for other clubs to follow, so surely it would be wrong not to adopt the person who had stuck by it through thick and thin? I consulted Trevor Birch, who knew his football, and he assured me Guy was committed, comfortable to work with and a good coach. I tried to get Andy Awford to do it with him, but, in fairness to Andy, he didn't want to hitch his wagon at that moment and preferred to remain as the Academy manager.

'I didn't want to sack Guy. In my businesses, we promote loyalty and continuity, which has cost me numerous gold watches. We have given seven people Gucci watches to mark twenty years of service. In the electronics industry that just doesn't happen. Despite the caricature, my modus operandi is one of complete and utter loyalty, so my feeling was, "No, we don't want to sack Guy because you then damage the whole concept."

'As manager, the one thing he never did, and I can say the same about Andy when he later became boss, was bring in somebody from outside the club to assist. Instead he went with a bunch of people who were his mates and paid the price, basically what managers do in any walk of life. Eventually it occurred to me that it wasn't going to work. When he met at my house for the news, it was the worst day of my business life. He didn't have a clue what was coming and, I'll tell you now, if people don't have a clue that you're thinking of firing them then you're doing something wrong. Clearly, we didn't get the right message across and that was because Guy and I were so close.

'We hug now when we see each other, but his wife has never forgiven me. I saw Martha at the start of the following season for a Havant & Waterlooville friendly when she sat two rows in front.

I went up to her and said: "Look, before I come for a hug, you can choose the cold shoulder." I remained in the cold and good on her for defending her husband, I say. Did we sack Guy too early? No, with hindsight we gave him the job too early and should have thought about it more dispassionately.'

Among the four-man shortlist to replace Whittingham was Chris Wilder, who had steered Oxford United back into the Football League and then achieved stability as a League Two presence, several times flirting with play-off qualification. Instead, McInnes' preference, along with the board's majority vote, went to former Crawley Town boss Richie Barker, who was accompanied by Steve Coppell as a director of football. That managerial spell proved ill-fated, spanning 109 days with just four wins from twenty matches in all competitions.

As for Wilder, a month after being snubbed for the Pompey job, he quit Oxford for Northampton Town, saving them from relegation to non-league before leading them to the League Two title. He subsequently joined boyhood club Sheffield United in May 2016, winning the League One title before reaching the Premier League, where they are presently seventh in the stalled table. Yet McInnes has no regrets about overlooking Wilder more than six years earlier.

He added: 'When we advertised for Guy's replacement, we received all kinds of applications. I thought the only way to go through them was to split ourselves into two groups to conduct first interviews, then use that feedback during the next stage, with all members of the board involved. Chris Wilder was among a shortlist of four, although he didn't come back with any glowing references. I spoke to his Oxford United chairman, Ian Lenagan, who was not complimentary. I later ended up having a row with Lenagan because he publicly criticised us for approaching his manager, even though Wilder had applied. To be fair, he accepted the retort and was very hospitable the next time we visited the Kassam Stadium.

'Some of the board strongly favoured Exeter City manager Paul Tisdale, particularly Ashley Brown, but most were put off by him saying that Saturday wasn't the most important day of the week in football. If I was starting a club tomorrow and wanted an architect to build me a successful model, Tisdale would be the best candidate. However, I don't think he would have gone down well at Pompey – he was too laid-back and wore that country casual attire.

'Ash and I met Chris Wilder for the first time in a hotel outside Newbury. He was very tentative and unsure of himself, while the feedback hadn't been impressive. He didn't make a compelling argument on the day, his track record didn't particularly appeal and he was actually struggling at Oxford, who accepted his resignation six weeks later. I text him every now and again. What a wonderful job he has done at Sheffield United.

'Instead Richie Barker was appointed as Guy's replacement, although it was the prospect of Steve Coppell arriving with him that weighed heavily on the decision. If you think about it, we voted with our hearts in Guy's case, the common denominator being no experience. As soon as Coppell walked through the door, he had not only been there and done it, but worn the T-shirt and written the book. If we were looking for some credibility, here was the man – and alongside him was a young coach who had taken Bury to promotion from League Two a few years earlier.

'There is no way Mark Catlin influenced Barker's appointment, and to claim that would be unfair and untrue. Granted, they previously worked together at Bury and, whether he'd had conversations with Richie prior to me, I really don't know. If he did, it never showed. I voted for Barker, as did Mark, and he won by one vote. In fact, the only unanimous vote the board ever delivered for a manager was Paul Cook.'

John Kimbell was summoned to the City of London offices of Mondrian Investment Partners in Gresham Street for his maiden Pompey boardroom meeting to vote on the sacking of Andy Awford. In March 2015, the digital media businessman had been promoted from the Pompey Supporters' Trust board to replace Mick Williams in the Fratton Park hierarchy, joining fellow fan representatives Ashley Brown and Mark Trapani on the club board. Congregating at the business offices of fellow board members Chris Moth and John Kirk, a pressing topic was the future of Awford, who only eleven months earlier had kept the Blues in the Football League.

Replacing Barker with the club languishing 22nd in League Two, the caretaker boss had pulled off four straight victories to avoid relegation with three matches to spare. Such was the seismic achievement, McInnes still jokes that a gold statue of the Pompey Hall of Famer should be constructed outside Fratton Park in Awford's honour. However, following Awford's permanent appointment in the summer of 2014, Pompey were residing a disappointing fourteenth in League Two. Now, at his inaugural board meeting, Kimbell was voting on the manager's dismissal.

He said: 'I had gone from the South Stand eating a pie with my dad the week before to sitting among Pompey's board being asked my opinion on sacking the manager and club budgets. You could say it was a baptism of fire! Andy Awford was struggling and what emerged from my first board meeting was that unless results rapidly improved then we'd have to decide what to do with him.

'There were one or two who wanted to keep him, but the majority felt he should go. It wasn't just me who tipped the balance, as we could see something needed to be done. Andy will not thank me for saying it, but I didn't feel he was the right person at that time. It was the correct thing to do. It felt like we were at the tipping point and the next managerial decision would be crucial in terms of driving the club forward. What an honour to be part of that process.

'Everything came to a head at Morecambe, two weeks after that board meeting. I sat next to Iain McInnes and we sank lower and lower into our seats as we witnessed a 3–1 defeat, all the time thinking: "This can't go on. It is dreadful, dreadful, dreadful football." Our fans in the away end were jumping up and down singing "Let's all have a disco" and performing a topless conga, which in itself was embarrassing. It was great that they were doing that, but how awful to see them being forced to celebrate how bad we were. Iain asked what I thought. Well, you could see for yourself;

we can't be losing 3–1 at Morecambe. Admittedly, Pompey do not have the divine right to beat anybody, but considering the playing resources we had out there, we should have been capable of getting at least a draw.

'As I left the Globe Arena afterwards, I headed through the reception area and Andy spotted me, asking, "How are you, John? How are things?" For me, that was a very difficult moment as I knew what was in store. That's football – what could I do? I shook his hand and wished him all the best for the rest of the season. Andy left the club 48 hours later, with his assistant, Gary Waddock, stepping up as caretaker for the final four matches and he did pretty well, stabilising things. That summer the board each drew up a list of people we thought were suitable.

'Chesterfield were flying at the time and, unsurprisingly, Paul Cook's name was on all of our lists, topping mine. He wasn't going to come cheap compared to other options, but if Paul Cook couldn't get us into League One, then who would and what options were there after that? He was a manager with a pedigree for winning promotion; we had to go for it. His budget was slightly bigger than Andy's, although not significantly. I just think Paul was smarter with how he used the money, no disrespect to Guy Whittingham or Andy. His pool of contacts and scouting network was larger, while he recruited a lot from the north, such as Liverpool and Manchester, when traditionally we signed many players from London and the south.'

Cook and his assistant Leam Richardson were appointed in May 2015, fresh from steering Chesterfield to the League One play-off semi-finals, where they suffered defeat to Preston North End. Among the fourteen new Fratton Park recruits that summer were Christian Burgess and Gareth Evans, who remain key figures in the current set-up , with others including Enda Stevens, Michael Doyle, Kal Naismith and Gary Roberts. That 2015–16 campaign concluded with the heartbreak of play-off semi-final elimination at the hands of Plymouth Argyle, following Peter Hartley's stoppage-time aggregate winner, with a visibly emotional Cook declining to carry out all press duties afterwards. The following season, however, would finally yield that prized promotion, claiming the League Two crown in the process.

Kimbell added: 'Paul was very charismatic and a real Jekyll and Hyde character. I really liked him. He saw a player, wanted him and that was it, irrespective of what form they were in at that time. He would have recruited most of Chesterfield's squad if he could, putting forward Jay O'Shea, Tendayi Darikwa, Sam Clucas, Rommy Boco, Sam Morsy, Gary Roberts and Eoin Doyle. We got a few of them in the end, though! In the case of O'Shea, for the first and only time Paul created a video presentation on why we should sign him. It was very interesting, and quite a compelling pitch, but at the time not financially right.

'We never put any pressure on Paul as a board – firing him didn't come into any conversation – but he put pressure on himself and was very aware of occasional rumblings from the fans, which got to him. Through it all, though, he stood by his players, which was admirable. In November 2016, a board meeting was held at Verisona Law's offices at Lakeside to discuss Michael Doyle's future following that infamous dressing-room fight with Christian Burgess. Three or four of the board present absolutely felt Doyle should be sacked. We talked about it at length and it was argued that, considering he was the captain and leader of that team, he should be fired for such behaviour. It wasn't what was expected of any professional in any job, and certainly if it happened in any office, that person would be sacked immediately. So why should Michael Doyle be treated differently?

'With any board meeting, we'd talk among ourselves before Paul later joined us for half an hour. What followed was the manager putting forward a very compelling argument for why his captain should stay. Michael should be grateful for how persuasive that speech was. It was a split board, then Paul arrived and made it clear he didn't want Doyle sacked. Although he understood our reasoning should we decide to act, admitting the Irishman's behaviour was unacceptable, Paul insisted he needed him to remain. It was explained this was about getting out of League Two and, in order to achieve that, we had to ensure our best players were available. At the end of that meeting we voted: Michael Doyle was staying, but it was close.

'Paul was obviously right. I don't believe we would have gone up without Michael. Who would we have replaced him with? To this day, he is still performing for Notts County and in February made his 800th career appearance. Personally, I voted to keep him, but wanted it recorded that a repeat of such behaviour should see him fired for unprofessional conduct. From what I learnt during my time on Pompey's board and now through my current job as a football intermediary, football is like no other profession. What happens at clubs is just incredible; it's something you need to ring-fence and do your own thing.'

Cook rocked Fratton Park by quitting for Wigan Athletic just 26 days after claiming the League Two title. During the promotion campaign, there were several occasions when those among the Blues hierarchy felt their manager may walk, amid supporter criticism and escalating expectations. Then, with mission accomplished, he followed through with that occasional threat, accompanied by assistant Leam Richardson and first-team physios Nick Meace and Andy Procter in exiting for their League One rivals.

'Mark Catlin would sometimes come to us and relate that he'd spoken with Paul, who wasn't happy for one reason or another. Two or three times we'd heard rumblings about him potentially walking, but the manager never mentioned it to us at boardroom level,' said Kimbell. 'The first occasion was around November 2016, when things weren't going particularly well. While watching Channel 5's *Football League Tonight*, I noticed Kenny Jackett was a studio guest, so Googled him and discovered he'd just left Rotherham United. That evening I emailed Mark Catlin, writing: "If Paul is going to leave, Kenny Jackett is available. We should be looking at him." Then things at Pompey picked up again.

'I don't think he was ever really close to quitting – it was just his character. He wore his heart on his sleeve and if ever he was upset about a performance or a player then he wouldn't hold back. That's the emotional guy he is. Paul's departure happened very quickly. On the Friday evening, Wigan's chief executive, Jonathan Jackson, requested permission to talk to him about their vacant position, with Mark making clear we didn't want him to leave. That night, emails flew back and forth between the board. We voted to do what we could to keep our manager, but was there a decision to make? Had Paul already made up his mind?

'The following morning, Mark spoke to Paul and Leam, who stated that they didn't want to leave but were seeking improvements on their respective contracts. Paul had already received a significant pay rise following promotion, a stipulation built into his contract. Now he wanted a further salary increase, in addition to pay rises for three backroom staff in Leam, Nick Meace and Andy Procter. In the case of Paul, fair enough, maybe Leam too, then you start going into additional thousands for Nick and Andy, so where do you draw the line?

'We returned with an increase for Paul and his staff, but it wasn't enough, Wigan were offering a lot more. You get to the point that if money is really that important, you have to move on. Within our budgets, we had committed all we could without being financially stupid. Subsequently there were supporter comments about how the board supposedly didn't do enough to keep Paul, but that wasn't the case whatsoever. We'd had two decent seasons with him. He won us promotion as champions and we were looking forward to him building a squad for League One, but it's football. He had probably already made up his mind.'

Jackett was installed as Cook's replacement, the sole candidate to be interviewed, despite early interest registered by former Pompey boss Steve Cotterill, Jimmy Floyd Hasselbaink and Alex McLeish. Keen to avoid prying eyes, initial talks were held around the kitchen table at Kimbell's former Godalming home, with the ex-Wolverhampton Wanderers boss later signing a two-year deal. As for Kimbell, following the Tornante takeover two months later, he departed Pompey's board, before also stepping down from Trust involvement in October 2017 to return to his South Stand seat.

The 44-year-old added: 'To be fair to the Eisners, the management situation was occurring during the early stages of their takeover. They were very much, "Look, it's your call; it's not our club. You do what you think is right as you are the guys in control." Personally, I don't think they would have got on with Paul. Admittedly, it has been Mark Catlin still running things, but there would have been clashes with the Americans. Paul's a very combustible character and they would have struggled to handle him, which is why Kenny is the perfect match for the Eisners. He's a steady hand who is experienced and trusted. I think the owners like the stability he offers.

'We contacted him on the day Paul officially left and he became the only person we interviewed. Everyone warmed to him very quickly. He's a likeable guy and you can't question his credentials, while he possessed a very clear vision of where he saw the club. He's also the complete opposite to Paul, which kind of appealed, and I think he's done a great job so far. We may sometimes question his decisions and preferred style of play, but we've been knocking on the door of automatic promotion again this season. If you were told two years ago that Kenny was going to deliver two Wembley finals, the play-offs, be top of League One for almost four months last season and possess a 52.72 per cent win percentage, any Pompey fan would have taken that, surely? I am obviously a Kenny advocate, but I believe he has done a good job for us.'

JOHN KEELEY AND ALEX BASS

20 April 2020

John Keeley is aching, his debut in the Pompey goalkeeping collective's Zoom fitness session instantly taking its toll. The regular early-morning bike ride, negotiating a 26-mile coastal journey from Worthing to Brighton Marina, has sufficiently maintained his physical wellbeing since football's suspension. The Blues' keeping coach has put his faith in the yellow Raleigh Max mountain bike purchased second-hand for £75 on the day the nation's lockdown began. With a snood pulled over his mouth, his six-day-a-week route has been both invigorating and socially responsible.

Still, Keeley, who has been furloughed along with the majority of Fratton Park's coaching staff and office workers, yesterday sought an extra workout alongside his four goalkeeping charges. Ex-England conditioning coach Chris Neville has utilised video conferencing platform Zoom to host twice-weekly sessions for first-team custodians Craig MacGillivray and Alex Bass. They are joined by youngster Taylor Seymour, with recent recruit Duncan Turnbull also participating from his Illinois home and negotiating the six-hour time difference, having returned to his native USA during the coronavirus crisis.

Neville spent six years as the Blues' head of strength and conditioning during their Premier League pomp, a club connection which prompted the offer of his services on a voluntary basis during a time of training inactivity for footballers. Now the ever-amiable Keeley has opted to sign up, much to his body's disgust.

'I'm trying to keep fit and yesterday joined one of the Zoom sessions for the first time, although I'm aching now,' laughed the former Brighton & Hove Albion stalwart. 'This is Chris' domain. He's a good friend of mine and offered to help out with our lads during this difficult time. Sessions last an hour, with breaks, and not only maintain fitness but also keep the banter going between the boys and help everyone stay chirpy.

'On Tuesdays it's more fitness based, with star jumps, squats and strengthening, while Thursdays is weight work, with the players using equipment they have at home. It is hugely beneficial to the lads and we really appreciate Chris' input. We now have four goalkeepers at the club. In the hope that this season resumes, it is crucial that they have followed their individual training programmes to ensure they're ready for action. These Zoom sessions are a little extra and the boys enjoy their involvement. I'm someone who also keeps himself fit. Obviously, I'm unable to use my gym membership at present, so the next best thing has been using the bike, which has quickly escalated into putting the miles in. I love it. I'm not sure when I'll be back on Zoom, though!'

Keeley's Pompey association began in July 2007, when he relinquished his role as League One Brighton's first-team goalkeeping coach to work under Paul Hart in the Academy. Following Avram Grant's decision to manage West Ham United in May 2010, taking Dave Coles along with him, Keeley was promoted to a first-team set-up now overseen by Steve Cotterill. Subsequently working with David James, Asmir Begović and Jamie Ashdown, he quit a financially ravaged Fratton Park in January 2013, joining Neville in following Michael Appleton to Blackburn Rovers. However, he returned for a second spell in the summer of 2016, following a four-month period with Chinese Super League side Guangzhou R&F.

Keeley was immediately faced with a goalkeeping department comprised of teenager Alex Bass and triallists Michael Crowe and Eric Grimes. With Paul Cook's Pompey striving for promotion in the 2016–17 season following the previous campaign's League Two play-off semi-final defeat with emergency loanee Ryan Allsop in goal, the challenge was laid down to the newcomer.

Keeley added: 'Basically, my remit was to find a goalkeeper who could win us promotion. I gathered that the previous season we'd had a bit of bad luck in that position, using five in total, with a number of injuries having a big impact. I know people have a go at Ryan Allsop about his play-off performances, but he'd just come in on loan from Bournemouth and hadn't trained for a while because the season had finished. At least he showed a bit of grit and put himself up to play, and you can't knock that.

'It was the agent Eamonn Collins, a friend of Paul Cook, who suggested David Forde and straight away I agreed. I've always had Fordie's number and been friendly with him. Funnily enough, when I was at Pompey first time around, with the club in administration and looking to get me off the wage bill, I went for an interview as Millwall's goalkeeping coach and Kenny Jackett offered me the job. I turned it down, though, as it would have involved too much travelling from my Worthing home. Had I taken it, I would have worked with Fordie much earlier. I ended up going to Blackburn Rovers with Michael Appleton and would have liked to have signed him then, when he was three years younger.

'Still, Fordie was exactly what Pompey needed: a keeper with the ability to collect crosses. We required somebody to dominate his area, taking the pressure off the back four, while also being able to strike a nice ball. Although contracted to Millwall for another twelve months and on good money, he was keen and we signed him on a season-long loan. He was brilliant that season. He was aged 36 when he arrived and didn't train every day. We gave him Mondays off in addition to the usual Wednesday. Footballers like to feel they're being looked after, which means they give you a little extra. These days, Mondays are effectively a second recovery day anyway. Besides, Fordie would use that day off constructively, taking part in yoga sessions. Everyone had respect for him. He walks into the training ground and he's a man, taking no nonsense off anyone, but he was good with people. He did exactly what we wanted him to do – I couldn't have asked for any more.

'Paul Cook told me that we were never attacked that much at home. People came and set up defensively, yet there was a problem keeping clean sheets. Fordie fitted the bill. His first game was a friendly at Championship side Bristol City in July 2016. It finished in a goalless draw and he was coming for crosses – it was brilliant to watch. Yes, he let in goals which he should have saved, but I wasn't too worried that he wasn't as agile as he had been. It was the fact he could come and take the crosses, while his distribution off the floor was excellent; he could put the ball anywhere.

'That summer we also required a number two which was going to be cheap and cheerful and able to train every day, so we signed Liam O'Brien as a free agent from Dagenham & Redbridge. We had previously recruited him from QPR for the Academy in 2008, but it didn't really work and he went off doing his own thing. When he returned, he was a superb number two, playing in all the reserve-team games and not missing a day's training, which allowed Alex Bass to go on loan to non-league Salisbury for the season to aid his development. Following promotion to League One, Cookie left for Wigan Athletic and then Kenny came in. Fordie was told there was unfortunately no chance of a contract and that they were looking for someone younger. Even if Cookie had stayed, I think it would have been the same outcome.'

Jackett's arrival as Pompey manager in June 2017 prompted the recruitment of Luke McGee from Tottenham Hotspur to fill the goalkeeping vacancy. Having earned plaudits for his performances while on a season-long loan at Peterborough United the previous campaign, the keeper was signed on a three-year deal for an undisclosed fee. The 2017–18 season would see the Spurs Academy product finish as leading appearance maker, featuring 50 times as the Blues finished an encouraging eighth upon their return to League One level.

Then, in June 2018, Pompey's boss plucked Craig MacGillivray from Shrewsbury Town on a free transfer, which proved to be an inspired piece of business. The former PE teacher dislodged McGee to establish himself as the undisputed number one, saving a vital spot-kick from Lee Cattermole in their Checkatrade Trophy penalty shoot-out win over Sunderland.

Keeley said: 'I was unaware of Luke when he arrived. I believed we were getting Christian Walton on loan from Brighton and thought the deal was done. Then I walked into training and Luke was sitting there signing. Walton would have been my choice, but Luke went on to play 45 league games that season, with Kenny giving Bassy the final match against Peterborough for his Football League debut.

'To be fair, with Craig MacGillivray a year later, Kenny asked me to look at his clips and give my opinion. To be totally honest, there wasn't that much footage, but, from the clips which were available, he could make some unbelievable saves. Craig played against us for Shrewsbury in January 2018 because Dean Henderson was serving a suspension and had a really good game.

'We didn't have a great deal of money to spend on a goalie and I believed I could work with Craig. He has been an excellent signing. His shot stopping is really good, if the ball is hung up then he'll come and catch a cross, while he reads the ball well with through balls and he's so quick off his line. The only thing he probably needs to practise is his kicking off the floor, which he will probably admit. You don't get into a Scotland squad playing for a League One side unless you have something about you.

'I go to work every day looking to improve someone – that's my aim with all our goalkeepers. I love seeing people improve and then going on to achieve more; that gives me a lot of pride. When I was at Blackburn, I brought through David Raya. He made his debut at the age of nineteen away at Leeds United and he hasn't looked back since, subsequently earning a £3m move to Brentford. Things like that give me a lot of pleasure because I helped him at the start of his career.'

On New Year's Day, Jackett delivered a shock by dropping MacGillivray in favour of Bass for the League One trip to Gillingham. The then

21-year-old had previously deputised when Pompey's first choice was away on international duty with Scotland, earning six appearances by the season's midway point. Among those outings was a stunning Leasing.com Trophy display at Oxford United, followed by a clean sheet in the Fratton Park league encounter with the Gills. However, in the aftermath of a deeply disappointing 3–1 defeat at MK Dons, the Blues boss opted for a goalkeeping change three days later, a decision which caught all by surprise, including Keeley.

He said: 'Listen, Alex has been ready for more than a year now. I know everyone's a bit surprised at Craig getting left out – and so was I at the time – but I have always said Alex has been ready. You can just tell. It's the way he was in training, making save after save, then playing in the Premier League Cup against teams like Everton and being absolutely brilliant. The players have been saying, "Bassy was unbelievable again this morning in training," and I think seeing how good he was wore Craig down a little.

'When Craig was left out at Gillingham, everyone was surprised, but it has proven to be the right decision, because Bassy has been unbelievable ever since. To be honest, I had no input. We have a team meeting every morning and, on that occasion, Kenny told us the only change would be Gaz Evans coming in for Andy Cannon. I then saw Craig and we began discussing the game, focusing on topics such as who takes Gillingham's corners, which opposition player stands on the keeper, just general match issues. The next thing, Kenny shouts, "Craig, Craig," and pulled him into his office. After twenty minutes, Craig emerged. He had been left out of the side.

'Craig asked to talk to me. As soon as he said that, I knew. I could read his face, and then he explained what had happened. I pulled Bassy over and said, "You're playing tomorrow." And he said, "Am I?" He didn't know. The thing is, he had been ready for ages. Now Kenny had selected him on the basis of a gut feeling. I would have played Bassy from the start of the 2017–18 season when Luke McGee arrived. Every Monday morning we have the chance to say who should play and I always suggested Bassy, always. I have nothing against Luke, I love him as a kid, and he's a really nice lad, but I just think Bassy is up there.'

Bass was in line to make his fourteenth consecutive league start before the suspension of March's visit of Accrington Stanley, along with the entire Premier League and Football League programme.

Such has been the 22-year-old's eye-catching impact following Jackett's remarkable show of faith, he has so far missed just two of Pompey's nineteen fixtures in all competitions during 2020. MacGillivray had been handed two Leasing.com Trophy opportunities in January but, beyond that, was forced to watch from the bench as his former understudy grasped his surprise first-team chance. Pompey's regard for the Academy product also saw him presented with a new three-and-a-half-year deal in January, despite having another eighteen months on his existing contract. Keeley recognises the talents of the protégé he has been honing for the last three years.

'I honestly think Bassy will go all the way to the top. He can play international football. But don't tell him!' said Keeley. 'That's my opinion, but I think he has it in him to go all the way. He could be fighting Dean Henderson for a place in the England team in the future. He comes and catches crosses, he makes good saves, he's very good at dealing with through balls and his kicking is good. His positional sense around the goal for shot stopping is excellent. Look at the save he made against Bolton going down to his left, the saves he made against Peterborough in the second half which stopped us getting trollied. He gets his angles right and these are the little things we have practised all the time in training – the difference between making a save or a goal being conceded.

'Craig is good at it as well, don't get me wrong, but Bassy is the best keeper I have seen at that age. David Raya at Blackburn was brilliant, but Bassy is above him; he has the whole package. He works unbelievably hard. He'll train with me in the morning and afterwards does all his gym work, never cheating on anything. All the times you hear players saying, "I don't want to do shooting, I don't want to do this," well he wants to. For a young lad like that, they're the things that help you come through. Since coming into the side against Gillingham, he has grown in strength and is getting better and better. I'm not just saying this, because everyone is talking about him, everyone. I get agents on to me all the time about him.

'Only this morning, Cheltenham keeper Scott Flinders texted me saying: "Your goalie is really good. How good do you think he is?" Obviously, I told him. I think a lot are looking at him. Former Wolves keeper Matt Murray, who now works for Sky Sports and is also an agent, absolutely loves him. He tried to get Bassy on his books a few years ago after seeing him play against Barnsley in a Premier League Cup game. He messaged me and said: "He's the best young goalie I have seen in our country."

'He's such a nice kid and everyone loves him. He's polite, level-headed, not a show-off, not loud, just a very nice kid. The club signed him to a three-and-a-half-year deal in January, but they didn't have a choice as someone would have been on to him. The club have backed themselves and that is only right. Should someone come in for him when he is on a long-term deal, they are able to ask what they want. You can't knock Craig at all, because he has been absolutely brilliant. Unfortunately, he's got someone who has overtaken him and possesses that much more at the moment.'

Pompey's goalkeeping pool has undergone something of an overhaul since the turn of the year. During the January transfer window, Bradford City offered McGee the chance of regular football for the remainder of the campaign, a loan opportunity he gratefully accepted. It had been thirteen months since his last Blues outing and, with the 24-year-old's contract expiring in the summer, the brutal truth is that he has no Fratton Park future.

McGee's Valley Parade exit created an opening for a third-choice custodian, with 6ft 7in Duncan Turnbull invited to trial after video clips supplied by his agent had impressed Keeley. An accountancy graduate from the University of Notre Dame, Indiana, in December, he had been drafted by MLS side Houston Dynamo before opting to try his luck in Europe instead. The 22-year-old subsequently spent two weeks with

Manchester United in January, training with their first team and under-23s, among them David de Gea. Last winter also saw spells at Aberdeen and Huddersfield Town. Coincidentally, Turnbull possesses family links with the area, with grandparents, Bob and Sheena, living in Fareham. Bob is also a former Fratton Park season-ticket holder.

The family had originally relocated to the south coast from East Kilbride, where they lived across the road from St Mirren manager Alex Ferguson. Their son, Neil, would later spend a season as centre-half for Bognor Regis Town under the timeless Jack Pearce, still in charge at Nyewood Lane even now. When Neil left England as an 18-year-old to study at the University of Akron in Ohio, he met future wife Sue. Now their son, Duncan, is on Pompey's books, signing a deal until the summer of 2021 just days before the season was paused.

Another new arrival has been eighteen-year-old keeper Taylor Seymour, earning the offer of a third-year scholarship after training with the club from December. Currently studying electrical installations at Chichester College, he progressed through Lewes' under-18s to warrant first-team recognition with the Isthmian Premier League side, making two appearances during the current campaign. The Worthing-based youngster has represented the Academy on occasion this term and the eighteen-year-old, who has appeared for England Colleges, remains a work in progress for Keeley.

Pompey's youth set-up has also swelled its coaching ranks by appointing ex-Pompey keeper Michael Poke as head of goalkeeping, his remit including coaching the under-18s and a prospective reserve team. An appointment driven by Keeley, the 34-year-old made the switch after quitting a role at Southampton working with the 9–15 age groups. For Keeley, however, there was sadness at the February departure of Croatian under-18 keeper Petar Durin by mutual consent. Recruited nineteen months earlier from Italian side Atalanta, the Blues had high hopes for the youngster, yet the move did not work.

'I felt sorry for Petar in the end. That kid had lived away from home since he was thirteen, having been to Italy by the time he came to us,' said Keeley. 'When he arrived in July 2018, I looked at him in training and thought, "Wow, we definitely have a goalie here," but the time away from home had taken its toll. Every day there was something different: his head was down, he wasn't coming in, he wasn't training. He believed he was going to be first-team goalie after a year – that was in his mind. He had no concept of how it works. Then, when he realised he wasn't as good as the others, it really hit him. He lost heart and went on loan to Bognor and couldn't hack it. He had an awful time there and returned early after six appearances. That is when I said to him: "Look, Petar, I think you're better going back to Croatia and spending some time at home. Don't even worry about football for a little while, just enjoy yourself."

'I would bring him over to my house for some weekends, otherwise I don't think he was doing a great deal. His best friend was at Chelsea – they're the same age and would meet up in London – but other than that it was the same old, same old for Petar every weekend. My partner has a huge family, so there's always something going on at weekends, such as a barbecue, and I'd invite him. He's such a nice kid and I wouldn't want anyone to go through what he did.

'On the football side, it initially took a few months for his work permit to come through, then, when it finally arrived, his thigh went while kicking during a warm-up ahead of a game, knocking him back for two months. It happened again when he returned. Petar didn't have the best of times, and mentally that took its toll on him. Someone will always be interested in him and he has been playing for Croatia at under-18 level, but first and foremost he has to start enjoying life again.

'I spoke to him last week to see how he was. Apparently, Dinamo Zagreb are looking at him. They were interested last year, prompting him to come to me and ask if we would let him go out on loan. I told him "without a doubt", but it never materialised. Hopefully he sorts himself out.'

The Bass family are woven through the fabric of Fair Oak Cricket Club, a dynasty synonymous with the Southern Premier League outfit. For almost two decades, Ian Bass has been a batting mainstay, registering in excess of 4,200 runs in local cricket and these days lending his considerable experience as skipper of an otherwise youthful IV team. With wife Jo once a fixture on cricket tea duty, the lure was inescapable for sons Nick and Alex.

All-rounder Nick remains largely a first XI presence, so far capturing 213 wickets with searing pace for the club. Alex is different. As a wicketkeeper, the youngest of the Horton Heath brood possessed rich promise, earning Hampshire recognition from under-9s level and subsequently elevated through the county's age groups. Having reached Hampshire under-16s as a fourteen-year-old, he counted future England leg-spinner Mason Crane among his team-mates, along with Hampshire first-class performers Brad Taylor, Michael Bates, Tom Alsop and Oli Soames. Then a football career came calling.

'Cricket was my first love,' said Bass. 'I became involved at the age of four or five and carried it on from there, representing Fair Oak, where my dad and brother also played. I was never told by Pompey that I could no longer play cricket, but it seemed the sensible decision. I've never liked running the risk. Being a goalkeeper, you don't want to break a finger in cricket. That would be stupid.

'I was a wicketkeeper and I would like to think of myself as a good batsman, but was a classic bat at seven keeper. I was definitely known for my work behind the stumps, getting the occasional good score with the bat, with a best of 85 against Hayling Island, but I was never someone in the top order. Former player Bobby Parks was the wicketkeeping coach at Hampshire and, once a month, would bring Michael Bates to sessions as his demo man. It was basically, "I want you to keep wicket like this." Bobby thought Bates was going to be Hampshire's wicketkeeper for years and years, and he did play 52 first-team matches, but unfortunately his batting was not quite up to his other abilities. Bates' hands were unbelievable and he is now Hampshire's wicketkeeping coach.

'There were occasions when I kept wicket to Mason Crane for Hampshire. He was a nightmare, I'm not going to lie. I couldn't pick his googlies whatsoever, so God knows how the batsmen managed. I have to admit, there were a lot of byes conceded. In two-day cricket, there would be him from one end and Brad Taylor from the other. I'd be standing up to the stumps with a helmet in the beating sun all day as they bowled away.

'Crane would take me to one side and try to explain what he was going to do for a googly, but I just couldn't work it out – it was too hard to pick. It got to the stage where, after a missed catch or stumping, he said: "If I shine the ball before I bowl it's going to be a googly. If I rub it on the back of my leg, then it's going to be a drifter." There must have been four different signals in the end and I still couldn't get it!

'He was a good lad, and you could tell he was going to go far in the game just because of his sheer love for it – he was always bowling. I was with Hampshire under-16s and regularly taking part in winter nets when Pompey offered me a scholarship in December 2013. There wasn't a massive decision. I opted to throw everything at it rather than going down the cricket route. Besides, I felt I was too tall to be a wicketkeeper and far better equipped for football.

'You can't compare keeping wicket to goalkeeping; it's very different. Of course, there's your hand-eye coordination, in terms of catching the ball, but other than that there isn't any similarity. For a start, your positioning is dissimilar, as is the diving. In cricket, you are told to tumble roll when catching the ball, whereas in football you dive on your side. Really there aren't a lot of comparisons other than attempting to catch a ball.'

An Arsenal fan, influenced by his dad and granddad, who originally hailed from North London, Bass' pathway into football with Pompey had kicked off with rejection. Turned away as an eight-year-old, he would eventually earn entrance into the youth set-up at the age of fourteen and within two years featured in pre-season fixtures during the summer of 2016. To date he has made 27 first-team appearances, including one against his beloved Arsenal in March's FA Cup defeat. Afterwards, the 22-year-old claimed the shirt of opposite number Bernd Leno, although the Gunners' first-choice keeper had been an unused substitute to allow understudy Emiliano Martinez game time. It has certainly been an eventful ride for the 6ft 3in stopper.

> He added: 'At the age of eight, I began as a centre-half for Bashley Cobras. Then, after a year, the goalkeeper decided to leave and, being tall even as a kid, I volunteered to take over. I never really enjoyed it that much on the pitch, so thought I'd give it a go. Funnily enough, my dad had been a goalkeeper, playing for Burridge, but never pushed me into a position. He felt it more beneficial to allow me to discover the role I preferred. Then, after playing in three or four summer under-9s tournaments, my dad was approached by four or five clubs interested in me, among them Pompey and Southampton. As Pompey spoke to us first, I attended a six-week trial, but unfortunately didn't do enough to be taken on.
>
> 'Then, at the age of fourteen, I went along to a League Training Centre in Eastleigh run by Andy Rowles, who had been my PE teacher at Botley Church of England Primary School. Coincidentally, his dad, Jan, was a scout in Pompey's Academy and I was invited back there for another trial, basically six years later. This time I was with the club for six months, with two other goalkeepers also around, so I was never 100 per cent certain I'd get anything. However, I ended up signing and have been here ever since.'

Bass became a first-year scholar in July 2014, the eight-strong intake also including Adam May, Calvin Davies and Christian Oxlade-Chamberlain. Within eighteen days, the sixteen-year-old was thrust into the first-team glare following a 59th-minute introduction as a substitute in Andy Awford's side's 6–1 friendly win at Bognor Town. With Michael Poke injured, the following week he attended Pompey's pre-season tour to the Five Lakes Resort in Maldon, Essex, serving as back up to Paul Jones and featuring in a 2–0 win at Thurrock.

During the subsequent 2014–15 campaign, Bass occupied the bench as an unused substitute in four outings, with Jones ever-present for all 52 fixtures that term. Nonetheless, it established a first-team connection which exists to the present day. A season-long loan at non-league Salisbury in 2016–17 provided a crucial opportunity for development, making 46 appearances for Steve Claridge's side before suffering an Evo-Stik Southern League Division One South & West play-off final defeat to Tiverton Town.

There was an injury-hampered spell at Torquay United, comprising eight games and five clean sheets, before Bass was recalled to Fratton Park in December 2018 following a wrist problem sustained by number two McGee. It ensured that the rookie was on the bench at Wembley for Pompey's Checkatrade Trophy success over Sunderland in March 2019 and began this campaign ahead of McGee as MacGillivray's back-up.

> He said: 'I was thrown in early doors, which I think helped. It was good to be in that first-team environment from the start, training with experienced keepers and allowing you to compare yourself. You look at what they're doing, learning from people without them telling you what to do.
>
> 'I went on loan to Salisbury for a season as an eighteen-year-old, which was so important to my development. At such a young age, I played in a competitive environment, where men are bigger, stronger and going to kick you, but eventually you overcome that. I took the confidence back to Pompey. I thoroughly enjoyed my time there as it's a great little club, although I was pretty scared of Steve Claridge when I first went in! He wasn't my biggest fan for the first couple of games and was critical early on. I didn't hit the ground running, as much as I would have liked to. It was a complete change from Academy football and I was a tall, skinny boy at the time who got beaten up on the pitch a bit.
>
> 'Steve didn't hold back from things he'd say to us in the dressing room. As an eighteen-year-old, when you know you've made a mistake it's quite hard to take, but I learnt and suddenly we had a successful season. I managed to win over the manager – he's a great guy and I really enjoyed it there. I thought Torquay last season was also going to be a great loan for me in National League South. They were a club with ambitions of bouncing back following relegation and the manager, Gary Owers, made it clear I was his first choice.

'I played four pre-season games before feeling something tight in my groin. It turned out to be a grade-two tear, so I missed the opening four matches. When I returned, I was back in the team, only to sustain a grade-two tear in the medial knee ligament in my left leg during a draw with Woking at the end of September, putting me out for another two months. Then, in December, Keelo called one afternoon to tell me Luke's wrist was sore, so Pompey wanted me back as soon as possible and I stayed at Fratton Park for the rest of the season.'

This term, MacGillivray's elevation to Scotland's squad in September presented understudy Bass with game time in Leasing.com Trophy victories over Crawley Town and Norwich under-21s in his absence. Upon the following month's international weekend, the youngster was recalled for the trip to Oxford United for the final Southern Group B fixture, with the holders' qualification for the next stage already assured.

What unfolded that evening was a stunning display of goalkeeping from Bass in front of those 1,548 present. Pompey's undisputed man of the match performance helped his side to a 2–2 draw before pulling off a penalty save in the subsequent 5–4 shoot-out triumph. It represented a key performance in the career of the Academy product who, almost three months later, would earn Jackett's preference over MacGillivray.

Bass said: 'I'd like to think Oxford was the match which showed everybody what I was about. That game kind of pushed me to where I am now. Sometimes you make loads of saves in a match and sometimes you don't – that's the way it goes. You don't want to be big-headed, but I knew I'd played well that day. It was the final game of the group stages which we had won on penalties, so it was a good feeling. Regardless, it's important I remain level-headed. I was happy with how I played, but I didn't start going around saying I had finally arrived or anything like that.

'To be honest, receiving a first-team call-up ahead of Craig for the trip to Gillingham a few months later was a massive shock. Initially I thought someone was taking the mickey. The previous match was a 3–1 defeat at MK Dons, but I wouldn't say anyone had a stinker or that it required drastic change. I was as surprised as anyone looking at the team sheet knowing I was playing.

'It wasn't expected, but that's football; it's how it goes. Later in life it may even happen to me. Craig has been really good about the situation. Alan Knight always tells me about the nightmares he had as goalkeeping coach with John Sullivan and Phil Smith, who couldn't stand each other, but it's definitely not like that between me and Craig. Everyone mentions the goalkeepers' union, but it's an odd one. As a number two, you're trying to get his shirt; as number one, you're trying to make sure he doesn't get it. It's going to be a competitive battle, but that's football. As a keeper, if you're out of the team there usually won't be a chance to return unless there's an injury. When you have that spot, you have to do well enough to ensure nobody can replace you.

'Craig and I still room together on away trips. There's a good, competitive working relationship there, both trying to be better than the other, striving to be Pompey's number one. Undoubtedly, I felt a hell of a lot of pressure for that Gillingham match. Craig has performed superbly for so long and is well regarded among supporters. Now I had the challenge to keep him out and it has pushed me to become better. Should you make a mistake, you know that next time you won't repeat it. It's about learning. I'm still young and I know I'm going to commit errors in games, but hopefully it doesn't cost the team. I am still learning.

'I believe I've been solid enough during my current run of matches, although I'm not claiming I've been perfect. There are times when things haven't gone our way, while we haven't won every match with a clean sheet. There are little things for me to work on. I haven't played as many games in my career as some people my age would have, but you must learn on the job. I've done well enough to keep my place and hopefully can continue to get better and better.'

It's approaching seven weeks since the Blues were last in action, when a midweek home encounter with Fleetwood Town yielded a 2–2 draw. It represented Bass' 23rd start in what will be regarded as his breakthrough season at Fratton Park and one which now raises questions over the future of goalkeeping rival MacGillivray. During the campaign's suspension, five of Pompey's squad tested positive for coronavirus, a development Bass learnt through the players' WhatsApp group following confirmation in March.

Meanwhile, the Football League have reiterated their intention to resume the campaign, with chairman Rick Parry writing to all 72 member clubs detailing estimates of 56 days being required to complete the fixture list. In addition, players have been advised that a return to training will not be possible until 16 May at the earliest. There is growing belief, however, that the Football League will not be able to keep pace with the financially flexible Premier League's aspirations for resumption. Bass harbours doubts over whether fourth-placed Pompey will be able to continue their promotion push.

'If I am being perfectly honest, I cannot see the season restarting,' said the keeper. 'There is talk about behind-closed-doors games, but how are we going to cope without the revenue provided by 18,000 supporters at Fratton Park every weekend? It's a tough one.

'The French and Dutch leagues have already been cancelled. Personally I can see the same happening to us, but you must keep yourself in the best possible shape should the League One season resume. Looking at the League One table, we're in a good position with nine matches to play. Obviously, some clubs have their own reasons for not getting it started, but for us there's the massive incentive of potential promotion. Let's hope so.'

SARAH MERRIX AND IAN BURRELL

29 April 2020

Dom Merrix refused to allow red into his North End home on account of its association with fierce rivals Southampton. Such was the passionate Pompey fan's loathing, anything bearing the remotest resemblance was banished. Even this season's first-team shirt incurred his wrath, refusing to buy it because of the four red markings intruding upon the customary royal blue.

Cherished recollections of the North Stand season-ticket holder's quirks invite laughter from partner Sarah. It has been a month since Dom's tragic passing at the age of 48, having contracted coronavirus. He leaves behind Sarah and ten-year-old daughter, Ellie-Mai. Pompey supporters rallied to raise £12,627 for the funeral of one of their own, whose story touched the heart of a city.

'Dom was very, very passionate. He was vocal, backed the team 100 per cent and was Pompey through and through,' said Sarah. 'He wouldn't have anything in the house that was red, purely because of his hatred of Southampton. When Virgin Media became their sponsor, he insisted we changed to Sky. If anything red entered our house, the message was, "Get it out." Our wardrobe contains all three Pompey shirts from each season, apart from this year. He complained there was too much red under the arm. Apparently, if the stripe had been thinner, it would have been okay. He was not a red person.

'I came home from work one day and, while looking in my wardrobe, couldn't see my pair of burgundy high-heel shoes. When I asked Dom if he knew where they'd gone, he insisted he didn't have any idea. I later discovered them in a massive tree at the bottom of our garden – where he'd thrown them. They're still up there now as I can't reach them.

'Dom wouldn't even visit Southampton other than for a Pompey match. When he cracked the screen on his iPhone, he refused to take it to the Apple store in Westquay Shopping Centre for repair. Instead he just left it, before eventually getting an upgrade.

'On one occasion, our daughter, Ellie-Mai, came home from nursery aged three or four. She was crying her eyes out saying, "Mum, Mum, Mum! Dad's not going to love me any more." When I asked why, she was upset that she'd been put into the ladybird group at her new infant school. She was saying: "I have to go to the red team. I'm a scummer." It's not hard to see where she picked it up from, and she was never allowed to wear red as a baby. At one stage she wasn't allowed a red pen or red colouring pencil at home. I mentioned to Dom that he really had to lay off. He agreed. Mind you, a few years ago I went to buy a new car and, as we walked into the showroom, Ellie-Mai said: "Don't buy red, Mum. I won't get in it." That was pure Dom. A friend of mine even wouldn't drive a red car to his funeral because she knew he wouldn't like it.'

At Pompey's 2010 FA Cup final against Chelsea, Sarah proposed to Dom on Wembley Way. Joined by three friends for the gesture, they revealed white shirts with a word written on each in a blue marker pen. When standing together, it read 'Will You Marry Me?'. Despite playful Chelsea supporters urging him to reject the offer, her boyfriend accepted. The engagement was a long one, with Sarah changing her surname by deed poll in the meantime to prevent confusion, but the year 2022 had been pencilled in as the wedding date.

That represented sufficient time to save after the family embarked on the holiday of a lifetime in October, spending three weeks in Orlando, in Florida, with Walt Disney World inevitably dominating the itinerary. However, the family suffered a blow when Dom was made redundant as a fault dispatcher with energy supplier SSE in March, ending fifteen years of employment with the Havant-based company. Then, earlier this month, he passed away suddenly in heartbreaking circumstances, having seemingly recovered from coronavirus.

Sarah added: 'Dom never got ill, never caught a cold and never got poorly, which is why it was such a shock. The day before Mother's Day, we picked up a new car and, after returning home, he complained of feeling a little dizzy, so I got him to sit down and made some food. He didn't eat much, just kind of nibbled away at it, and we watched TV then went to bed.

'The following morning, he was so hot. We don't own a thermometer, but I touched his chest and it was clear he had a temperature. As the days went on, his taste went and his mouth became sore as it was constantly dry, while he struggled to eat. We just couldn't get Dom's temperature down, so, after seven days, I rang 111. At that stage his breathing was fine and we certainly didn't think it was coronavirus, but perhaps a cold or something similar.

'However, we were advised the symptoms meant one thing, but not to bring him to hospital until he was unable to hold his breath. The test was to count to 30 while holding his breath. Should he fail to get past eight, then we were told to phone 999. The lowest Dom reached was seventeen, so his breathing was okay, and it appeared his symptoms were mild.

'He started getting better and became hungry. I'd previously been advised that should he ask for more food to make sure it was high calorie, as he had lost two stone in two weeks. 'Initially it was a Chinese takeaway, a small portion, but he ate the lot. Over the next four days he was asking to drink orange juice or strawberry milkshake. His health was improving, his colour was returning and he was moving around a lot more. Dom still couldn't get upstairs as it made him breathless, so he had been living downstairs on the sofa for nearly three weeks. We hadn't slept in the same bed, Ellie-Mai hadn't cuddled him, I hadn't kissed him or held his hand, instead we fist-bumped and then I would wash. We stayed upstairs, only coming together as a family to eat, that was it.

'On the Thursday morning, I came downstairs and he asked for a cup of tea, even though he usually never drank it. The night before we had all shared a pizza from Domino's. He had turned a corner, didn't have a temperature and seemed fine. He put the bins out that day and at 9.30am was texting his friend, Steve, about how he was feeling better and was talking about playing golf. He passed away two and a half hours later.

'It began with Dom calling for Ellie-Mai to come downstairs and open the front-room window because he was hot. She did so and returned to her room. Then, at 11am, I received a text message saying: "Babe, can you come down? I really need your help." I was on the phone because I work in a call centre, so took off the headset and ran downstairs. He was on all fours in front of me, unable to catch his breath. He told me he was fine, but I touched his head and beads of sweat were coming off it and he was panicking. I insisted on calling an ambulance.

'What happened next is a blur, as it flashed by incredibly quickly. The medics put a mask on Dom's face, but he couldn't breathe and was getting frustrated. They managed to get oxygen into him and asked him to sit back, but he couldn't and he kept telling them, "It hurts."

'I will never forget what he said next: "Sarah, I'm going to go." They were his last words. He crawled towards the front door on all fours, they helped him into the ambulance, and I was told I couldn't go with him.

'It didn't occur to me that I would never see him again. I phoned Dom's mum and dad, explaining that he was on his way to hospital. Then I looked out of the window. Fifteen minutes after the ambulance should have left, it was still there in our road. It was stationary, but moving up and down. Then three more ambulances turned up containing people in white suits.'

After losing consciousness in the ambulance, Dom stopped breathing and could not be resuscitated. He died at Queen Alexandra Hospital, although his partner is convinced his heart stopped in that ambulance.

The family have long agonised over the point of contact for coronavirus. At the start of March, on the occasion of Dom's 48th birthday, he had joined Sarah and Ellie-Mai in attending the FA Cup game against Arsenal at Fratton Park. The Gunners were overseen by Mikel Arteta, whose positive test for the virus subsequently sparked the Premier League and Football League's lockdown. According to Sarah, her partner didn't come into contact with any Arsenal representatives, leaving her at a loss to explain the cause of infection. Reassuringly, she was declared negative after taking a test two weeks following his passing. Ellie-Mai has also never shown symptoms.

'Dom was getting better, which is why I have been struggling to come to terms with it,' said Sarah. 'The nurse explained to me that it was a secondary infection. They appear to be getting better, having successfully battled against it, but remain weak as the immune system is low. When it returns, it attacks the lungs, which can no longer fight it. Dom's death has been put down to cardiac arrest, not coronavirus. We'll have to wait between six and twelve months to find out the truth as toxicology and histology tests need to be carried out on his organs to determine the cause of death. As he was getting better, at the moment they cannot record it as coronavirus. Tests carried out five days after he passed came back negative, which is to be expected. The virus will have died with him, and it was no longer in his system. He should have been tested when the ambulance turned up, not five days later.

'I've been thinking about it non-stop. It will remain that way until I know what really happened. Maybe if I had got him to hospital two weeks prior, or taken him to the doctors two weeks earlier, he might still be here. They could have treated him, got his breathing right, brought his oxygen levels up. Instead he was sitting at home for two weeks with his lungs worsening. Dom received his SSE redundancy money on the morning of his death, which I didn't know about until I later spoke to one of his friends. It was £4,000 less than it should have been, so did he stress about that? Had he got himself so worked up that it caused the heart attack? I can't get it through my head why it happened.

'Poor Ellie-Mai saw all of it that day, I couldn't shield her. We were at home, in lockdown, and there was nowhere for her to go. She blames herself a little. When he called her down to open the window, he was on all fours. She has since said to me: "Mummy, I should have told you." But she didn't know. Daddy didn't say to her: "I'm struggling to breathe." He said he was hot and she opened the window before toddling off back upstairs to her bedroom. Then, ten minutes later, he texted me. Even the ambulance people said they did not expect that outcome considering he was talking when they turned up.

'Dom's final words continue to play on my mind. "I'm going to go." What did that mean? Did he think he was going to die? Or was he referring to being taken to hospital in an ambulance? Everything goes around my head because I just don't know. I have no answers. What did he mean? Did he know he was going to pass away? It's horrible to think that I didn't have a chance for that last goodbye; I didn't say, "I love you." It's horrible.'

Following Dom's death, Sarah's friend, Rachel Hibbert, launched a GoFundMe campaign to help raise money for funeral expenses. The outcome was £12,627 in little more than a month during a stunning demonstration of support from family, friends and complete strangers. Among those to donate were Fleur De Lys Football Club, handing over £1,000 to the fund. Dom was a highly regarded member of the Drayton-based club, having formed the under-10 girls' team with Dave Sykes. Ellie-Mai features at left-back and her dad had assisted in coaching, possessing aspirations to take his FA Level 1 in Coaching badge.

Other notable names to contribute included Pompey board member Eric Eisner, chief executive Mark Catlin, chief commercial officer Anna Mitchell, former Trust and board member Mick Williams, Ellie-Mai's 6th Portsmouth Brownies pack and ex-Blues players Conor Chaplin, Danny Rose and Jed Wallace. In the midst of lockdown, a number of well-wishers lined the city's streets for the funeral, albeit maintaining social distancing as the procession passed Dom's beloved Fratton Park. Sarah and Ellie-Mai chose to wear club-donated shirts for the occasion, each sporting the name 'Dom' on its back. It was a remarkable display of unity from the Pompey family which touched the grieving pair.

Sarah added: 'I was in a bit of a mess and people's support has blown me out of the water. The donations didn't just help pay for Dom's funeral, they covered the lot. We would never have been able to afford it otherwise. We'd spent our savings in October on a family holiday in Orlando and I had nothing to fall back on, so it would have been a struggle to pay anything towards the funeral.

'As Dom died so suddenly, we don't know if he had a will. It's something he claimed to have written, but I can't find it. We've lost his wage, with his redundancy put into his bank account, which I can't access. I'm now having to go part-time, so there are a lot of problems at the moment. People will not realise how much that money means to us. If it wasn't for them, I don't know where we'd be right now, I really don't. Thank you so, so much.

'We've had hampers delivered to our house; people have really rallied round. One day Sean Raggett came round with a bag of goodies such as hand sanitiser and bubble bath. He then learnt that we were avid Pompey fans and the next day returned to give Ellie-Mai the shirt he wore against Arsenal. He also handed over his phone number and said to text him if we needed anything, such as shopping. What a gesture, it was absolutely amazing.

'For the funeral, the club allowed us to use their copyrighted badge on his coffin and kindly donated two shirts with Dom's name on. I also received video messages for Ellie-Mai on WhatsApp from Ronan Curtis and Christian Burgess, along with former players Jed Wallace, Conor Chaplin and Carl Baker. My daughter was overwhelmed; she absolutely loved the fact they took time out for her. Yes, they are footballers, but they're genuine people as well. They have got lives and can be affected by the current problems too. It doesn't matter who you are – footballers are people at the end of the day. We're all in a crisis and they have decided to help somebody who just goes to watch them play football.'

✳ ☽ ✳

The residents of Galt Road ventured outside during lockdown to pay their respects to Merrick Burrell's passing hearse. His sporting loves were unmistakable, the casket accompanied by a spray of blue and white flowers and a cricket bat on its journey from his Farlington home that Friday afternoon. The Pompey season-ticket holder had passed away at the age of 84, some two weeks after contracting coronavirus. Burrell had witnessed the Blues' glorious two-year reign as champions of England with Jimmy Dickinson, Peter Harris and Len Phillips in their prime. Almost seven decades later, the FA Cup visit of Arsenal represented his final Fratton Park visit.

Maintaining self-isolation guidelines, widow Julia, his wife of nearly 59 years, climbed into her car alone, behind the hearse during the funeral procession with nobody to hold her hand or wipe her tears. The lockdown dictated that no funeral limousines were allowed. Ian, the eldest of her two children, occupied a separate car as the mourners headed towards The Oaks crematorium in Havant. Then something caught his attention.

He said: 'I noticed a family across the road had emerged from their house wearing Pompey tops. It seemed some sort of Friday afternoon gathering was going on. For the first few seconds, I couldn't really work out why. Then I realised. It was for Dad.

'Those neighbours stood outside, holding Pompey scarves aloft as the hearse pulled away from our family home. It was a lovely touch, a show of strength from fellow fans. They knew Dad and his dedication to the Blues and wanted to show solidarity. As the hearse made its way down the street, others came out to see him off from the surrounding houses. It was incredibly moving.

'Due to lockdown restrictions, there were only nine of us present, including the pastor. It was socially distanced; I couldn't even comfort my own mum at her husband's funeral. It wasn't as you'd imagine, though. Dad was someone well known in the city with a big social network and lots of friends. He was connected with many people through his work and a lifetime love of sport. He was a governor at Crookhorn College and active with the Rotary Club of Cosham.

'Certainly, we never expected his funeral to ever be such a small-scale affair, but we found that only having close relatives present made it a very intense experience. In some ways, it was more special than it may have been. That was the positive aspect to it, balancing the sadness of Mum having to drive herself behind her husband's hearse at the age of 81.'

Ian first accompanied his dad to Fratton Park in December 1969. The outcome was a 3–2 home loss for George Smith's side, yet the six-year-old was captivated from his North Terrace vantage point. Merrick and his son continued to attend Blues matches, although Ian has, in recent times, relocated to the South Stand to be with friends. His dad, though, maintained his season ticket in Block F of North Stand Lower, positioned level with the halfway line.

Merrick had issues with an irregular heartbeat, requiring medication, yet remained active, devoting his summers to watching his beloved Hampshire at the Ageas Rose Bowl, where he was a member. He spent 40 years working at North End-based estate agents Waterfield & Stanford, while in retirement was known to don a Santa suit and participate in bucket collections outside Morrisons in Anchorage Park and Cosham High Street's Tesco and had every intention of doing so again.

Ian added: 'I've thought about it and my mum has inevitably turned it over in her mind many times. There are numerous possibilities how Dad caught coronavirus considering it's an invisible threat. With so many people having died from it, we now realise how big a threat it is. In those early times, when there was no social distancing, there was very little awareness of exactly what it was.

'Dad became sick in the days after the Arsenal match, which we initially believed was the flu or some kind of bug. The chances of him having coronavirus were very low. At that stage, it was almost unknown in Portsmouth, and it seemed to be happening outside the UK. We assumed his illness was something else. Football was slow to react and, in hindsight, you can say that Arsenal game probably shouldn't have happened – then things might have turned out differently for a lot of people.

'We were later made aware that Mikel Arteta had coronavirus. Even then, at that stage, hardly anyone knew somebody personally who had caught it, so it still seemed pretty remote that my dad was infected. Dad wasn't in the South Stand near the dugout or changing rooms during that FA Cup match. He was on the other side of the pitch. He always parked on the site of a car wash on the Anson Road industrial estate. Entering the ground from that direction, he would have passed the Arsenal supporters' coaches. Perhaps he crossed paths with fans from London where the virus might have been more prevalent? My mum later told me that someone won the free Domino's pizza in Dad's section of the North Lower that night and slices were handed around. It's impossible to know, but you do wonder.

'The virus was out and among the population by then. It makes you realise how vulnerable the people attending that game were. A few days later, he fell ill. When Pompey played at Peterborough the following Saturday, we texted each other about the disappointing 2–0 defeat. By then he was ill. Three days later, Dad couldn't go to Fratton Park for the visit of Fleetwood as he wasn't feeling great. It was a cold night and he thought he was suffering with some kind of flu.

'For two long weeks my mum nursed him day after day at their Farlington home. He was convinced he had the virus and they spent a long time trying to get through on the phone for medical help, but the doctors were not coming out to see patients. People had been told to stay in and deal with it themselves and Dad was prescribed antibiotics by phone on the basis he had a cold.

'After a fortnight, he appeared to be improving. No longer was he confined to bed, and he was downstairs watching TV and eating. Then, during the night, he developed breathing difficulties. An ambulance was called, and he was still talking when they arrived. That was the last time my mum saw him alive. He was taken to Queen Alexandra Hospital and put straight into intensive care to give his body a chance to recover. Dad died five days after being admitted into hospital. He had tested positive for coronavirus and we were never allowed to visit or call him. The only time I was allowed to go to QA was to pick up his things after he died.'

Ian and his dad had bought tickets to attend Pompey's Leasing.com Trophy final against Salford City, a fixture scheduled for 5 April. It would have represented the seventh time since 2008 that the Burrells had attended Wembley together for the Pompey cause, experiences the pair cherished. They had sat alongside each other for February's remarkable 3–2 win over Exeter City, which booked the Blues a place in the EFL Trophy final for a second consecutive year. However, Merrick will no longer be attending a fixture which has yet to be rescheduled following its postponement.

'Dad had been really invigorated by Pompey since December,' said Ian, who lives near Chichester. 'Before then it had been a disappointing season, yet he had faithfully continued to attend every game. For that 3–3 draw with Coventry City in August, I was on holiday in France, so dodged that terrible outcome, but he filled me in on the ugly details. He was feeling enthusiastic about the way the season was developing after the slow start.

'The last time we sat together was in the North Stand against Exeter City for the Leasing.com Trophy semi-final. We spent most of the game gnashing our teeth in despair at a pretty terrible performance, but Pompey ended up winning 3–2. It has to be the most incredible finale I have ever seen and we were hugging each other at the thought of returning to Wembley.

'Mum has since told me that returning to the home of football for the final was at the forefront of his mind. It had given him a lot of energy and positivity about the future while he was ill. Last season, there were ten of our family in attendance at Wembley to watch us beat Sunderland on penalties in the Checkatrade Trophy. There would have been a similar number this time around, representing three generations of supporters.

'Dad was so proud of himself last year. He was 83 and still able to travel around London, keeping up with everybody, going to the pub before the match and coping with the Wembley escalators. For him, the latest trip would have been the ultimate day. He was so looking forward to doing it all over again. Unfortunately, our dream of going through that old Wembley routine once more was not to be realised. Still, I'm grateful I managed to experience sitting there alongside Dad for six games. I never imagined that would be possible when I started going. Back then and for most of the 1970s we were a mediocre second-flight team that never seemed to challenge for silverware or have any prospect of any great achievements.'

Merrick's widow, Julia, has not tested positive for coronavirus, yet remains at home, following guidelines tabled by the government. The 81-year-old is gazing to the future, which will involve maintaining the Burrell family tradition.

Ian said: 'It has been difficult for us to comprehend how Mum has lived with and nursed someone who has died from the virus, then been forced to grieve, confined in the same house without any support. On what would turn out to be the day Dad died, I went to see her from a distance, sitting outside in the garden while she was by the conservatory door at their house. We knew Dad might not have long to live and I put my sister in London on speakerphone before we all took turns to express out loud our thanks and love to Dad. We found out later that he had passed away very shortly afterwards. We like to feel he felt that love. Two months later I still want to give Mum a hug but can't.

'She has talked about putting up a plaque in Fratton Park in Dad's memory and has also expressed a wish to take over his season ticket. One of their first dates was at Pompey, and she recalls the dashing Jackie Henderson in the forward line. She's been to Fratton many times herself and lived her life looking out for the scores to gauge our moods ahead of our return home after the game. I wouldn't say she was a fan to the point of knowing who the current team are, but she has been going on and off for some 60 years.

'I have already emailed Mark Catlin to ask if I can relocate my seat from the South Stand to be with her. He has been very good and put me in touch with a senior ticket office person, although obviously nothing can be done at this stage. I'm also hoping that my six-year-old son Joel will go to his first game next season, when it finally begins. I can't believe that for the first time in my life Dad won't be around when football kicks off again at Fratton. But we will keep the family's Pompey tradition going and he'll be there in our hearts.'

The Premier League and Football League have decreed that fixtures will take place behind closed doors should the 2019–20 campaign resume. With the government guidance prohibiting mass gatherings, football must operate without supporters for the foreseeable future. Pompey fans will instead have to rely on live streaming platform iFollow for the remainder of their team's League One promotion bid, with nine matches left to play. Sarah Merrix, however, can muster little enthusiasm for football's resumption with coronavirus cases and deaths continuing to soar.

She said: 'Going back to Fratton Park will be the hardest. For eight years we've been to almost every home match as a family, so it's going to be hard seeing an empty seat. I think I am going to renew Dom's seat because I don't want anyone else sitting in it yet. I could buy a season ticket for another year and give it to family or friends. I don't think I've got the strength to see someone else in it just at the minute.

'Football was a big part of our lives, and we do love it, but we have to make sure it's safe for everybody to return. I don't want people rushing back to Fratton Park, because I never, ever, ever want anyone to experience what I'm going through. I'd rather they wrote off this campaign and announce that the next won't start until the beginning of 2021, just to be sure everything has cleared. Coronavirus can be life-changing, it can be instant and it's affecting people. I wouldn't wish it on anybody, I really wouldn't.'

SEAN RAGGETT, CHRISTIAN BURGESS AND CLARE MARTIN

22 May 2020

Sean Raggett did not require hospital treatment. Fortunately, his coronavirus infection dispersed naturally, a loss of taste the only symptom. The central defender was among five Pompey players to test positive for the virus, along with James Bolton, Andy Cannon, Ross McCrorie and Haji Mnoga. All but second-year scholar Mnoga had been involved in March's FA Cup visit of Arsenal, a potentially significant fixture when attempting to trace the potential source of contamination for the Blues. Considering Mikel Arteta was present, suspicions are strong.

Raggett cannot be certain of the point of contact. His only symptom had subsided by the time physio Bobby Bacic delivered the bombshell that a test conducted three days earlier had registered positive. Back in his native Gillingham when handed the shock news, the 26-year-old immediately returned to his Old Portsmouth home for the advised self-isolation period, along with girlfriend Eleanor.

Once fulfilled, the community-conscious couple pledged to help others, stepping forward to apply for the NHS Volunteer Responders scheme, launched in March. Their offer was rejected. Then arrived Christian Burgess' call to arms among Pompey's players, keen for furloughed players to lend assistance to charitable causes. Inevitably, Raggett embraced the opportunity with customary enthusiasm.

He said: 'When the NHS were appealing for volunteers, Eleanor and I were turned away. As I've had coronavirus, I thought I would try to help. Although it's not confirmed that you can't catch it again, it's still likely I'll be safer. So, it makes sense for me to go out there to help others. For our application form, we had to give our Portsmouth address but, as our driving licences are registered to places in Gillingham and Colchester, which is where we are from, our identity unfortunately couldn't be validated, so we couldn't be accepted.

'Then Burge asked on the players' group chat whether anyone wanted to get involved with HIVE Portsmouth, which sounded ideal. I've been in the kitchen at Landport Community Centre preparing food and also making deliveries in my car. I'm not the best in the kitchen, concentrating on peeling potatoes and apples, and leaving the cooking to people like Burge and others working there. I can definitely drive, though!

'I've been three or four times now and will probably get down there again next week at some point to help out. There are some really good people involved. It's about helping the vulnerable, the disabled, people who can't get out, like a lot of elderly. This is a tough time for all of us and they're finding it the hardest, so we're doing the best we can to help.

'I've heard the criticism directed at footballers from clubs higher up the leagues about supposedly not helping during the coronavirus crisis and it's unfair. A lot of players are doing good things for the community but aren't seeking publicity. Take Tottenham Hotspur's Danny Rose, who has donated money to two domestic abuse charities, while giving £19,000 and hundreds of Domino's pizzas to North Middlesex University Hospital in Enfield.

'I don't see that whenever I turn on Sky Sports News, in fact I've never seen that mentioned by them once. The majority of people probably think these players are sitting at home counting their money, when actually a lot are doing plenty of good with the resources they have. The criticism they receive is wrong.

'At Norwich, the playing squad volunteered to donate part of our wage towards the Canaries Covid-19 Community Support Project, which is doing brilliant work in the local area. That's in addition to #PlayersTogether, which Premier League players have contributed towards with a view to helping NHS funds. Any little thing you can do to help people is important. I recently met the Merrix family, who are massive Pompey fans. I cannot imagine what it's like to lose a family member to coronavirus. They've had such a tough time that I decided to give Ellie-Mai my shirt from the Arsenal game. As it was the FA Cup, with different sponsors on your shirt, we can keep them, so I handed mine over, along with my phone number. There isn't loads you can do, but they are welcome to give me a shout should they ever require anything. I'm there to help. Little gestures like that are important.'

Raggett's ongoing assistance is admirable, particularly considering the temporary nature of a loan player's situation. Despite only being contracted to Pompey for the duration of the season, the former Lincoln City man has joined another loanee in Cameron McGeehan in throwing his weight behind community projects. Raggett can empathise with the social impact of the global pandemic following first-hand experience.

'My only coronavirus symptom was losing taste for two or three days, not that I realised what it meant at the time,' he added. 'I have been without a top front tooth for a while, so, ahead of receiving an implant to fill the gap, I had braces applied at a dentist in Fareham to straighten my bottom row of teeth. When I realised that I could no longer taste, I put it down to that dental work a few days earlier. It never came into my head that it was anything to do with coronavirus. I felt completely fine. Once I tested positive and looked up potential symptoms, that's when it made sense, although when Bobby Bacic told me the news, my taste had already returned. The truth is, had it not been for the test, I wouldn't have a clue that I'd ever had coronavirus. It came and went without me realising.

'Everyone, of course, will point to the Arsenal game as a possible source of infection, purely because of Mikel Arteta, but I was an unused substitute and didn't come into contact with him. Being an Arsenal fan, I would have been aware if I had. I didn't even walk past him. We'll never really know how it happened; it's impossible to be sure. I could have caught it from anyone, and certainly no one was ill in training sessions during the week before football was put into lockdown. I ended up self-isolating with my girlfriend at our Old Portsmouth home, but she never showed any symptoms, so we don't know whether she had it.'

On doctor's advice, Clare Martin is directing community matters from afar, medically shielding in her Purbrook home. Required to take medication for an underlying health issue, her sole forays outside are restricted to daily 7.30am walks with her Shih Tzu dog, Poppy, around the deserted Portsmouth Golf Course. The frontline absence of Pompey in the Community's inspirational chief executive is a blow partially cushioned by her ability to continue to oversee efforts from her socially distanced vantage point. The multi-award-winning charity arm of Pompey have joined forces with HIVE Portsmouth during the coronavirus crisis to deliver food, medicine and other essentials to those forced indoors by the pandemic.

With around 60 per cent of the Pompey in the Community workforce having been furloughed, they have instead offered up their voluntary assistance to the HIVE Portsmouth project, utilising their Anson Road base and existing transportation. Since the middle of March, 2,134 food parcels have been supplied across the city, with those carrying out door-to-door deliveries including Pompey players Cameron McGeehan, Ben Close, Tom Naylor, Andy Cannon and, of course, Burgess and Raggett.

Martin said: 'Initially we focused on helping older people left isolated or shielding during the coronavirus crisis, particularly those who hadn't received their government parcels. Now it has evolved to those who cannot afford to buy food. Sometimes the poverty out there is quite terrifying.

'I spoke to one lady who said: "Don't worry love, we have a tin of peas in the cupboard, we can eat that tonight. Just get us something tomorrow." That's awful. HIVE Portsmouth was set up eighteen months ago and was recently awarded charitable status. It acts as central support, the conduit between community organisations, businesses and the city council. Referrals come into them, with their staff working with pharmacy teams to sort out the distribution of medicines. Should there be requests for food or supplies, we are then informed and carry out those duties.

'I have three teams of Pompey in the Community volunteers who put parcels together and they are delivered to those who really need them. People continue to be incredibly generous, donating food, products and money. We are so thankful for all their help during this time. When lockdown was announced, Pompey had two forthcoming home matches cancelled, but had just bought in £4,000 worth of pies, so they kindly contacted me to see if we had any use for them. Well, I filled the two freezers in our kitchen classroom at the Study Centre with those leftover pies and we soon found good homes for them.

'Basher Benfield is among those on our delivery rounds. He's so lovely – he closed his eyes while eating one, pretending he was back at Fratton Park. Landsec, who own Gunwharf Quays, donated a load of Easter eggs which could no longer be sold, while their shopping outlets have supplied the bags for life which all our deliveries arrive in. In addition, with a number of takeaway restaurants temporarily closing during lockdown, we were invited to collect food from seven branches of McDonald's across the city. That included patties, rolls, muffins and sauce sachets. Kentucky Fried Chicken have also helped.

'The most humbling part of the whole response has been the Pompey in the Community team. Being furloughed, they could have simply chosen to stay at home and enjoy the sunshine. Instead they virtually all signed up to volunteer with HIVE Portsmouth and have given 100 per cent to serve their city and help ensure that no one has gone hungry. They are proof that true spirit shines through in tough times.'

Remarkably, the kitchens of Landport Community Centre are producing 200 meals on a weekly basis, with Burgess and Raggett often lending assistance in terms of food preparation and cooking. In addition to that output, The Queens Hotel, in Southsea, are presently making 450 meals per week to include in food parcels, assisted by contributions from The Akash Indian Restaurant, La Casa Flamenca, Madani Academy Primary School and Quattro Foods.

Pompey in the Community remains at the heart of the effort, maintaining outstanding work which has seen it claim seven prestigious EFL titles since 2016, in recognition of a procession of trailblazing projects. The most recent honour arrived at the 2019 EFL Awards, when Portsmouth were crowned Checkatrade Community Club of the Year for the second time in three years. The charity bears a close affiliation with Pompey, trustees including Mark Catlin, Anna Mitchell, Burgess and Trent Stamp, the long-serving CEO of the California-based Eisner Foundation. Similarly, the ubiquitous Martin, who has presided over Pompey in the Community for approaching twenty years, occupies the Pompey Supporters' Trust board, while she also sits on the club's Heritage & Advisory Board.

'After all the bad press football received at the beginning of the situation, a lot of people, certainly in Pompey's case, are going to have to eat their words,' said Martin. 'Normally, I have to put in a player request to help with our projects, but this has been driven by the players themselves. You couldn't ask for anything more. They're not contributing to the community effort as footballers; they are doing it as human beings. That's the difference. Everyone is in it together at Pompey.

'Christian is such an incredible role model for the other players, and they want to follow his example and lend a hand. He'll phone me on a Sunday and let me know who is available during the coming week. They are helping a lot more than people realise and for no other reason than genuinely wanting to. That's what makes it special. Nobody knows how many little requests I have forwarded to people, who have then worked quietly behind the scenes with the sole aim of helping others rather than seeking publicity.

'You look at Ben Close, who goes about things in his usual understated manner, not making a song and dance about it. He carries out deliveries in his own car almost every Wednesday, with the minimum of fuss. I've known him since he was four, when he would sit in the Study Centre and eat his breakfast. His mum, Kat, was our admin at the time, and she would walk him to school before coming back to work.

'Ben agrees to everything we ask of him. Mind you, if he doesn't then I'll tell his mum and she'll make him! I'm only joking, of course. It's not just the players but also club staff, some of which are furloughed but help out voluntarily. Pompey ambassador Alan Knight is out every morning carrying out food deliveries to some of our season-ticket holders and wheelchair users, often heading into West Sussex and further north in Hampshire. He has a heart of gold.

'Our kitman, Kev McCormack, has been doing pick-ups from The Queens Hotel in his van, where they are cooking meals to send out into the community. Tanya Robins, the club's finance manager, has made herself available to fulfil deliveries after finishing work at 4pm each day. There's also Abi Urmston, the Academy's lead therapist, and the lovely Fratton End gateman Abdul Khalique has helped in the Landport Community Centre with cooking – it really is a club effort.'

Christian Burgess hasn't seen girlfriend Méabh for more than two months, socially distanced by 250 miles. While the central defender remains on the south coast and is instrumental in the club's community collaboration, junior doctor Méabh serves on the NHS frontline in Southport Hospital, Merseyside. Since the government-enforced lockdown, the pair have been restricted to phone calls and FaceTime chats, their respective working commitments taking precedence. For Burgess, maintaining an individual training programme monitored by Pompey is complemented by spearheading the admirable player effort to support the city's most vulnerable residents.

He said: 'Méabh and I haven't seen each other in person since the lockdown. The rules have recently relaxed, but it's probably still a bit too far to travel just to socially distance before coming back. Méabh is approaching the end of her first year, so has been rotated through different wards and different jobs. They may have surgery duties or a medicine job or work in A&E, and sometimes it could be a GP role. When this kicked off, the rotation was stopped for logistical reasons. She was on the cardiology ward at the time, before moving onto the Covid-19 ward, dealing with patients. It has been tough for her, but she has done really well. I'm proud of her.

'As footballers, we can see the scale of the virus in this country and the effect it has had on the community. Naturally, we also wanted to help. I've known Clare Martin for a number of years through Pompey in the Community, so should I have any ideas to help or propositions, I pop them on to our player WhatsApp group. Whoever comes back, I liaise with them, organising times and dates.

'Cameron McGeehan is usually the first to volunteer; he's incredibly keen and a really, really good guy. Every time he has helped, I've later asked how he found it and he's always buzzing. Cam's very down to earth and loves what we are trying to do in the community. He has been on deliveries so far, sometimes twice a week, but is now talking about going into the kitchen at Landport Community Centre. That role mainly involves preparing the food, so there's lots of slicing and dicing, chucking things into frying pans, stirring pots on the hob, sometimes baking cakes, while I've made curries and stir fries. There's also a bit of washing-up required – I try to steer clear of that!'

While Burgess has been orchestrating the Pompey players' community contribution, other groups have also received his considerable support. The Heart of Hayling Boxing Academy, in partnership with Hayling

Helpers, has been working with four local chemists to distribute medicine to residents. With Burgess on board, his round once included former Pompey winger John McClelland who, aged 85, is among the club's oldest living players. McClelland's wife is Heather Armitage, whose own impressive sporting background includes Olympic medals in the 4x100m relay at Helsinki in 1952 and Melbourne in 1956.

On VE Day, Burgess even conducted deliveries from an FV101 Scorpion tank, decorated in flags and playing music of the period as it clattered through the streets of Hayling Island. He has been in fine company, with team-mate John Marquis overseeing the creation of a players' fund, resulting in the squad donating more than £4,000 for community causes. The fourteen-goal striker has also reached out to George Carnell, the Pompey supporter who posted a suicide note on Twitter.

Carnell was subsequently found unconscious on his kitchen floor after overdosing on antidepressants, requiring him to be taken to Queen Alexandra Hospital. After coming round, the 20-year-old discovered a message on his phone from Marquis, wishing to talk. The touching gesture from the striker, who has worked with mental health charities in the past, is credited by the Pompey fan with saving his life.

Burgess added: 'We are an honest bunch of lads who have been touched by what has happened during this period and are keen to help in whichever way we can. While loads of the boys want to assist with deliveries, some can't, which I understand. For instance, those with young families have to be a bit more aware. It's easy for me, because I have no dependents. However, all the boys have contributed financially, with every member of the squad donating towards our player fund. It wasn't mandatory and there was no minimum amount or limit. We're lucky that Pompey are still paying us in full while the season is suspended and I guess the boys wanted to give something back to the community.

'Through the WhatsApp group, we debated how to best utilise that money. It was agreed that half of our collection should be put towards the Portsmouth Hospitals' Thank You Appeal, with the remainder split between care packages for disabled season-ticket holders, Pompey in the Community food packages and also LunchBank PO9. Everyone has seen the scale of the virus and how it is affecting the community, so we wanted to do something. With the flexibility we currently possess in terms of training programmes, we have a little more time on our hands. The guys aren't doing this as one-offs, they are returning every week, incorporating it into their routines. When full-time training returns, I'd still like to continue helping with deliveries in the afternoons during my spare time, hopefully until those services aren't required any more.'

With football still yet to resume, Sean Raggett can reflect on the frustrating intermission having impressively conquered a difficult start to his season-long Fratton Park stay. The central defender arrived off the back of an injury-ravaged 2018–19 campaign while on loan at Championship club Rotherham United, restricting him to just ten outings. His injury woes can be traced back to September 2018, when he broke a bone on the inside of his right ankle after his studs caught in the turf while clearing the ball. Sidelined for four months, within five matches of his comeback, misfortune struck once more as a Leeds United opponent again fractured the bone during a tackle. As a consequence, Raggett's Pompey appearance in August's 3–3 draw with Coventry City signified his first competitive start in almost seven months.

He said: 'I actually started the season playing with quite a bit of pain in my ankle, and it was affecting me. The first game I felt good in was at Doncaster Rovers in October, when we won 2–1. About ten minutes into the match, it occurred to me that everything felt fine. From that point, I was able to kick on.

'The issue centred on the back of my ankle, which was tight and would become inflamed. It was unconnected with previous injuries, simply a consequence of my ankle being in a protective boot for so long. Having not walked on it much during that time, it became a little weak and required building up. It wasn't my original injury, so I knew it wouldn't be a long-term problem and it was just a case of getting through it.

'In truth, I think I may have come back a little too soon. When I joined Pompey, I did my medical and went straight into pre-season. Maybe I should have spent longer strengthening my ankle, but I was keen to get back playing. I was a little naive. I had never suffered a serious injury before, and I just assumed I'd come back and be the same as before. It doesn't quite work out like that. You return and there's that natural rustiness, so it takes time to get that match fitness back.

'Looking back, I felt good going into that Coventry game for my full Pompey debut. I wouldn't have put the result at risk if I didn't feel I was capable of playing. However, during that fixture, I realised I probably wasn't quite ready to play. My ankle was sore and I didn't feel match sharp, so it impacted upon my performance. I don't like making excuses, so it's a tough one, but obviously I hadn't played for a while.

'Any player will perform better when they have a run of games under their belt and Kenny Jackett was very good with me. I returned to the side against Bolton Wanderers at the end of September and he told me I'd be given a run of fixtures to get me back up to match sharpness. My form improved and, since the turn of the year, I believe I've been playing really well. Even so, I was still not quite at my best and had more to offer. I was definitely getting towards that, only for the season to be halted.'

Raggett's early Pompey displays attracted criticism from sections of the Fratton faithful, unconvinced of the talents of a player associated with a Premier League club. Tellingly, Jackett also had his say in the aftermath of the loanee's debut, omitting him from the League One starting XI for the next five weeks. It was a difficult time for the former Gillingham apprentice, who became the subject of vile abuse directed towards his Twitter account. However, Raggett is adamant he always believed he would turn around public opinion once granted a regular first-team presence free from injury and niggles.

'I was always confident in myself. I featured in the Championship last season and, if not for the injury, I would hopefully have played the whole season as a regular,' he added. 'I believe I performed well for Rotherham when I did play, and I scored in a win over Millwall, so, in my mind, there were no doubts I could then do well at Pompey. I just needed that run of matches. Everyone has bad games. When you do, it's terrible. You return home and replay it in your head. Then you wake up the next day and say to yourself: "Right, I know I can play better than that. I know I'm a better player than that; my performances will come back." It's not about ramming words down people's throats, it's more to do with proving it to yourself. If I've had a good game, I'm not thinking about how I've shown a person that they're wrong, I'm just happy with myself because I want to do well.

'Criticism is fair enough, and I can handle it. I'm 26 years old and a pretty tough guy, but it does get below the belt with football fans sometimes. People get too personal. I will never go looking for what fans are saying about me on social media, but should people direct message you, then obviously you can't avoid seeing their comments. You get some bad messages on social media sometimes, pretty dark stuff which people seem to think is okay to write to footballers. You see it up and down the country, with players getting grief from people who sit behind a computer screen.

'We're all grown men, and we can take a bit of post-match criticism, but when you start sending people personal insults and threatening their wellbeing, their family's wellbeing, that's when it oversteps the mark. I'm on Twitter, but don't use my account a lot. I like to see how my pals who play for other teams are doing rather than tweeting that much myself.

'I'm a centre-back, and centre-backs will make mistakes. Both Burge and I have made mistakes which have led to goals this season. I know what happened at MK Dons in December is mentioned, but we had just come off back-to-back wins and clean sheets against Ipswich Town and Wycombe Wanderers, who were both in League One's top two at the time. I felt like I was on form entering that match and then made a mistake for the first goal. That happens. Overall, the team was pretty terrible for that 3–1 defeat, surely our worst performance of the season, other than at Accrington when we had a makeshift back four.

'It has been nice to receive more backing from the fans as the season has progressed, though. Their comments about me receiving the Ballon d'Or crack me up. I also once heard the "Raggett for England" chants. I can't remember the game as I normally don't really pay attention to the crowd noise. Then the ball went out of play and I caught the end of it, which was quite funny. My family have also heard those songs when attending matches, although my dad is Irish and my mum English, so I could play for both countries!'

The remarkable resurgence in Raggett's Pompey fortunes has seen him emerge as an outsider to win player of the season. Jackett's belief in the defender was reflected by a run of twenty successive starts in all competitions up until the visit of boyhood team Arsenal. With a two-match suspension looming for Christian Burgess, Jackett opted to pair him with James Bolton in the centre of defence, with Raggett rested on the bench.

Inevitably, the Norwich loanee was immediately restored to first-team duty once League One fixtures resumed, although the Blues disappointingly took just one point from the next two matches. A hamstring tweak ruled Raggett out of the Fratton Park visit of Accrington Stanley, a match that never took place following the intervention of coronavirus. The former Lincoln defender now awaits to discover when he will again play for the Blues before his scheduled Carrow Road return.

He said: 'Last summer I had quite a few options in League One, but Pompey stuck out to me. Being such a big club, it was a challenge which really appealed. When you join a team, it's important that you're excited and that's definitely the feeling I had. My Norwich contract is up this summer, but the club have a one-year option, so I'm waiting to hear what's going on. Should they not take that up, I will be out of contract, which is the first time I'll have been in this situation, but I don't really get involved in all that, I leave it to my agent.

'At the moment, there's not a lot happening on that front and that will most likely remain the case until clubs know what will happen to this season. It sounds like the Football League will be decided fairly soon. When it is, I'm sure I can resolve my future and I would be open to any options that come my way, including Pompey. We'll just have to wait and see.'

JAMES BOLTON
AND ANDY CANNON

9 June 2020

James Bolton is far from a medical marvel but, having tested positive for coronavirus twice within three months, has defied convention. On the day Pompey toasted the return of League One and the cranking up of their promotion ambition, soaring spirits were diluted with sobering news concerning two members of their squad.

Having adopted the Football League's 'Return to Training' protocol ahead of an anticipated resumption of competitive fixtures, the first round of coronavirus testing among players and staff delivered a resounding all-clear. However, in line with requirements to implement twice-weekly testing at their Hilsea training base, James Bolton and Academy product Harry Kavanagh were diagnosed with coronavirus days later. An intriguing outcome for Bolton, in particular, for the right-back was among five Blues players to have tested positive in March.

Whether immunity to coronavirus exists for those previously infected remains a subject of ongoing debate, with medical research presently inconclusive. Nonetheless, Bolton's situation has been put down to a flawed testing process rather than scientific abnormality.

'I actually haven't contracted coronavirus again,' he said. 'Following that result, I then got a test from the NHS, which came back negative. So, it has been a bit of a weird one, to be honest. Something has clearly gone wrong. I know what it's like to have coronavirus and this wasn't it. I've felt absolutely fine.

'When the club test came back positive, Bobby Bacic advised I got a second opinion. Apparently, it has been known for people to have positive negatives, so it was important I made sure. On the same day, I travelled to Guildford for a drive-through test with the NHS and it returned negative, which then raises other questions. Perhaps they got the results of my first test mixed up? Maybe it didn't work properly? I haven't got a clue what the answer is; it's just a strange situation.

'If people thought you could catch coronavirus again it would change the whole dynamic of how we approach this pandemic. Thankfully, I'm okay and I felt fine anyway, unlike back in March.'

Pompey have been paired with Oxford United in the play-off semi-finals after a Football League EGM. With games instructed to take place behind closed doors for the foreseeable future, these remain bleak times for lower-league members deprived of essential match-day revenue, including ticket and corporate sales. There has been a reticence among League One clubs to fulfil the remaining fixture programme. Crucially, the commitment would require the unfurloughing of staff, leading to even greater financial losses.

In a footballing context, two points separate Pompey from second-placed Rotherham United. Their strong position with nine fixtures remaining prompted them to align with fellow promotion hopefuls Peterborough, Sunderland, Oxford United, Fleetwood Town and Ipswich Town in seeking the campaign's completion. It's a pathway already followed by the Premier League and Championship, yet garnered just four shows of support in the subsequent vote among League One's 23 members.

With the fixture list curtailed, an unweighted points per game model was employed to calculate the final table, with Pompey finishing in fifth, securing a place in the play-offs. Joy then for Coventry City, promoted as champions, joined by Rotherham. Neither club wished the campaign to continue, as self-preservation dominated the voting process. Reinvigorated by the Football League's clarification, Kenny Jackett's side have returned to full training, beginning play-off preparation on Sunday with a 3–1 friendly defeat at Reading. Despite his reaffirming second test, Bolton was not involved in the Madejski Stadium encounter, sidelined by a knock to the knee collected in training.

He added: 'I knew the Premier League would get back eventually. There's so much money and interest at that level, there's no way it could not finish. I must admit, there was a point where I thought League One would not return, but we're back in action now and have a good chance. If we can claw back a bit of the form we showed before the lockdown, it will stand us in good stead. On paper, we've been deemed the bookies' favourites, but there are some good teams in there, sides who have given us good games when we've met previously.

'You can see why Peterborough are upset at how the season has ended, but we had just come off a really good run and deserve to be in there. Peterborough were very good, but their failure to qualify for the play-offs means they're now likely to lose the division's top scorer, Ivan Toney, in the transfer window. It's harsh, but I think the way the league has been calculated is the fairest.

'You look at our games this season and there have been some mad ones, such as being beaten in the last minute at AFC Wimbledon and losing the lead late on to Coventry at our place. There have been loads of games in which we've thrown points away. It's fine margins, but now we have a chance and must be positive.'

For a Pompey career which got off to a frustratingly low-key start, the summer recruit from Shrewsbury Town was thrust firmly into the spotlight in March during the FA Cup encounter with Arsenal, entrusted with centre-half duties. Informed of the responsibility hours before kick-off, it was a position he had occupied during his formative years, before Halifax Town boss Neil Aspin initiated his conversion into a right-back.

Partnering Christian Burgess at the heart of the Blues' defence for the visit of Mikel Arteta's side, Bolton was challenged with nullifying the threat of Eddie Nketiah, who had netted in a Premier League triumph over Everton a week earlier. The England under-21 international would score for the Gunners in their 2–0 Fratton Park victory, yet post-match proceedings were dominated by a tackle which left Lucas Torreira with a fractured right ankle. Bolton's first-half challenge on the Uruguayan midfielder was not deemed a foul, yet the backlash from angry Arsenal supporters was fierce.

He said: 'I had Instagram messages from a few Uruguayans. One was in broken English, the other in his own language, so I didn't have a clue what he was saying. He seemed angry, though. I thought it was a good tackle on Torreira, a fair one. I didn't go in to hurt him but, unfortunately, he broke his ankle. It was the first time in my career I've seen an opponent come off having gas and air following one of my challenges. It wasn't nice to see. I must admit, the incident played on my mind a little for the remainder of the game. I knew it was a good tackle though, which put me at ease.

'To be honest, I couldn't understand the criticism from Arsenal supporters afterwards. I'm a bit old school, and if the ball is won then it's a good tackle. The older generation, such as Stuart Pearce, publicly agreed that the challenge was fine, but the game has changed a little. I've played non-league football and anything goes down there. It's a little different playing against the Premier League boys. The referee was Mike Dean, a very experienced match official, and he saw no problem with the tackle. Not many Arsenal players gathered around him either, surely a sign that few thought it was bad.

'Things were at their noisiest in the hours after the match. With my Twitter account on private, I missed a lot of it but my parents showed me stuff. At the end of the day, I suppose their supporters will view it like that because he's their player. I went to Torreira at the time to see if he was okay, and later I asked their players if they could send him my best. I genuinely didn't wish to injure him.'

Football's enforced break has allowed Torreira to return from what was purported to be a season-ending injury to emerge as a potential selection choice against Manchester City upon the Premier League's restart. The Gunners head to the Etihad Stadium on the opening day of the recommenced top-flight season, the televised evening kick-off following on from the Aston Villa and Sheffield United curtain-raiser. The restart came 100 days after Premier League football was suspended and 107 days after Arsenal had travelled to Portsmouth for that FA Cup meeting.

'I cannot be sure where I contracted coronavirus, but I would look towards the Arsenal match,' said Bolton. 'I didn't come into contact with Mikel Arteta, but it stands to reason that if the manager got it then a number of their players could have too.

'Our next match was at Peterborough and, afterwards, I mentioned to Bobby Bacic how my muscles had fatigued, and I wasn't recovering the way I usually do. Something wasn't quite right with my body. I've played plenty of games in my career, so I know my body and you recognise when something's not how it should be. When I later discovered I'd had coronavirus, I wasn't surprised. In the build-up to Fleetwood I was at my worst. I came in on the Monday, after the Peterborough game, and felt a bit leggy – my body was quite achy and the muscles weren't behaving normally. There was something different about me.

'I'm a footballer, though. You bat it off and get on with it. I played against Fleetwood and was still coming into training and involved in everything. I don't think any of us missed any days. If I'm honest, as it wasn't too bad. Obviously there have been serious cases across the world, but I must have had a milder version and my body had the power to fight it off. I was quite lucky. I also lost my taste and sense of smell for a week, which is something you really notice. It's not pleasant being unable to appreciate what you eat. I was probably a miserable so-and-so during that period!

'Strangely, my mum lost her taste and smell the other week, although when tested it came out negative. Looking back, I do think the virus had been going around a good while before it even hit football. A lot of people have probably had it but aren't privileged enough to be able to get tested so don't realise. My dad was really struggling before that Arsenal game. He couldn't shake off a cold for two weeks before and didn't feel well that night, struggling to sleep after the game. Had I not been tested, I would have passed it off as the flu and been none the wiser.

'I drive into training with Craig MacGillivray and thankfully he tested negative. However, he could well have had it before. I remember him coming into training for a period with a few coughs and colds. You don't know how it has been transmitted. I also room with Sean Raggett, who is another who has struggled with coughs and colds at times. When we played at Fleetwood Town in the FA Cup in January, Raggy was quite ill, but still played. People will assume it's nothing more than a cough or a cold, unless you're lucky enough to get tested.'

Andy Cannon had been left reeling after Jackett condemned him to bench duty for the FA Cup visit of Arsenal. Having started in successive Fratton Park victories over MK Dons and Rochdale, scoring his first Blues goal against the former in his 24th outing for the club, he was among six changes for the Gunners fixture. It wasn't until the 76th minute that the tireless midfielder made his entrance, replacing skipper Gareth Evans with Arsenal having already established an unassailable 2–0 lead. Upon the final whistle, as Pompey's disappointed players trudged off the pitch, he paused to shake hands with Arsenal's manager. Twenty days later he was among five Pompey players who tested positive for coronavirus.

'I came off the bench for the final sixteen minutes and was fine, then a few days later suddenly didn't feel myself,' said Cannon. 'It was a weird one. I could have caught coronavirus in a shop, you just don't know. Anyone can get it and it's hard to pinpoint exactly where it happened. However, I ended up not feeling great, so there is every possibility it can be traced to that Arsenal match.

When Arteta tested positive a few weeks later, obviously it got me thinking. We had played them, I had shaken his hand, and it was all around the time when I didn't start feeling well. You can't be 100 per cent sure, but it fits.

'In the build-up to our following match at Peterborough, I felt unusually lethargic; it was really strange. There was also a little cough, but I get coughs quite a bit, so in that respect it wasn't anything I was concerned about. Then in the hotel the night before the game, I recall going to sleep really early by 9.45pm. I woke up about 8.45am the next day. That is a stupid amount of sleep compared to what I normally get. Usually I go to bed at midnight, but I just didn't feel right. At breakfast, I felt so spaced out. There was definitely something wrong with me.

'That evening, after the game, I fell asleep around 10pm, and I just couldn't keep my eyes open while attempting to watch TV. Things weren't right. To be honest, I cannot remember the Peterborough game itself. I came on as a substitute in the second half and it's all a bit of a blank. You're never happy when told you aren't starting, but at the time I wasn't really bothered, which isn't me. I definitely would be normally. Half of me inside was thinking, "I'm actually kind of glad because I don't feel myself at all."

'Being told I had coronavirus came as a bit of a shock. I felt fine at the time, yet obviously it was still in my system. Suddenly everything made sense and I understood why I felt how I did around the Peterborough game. Other people have had coronavirus at other clubs, but I don't think many have had it as bad as Pompey.'

A recruit from Rochdale in January 2019, injury wiped out Cannon's opening six months with his new club. Despite that difficult period of adjustment, the 24-year-old forged an instant friendship with team-mate Ronan Curtis. Initially living on his own in a Port Solent apartment, the Irishman has provided Cannon with crucial companionship while separated from his Glossop-based family 250 miles away.

The energetic midfielder has also been welcomed by Marie and Dave Curtis, keen to put a supportive arm around his shoulder during their spells of staying at son Ronan's Old Portsmouth home.

On occasions, Cannon has even joined the Curtis family for visits to Cosham Crown Bingo, where manager Darren Bessey has allocated them a regular table, with Ronan served his favourite dish of cheesy chips with curry sauce. The Curtis' immense support helped nurse Cannon through that period of incubation with coronavirus.

> He added: 'Ronan is one of my best mates and his family are really good people. They are some of the most caring people I know and incredibly down to earth. They were always there for me when I was self-isolating, checking up almost every day. If I ever needed food, Marie would insist on making it. She's a great cook and they'd deliver a plate of Sunday roast or spaghetti bolognese to my doorstep, ringing me up to let me know when it had been dropped off outside. They didn't have to do that, but it says a lot about the family. They'd do anything for anyone and have treated me like another son. I'm so grateful for that.'

Since July 2019, Cannon has lived with Blues skipper Tony Naylor in the Berewood estate in Waterlooville. Naylor, a popular and highly respected presence in Pompey's squad worthy of his captaincy status, represents a perfect housemate for the softly spoken youngster. The duo are the only senior members of Jackett's side that live together, yet it's an arrangement which suits both parties being so far from their native north.

> 'I was mostly on my own during the lockdown period, with Nayls going back up to his family home near Mansfield, but Fortnite helped get me through,' said Cannon. 'I'm quite a gamer, so am always on my Xbox, which passed the time. I was also regularly on the phone to people, while team-mates were good, messaging to check how I was.
>
> 'I like company, which is the reason why I moved in with Nayls in the first place. It's just good having someone there. Initially I lived in a Port Solent apartment on my own and, with Nayls' missus still back up north, he was in the same situation. He was already in the house, so it made sense to move in together and go halves on

everything. I know of quite a few players at other clubs who live together. It makes it easier. You don't want to be on your own all the time, especially me; I enjoy being around people.

'Thankfully we get on. I shop for food one week, he gets it the other, although Nayls does most of the cooking, I have to admit. We also travel into training together, but Marcus Harness is my roommate for away games, so I'm not with him all the time! I also managed to go back to my family home in Glossop, near Manchester, for four weeks, which I really needed. It was a chance to spend time with my mum, dad and brother. I just don't get the opportunity during a football season. That was important to me and now we're back in the swing of football and looking forward to the play-offs.'

A quad problem restricted Cannon to just 40 minutes of football during the second half of last season following his Fratton Park arrival. Entering the current campaign with a clean bill of health, he set about the task of convincing supporters of his worth with vigour, rapidly establishing himself as a popular Fratton figure.

Nonetheless, there have been periods of immense frustration for the down-to-earth Lancastrian, forced to spend time on the bench while Pompey's boss has strived to identify his most effective first-team role. Cannon's drive with the ball at his feet and boundless energy earmarks him as an attacking option, on occasions employed as a number ten or the most attacking central midfielder. His first-team absence is usually met with criticism from sections of the Fratton faithful, who believe he should be a regular starter.

He said: 'When I moved to Pompey, I had a bad start, but it has been fine this season. I would never say I've had a bad time at the club. I've had one nasty injury, but, other than that, have only been out for a couple of weeks when my hamstring has been a bit sore. I've been available for almost all of this season and feel I've been able to prove what I'm capable of doing.

'I think I've done well. When you look at the stats, there are high win percentages when I've been playing. That's a great stat to have behind me because the main thing is to be winning matches. If I'm helping the team to achieve that, then all is good.

'The fans seem to have really taken to me this season, not that I take much notice of social media. You're always going to get some kind of criticism regardless. But if I'm making the fans happy then that's good.'

Bolton can empathise with Cannon's teething problems after a Fratton Park switch. Likewise, he was emerging strongly through such difficulties when the season stalled in mid-March. Recruited from Shrewsbury Town on a free transfer in June 2019, he was handed a three-year deal and earmarked to replace the reliable Nathan Thompson at right-back. However, a groin injury sustained during the opening 45 minutes of pre-season friendly action initiated a stuttering start to life at Fratton Park for the ex-Stoke City youth player.

He returned to feature in the final friendly at Woking and was named on the bench for the League One opener at Shrewsbury, only to damage his ankle during a substitute appearance. Bolton was finally handed his maiden league start at Wycombe in mid-September, the Blues' seventh League One fixture of the season. A 1–0 defeat at Adams Park that afternoon left them twentieth in the table.

He said: 'You're at a new club and keen to hit the ground running, but I had to deal with a lot at the beginning. There's no reserve league, so you get your fitness from going straight into games, picking it up on the job. You can train all you like, but it cannot replicate matches.

'It started in Dublin, when I picked up a slight groin nick in our first friendly against UCD. I had never suffered that type of injury before, but I felt it towards the end of the first half. I thought I'd play through it and get to half-time as I knew I was coming off, with eleven substitutions pre-determined. It actually made the injury a little worse.

'Looking back, it wasn't a great thing to do, but when you're at a new club you want to stay on the pitch and do well. It was a stupid decision, but that's just the way I am, I want to play. We were winning by a big margin and playing well – it was a really good start for me. Then a nick towards the end put a dampener on it. When I returned, I was substitute for the opening game of the season at Shrewsbury, only to collect another injury, which was incredibly frustrating.

'I'd had a problem with my right ankle the previous season, having injections to get me through games. Then my mate, Shaun Whalley, tackled me and put me out for a couple of weeks. I knew it was a bad one and how long it takes an ankle to heal. I was miserable to say the least after that game, especially having lost 1–0. When I was right-back at Shrewsbury, Shaun was on the right wing, so we built up quite a close relationship. He had also been my roommate there on occasions. Then, on my Pompey debut, he was slow into a tackle and caught me late, right on the bone. It wasn't malicious whatsoever, but he's better at crossing balls rather than tackling people!

'A scan showed it up to be bad bone bruising, with a chip already there from a previous injury. I was struggling to walk for the first week and constantly had my foot in an ice bucket trying to get it right, but it wasn't budging. It took forever to heal. I came back at the start of September and was in and out of the team for a bit. You just have to carry on waiting for your chance again and build from there. It's hard, but that's the way football is. Some players can dive in and play, whereas I need that flow and rhythm of playing games regularly.'

Following October's last-gasp 1–0 defeat at AFC Wimbledon, Jackett opted to head in a different direction. Bolton was the sole casualty from that starting line-up, with Ross McCrorie instead pressed into action at right-back for the following match against Lincoln City. McCrorie had arrived on a season-long loan from Rangers as a highly regarded holding midfielder, despite skippering Scotland's under-21s as a right-back. When the Scot was struck down by a hamstring injury in the first half of November's visit of Southend, Bolton was not present on the bench to deputise, having failed to earn selection. Instead left-back Brandon Haunstrup was called into the fray to take on an unfamiliar position and became the latest to earn consistent selection ahead of the man recruited in the summer. Yet Bolton battled back to become a fixture in the side which would establish a club record nine successive victories in the Football League to catapult them into League One's top five.

'There's no point moping about thinking, "I'm not in the team, so what's the point?" You've got to roll your sleeves up,' he said. 'I'm a hard worker, but I will say it myself – I am not the most naturally gifted footballer. However, hard work and determination have probably lifted me higher than perhaps people would have thought.

'You get lads who sulk if they're not in the team but you are not helping yourself. They think people don't notice, but we can see. It's all right to have a bit of a sulk at the start, but you have to dust yourself down, try to be upbeat and get yourself back into the team. I've played from the very bottom at Stafford Rangers to reach where I am now, so I understand graft.

'During my time out of Pompey's team, I'd be working in the gym after training, doing a little extra on aspects I thought needed improvement. It's not a chore, I enjoy it, and it's good for me. You have to keep it relatable to match situations. There's no point me practising shooting from ten yards because realistically that's not going to happen. Instead, I've worked on crossing, longer passing, channel balls, generally things I'd be doing in a game which can be improved. When out of the team, you continue to work hard – there's not much else you can do. You must impress the manager and you do that in training.

'The big turning point was probably against Ipswich in December, when I came on as a substitute for Ross McCrorie late in the first half. On a personal level and as a team, I felt everything kicked on from that point. We beat them 1–0 in a tight game, which was a massive relief. Next up was Wycombe Wanderers, and suddenly we were churning out results while I was handed my longest run of games. A lot of managers appreciate a player with a good attitude – it goes a long way. That has helped me a lot in my career.'

❋ ◡ ❋

On the day of Dom Merrix's funeral, Bolton joined Pompey supporter Gemma Raggett in releasing five blue balloons beside the River Wey for a touching tribute. Fellow Godalming resident Raggett, a committee member of Portsmouth Football Supporters' Club London, reached out to the right-back via Instagram to see if he would be willing to assist. A family friend of the Merrix's, lockdown rules prevented Gemma from attending the Portsmouth-based funeral. Instead, with the help of Pompey's right-back, she staged her own commemorative ceremony.

Bolton has become a regular sight in the Surrey market town during lockdown, maintaining his fitness regime in hope of this season's resumption. The 25-year-old has previous with the play-offs as a member of the Shrewsbury side that lost 2–1 during extra-time in the League One final at Wembley in May 2018. Now he's eyeing a more successful outcome as Pompey prepare for next month's semi-final encounter with Oxford.

> He added: 'I know what play-offs are like. To win one with Pompey would be a dream. You can do all you want in training, but when it comes to those competitive games it will be completely different. Whoever handles that situation the best will go up. The club have been using the Strava app to monitor our work away from the training ground and, as a team, we've been staying fit throughout this. It will stand us in good stead and help get us through these games. I have a bike and have been running around a rugby pitch near my house, trying to do as much as I can. I've always liked to keep fit and stay active anyway.
>
> 'Playing in front of no crowds will feel like a bit of a friendly, while nobody knows what kind of shape any of the teams are in – there's no form book. It's going to be a bit of a shoot-out and hopefully we can handle the situation and put in the performances to get us into the Championship.'

JOHNNY MOORE,
ABDUL KHALIQUE
AND SIMON MILNE

3 July 2020

Inspired by DVDs of 1970s TV series *Secret Army*, Johnny Moore
chose to use his enforced sabbatical from Pompey to learn German.
Enrolling on a free online course, the 61-year-old sailed through
three volumes of lessons in two and a half weeks of encouraging
progress, before his enthusiasm was dampened. Moore baulked at the
subscription fee required to maintain his learning. His new-found
passion was swiftly dropped in favour of poring over newspapers while
sitting in the gazebo in his back garden.

It has been almost three months since Pompey's long-serving
supporter liaison officer was instructed to remain at his house in
Havant. Chief executive Mark Catlin personally intervened, urging
Moore to work from home for his own wellbeing as the coronavirus
crisis headed towards lockdown status. Within a month, he was among
a large number of staff furloughed. During 22 years at Pompey, Moore
had kept his job through three administrations. Now, a pandemic

forced his absence. Still, it was a touching moment when he cut through Tesco's petrol station to emerge at Fratton Park for the first leg play-off semi-final encounter with Oxford United. Invited back as the club's guest, the separation had spanned twelve weeks. Now football – and Johnny Moore – were back in PO4.

'I remember the exact date I was last at Fratton Park: Thursday, 12 March,' he said. 'My final duty was interviewing our former player Chris Kamara on the phone. I caught the train back to Havant that night and have stayed away since.

'It's been twelve weeks, the longest time I've been apart from Pompey since starting work there in September 1998. Funnily enough, I came into this club through the back door and have remained here. Back then, the Martin Gregory era was reaching its end, but I went to see his right-hand man, Peter Hinkinson, the managing director, to explain how they needed to build a bridge between the fans and the club.

'Martin didn't trust me at the time as the supporters club which I chaired had staged several protests. I'd also written some uncomplimentary pieces in my *Sports Mail* column concerning his regime. However, Hinkinson, obviously thinking there was nothing to lose, replied: "You're right. We'll find you an office at Fratton Park and start that process. I think it will be good." Then he had a heart attack and never returned! It was a great shame as the relationship between club and supporters was at an all-time low, with zero communication.

'Still, nothing was going to stop me. I went there and found a room in the attic to serve as my office. It used to be an accounts room, so I decorated it, put a telly in there, installed a computer and sat there for two months before anybody realised. Then, one day, somebody from the accounts department rang my phone and said, "Who's that?"

'When Milan Mandarić became owner, he told me: "Johnny, we need to put bread on your table." I replied: "A few Carlsberg will be fine, Milan." David Deacon was the chief executive and another not too keen on me, but Milan was his own man. We got on famously from the day he entered the football club. He's such a genuine bloke, so down to earth. I had to pinch myself when the owner of Portsmouth Football Club gave me a lift to Wetherspoons. He had offered to drive me home to Havant after a late-night meeting and, as we pulled up at the Parchment Makers pub where I asked to be dropped off, he stared and said: "Johnny, that's a big home."

'I remember Paul Weld, the club secretary, and I were leaving one night and found Milan with his head in his hands. He hadn't been there a year as owner but was starting to understand all the skeletons he was finding in cupboards. I know Milan wasn't everyone's cup of tea when he left, but, for me, you couldn't have wished for a better owner at that time after all the club had been through. Apart from the stadium, he fulfilled every promise and gave generations of fans times they could not have dreamed of just a decade earlier. He once told me his biggest regret was going to Leicester City and all the problems that brought on to Pompey. I saw him quite a few times as owner of Leicester and Sheffield Wednesday and I don't think he found the same love and affinity.

'In contrast, Sacha Gaydamak was cold and didn't have a connection with anyone. I had nothing to do with Gaydamak because he wouldn't have anything to do with me. His sidekick and vice-chairman, David Chissick, wanted to take bad news off the club website. If we lost a game, he insisted that it be put at the bottom of the page. When we fell to a 2–1 defeat to Southend United in July 2006 as part of pre-season, he said: "Don't put it up." It demonstrated their appalling lack of understanding of football. If you look at Milan's history, he repairs football clubs, takes them to the next level and then moves on. At Pompey, he wanted to sell it on to someone he thought was better, but they weren't the right people.'

While Moore was offered a seat in the directors' box, there was no such Fratton Park recall for boot man Barry Harris. The 76-year-old has a slight shadow on his outer lung, diagnosed as pleural plaque, following asbestos exposure. It's a consequence of working as a scaffolder in Portsmouth's Dockyard for sixteen years, before leaving in 1981. Harris was diagnosed in 2004, earning a compensation payout, yet considers himself fortunate that his treatment involves nothing more serious than using an inhaler morning and night of each day.

Still, he believed it wise to give a Pompey fixture a rare miss in favour of remaining at his Southsea home to watch the match on Sky Sports. As two of Pompey's longest-serving employees, Moore and Harris were present when Harry Redknapp took up the managerial reins in March 2002 to lead the club into the Premier League. Moore has remained in touch with the man he regards as his favourite boss during 22 years at the club.

'There was an occasion when I had been in the Old House at Home pub in Havant and phoned up for my regular Chinese takeaway,' he added. 'The call was answered and I gave my order: chicken curry, egg fried rice and chips. However, something was wrong. "Who the hell is that?" came the reply from the person on the other end. I'd rung the wrong number, so quickly hung up. Then I realised who the person was – Harry Redknapp! In my phone directory, his name was just above Havant Chinese Food Centre, so it was an easy mistake to make. Thankfully, he never found out.

'I loved working with Harry – he was always open with me. I recall in the summer of 2008, having won the FA Cup a few months earlier, we signed Israeli international Ben Sahar on loan from Chelsea. Naturally, with any signing, the club wanted to interview him, but firstly I was keen to speak to Harry for his take on the newcomer. There was no answer, so I left a message. He never returned the call, which was unlike him as Harry would always ring back.

'On the first day of pre-season training, he came up to me and said: "Johnny, I'm sorry I didn't reply, but I don't want Ben Sahar; he's never going to play for me." It turned out Sacha Gaydamak had arranged the deal with Roman Abramovich, purely as a favour to Chelsea. Then Harry continued: "Do you know what? We haven't got any money. Can you believe that? We've just won the FA Cup and have no money." Mind you, not long after we somehow found the funds to buy Peter Crouch from Liverpool in an £11m deal. As for Sahar, he never did play for the club and only made three squads.

'In October 2008, we lost 3–0 at Braga in the UEFA Cup and, on the flight back, Harry sat at the front of the plane with Peter

Storrie beside him. Something wasn't right and 48 hours later he had left for Tottenham Hotspur. I'm quite good at sensing things. On that evening in Braga, Harry stood there during the game not looking interested. We later found out why.'

Having attended his first Pompey match on the opening day of the 1967–68 season, Moore's Pompey affiliation was irreversible. He went on to form Portsmouth Supporters Club (Central Branch) with Kev Ryan, becoming chairman in the mid-1990s. Meanwhile, for eight years, his *Sports Mail* column 'Voice From The Terraces' was well received among fans, although on occasions incurred the wrath of Pompey's hierarchy.

Having later been admitted into Fratton Park as an employee, Moore occupied a ringside seat as Pompey unravelled financially while inhabiting the wealthiest league in world football. During the 2009–10 season, their last in the Premier League, the Blues were burdened with four different owners in 146 days, before being placed into administration with fifteen matches remaining.

He said: 'It was a Mad Hatter's Tea Party during that time, with all these strange characters coming in and out. I once took a call from our director of communications, Gary Double, asking me to come to Fratton Park as quickly as possible as we were gathering a group of supporters to meet the new owner, Sulaiman Al-Fahim. I was in the doctors' waiting room at the time awaiting a check-up. "Your blood pressure is quite high," the doctor told me a few minutes later.

'Anyhow, I managed to bring together a number of representatives from various supporter groups. We sat in a boiling-hot room on a sweltering summer's day waiting for this character who must have been three or four hours late. Then the door opened and a bloke with holes in his jeans walked in. I asked: "Can I help you?" He replied: "Yes, I'm Sulaiman Al-Fahim." I was expecting loads of henchmen, as he was meant to be a billionaire, but it was just a man in holey jeans. I don't think my blood pressure had lowered. The thing is, you put someone false in front of football fans and they are soon caught out. Nothing he said rang true and that continued to be the case during his short time with the club.

'It was then arranged for Al-Fahim to meet supporters in the Victory Lounge, except his advisor rang us the night before to let us know it would no longer be happening. It was chaos, and our chief executive Peter Storrie didn't know what was going on. Then suddenly it was back on again, which prompted the bizarre sight of Storrie and a few others from the club hierarchy coming along to hear what the new owner had to say. They were looking at Al-Fahim with daggers, throwing in the occasional question themselves. He was replaced as Pompey owner by Ali Al Faraj, but none of us ever saw him before he vanished and someone else came in.

'I must admit, I was once travelling with Peter Storrie and his car phone went off, with somebody purporting to be Al Faraj on the other end. Whether it was him or not, I cannot be certain, but they were talking about bills to be paid. It was a very short conversation. I don't think you can come up with a character which didn't exist.

'I got on famously with Peter Storrie. As chief executive, he was wrongly blamed for a lot of stuff. At the end of the day, he was employed like everyone else. Pompey were put into administration in February 2010, the day before facing Burnley at Turf Moor in the Premier League. That brought Andrew Andronikou, a very abrasive character, into the club as administrator. 'At that stage we were based in offices in Rodney Road and, following a staff meeting, we were told to head upstairs in turn, where we would enter one of two designated rooms. It was barbaric. One room meant you were safe, the other would see you dismissed. A lot of people didn't have a clue what would happen to them. One lady, who was reasonably long-serving, was directed to the wrong room and nearly fainted. How can that happen? I offered for my wages to be cut, and I was even prepared to work for nothing. I had done it before and would do it again for my club. Fortunately, I was told to enter the right room.'

With Pompey remaining in administration that summer, Andronikou set about appointing a new chief executive to replace the departed Storrie.

David Lampitt was the June 2010 selection, a candidate possessing an impressive pedigree. The qualified chartered accountant had seen six years' service with the FA, rising to the position of head of financial regulation. Handed the remit of stabilising the club, Lampitt joined Andronikou in the managerial interview process which would identify Steve Cotterill to fill the vacancy created by Avram Grant's departure for West Ham United. However, financial turmoil struck once more when latest owners Convers Sports Initiatives entered administration.

In February 2012, Lampitt was among 33 members of staff made redundant by Trevor Birch from administrators PKF. When fan ownership seized control, Mark Catlin was their choice to occupy the chief executive role.

Moore said: 'In the mornings, I would sit and have a 7am chat with Trevor Birch at Fratton Park, and he was always open with me. He also got rid of the only bloke I've really struggled with during all my time at the club – David Lampitt. I've got on with every chief executive, from Barrie Pierpoint to even David Deacon in the end, but not Lampitt. I don't think he ever knew how I really felt about him.

'I remember early on in his time at the club. Lampitt voiced his displeasure at my sitting in the directors' box for games. Listen, I had no right to be there to be perfectly honest. It was something Milan Mandarić and Barrie Pierpoint had offered way back in 2000 and simply carried on. It was something I never took for granted.

'So, after a decade, if Lampitt had a problem with it he should have just told me, explained and moved on, but he didn't say a word to my face. Talk about double standards – his PA was allowed in there, with her mates sometimes, and the rest of his little crew. He relented in the end and I returned to the directors' box. It was such a petty situation. Mind you, at one time he insisted that if you wanted to be in the directors' box for an away game, you had to let his PA know and they would draw it out of a hat. Regularly, I was the only one in the hat.

'Former player Michael Brown hit the nail on the head recently in *The News* when he said the man was out of his depth. Obviously, he was playing his silly games with people far higher up than me. There was the time the club raised season-ticket prices a few days after commercial director Lucius Peart had promised supporters in a meeting that they wouldn't. As I remember, it was a massive hike. I was on the train to Leicester and Lampitt called. He said: "I need you to write a statement to all the fans and say this is the reason why we are doing this." Worst of all, he wanted me to sign it! I got off at Petersfield station and caught a taxi back to Fratton Park which went straight past my home. I felt like jumping out and leaving there and then. No other person or situation had driven me that close. For me to put my name to a hike in season-ticket prices that I had no discussions in and steadfastly opposed, thereby inevitably attracting all the flak from others, was as gutless as it got. In the end, he agreed to a general statement, but never thanked me for coming back. They still owe me for the £30 taxi fare back from Petersfield as well.

'The Tuesday he was laid off was the biggest release I ever felt. It was March and, as I walked down Goldsmith Avenue early the next day, the light mornings were reappearing and the sky above was pink. It was as if it was meant to be. When I arrived at Fratton Park, I looked at our receptionist, Debbie Knight, and we just smiled. No words were needed. His reign was over.

'Lampitt left a phone message saying he was sorry he didn't have the chance to say goodbye. I wasn't. In fact, I'd left for a wander round the ground to deliberately avoid him. He really didn't understand the depth of feeling. Many staff didn't like him as he had no idea how to manage people. Mark Catlin couldn't be more different. I have watched him grow into the best chief executive the club, and perhaps lower league football, has seen. More importantly, he has retained his natural down-to-earth demeanour and, despite his own hectic schedule, always has time for people.

'In terms of other chief executives, Peter Storrie wouldn't suffer fools and could be a little abrasive at times. He was a football man who had previously worked at West Ham and was very experienced in the game. They came into the club and realised that I had Pompey at heart, and money was secondary. I had worked there for free for two years. They all knew I wasn't there to fleece them or cut corners. I'm there because I love it.'

✳ ☽ ✳

Abdul Khalique is back on his feet again following a hospital stint, but his Fratton Park services aren't required on this occasion. The 49-year-old had recently been admitted to St Mary's Hospital to rectify ingrown nails on the big toes of both feet. He was discharged later that same day following the operation, though he was required to take a week off from work at Sumika Polymer Compounds, in Havant, to recuperate. Still, the infectiously positive Khalique has made a timely return to fitness to fulfil his customary Pompey match-day duties on the Victory South gate for the play-off semi-final first leg.

Few Blues stewards can match the popularity of the North End resident, whose sunshine personality and natural warmth have established him as a cult figure among the Fratton faithful. Khalique's photograph adorned Wembley Way for the 2019 Checkatrade Trophy final and he was once crowned the supporters' Pompey man of the match following an abysmal home defeat. However, with Fratton Park operating with a skeleton staff of ten stewards, he was asked to step down for football's return against Oxford. Inevitably, the news was greeted with good grace and a sizeable smile.

He said: 'Oh, my giddy aunt; you wouldn't believe it, would you? Ingrown toenails on each foot! That was a week ago and now I'm back fighting fit. I'm fine and have been given the all-clear to go back to work in time for Pompey's game. Unfortunately, on this occasion, I'm not needed as only a small number of staff are required with there being no supporters allowed into Fratton Park. I'll be watching it on Sky Sports at home, though, and I have every belief we can win this match. At the start of the season I thought we would get promoted and my opinion has never changed. Our form dipped a little at one point, but by some miracle we are in the play-offs. It's now in our hands and I believe we have the quality of players and squad to achieve the goal of returning to the Championship.

'I am well excited about it to be fair. It was announced the season would continue, then the penny dropped that we'd be in the play-offs, which was fabulous. I knew we would be there and we're in the mix – that's all that matters. Can you tell I'm enthusiastic? We now get some extra football on the TV and have the chance of being at Wembley for another final. There are so many positives. It will be strange not having fans there for these play-off games, but it's only for a short period. It's not for long, is it? We'll get over this and be back to normal.'

Born in Scunthorpe, Khalique moved to Portsmouth at the age of thirteen when Dad, Asir, moved to the area for a business opportunity following redundancy from a steelworks. Along with a friend, Asir opened a restaurant in Elm Grove, soon expanding with the launch of an Albert Road grocers, which the family lived above. While Abdul lost all traces of a northern accent, his passion for Pompey blossomed. That Fratton Park connection saw him volunteer his services as a steward for the 2008–09 season, when Harry Redknapp's men were reigning FA Cup holders and playing in the Premier League. For those who have encountered him on match days, it's clearly a job he adores.

He added: 'I'm a Pompey fan and a friendly person – I genuinely like chatting to people. So why not kill two birds with one stone and absorb the wonderful Fratton Park atmosphere every game. I love being there. As a steward, we are the first port of call when anyone comes to the club. We are the first impression and first impressions are the most important thing. We may not always get it right, but we strive to. I find it easy because I love doing it. In life, most of us want to help someone. My chance to do that is to give someone a good experience when they come to Fratton Park.

'I don't really see the game, although I get feedback from three quarters of the ground when they leave. That's the best opinion of how the game really went. Through my gate, I meet managers, football scouts and, best of all, Academy players. It gives me such a buzz seeing those youngsters who are here to help this club get better and achieve its goals. Hopefully they'll get us back into the Premier League at some point.

'Mind you, when Will Ferrell came to watch us in August, I only caught glimpses; I didn't actually have the chance to speak to him. He was walking around with a little entourage and didn't come into my gate, unfortunately. I've watched loads and loads of his films too. My favourite has to be *Step Brothers*, although we all love *Elf*, don't we? My general view is if you treat someone how you want to be treated, then 99 per cent of the time you can't go wrong. Should someone not be the most pleasant, perhaps they may be having a bad day. So, treat them even nicer on those occasions.

'I'm very lucky with the amount of lovely people I get to meet. People are generally nice; they come here to watch a good game of football and are hoping Pompey win. We're all the same. I am a person whose cup is half full rather than half empty. I'm never upset about anything. Life's too short. You must enjoy what you do and for me that's meeting people.'

Following Pompey's abject 1–0 defeat to Crewe Alexandra in March 2017, Twitter account PompeyNewsNow held a tongue-in-cheek vote to decide who was worthy of the man-of-the-match award. By an overwhelming majority, Khalique emerged as the winner, polling 48.4 per cent of the 525 votes and finishing ahead of Pompey Ladies, boxer Joel McIntyre and contestants of the dizzy stick half-time entertainment. Among those who registered their delight on Twitter at the outcome were the wife of ex-Blues right-back Ben Davies, and the dad of Jed Wallace, a former *The News/Sports Mail* Pompey Player of the Season who is now starring for Millwall. Abdul the Steward leaves an indelible mark on all who pass through Fratton Park.

'I do get recognised when I'm out. I am terrible with names, but I'm brilliant with faces,' he laughed. 'Once I was doing some work at the Queens Hotel in Southsea, and someone said: "I know you." Or, if I'm in the supermarket, people spot you, which is great. I will always stop to chat about Pompey with anybody who wants to listen.

'Ahead of last season's Checkatrade Trophy final against Sunderland, the Football League wanted to interview and do a photo shoot with someone who represented the club and I was nominated. I was told I could wear what I wanted but made sure I put on my steward's jacket. I'm only one part of a great group of people who do an amazing job.

'I am lucky that people recognise me, but there are so many other stewards who do the same job and work really, really hard. As a homage to them, I made sure I wore my steward's coat. It was a hot day as well! I went with my son, Qasin, to the Wembley final against Sunderland and we saw that picture. It was weird for him because, as we were going around Wembley Way, people spotted me and wanted photographs. The boy was flabbergasted. "Dad, really?" I replied: "I'm afraid so, son. Sorry." It was the best day out.

'I know I was once named man of the match and, don't get me wrong, it was very nice, but we must not forget that players give their all. Nobody goes on to the pitch and wants to play badly. It was just one of those days for them. I'm a positive guy. Even if somebody says they are not happy with a game, I will pick up on the positives. That's just the way I am.'

The resourceful Simon Milne had already managed to negotiate behind-closed-doors restrictions to observe Pompey's June friendly at Brentford. Equipped with a step stool usually employed during his work as a roof tiler, he peered over a Griffin Park wall to survey the Blues in action ahead of the play-off campaign. Accompanied by six-year-old son Ollie and friend John Westwood, they were the only Pompey fans to catch sight of the 1–1 draw with the Championship outfit.

Similarly denied entry to the play-off first leg against Oxford, the trio plotted to gather in a street outside Fratton Park during the match as an act of spiritual support. It has been almost nineteen years since Milne, from Petersfield, has missed a Blues game, a proud statistic he must now surrender.

The 34-year-old said: 'I've been to every Pompey game, home and away, since Boxing Day 2001. There's even been tours to Nigeria, Hong Kong, America, Canada, Gibraltar, the Republic of Ireland, France and Scotland. Some people think it's stupid. My son's like me though. Ollie has been everywhere following Pompey for the last two seasons. The only game he's missed during that time was Coventry City at home in August because he was with his nan. Oli Hawkins is his favourite player, although there is a story behind that. At Doncaster Rovers last season, during the warm-up, Oli smashed a shot into the crowd, hitting my son straight in the stomach and making him cry. So, he came up to us and handed Ollie his training top. Then, after the Sunderland game, he gave him his boots. My son will be devastated if Oli leaves at the end of the season when his contract is up.

'The boy travelled with me and John to Reading the other week for Pompey's first friendly since lockdown. It was behind closed doors and a bit of a secret. Unfortunately, we arrived ten minutes before the final whistle and couldn't get anywhere near the ground to watch it. At least it worked out for us going to Brentford. In one of the corners was a wall and we watched the whole game from there. A steward came over and said: "I'm going to have to ask you to move," but we weren't causing any harm and promised not to climb into the ground. Then a bloke in a suit and an earpiece, who must have been the top security person, asked if we were okay and walked off smiling. Nobody seemed too bothered about it. After the game, we stood on the opposite side of the road to where the players came out and Kenny Jackett and Joe Gallen came over for a chat. I don't even think they were surprised to see us there.'

A generous invite prompted Milne and his compatriots to abandon plans to stand in a neighbouring street for the duration of the Oxford match. Instead they relocated to the Frogmore Road home of former Blues steward Andy Johnston, whose house is situated just yards from where Pompey were in action. Having not missed a Fratton Park fixture for 21 years, Johnston shared their frustration and threw open his doors, creating an eclectic group, gathering around an iPhone on a garden table.

Johnston's friends, Will Kipling and George Hatton, were also present, thereby keeping to government guidelines by socialising in groups of no more than six people, while pizzas purchased from Lidl fed his house guests at half-time. Neighbours had also been consulted, yet no issues were raised about Westwood spending a few hours in the adjacent garden. Perhaps they were unaware the Petersfield bookshop owner would be accompanied by his faithful bell and bugle, two snare drums and full repertoire of Pompey songs during the 1–1 draw.

Milne added: 'I know Andy through football, and he dropped me a message asking if I fancied popping around. He hasn't got Sky, so the idea was to watch it on John's laptop, but we aren't very technical. Instead, a mobile phone propped up on a table outside was the best way. To be fair, John saw more of the football than usual! The weird thing is, I received a notification on my phone that Pompey had gone 1–0 up before we had seen it. There was even a little cheer a few doors down before we saw it for ourselves about a minute later.

'Having spent most of the match in the back garden, banging on the instruments and singing Pompey songs, we decided to go right outside the stadium ten minutes before the end and make a bit of a racket. Initially we thought there might be police and stewards about, so probably wouldn't be worth the hassle, but I popped my head out of the door and no one was there. Sod it, what's the worst that can happen? A policeman did appear, had a chat with John and soon disappeared. Apparently, he had spent ages that afternoon wondering where all the noise was coming from. The only people not happy were Sky. One of them came out asking us to be quiet because they were interviewing players after the match and it was difficult to hear!'

MARIE AND RONAN CURTIS

4 July 2020

Marie Curtis had laid on chicken wraps and Prosecco for the grand occasion, intent on ensuring that her fifteen house guests were substantially catered for. Pompey were in action but circumstances prevented the parents of Ronan Curtis from occupying their customary South Stand seats for the opening play-off semi-final fixture. The pair had returned to their home in Drumatoland three months earlier, having obtained permission from Portsmouth police to travel back to the Republic of Ireland during lockdown. Now, following the resumption of the Blues' season, the sizeable Curtis family had congregated at Marie and Dave's four-bedroom home, set in three acres of land in rural County Donegal.

Well watered and fully fed, each member donned a Pompey shirt in solidarity and gathered around the television to roar on their favourite left winger against Oxford United. They were cheered by Ronan turning in a scoring display and man-of-the-match performance in the play-off contest, although the majority of the Fratton faithful in their living room were a little underwhelmed by the 1–1 first leg outcome, which still leaves Pompey looking for a first play-off win after seven attempts.

Marie said: 'I think there'll probably be more of the family around ours for Monday's second leg, as some were working when the first match was shown. It will be the usual madhouse. I'm planning to give them curry for that game. There were fifteen of the family there on Friday, screaming at the television, and every single one of us had a Pompey shirt on, including the grandchildren.

'Even though Ronan had a brilliant game and scored from a very tight angle, Sky Sports gave Oxford's Rob Dickie man of the match. I suppose that shows how much pressure we put them under. We came out of the traps very well and were the better team to begin with. Ronan hit the upright and then, when he scored, we sat back, didn't push, didn't create anything. I don't know what happened.

'My husband, Dave, says he didn't mind a draw as it gives us something to go into the second leg with, but I wanted a win. We had three penalty shouts but the referee, Gavin Ward, didn't give anything. He was afraid to rock the boat and give a decision against either of the teams.

'Ronan had an appeal in stoppage time when Dan Agyei fouled him inside the box. Ronan thinks it definitely should have been a penalty. He's told me if it wasn't a foul then the referee should have him for diving, yet didn't. He says: "Mum, why would I go down when bearing down on goal with the defender coming in behind me?" For me, the one where Rob Dickie pulled Christian Burgess to the ground in the first half was also a blatant penalty. Think what the score would have been if both had been correctly awarded. I believe we'll win the second leg. We were the better team and we didn't look like we'd had three months off. Kenny Jackett must be doing something fantastic with their fitness.

'It really pleased me to see Lee Brown back at left-back. Him and Ronan work really well together and have that partnership. If Browny pushes on, then Ronan knows he has to get back into the full-back position. They've clicked since day one. What about the news of Christian Burgess leaving as well? That was a shock. I was really surprised because I thought he liked it at Pompey. Why go to the second division in Belgium when he could maybe get to the Championship here? Still, I thought we did pretty well against

Oxford. It's hard for the players being at Fratton Park with no fans, although towards the end of the game I could hear singing outside the stadium and someone on a drum.

'I haven't a clue what team Kenny will pick. Ronan always says to me: "I'm not telling you, Mother, because you'll put it up on Twitter!" He doesn't tell me anything now. I can't see Brett Pitman being involved either. That's what you get for telling me to shush when you've scored against Altrincham in the FA Cup!'

Curtis struck the post before breaking the first-leg deadlock on 32 minutes through an angled finish from the left, beating keeper Simon Eastwood at his near post. However, winger Marcus Browne, on loan from Middlesbrough, levelled two minutes before the break, placing a right-footed shot beyond Alex Bass, into the far corner. The 1–1 draw ensured Pompey finished the 2019–20 campaign undefeated at Fratton Park in the league in a truncated season which totalled eighteen home games, nineteen including the play-offs.

In the Football League, Liverpool were the only other team to go undefeated at home in league encounters, having completed nineteen matches. In all competitions, Jackett's men suffered two home losses in 29 fixtures, the only blots on their copybook coming at the hands of Premier League pair Southampton and Arsenal, while their last League One loss occurred on 30 April 2019, in a 3–2 defeat to Peterborough United which effectively condemned the Blues to the 2018–19 play-offs.

'I'm gutted we couldn't be at Fratton Park for the first leg as we've always watched Ronan's games, no matter what the club,' added Marie Curtis. 'We've not missed many since he has been at Pompey, while I was absent just once at Derry City because I was sick. We understand the reasons why it is behind closed doors, though. It's important we look after ourselves. We stayed for two weeks in Portsmouth after lockdown and then left for Ireland at the start of April. We've been here ever since.

'I had asked a police officer if it was okay as nobody was meant to be driving that far, but we don't live here, it isn't our home, and we just stay at Ronan's in a spare room, so it was fine. The policeman did ask which way we intended to go back to Ireland and advised us not to go the Dublin route as they weren't letting anybody in because of the coronavirus. We could have been kept in isolation. Instead we caught the overnight ferry from Liverpool, which took eight hours to reach Belfast. Then it was two hours from there to get home.

'Where we live has loads and loads of lanes. You can go on long walks which take you out into the country with cows and sheep. I can walk for three miles and not see anybody. I have a couple of neighbours, but they are few and far between around here. If ever we need anything, by car it takes fifteen minutes to Derry and you are fifteen minutes from Letterkenny. So we're fine.

'I don't think you're going to get any fans into football matches before Christmas, but Ronan's okay. I ring him twice a day, while his sister calls every day. His brother, Blain, has a building job in Portsmouth, so he's keeping him company. I know I'm not there at present, but thankfully Ronan isn't on his own.'

Ronan Curtis' Oxford strike signified his fourteenth of the campaign, drawing him level with John Marquis as Pompey's leading scorer. All but one of the left winger's impressive tally has arrived from open play, a direct free-kick at Lincoln City in January the sole exception. He has surpassed the twelve-goal haul from his maiden season with the Blues. Ahead of the semi-final first leg, he was declared runner-up behind Christian Burgess in *The News/Sports Mail*'s Player of the Season vote among supporters. It's fitting recognition for the remarkable resurgence in form since his September low against Bolton Wanderers when the 24-year-old subsequently used Twitter to lash out at a section of the Fratton faithful.

Ronan Curtis said: 'I was booed and jeered off the pitch by my own fans against Bolton. I had a go at them and that incident made me even stronger as a player. In my mind, it was: "Do you know what? I'm going to show these people who I really am. I'll show who the boss is on the pitch." When next handed the chance, I went on a mad scoring run and my confidence came back. I was a completely different player.

'Of course that supporter reaction hurt. If our supporters are doing that to their own players, how do you think the opposition felt on the pitch that day? I can tell you, they were buzzing. It lifted them. It touched a nerve with me. They were actually clapping and cheering when I was being substituted. I bit my tongue at the time, then reacted when I got home by putting out a tweet which they didn't like. A couple of weeks later, when I scored against Bristol Rovers, they were cheering in a different way.

'I don't regret putting that tweet out having a go at them. At the time I was hurt and upset, but when I'd calmed down and taken a breath, thinking about everything, it felt a bit bad. Upon reflection, I deleted it after an hour or so. Nobody instructed me to. It's in the past now. I forgive them for what they did and they have forgiven me for what I said on Twitter. It's over and done with.

'Every player has a bit of passion inside them, but mine is overwhelming – I love the game. I've been playing since the age of four or five. It's in my blood. I'm passionate about every club I represent, not just this one. Around that period I was getting loads of stick on Twitter and Instagram, while I was receiving abusive phone calls as well. I had to prove them wrong, I just had to. People wrote me off after the way I finished the first season. They said: "We'll see if he can perform again." And I did.

'The truth is, my form at the beginning of the campaign was down to confidence. Certainly not about fitness, as some were accusing me of. My running stats are among the highest at the club, so it's nothing to do with fitness or energy. It was a mental issue. Any striker or winger will get down if they fail to score for a few games. *When am I going to get a goal? When will I set one up?* It was getting to me.

'It came to a head against Bolton. Some players try their best and, if it doesn't work out on the day, they then try even harder. That's me. I was annoyed with myself and the fans' reaction also played its part. It sent me over the edge and I lost the plot. Then a knock in training forced me to miss Doncaster Rovers away and pull out of international duty with the Republic of Ireland for Euro 2020 qualifiers against Georgia and Switzerland. When I returned for Pompey, I was on the bench for three matches. Thankfully, it did change, otherwise we wouldn't be in the position we're in. I scored in a 2–2 draw against Bristol Rovers and my confidence returned. The goals came flooding back and the team were flying again.'

Restored to the starting eleven at Bristol Rovers in October, the Republic of Ireland international embarked on a staggering spell of nine goals in his next twelve appearances. That included goals in four successive League One fixtures in December, including games against high-flying pair Ipswich Town and Wycombe Wanderers.

With his contract scheduled to expire at the season's end, Curtis was rewarded with a new three-and-a-half-year deal in February, tying him to Fratton Park until the summer of 2023. He entered the play-offs on the back of 23 consecutive League One starts and, having previously rejected Championship advances in January, is undoubtedly one of Pompey's prized assets.

'Kenny gave me a chance to come to this club and I have repaid that,' he added. 'He obviously didn't think I was going to do as well as I did when I initially arrived from Irish football, but I've shown him how good I am and what I'm made of. I wanted to repay the club by signing another deal. There were other offers that came in from a couple of other teams such as Reading and Blackburn Rovers. I'm not sure of the full details; I just do my thing on the pitch and my agents do their thing off it. Still, my heart was telling me to stay here and try to win promotion.

'I had a feeling the gaffer would take me out of the team after Bolton because I really didn't play well. The outcome was hard to take, but I knew once I got my chance again, I wouldn't let it go – and I didn't. No matter how disheartening, you could say that break did me good. It was tough not to play, but it provided a mental break, having had no rest for two seasons, coming from the Irish league straight into League One. I returned to show what I could do and when Pompey offered a new deal, it wasn't a difficult choice.

I love the city, I love the fans – I love everything about the club. I want to achieve big things here and help get us back where we belong.

'Of course, every player wants to compete in the best leagues in the world. However, it has to come at the right time and this wasn't the right time for me. I would rather go up with Pompey than go straight into a better league with someone else. I have settled in well. I have family around me who love it down here on the south coast, I have team-mates I like being with and the club have looked after me and given me a chance.

'Thankfully being in League One also hasn't affected my involvement with the Republic of Ireland and I've won all three of my caps since being at Pompey. There are a lot of talented players in the Irish squad, mostly from the Premier League. I'm the only one from this league in the squad, which is an achievement in itself really. Stephen Kenny replaced Mick McCarthy as manager in April and we have spoken on the phone. He loves his young players and, hopefully, when we get back into the swing of things, I will be playing for my country.

'When I signed for Derry as a kid, he had just left as boss to join Shamrock Rovers, before going on to manage Dundalk. I went on to play against him loads of times in the League of Ireland Premier Division, and scored. He actually tried to sign me for Dundalk, but my heart was at Derry at the time. Stephen Kenny knows all about me as he's watched me loads and loads of times. I'm looking forward to working with him for Ireland.'

Curtis' improved form since October has coincided with the introduction of eve-of-game visits to Cosham Crown Bingo. Accompanied by his parents, brother Blain and, on the odd occasion, Blues team-mate Andy Cannon, the left winger's Friday night outings have proved to be the perfect pre-match preparation. Darren Bessey, who has managed Cosham Crown Bingo for the last seven years, and wife Donna have provided excellent hospitality, establishing a firm friendship with the Curtis family in the process.

'There are players who chill out in the house with their wives, girlfriends and families the night before a game,' said Curtis. 'With me, I like to take Mum and Dad to the bingo and then get an early night. It relaxes me. I'm sitting there having a laugh with my family, taking my mind away from the following day's game. I don't like to contemplate the match too much. I find you dwell on the possibility that you might do something wrong or think about the opposition you'll be facing.

'Donna and Darren are lovely, lovely people and make us feel so welcome and the food is really good. They give us our own table to sit at, away from everyone else, but I'm not stuck up. If people want to come over and ask for photos or for anything to be signed, then I'm very happy to do it. That's what life's about as a footballer. As a way of thanking Darren and Donna for looking after us at bingo, I volunteered to have a meet and greet there last Christmas Eve, which went really well.

'We are a close family and our nights at the bingo allow us to spend time together, along with Andy Cannon, who also joins us sometimes. Mum has eleven children – she loves kids and loves everyone's kids. Andy is like a brother to me and since he's come to the club I've looked after him and he has looked after me. We are best mates and when he was sick from coronavirus and stuck in a house on his own, we made dinners for him and I dropped them off.

'That's what Mum's like. She's the main woman in my life – she tells me what to do. She and Dad are straight up about my performances, whether they're good or bad, which is what you need from your family. They are honest and tell it to my face. She can be outspoken at times, like the tweet about Brett Pitman's weight after seeing him on TV, but she didn't mean anything by it – and he knew that. It was all a bit of banter. She apologised to him and he didn't take it badly. Brett was all right with me afterwards, although he initially thought Mum was being serious. She explained it to him and he accepted that there had been a misunderstanding. When she knows she's in the wrong, she will do that. I did tell her that she wasn't allowed to be on Twitter for a few weeks and, to be fair, she listened. When she returned, I had to make it clear: "Just don't be writing anything silly!" She's behaving herself now.

'I sent Mum and Dad back to Ireland because of the coronavirus situation, which was the right thing to do. There aren't many cases over there and she can watch our play-off games on Sky. Hopefully they'll be back at Fratton Park next season. Mum will be desperate.'

Such is Curtis' ongoing importance to Jackett's side, his place in the semi-final first leg was assured. However, among the four changes implemented by Pompey's boss since the last team sheet was submitted against Fleetwood Town almost four weeks ago was the shock omission of skipper Tom Naylor.

With 96 appearances in two seasons since his June 2018 arrival from Burton Albion, the midfielder has been a pivotal presence. The reigning Players' Player of the Season, his rare exclusions from the starting eleven have been influenced by suspension, injury or rest. Jackett, though, opted to drop the 28-year-old to the bench against Oxford for tactical reasons, handing Bryn Morris his first competitive outing in fourteen months. It represented the former Middlesbrough man's ninth match during an injury-ravaged Pompey career which earlier in the season saw him undergo an operation in Munich to resolve what was eventually identified as a double hernia.

Elsewhere, James Bolton, who had started fifteen of the Blues' last seventeen League One fixtures, was left out in favour of loanee Ross McCrorie at right-back, while Lee Brown was preferred to Steve Seddon at left-back. The final change saw Marcus Harness selected ahead of Ryan Williams on the right wing. It wasn't merely the removal of Naylor from the side which proved controversial among supporters – Ben Close was axed entirely from the squad. The 23-year-old had been a regular choice for Jackett, amassing 44 appearances during the season, of which 38 were starts. Yet despite match-day squads being expanded to twenty places during post-coronavirus football, there was no room.

It was a similar tale for Brett Pitman, although his exclusion was entirely predictable having been instructed to stay away from training and not required for friendly fixtures against Reading and Brentford.

Meanwhile, Jack Whatmough wasn't considered, having opted not to return to training alongside team-mates post-lockdown to safeguard the health of heavily pregnant fianceé Demi, who is classed as high risk with an iron deficiency. Their daughter, Esme, was born on the evening before the Oxford first leg. The club had elected against publicising his ongoing absence out of respect for the central defender, who had put his family ahead of football. Jackett's overhauled team was forced to settle for a 1–1 draw, despite an encouraging opening 30 minutes and the best intentions of the lively Curtis.

He added: 'I thought we battered them and should have had a couple of penalties. We took the lead through a great team goal. Christian Burgess put the ball down the line to Marcus Harness, who fed Ellis Harrison and his first-time lay-off was to Andy Cannon, who put me through down the left. I'm a goalscorer and I will shoot with my right or left foot – luckily it went through the keeper's legs. That goal showed what happens when we get the ball down and pass it. We don't always have to go long – we mixed it up in that game and caused them a lot of problems. Before that, I managed a good right-footed strike from outside the box which hit the post, but unfortunately Cannon couldn't collect the rebound to finish it off as it came at him too quickly.

'We deserved more from that game though, especially with those penalty shouts. I was clean through when Agyei made that challenge on me inside the box during stoppage time. It's either a yellow card for me and a free-kick, or a yellow card for him and a spot-kick. The referee didn't believe me, unfortunately. I've seen the replay. Their guy has pushed me. I'm not going to go down if he hasn't touched me, but it's a push in the back when I am clean through. If I get clipped, obviously I'm going to want a penalty. If not, then I won't be going down in that position with the chance to shoot. I'm not one for diving around. I thought it was a pen, their manager Karl Robinson thought it was a pen, our manager thought it was a pen, and the only one who didn't was the referee.

'There were at least three good shouts in the whole game. For one of them, Dickie had his hands raised above his head and handled. The new rules state that, should that happen, then it's a penalty. If you aren't going to play to the rules, then what's the point of having them? The other was when Christian Burgess was dragged to the floor by Dickie. That's three shouts and the referee didn't give any of them. I don't know whether he saw them, but there are linesmen and a fourth official to help. We're not cheaters. We don't just dive around in the box. We like to play fairly and they were penalties.

'Had the crowd been at Fratton Park they definitely would have played a big part in my penalty shout. They're going to go wild after seeing what happened. That's helped the ref. There's no crowd to get into his head. Still, he's the referee at the end of the day and he calls the shots on the pitch, so it's up to him. It's in the past and we must go to Oxford, keep our heads and win. Without fans present, it's not really an advantage to play at home, so we'll go there full of confidence, looking to turn them over on their own patch.

'As a footballer, I want to get to the highest level I can play. If I'm good enough for the Premier League then it's that; if I'm good enough for the Championship then it's there. Hopefully we can reach the Championship this season. Win at the Kassam Stadium and it's off to Wembley against either Fleetwood Town or Wycombe Wanderers. At the start of the season we set ourselves the task of winning promotion. We're still on track for that. We will know more on Monday.'

LEE BROWN

6 July 2020

Lee Brown can garner no pleasure from being a footballer with a contingency plan. Second-leg defeat at Oxford United on Monday evening would end Pompey's play-off involvement, and potentially the left-back's Fratton Park stay. With his two-year contract expiring at the end of the season, the 29-year-old's future is uncertain. Certainly in football, anyway.

Brown's back-up career is represented by B3 Homes, a property development company he founded in 2017. Its slick website proclaims 'niche, high-end residential homes' across London and the south-east, with the defender listed as the sole director. With lower-division squad numbers expected to be slashed in football's post-coronavirus existence amid ongoing debate over the implementation of a £2.5m salary cap at League One level, these are worrying times for those deemed surplus to requirements by their clubs.

While the Blues' campaign remains active, Brown is unaware of the club's stance on retaining his services. A possible Kassam Stadium swansong is looming, yet, unlike the vast majority of fellow professionals, he is comfortable with the situation.

'There are many players out there deluded in the belief that football is going to last forever. It won't, it really won't,' said Brown. 'I reckon 90 to 95 per cent of them haven't got anything organised outside the game. The thing is, we have so much spare time as footballers. We finish training at 12pm, so what are you doing from 12pm to 5pm?

'The second leg against Oxford could be my last Pompey game. Then again, it might not be. I really don't know. This summer, out-of-contract footballers will be concerned about what happens next. Will they get the same money elsewhere? Do clubs still want you because they must now operate with smaller squads? Most of all, the majority will be worried because they haven't got anything else beyond football and still have families to feed. To be honest, I've worked really, really hard away from the game to ensure I am not in that situation. I've been planning for five or six years, maybe longer. Okay, I'm out of contract, but far from worried. If my time at Pompey ends in a week, it ends in a week. It's one of those things.

'While I've been getting on with my football career, my property development company has done okay. It largely takes care of itself thanks to a good middle management. I could move into a full-time role whenever I want – it's sitting there waiting for me. Could I do it tomorrow? Yes. Do I want to do it tomorrow? I'm not so sure. Regardless, I'm focusing on the Oxford game before heading into the summer and assessing what I want to do.

'My business leaves me in a position where, irrespective of what Pompey decide to do with me or whatever they may offer, I can make my own decisions. I won't be forced into anything or required to move to the other end of the country to provide for my family. That's the importance of having something outside of football which you can fall back on. This is a ruthless game and you could be let go tomorrow. It doesn't go on forever, but what remains is a family which needs providing for.

'Academically, I'm not the greatest, but I possess a business brain in terms of knowing what works. I have someone in the office who can do the paperwork side of things, which I'm not very good at. I'm the one who can see potential – what works and what doesn't.

That's where my strength lies. I've always dabbled in property in terms of refurbishment and things like that. It just got to the stage where I wanted to move on to bigger things, so I formed B3 Homes three years ago and it has really progressed.

'If Blackpool were the only club tabling a contract this summer, offering me a grand a week, I am fortunate that I don't have to take it. I'm settled so I can stay in Surrey and provide for my family. For other players, you're heading into a situation where coronavirus has hit, you're out of contract and now stressing about what happens next. Sorry to say it, but if you haven't thought about this, you only have yourself to blame, because this can happen to anyone, absolutely anyone.'

Brown cited the necessity to move closer to his London business as the driving force behind his exit from Bristol Rovers in the summer of 2018, turning down a new contract to depart on a free. The switch to Pompey fulfilled his needs, penning a two-year deal, which also contained a twelve-month extension clause for the club, while the family relocated to his home town of Kingswood, Surrey, an hour's drive from Fratton Park. To date, he has made 70 appearances and scored once, while he was a member of Kenny Jackett's side which triumphed at Wembley in the 2019 Checkatrade Trophy final during his maiden campaign. However, following a season hampered by an Achilles injury and the form of loanee Steve Seddon, Brown drifted out of the first-team picture. Nonetheless, he was restored to the side for the play-off semi-final first leg against Oxford and handed the captain's armband, a timely re-emergence with his Fratton Park contract scheduled to expire at the season's end.

Brown added: 'I've told the club I don't want to talk too much about contracts; let's get the play-offs out of the way first. Then we'll see where we are and have a chat afterwards. The club had an extension option, but that has now lapsed, so we're going to have to negotiate – or not, if that's the case. Of course I want to stay as Pompey is a fantastic football club. Do I feel I've got a bit of a point to prove here? Definitely. Does it wind me up that I have a point to prove? Yes. Does it give me the bit between my teeth to prove people wrong? Oh yes. Proving people wrong is probably the main reason why I'd want to remain at Fratton Park. You always have doubters. When you've suffered with an injury for so long, you want to prove you're better than people think you are. It winds you up and you want to show these people they are wrong.

'I'm open to seeing what Pompey have to say, but not at the moment. We have some massive games coming up – we're in the play-offs – and I don't want to make it about Lee Brown right now. It's about Portsmouth Football Club. I am nobody in terms of the club and its rich history. Life will go on without Lee Brown at Portsmouth Football Club. The sole focus has to be on returning to the Championship.

'I've plenty more years of football left in me. The main decision is do I want to carry on in the game? I have no doubt I can still do it, but it's just a case of what's right for me and what gets put on the table by Pompey.'

Encouragingly for Brown, he seems to be over the long-standing Achilles problem in his left leg. It's an injury he is convinced has impeded his Pompey performances for the last eighteen months. The complaint forced him out of the first leg of the previous campaign's League One play-off semi-final at Sunderland in May 2019. Following a third injection into the problematic tendon days before that Stadium of Light encounter, he was forced to sit out while the affected area settled down. Instead, the versatile Anton Walkes was challenged to stand-in at left-back for the 1–0 defeat.

Brown returned for the decisive second leg which ended in a goalless draw and saw Jackett's side eliminated on aggregate. The Achilles issue continued to blight him this term and, after scoring his first Blues goal in a 2–2 Fratton Park draw against Peterborough United in December, he conceded that it was time to go under the surgeon's knife. Now in July, the defender's outing in the first leg against Oxford was only his third start of 2020. Nonetheless, Brown turned in one of Pompey's best performances, silencing the talismanic James Henry to justify Jackett's selection.

He added: 'I remember watching that Peterborough game back and noticing that I actually couldn't move when I scored my goal. I was in agony, hobbling with every step. People probably didn't notice it but, analysing my own performance, it was obvious to me. When I received my playing stats the next morning, the distance I'd covered during the game was probably the lowest of my entire career. The average is 9.5–10km. I came in at 8.5km, which was very unlike me.

'Enough was enough as it was starting to get embarrassing and there was no point in soldiering on. I knew it was time to have an operation. Those in-house knew I was struggling with my Achilles, of course they did – I was receiving treatment on it every day. The manager wanted me to play on, but it came to a point where I physically couldn't do it any more. So, I had to make the decision.

'It had initially flared up around Christmas during my first season. I was playing with a nagging injury which progressively got worse. It becomes incredibly demoralising when you can't get your fitness levels up as you're in constant pain. Every time you strike a ball, there's a shooting pain. Then there's the knock-on effect of overcompensating because you're frightened to kick it properly.

'It reached the stage where I couldn't get out of bed in the morning. If I ever needed to use the toilet in the night, I had to either hop on one leg or use a walking stick. It really got that bad. You end up doing yourself and the team no justice. You're being judged with every game and letting down your team-mates because you're nowhere near the levels of performance you've been at for many years.

'I was booked in for an operation in London, then something happened. The night before it was scheduled to take place, I was informed it had been switched to Sweden, where the surgeon, Professor Hakan Alfredson, was based. He's the best in the business so I flew to Stockholm before catching an interconnecting flight to take me to Umea, where the Alfredson Tendon Clinic is based. I don't know how I made it there. I was on a poxy plane in the middle of a snowstorm being thrown all over the place.

'There were ten inches of snow on the ground and, when I arrived at my hotel, was checked in by the geezer who was the chef, taxi driver and housekeeper. It was down the road from the clinic, so the following morning I walked through those ten inches of snow to get there. The operation was done and three hours later I was making my way back on crutches with studs on the bottom to give me grip in the snow.

'Thinking about it now, it was madness. It was about 300 yards from the hotel, but felt a long way, let me tell you. The following afternoon, I flew back through another snowstorm. I remember ringing Mark Catlin laughing and saying, "What the hell have you booked me into here?" Still, it did the job superbly, so I can't complain too much. It's all good fun, isn't it!'

The play-off first leg signified Brown's first 90 minutes since December, his final appearance before undergoing surgery. In that same Peterborough fixture, Brown's usual deputy, Brandon Haunstrup, tore the meniscus in his right knee while serving at right-back. It required an operation and Pompey were out of left-back options. Walkes stepped forward, featuring for five successive matches, before Seddon's arrival on loan from Championship Birmingham City for the remainder of the campaign.

Upon Brown's return to fitness, he had two first-team outings at the end of February, but his young rival reclaimed the spot for the three matches which preceded football's lockdown. Then arrived the sixteen-week break which would signal Brown's re-emergence as Jackett's left-back preference.

He said: 'The extended season actually helped my recovery. It takes six months to finally break the scar tissue down following an operation. You can play during that time, but there's still a niggle. I know it's not as painful as previously, but it continued to be present. It's never completely right until you get rid of that scar tissue, which takes some time. That's why the break did me the world of good, enabling me to fully get over it. I'm fine now.

'When I came back from my injury in January, Steve was on a good run of form and rightly stayed in the team. However, we've all returned from lockdown with a clean slate and the manager chose me for the first leg. Following that long time off, some were coming back from injury, while others had previously been fatigued after a long campaign, so it's like a fresh start. Suddenly other players are considered, with Bryn Morris another instance. The break probably did him good too.

'We discovered the starting line-up on the day of the Oxford game, although we had an inkling during the build-up. It was kind of confirmed the previous day when we worked on a few set-pieces. Admittedly, there were a few surprise team selections, but the manager has seen something and wanted to go with it.

'I felt I did okay in the first leg. I can probably do a bit better, but it's a case of getting back. I played my first 90 minutes in almost seven months, so it's one you'd like to think you can build on. The match was a bit cagey between two evenly matched teams, but you could see the players had been off for a long time as we were a little rusty. Having said that, I'm quietly confident going into the second leg. We'll be fitter than Oxford over the two legs and definitely possess the squad strength to take them, especially when there's a quick turnaround between the first and second leg.

'Encouragingly, they were really, really struggling at Fratton Park fitness-wise, especially around the hour mark. Players were even asking to be substituted. It gives you a bit of a lift knowing they were dead on their heels. Their goalscorer, Marcus Browne, was gone – he said he couldn't run any more and had to come off. It was probably handy that he could no longer move! A few other players were also calling to the bench, which was crazy. I definitely believe we're fitter than them and you could also see that in the way we finished the game.'

With Tom Naylor controversially dropped from the first-leg starting eleven, vice-captain Brown was promoted to the role of skipper for the occasion. The duo were appointed to the positions by Jackett at the start of September, much to the disappointment of deposed pair Brett Pitman and Gareth Evans. A bubbly personality around the Pompey camp and strong voice on the pitch, the highly popular Brown's influence is unmistakable. Certainly for such a pivotal fixture, Jackett had no qualms handing over the captain's armband to the chirpy 29-year-old, who is quick to remind people he has now never lost in four outings as Pompey skipper.

'We had a lively group at Bristol Rovers. When I arrived at Pompey, the dressing room was very quiet, like a morgue,' laughed Brown. 'There were a lot of young lads in there to start with, who were probably a bit timid, but they've now got another couple of years into them. The more games people play, the more they come out of their shell and feel confident around everyone. First and foremost, you've got to bond and feel comfortable with each other. As soon as that happens, it should flow naturally.

'I believe in having a laugh and a joke, not taking life too seriously, but it's hard as some people aren't like that; everyone is different. The dressing room has probably changed slightly since I arrived, but those characters are still the same people, so it's not going to alter too much. Of course sometimes the atmosphere is created by what the manager encourages, in terms of what he wants from his players.

'Regardless of whether I'm wearing the armband, I've always spoken on the pitch, and I wouldn't need the captaincy to do that. I'd still talk to people, simply because it makes your life a lot, lot easier in terms of positioning team-mates where I want them in games. People underrate the ability to organise; it's a dying art. If no one is organising, everyone's doing their own thing, especially the back four. The defence have to talk to the midfield and the midfield have to talk to the strikers. You need organisation.'

Unfortunately for Brown, the captaincy he prized was removed for the play-off second leg, as was his place in Pompey's starting eleven at the Kassam Stadium. Jackett opted to make three changes, with Seddon coming in at left-back and James Bolton replacing Ross McCrorie at right-back. The final alteration saw Ryan Williams handed a recall, with Andy Cannon dropping to the bench. The Australian international operated in his customary role on the right flank, allowing Marcus

Harness to come inside to start in the number ten position for only the second time in his Pompey career.

With Naylor surprisingly condemned to the bench once more, the captaincy this time transferred to Christian Burgess on what could potentially be a final outing. It was the first time the central defender had skippered Pompey for a league or play-off fixture during five years spent at Fratton Park. It was merely a happy coincidence, as Jackett is certainly not one for sentimental footballing gestures.

As with the first leg, Pompey broke the deadlock in the first half. Ellis Harrison rose high to flick the ball on to Harness who, with his back to goal, controlled the ball on his left thigh, swivelled and then took a touch, before drilling a right-footed shot into the bottom corner of Simon Eastwood's net. It was a classy finish from the summer recruit from Burton Albion, his ninth goal of the season. However, three minutes into first-half stoppage time, Oxford were gifted a leveller through catastrophic defending from Henry's left-wing corner. Harrison unwittingly went up against his keeper, Alex Bass, in an aerial challenge, succeeding only in glancing the ball off the top of his head towards the vacant net behind him. Sean Raggett desperately swung a right foot to hook it clear, however referee Darren England was alerted by Hawk-Eye that the ball had crossed the line: 1–1.

Brown was called from the bench on the hour mark, replacing the disappointing Seddon, in a double substitution which also introduced John Marquis for Harrison. Within eight minutes, Marquis had headed a Ronan Curtis cross against the outside of the post. As fear of defeat strangled the contest as a spectacle, it limped uneventfully through extra-time to reach a penalty shoot-out, with the aggregate score deadlocked at 2–2. Marquis, substitute Gareth Evans and Brown had successfully converted, with the score poised at 3–3, by the time Cameron McGeehan stepped forward for the Blues' fourth spot-kick. His right-footed shot was comfortably stopped by Simon Eastwood, the keeper flinging himself to his right, to put Oxford in control of proceedings.

Despite another substitute, Oli Hawkins, registering for the Blues, it was left to Cameron Brannagan to settle the fixture. He finished confidently to earn Karl Robinson's side a place against Wycombe in the League One play-off final. For the third time in five years, Pompey had perished at the semi-final stage of the play-offs. Their miserable overall record in the format reads eight matches and no victories. Lee Brown's final touch of the season was crashing a left-footed penalty into Oxford's net. It remains to be seen whether that will be his last contribution for Pompey.

CHRISTIAN BURGESS
AND BRETT PITMAN
9 July 2020

The grey Mercedes-Benz C-Class was loaded with three suitcases, two holdalls, a backpack and a large box. Hardly Christian Burgess' worldly possessions, but nonetheless it was sufficiently stocked with football equipment and protein powders to help him acclimatise swiftly. Little short of 72 hours after Pompey's play-off elimination at Oxford United and the central defender's footballing journey was leading to Belgium. The ever-patient Royale Union Saint-Gilloise could wait no longer, and Burgess was summoned to training ahead of the forthcoming weekend's opening pre-season friendly. That Thursday afternoon, the 28-year-old quit his Old Portsmouth home of five years to embark on a fresh adventure. Driving to Folkestone's Eurotunnel to catch a double-deck shuttle to Calais, he reflected on the decision to depart the city that had changed his life.

He said: 'I've always wanted to live abroad. When I became a footballer, I thought maybe I could play overseas. I never knew when or where, but always fancied it. So, when this opportunity came along it really interested me. It wouldn't suit some players, and there are those who wouldn't be keen to go down that route, but my ears pricked up. Let's have a look.

'I went out to Union for a short trip to look around the place and meet their sporting director, Chris O'Loughlin. I really liked him and their set-up. It's a new city, a new culture and a different language. It really appealed. Royale Union Saint-Gilloise is a French-speaking club, although they coach in English. I'm looking to live in Antwerp, where they speak Dutch. The club put on French lessons for the players in the afternoon, which I'll attend. I never studied it at school but I've been learning using the app Duolingo for quite a while.

'I room share with Gaz Evans, so have been practising at times. I'm sure he was thinking: "What the hell are you trying to speak French for?" At that stage, though, I couldn't let on the real reason, so told him I just fancied learning the language. This is an adventure and the chance to immerse myself into a new culture. I've loved my time at Pompey – five years is a long time – but you never know whether you'll get this opportunity again.

'I've been to Belgium before, although only as a kid. I played a couple of football tournaments for Arsenal over there and visited Ypres on a school history trip to study the First World War, but nothing since. They were the only club outside the UK that showed an interest. It's not like I had a desire for any country in particular; I wasn't looking for the Netherlands, Germany, America or Australia. What mattered was the opportunity of a fresh challenge and new experience.

'In the end, it has all been a bit of a mad rush. The day after our play-off defeat, I found out I had to go. From that point I needed to get things packed up and visit people to say goodbye. I don't think it has sunk in yet. Last night I was going through lots and lots of messages on social media, which was very emotional, and today I've been running around like a headless chicken, packing up my house and delivering cards and flowers to neighbours. My mum and dad actually came to Portsmouth to help, taking some things back to the family home in Ilford, Essex.

'I start training tomorrow, and it's down for a double session too. Then I'm scheduled to play 45 minutes on Saturday against

Crossing Schaerbeek in the club's first pre-season friendly. Next, we travel to Genk on Wednesday, so it's straight into the thick of things.'

Royale Union Saint-Gilloise compete in the Belgian First Division B, with Brighton & Hove Albion owner Tony Bloom the majority shareholder. The Seagulls had recruited Matt Clarke from Pompey in June 2019 and six months later their Brussels-based sister club were pursuing his former central-defensive colleague. Union made their move at the turn of the year for a 28-year-old whose Fratton Park contract was scheduled to expire at this season's end. Burgess subsequently settled on a three-year deal plus a twelve-month option, signing a pre-contract agreement which kicked into action on 1 July.

However, complications arose when the coronavirus crisis forced the English season to be extended, with Pompey set to return to action in the play-off semi-final first leg against Oxford on 3 July. Suddenly, the defender required permission from his new club to remain for the duration of the Blues' play-off programme.

Burgess added: 'Union did me a huge favour and I owe them a big thank you. It's a good footing to start on in terms of trust and building a relationship. Having signed a pre-contract agreement, I was originally scheduled to join them on 1 July. Once Pompey's season was extended, Union were well within their rights to not allow me to play as they were taking all the risk of me sustaining possible injury.

'One of the reasons they allowed me to remain for the play-offs is because I really pushed to play and they liked the fact I was keen to finish things off properly. I wanted to do things right, not leave Pompey in the lurch. There was still a promotion to be won. Union took the risk for no reward. It's not like they got anything out of it from their side but they appreciated my reasoning.

'I can recall the moment in training, in early June, when the assistant manager, Joe Gallen, mentioned the possibility of the League One play-off final taking place on 13 July, with the semi-finals starting at the beginning of the same month. My heart sank. Nobody at the club was aware that I'd no longer be there during that period as I had already signed for somebody else. After training, I got on the phone to my agent straight away. It was then a case of warning Pompey, explaining the predicament and the details of my departure. Mark Catlin congratulated me and wished me all the best, then it was about getting permission from Union to play. I went to bed on 22 June, the night before the registration deadline, not knowing whether I would be allowed to feature in the play-offs.

'Understandably, my new club were quite nervous about me getting injured. There was the issue of insurance and also the need to draw up contingency plans to maybe sign a player should I pick up a long-term injury. You cannot reassure anyone that you won't get injured. My agents, Brian Howard and Phil Korklin, were brilliant. Phil did so much work, acting as the middleman between Union and Pompey, dealing with the paperwork, legal issues and insurance. There were three different contracts drawn up because of the required extensions and cancellations.

'On that final day of the play-off registration deadline we had no training, and I was waiting by my phone. Every time Phil rang, I was on the edge of my seat wondering whether it was good news or bad. Phil's a bit more of a pessimist, but I'm an optimist. I had spoken to Union's sporting director on several occasions and got the feeling he was a good guy. We were on the same page. Their club board, however, were a little nervous, but Chris O'Loughlin was attempting to make it happen because he understood it from my point of view. Then, in the afternoon, while I was on Southsea Common, I received the phone call with good news. I had the all-clear. I would have been heartbroken if I hadn't been able to play. I didn't want my Pompey career to end that way, without kicking a ball. After we were knocked out at the Kassam Stadium, Union expressed their wish for me to go there as soon as possible. It was only fair after everything they had done for me.'

Such was the scale of Burgess' Fratton Park performances, he was named *The News/Sports Mail*'s Player of the Season. The fact he reaped 69 per cent of the supporter vote signified a comprehensive victory over nearest rivals Ronan Curtis and Tom Naylor. Once engravers are back open for business, his name will be etched on to the 41-year-old trophy alongside the likes of David James, Alan Knight, Neil Webb, Peter Crouch, Enda Stevens and Paul Walsh. Following five Blues seasons, consisting of 210 appearances, twelve goals, a League Two title and a Checkatrade Trophy medal, Burgess elected to quit the south coast, arguably at the height of his powers.

He said: 'Had Pompey offered me something concrete in December, before I was aware of the opportunity in Belgium, then I would very, very possibly have signed a new deal. I definitely wanted an offer. As matters developed, there was interest from a Championship club. Yet, realistically, it was always between Pompey and Union.

'In January, we told Pompey that there was an option of a pre-contract agreement and there had been foreign offers. We asked them to put something on the table. I know my agent and Mark Catlin spoke and even discussed numbers, but their policy at the time was to wait until the club was in a healthier league position. They didn't feel it was the right time to be discussing new deals.

'Union weren't going to hold their offer forever and let me use it as a bargaining chip all the way through to the season's end. If I waited, that may have gone. We offered Pompey the chance and, at the time, it wasn't right for the business. That's football, and there was no ill will at all. Mark Catlin has been fantastic throughout.

'The contract length tabled by Union was an obvious factor in my decision, especially when you're looking at it from a financial security point of view. My agents were happy with the offer, which represented a long-term deal enabling me to be secure. Some supporters jumped to the conclusion that Pompey were only prepared to give me one year. That wasn't the case as we never actually discussed any of the finer contractual details.

'What my agents and I did was estimate the length of contract I may get with the Blues and we surmised that I probably wouldn't be given three years. It was about analysing previous situations in the club's recent history. I won't name names but, using those examples, we thought the offer might be one year. What had gone before appeared to be the club's policy.

'It wasn't even about money. It's a small wage increase, but nothing outrageous. When you see people claiming I was going just for the money, it really wasn't the case. If I'd been part of a Pompey team that reached the Championship, I would have been better off financially than what Union offered. Pompey actually came back to me in February, when I was up Mount Snowdon in Wales during a short break. They wanted to let me know they were going to offer me something at some point. I thanked them and spoke to my agents. It was just too late unfortunately. I had decided on Union and didn't want to lead Pompey on. I didn't even ask what they would likely offer as there was no point.

'Funnily enough, after I had signed my pre-contract agreement, I probably had my best run of form. I remember hearing people say that I was playing so well because I wanted a new Pompey contract. Little did they know I had already signed elsewhere! It was simply down to me being keen to do my best for the club. However, I was wary about my summer departure being made public, so kept it close to my chest. My parents, girlfriend, agents and a few people in Belgium were the only ones who knew about it. I didn't want to be treated differently if the news was announced. I didn't want it to influence anything on the pitch, though I don't actually believe Kenny would have allowed it to. You never know how fans are going to react, though. I remember what happened with Nathan Thompson. In the end, my hand was forced because of the play-offs and my move to Union became common knowledge.'

To mark the popular central defender's exit, Pompey's club shop unveiled their 'Ultimate Christian Burgess Bundle' at a cost of £29.99. The commemorative package consists of a mug, a piece of his match-worn shirt from the 2019 Checkatrade Trophy final triumph and a signed copy of the match programme against Shrewsbury Town.

No such grand fanfare, however, for fellow departee Brett Pitman. The deposed skipper struck 42 goals during three Fratton Park seasons, with Yakubu Aiyegbeni the only player to have netted more for the Blues in the last 22 years. Pitman's 99th and final appearance came on 29 December, signified by a 72nd-minute entrance from the bench in the disappointing 3–1 defeat at struggling MK Dons. He spent the remainder of the campaign in exile, aside from a flurry of four outings as an unused substitute before football's lockdown.

Kenny Jackett had demonstrated professional courtesy by calling the 32-year-old to inform him of his Fratton Park release, along with Oli Hawkins, Adam May, Luke McGee and Matt Casey. While Pitman's departure was widely anticipated, it still reflected a remarkable fall from favour for a player who had registered 25 goals in his maiden Blues season just two years previous.

'Speaking on a personal level, the first year was very good. The second year ended up being very good in the second half, while this last season was pretty much a non-event,' said Pitman. 'I think my record on the pitch speaks for itself. If I had played the majority of games this season, I'm pretty confident I would have scored fifteen to twenty goals.

'I was desperate to be involved in the play-offs and was fit, really fit. I was never asked to return to training at Pompey, so I looked after my own fitness, running and biking most days during lockdown. We players used an app called Strava, which logged our sessions and allowed the fitness coaches to keep track. I was fit and definitely ready to be considered for duty.

'I signed a three-year contract when I arrived at Pompey and that didn't change for me. I wanted to be involved in the play-offs and also agreed to extend my stay to cover that period. I remained on the players' WhatsApp group chat, while the manager called me a couple of times, mainly after lockdown when they had started training again. I guess it was to touch base. I wasn't wanted back, though. I knew I wasn't required for the first leg but thought there was a chance for the next match at the Kassam Stadium. I believed I'd be a good option. Obviously, though, it's the manager's decision. I ended up watching both play-off games on TV.'

Pitman burst on to the Pompey scene in July 2017, following his arrival from Ipswich Town for an undisclosed fee. Newly appointed boss Kenny Jackett wanted the former Bournemouth man to spearhead the Blues' attack upon their League One return and instantly installed him as captain. Pitman responded by scoring 25 times, becoming the first Pompey player to break the twenty-goal barrier since Svetoslav Todorov's 26-goal haul fifteen years earlier. Only Peterborough United's Jack Marriott netted more times in League One that term, while Pompey's striker finished as runner-up to Matt Clarke in *The News/Sports Mail*'s Player of the Season.

However, ominous signs of an uneasy relationship with boss Jackett emerged during the following campaign in 2018–19. Pitman was informed that he was no longer required to train with the club and, from January 2019, was only included in the match-day squad for one of six Pompey fixtures. Within 34 days of his subsequent first-team squad recall, he skippered Jackett's side to Checkatrade Trophy success over Sunderland at Wembley.

He added: 'We travelled to Luton Town in January 2019. I didn't play particularly well, and the team didn't play particularly well. I was taken off at half-time and exiled for a while. Pompey didn't win any of the five games I was out of the squad for, so I ended up coming back in. During that period, most of the time I was training on my own in Whitecliff Park near my Poole home, or running on Sandbanks beach. On occasions I'd come into the training ground to carry out running work under Jeff Lewis, the fitness coach.

'On Saturdays, I'd run in the morning and sometimes watch Bournemouth under-18s, where my friend Alan Connell is coach, or watch Bournemouth's first team if Pompey were playing away. Often I'd watch Jeff Stelling on Sky Sports' *Soccer Saturday*. For fifteen years, all I'd known was being involved in a squad on a Saturday. It's difficult when 3pm comes and you're sitting at home watching the scores roll in. You don't give up, though, as you never know what's going to happen. More than anything, you carry on for yourself. You've got to be ready for whatever. Luckily, I was fit and, when I got a chance at Pompey again, managed to take it.

'My comeback was at Charlton Athletic in March 2019 and I did well, although ultimately we lost. The following match, at Walsall, I scored once and was involved in another in a 3–2 win. I netted six goals in thirteen games from that point. That's what it was like throughout my career. If I play regularly, I score. Unfortunately, we lost in the play-off semi-final to Sunderland that season. In all honesty, probably my one regret of my time at Pompey was playing in that second leg – I shouldn't have. I damaged my hamstring in training the day before the first leg at the Stadium of Light. It was innocuous as I wasn't really doing anything, but I was out of a match which we lost 1–0.

'We did everything we could to get me back, including blood-spinning injections, which I'd never had before. It's actually called platelet-rich plasma (PRP) therapy, involving taking the blood out, putting it into a machine to spin it and then injecting it back into the injury to speed up the healing process. It worked to a degree, and I was close, but probably needed another two or three days. We didn't have that luxury and I tried to get through. In hindsight, I shouldn't have played the second leg at Fratton Park. I could still perform, but you're playing within yourself to a degree. I played the full 90 minutes, but it ended goalless and we were eliminated 1–0 on aggregate.'

Last summer saw the acquisitions of John Marquis and Ellis Harrison to bolster Pompey's striking options. Nonetheless, Pitman scored seven times in pre-season, including a twenty-minute hat-trick against Irish side UCD, as he pushed for consideration in the number ten role behind the lone forward. However, when this season kicked off, he was condemned to a substitute role in the opening seven matches in all competitions. Then, in September, following a 1–1 draw at Blackpool, a match in which Pitman was unused from the bench, Jackett declared he was removing the armband. Similarly, vice-captain Gareth Evans was also demoted. Instead Tom Naylor, a widely respected figure among the squad, was installed as skipper, with Lee Brown his second in command.

Pitman explained: 'The manager told me, "I'm going to make a change." Basically, that was it. I wasn't playing as regularly as I wanted, but still felt I could have an influence around the dressing room. Ultimately, he made the change and that's his decision. I did think retaining me as club captain was an avenue they could have gone down, but it was quite clear that the manager no longer wanted me and Gaz to be captain or vice-captain, so changed both.

'The following night, I came off the bench at half-time against Crawley Town in the Leasing.com Trophy and scored to give us a 1–0 victory. I think that tells you everything you need to know about how I took that captaincy decision. A lot of people would have sulked. That's not my character. Without doubt I was angry and disappointed by the manager's actions. Ultimately, however, whether captain or not, I just wanted to play. I wouldn't be downing tools; I wanted to get back into the team. I actually didn't see it coming, and certainly there had been no argument. We probably hadn't said more than "Good morning" to each other for the best part of a month, so it wasn't influenced by a fallout. As I hadn't really played, it wasn't caused by anything I'd done on the pitch either.

'Regardless, after my goal against Crawley, I returned to the side and scored a penalty against Burton Albion, faced Southampton in the FA Cup, then missed from the spot against Bolton Wanderers only to then score the winner with a header. Then I picked up an injury against Gillingham in mid-October and that was really the end for me at Pompey. I pulled my adductor kicking a ball at the start of the game and lasted 54 minutes. I should have called to be substituted straight away, but I never like coming off. I want to fight on and to continue until I can't play any longer. That was the last League One match I ever started for Pompey.'

Having recovered from his injury, Pitman would be restricted to substitute duty upon his return, except for a rare start in December's 2–1 success over Northampton Town in the Leasing.com Trophy. In the previous match, his stoppage-time winner had overcome Altrincham in the FA Cup at Fratton Park, avoiding a replay at the home of the non-league club and preventing yet more fixture congestion. He made three more appearances but that was his 42nd and final Pompey goal.

Following the January transfer window, in which he declined to leave the Blues on loan after being linked with Plymouth Argyle and

Swindon Town, Pitman was condemned to his second training ground exile, only this time there was to be no comeback.

'Towards the end of the window, the manager told me I could go out on loan if I wanted. For me, it's difficult as I have a family and the two kids are in school. To up sticks and move for six months did not interest me,' he added. 'There were one or two clubs interested, but nothing concrete and nothing that suited me or my family, which was the main thing. I chose to stay and fight for my place.

'In all honesty, there was no big falling out at any point with the manager. However, a day or two following the transfer window's end, I received a phone call from him. Basically, we had too many bodies for training. I was told: "You don't have to come in any more." Once that conversation happens, you know your time at the club is up.

'I didn't want to work on my own for the remaining six months of my contract, so asked Pompey for permission to train with Bournemouth. I had spoken to Eddie Howe, who obviously I have a good relationship with, and explained the situation. He said it was no problem, so I trained between the under-21s, who are managed by one of my best mates in Shaun Cooper, and the under-18s. It was whichever group were training at the time. I worked hard and really, really enjoyed it. Of course it wasn't ideal as I was desperate to be involved with Pompey and playing matches, because that's what you're paid to do, but obviously that wasn't going to happen. It was good for me to train at Bournemouth and I'm thankful to them for letting me do that.

'At that point I was never overly hopeful of coming back. I hadn't really heard from Kenny Jackett while I was at Bournemouth. It was about maintaining my fitness, while providing an example for their younger players in return. It was a case of, "Look at this lad, he's 32 and he doesn't have to come here. He could be sitting at home, but he's here training hard and training properly because he wants to stay fit." On the odd occasion the under-21s or under-18s were not training, my friends, who were coaches, would put on a one-on-one session to help me.

'I had gone off my own back to train with Bournemouth, otherwise I'd have been left to my own devices. Then I received a phone call one Monday evening at the end of February. Pompey were hosting MK Dons the following night and the manager said I'd be on the bench. Of course I was fine with that because, ultimately, I wanted to be involved. We were winning that game, so I didn't come on. Next was Rochdale, which we won 3–0, so again I didn't come on. I wasn't on the bench against Arsenal in the FA Cup because we went with one up front, which the manager explained, and I was more than fine with his reasoning.

'Then I was on the bench at Peterborough. We were losing and I wasn't one of the three substitutes used. At that point, I thought to myself: "Well, if I'm not going to come on when we're losing, when am I going to?" That was it for me at Pompey. I was never involved again.'

Pitman sees a future in coaching beyond his playing days and, before lockdown, was helping with sessions for Bournemouth's under-13s. Meanwhile, the dynasty continues with the Cherries through son Harlow, an aspiring striker who next season will step up into the under-9s. Pitman senior is eager to resume a playing career in which he has scored 179 goals, having not featured in a competitive match during 2020 and now rendered a free agent.

He said: 'I've read comments from people saying, "He's finished, he's this, he's that." When you're an attacking player, if you're in the team for a game and then don't play for six weeks, it's difficult to remain sharp. You need a run of matches. Give me that and I'll score goals, without a doubt. I have never been dependent on speed – I have relied on my football brain, my technical ability and my finishing. You don't lose those attributes. I think I've got a lot to offer somebody.'

Unbeknown to Burgess, he would bow out for Pompey at the Kassam Stadium while sporting the captain's armband once worn by Pitman. He had previously been entrusted with the responsibility during

Checkatrade Trophy duty, but the play-off second leg was the first time he'd worn it when starting a league fixture.

With the ongoing exclusion of Tom Naylor, once again surprisingly named on the bench that evening, and Lee Brown replaced at left-back in the line-up by Steve Seddon, a new captain was required. Jackett's choice was Burgess, the player who had established himself at the heart of the dressing room through his outstanding displays and tireless community contribution.

'The captaincy was a weird one. It was obviously special in a way, but, at the same time, you're there by default,' said Burgess. 'Let's be honest, if any of Tom Naylor, Lee Brown or Gaz Evans had been playing then they'd have received the armband ahead of me. It was nice, but I didn't feel like I'd earned it. It wasn't for the sentiment of being potentially my final Pompey match either. It was because, for whatever reason, Tom and Lee weren't playing. Still, it was great to be ahead of Ellis Harrison, who always makes jokes about trying to be captain!

'A lot of people have asked me if something happened with Tom. Nothing did. It was just the manager's outlook on how to win a game of football. Did they fall out? Did they kick off? Genuinely, genuinely no. I'm not sure I would say even if something had happened, but there wasn't anything, so I don't have to! There was nothing untoward.

'When saying my goodbyes at the club, I spoke to one of the senior executives and they confirmed that the manager just wanted to go with something different in midfield at this time of year. Kenny sees the game as black and white. He is ruthless, but that's how he manages. Everything he does is in the best interests of winning that particular game. That's his style and I've been on the receiving end myself plenty of times.

'I've never thought of him as a horrible person or had ill wishes towards him; that's just football. It's a ruthless game and we must be professional, and ready when called upon. That's our job. Tom handled it pretty well considering. I didn't raise the issue with him; I don't think he would have wanted to talk too much about it or make it about him. I felt massively sorry for him and Ben Close as

486 POMPEY

it's hard to be left out of the play-offs when you've been part of it all season. Regardless, he showed great professionalism and a lot of class in how he handled the situation in front of the lads. He was gutted, but is still club captain, and continued to gee us up.

'Tom had actually been playing at centre-half for the opposition during in-house games ahead of the play-offs, which surprised me a little. Perhaps the manager was thinking of playing him in defence if Sean Raggett or I weren't available? Having said that, I still believed the manager had it in him to change the line-up after the friendlies. However, he stuck with Cameron McGeehan and Bryn Morris in midfield for both legs against Oxford.

'Tom has been a terrific player for us, by far the most consistent over the last two years. He has been a really, really important figure in midfield, a worthy recipient of the armband and a good leader. As a centre-half, having him in front doing the dirty work has made my life a hell of a lot easier. Without trying to say he should have been playing in those two play-off games, I have always been grateful to have him in the side. For me, Tom has been one of our best players over the past few years.'

As it was, Naylor remained on Pompey's bench for the duration of the second leg, which stretched into extra-time and a penalty shoot-out. The league encounter between the sides ended in a 1–1 draw, with Matty Taylor registering a last-gasp leveller at Fratton Park. The season's curtailment meant there was to be no Kassam Stadium league rematch. The teams did however meet in the Leasing.com Trophy in October, the encounter finishing 2–2 before the Blues claimed a spot-kick victory by a 5–4 scoreline. Only goal difference separated the clubs in the League One table, with both finishing on 60 points.

Perhaps it was inevitable that both play-off legs would be tight, cagey draws but Burgess felt Jackett's men were deprived of three cast-iron penalties during the Fratton Park first leg.

He said: 'We were the better side in the first leg and had the most chances, while there were some outrageous penalty shouts. I genuinely think there were three stonewall penalties. Even if you get just one of those, that gives us a huge, huge advantage. You never know how things would have changed if we'd gone into the second leg one up.

'There was one in the first half when Rob Dickie had his arms all around me, which was actually a hold. I just expected the linesman to be flagging and the referee to whistle for the penalty. When the ball came in from the left, I saw it early enough to go to the back post. Dickie was in the wrong position and he wasn't even watching the ball, just me. I think there's a weakness to his defending on set-pieces as he seems to do it a lot and he wasn't bothered where the ball was and grabbed me. He wouldn't let me get the ball legally and he had to be punished for that; it was a penalty. We got nothing.

'I actually ran off laughing. I'm used to that standard of refereeing. It happens so often in League One because the quality of refereeing is so poor. There was also a handball in that half, although I didn't see it at the time as my head was down trying to meet the ball. Looking back now, it's a handball. Marcus Harness puts a free-kick into the box and Dickie's hands are above his head in an unnatural position.

'The third penalty incident happened in stoppage time when Ronan Curtis was tripped by Daniel Agyei. It's clumsy, but you can't be clumsy like that in the box. If you trip somebody up when going for the ball it's a penalty. It doesn't matter whether or not you meant it, which was the point the Sky commentator raised when I watched it back. The referee said he thought Ronan had pulled the player first, but, in my eyes, there is absolutely nothing in that. As I said, three cast-iron penalties turned down.

'The second game was tighter and had more ups and downs and momentum swings. For much of the match, I thought we shaded it. Oxford's equaliser in first-half stoppage time was really, really unlucky and a tough one to take. It's one of those things that happen in football and we were unfortunate it came in such an important game. They won a corner down the left and I remember saying to the lads: "If we don't concede here, it's half-time," thinking this would be the worst time to let one in.

'I didn't see exactly what happened next as I was marking Dickie. When the ball came in from James Henry, it was nowhere near Dickie, so there's a bit of relief that your man's not getting it; I had done my job. Then I was looking for somebody else to head it out or catch it. Unfortunately, two players had gone for the ball. Even then, it's the finest of margins. Sean Raggett did well to clear it off the line, but I knew it was tight. I was watching the referee straight after it happened, then he looked at his watch and it was given.

'To go in 1–0 at the interval would have been a different game. I did speak to Alex Bass to check he was okay. I've been there myself and, while you want to moan, I had to ensure there was none of that. We needed to quickly get over it and had half-time to do that.

'When it came to penalties, I was in my usual slot of ninth, which was also my place in the order at Wembley for the Checkatrade Trophy final in 2019. We had practised quite a few times. Staging them properly, lining up on the halfway line, at one stage replicating the situation at Fratton Park as a practice. Unfortunately, in the play-offs, we came out on the wrong side.'

For Burgess, it signified a third play-off semi-final elimination in five seasons, with the central defender having started all six of those fixtures. The heartbreak began in May 2016, when Peter Hartley's last-gasp header handed Plymouth an aggregate 3–2 victory, sparking a Home Park pitch invasion. That was followed by last season, with the Blues' goalless draw at Fratton Park sealing a 1–0 aggregate loss against Sunderland. Now, he has added Oxford to the list of misery, a defeat which would also mark the end of Burgess' Pompey playing days.

He added: 'I have been dreaming about going to Wembley and leaving Pompey on a high. I've not managed to do that and it will always stick with me unfortunately, but you have to move on. I was particularly gutted at Plymouth and the manner of defeat in the last minute. We didn't like them and it was hard to take losing on their ground with supporters running on to the pitch. That was horrible. Yet, on that occasion, I was proud of the lads and how well we had fought with all the injuries we'd suffered in that game.

'Sunderland last season was probably the most disappointing in terms of our performance, considering we didn't score over the two legs. We fell out of the play-offs with a real whimper, not really threatening their goal at Fratton Park. Then there was Oxford. This one was heartbreaking because it meant it was all over for me. It was the end of my Pompey career and I knew it.

'The chapter's closed for now, but you never know what could happen in the future. I expect I'll come back to watch a game as a fan next season and I'll be keeping in touch with the boys and following the results. I really hope we get off to a good start in 2020–21 and finally do it. There will be no one happier than me when Pompey achieve promotion from League One.'

KEV MCCORMACK

17 July 2020

Kev McCormack had been instructed to join friends for a round of golf at Old Thorns, his wife believing it more beneficial in tough circumstances. For Sarah, an afternoon spent with Andy Awford, Paul Walsh and Neil Sillett offered Pompey's kit man a timely distraction and a favourable alternative to pacing the garden at home during the couple's excruciating wait.

McCormack was teeing off on the eighteenth hole at the Liphook-based golf club when the critical call arrived, his phone's vibration prompting him to shank his shot. Upon learning that his partner was free from cancer, he crumpled to the floor and cried. The Welshman's Pompey play-off absence had gone unnoticed in grounds deprived of supporters, his attentions focused on more important matters.

'I have been a fighter all my life, and now I have another fight on my hands,' said McCormack. 'You always think cancer will never happen to you or your family; it's some other poor soul who gets it. *Good luck with fighting it, thankfully we're all fine here*. Then, during lockdown, we learnt that Sarah had bowel cancer. It was two days before the play-off first leg against Oxford United. The club were brilliant, though; they understood.

'I was brought up a strict Catholic, with two Irish parents, but eventually shied away from it because I was forced to go as a kid. I still go to church at Christmas and Easter, but that's it. This summer, I started praying before I went to bed at night. We were worried it could be something bad, and I prayed for things to be okay. I prayed for Sarah.

'When she was diagnosed with cancer, I told him up there exactly what I thought of him. He hadn't listened; it didn't make any difference. It was like having the devil and angel on my shoulder. The angel reminded me that God had actually caught the cancer in time. I don't preach to anyone, but the day we received the news that Sarah had been given the all-clear following the operation, her grandmother died. She was 94. My mum is convinced she passed away to give Sarah more time. Whether you believe in praying or not is another thing. Everybody has different beliefs, but it did make me think.

'I was only on the golf course that day because of Sarah. A group of us normally spend the day at Goodwood Racecourse in the summer. With that postponed because of coronavirus, golf was the alternative. The hospital were supposed to call us with the results of the biopsy the previous day. When they did it was to say they still hadn't received all the details. It would be Friday instead. Then your mind starts playing tricks, and you're thinking: "There's something wrong here."

'Sarah told me to play golf as arranged that day, rather than have me pacing around the house. She obviously knows what I'm like. Then, on the last hole at Old Thorns, she rang with the news we'd been waiting for. I dropped to my knees and sobbed my heart out. We got the cancer in time and, by the grace of God, all had been removed. Sarah is still with us.'

Next year the couple celebrate 25 years of marriage, a romantic affiliation born in the NAAFI financial centre at HMS *Nelson* when a confident Royal Marine attempted to secure a loan. Kev McCormack's application was rejected due to a lack of credit, with not even a credit card to his name. Undeterred, he pushed for a date with the attractive financial manager who had delivered the blow. When Sarah Brooking first rejected Monday and then Tuesday as suggested nights to go for a drink, McCormack decided to give it one more go. That Wednesday evening, they headed to The Mermaid pub in Port Solent. In September 1996, three years later, they tied the knot at Portsmouth Cathedral.

'We've now been married 24 years. I've been paying her back with interest ever since,' laughed McCormack. 'Mind you, I didn't have the money to pay for the drinks on that first date because she had turned down my loan application! As Sarah always says to me, I wouldn't be where I am today without her. She's right, you know. She always is.

'Earlier this summer, she was suffering from persistent stomach problems, and it became quite a concern. The doctor thought laxatives and painkillers were the answer. Well, that was no good. So we rang him and were told: "I don't know what you want me to do." In the end, we were advised to visit Queen Alexandra Hospital, where blood tests were taken, but, annoyingly, no scans. Thankfully, Sarah has health insurance with Vitality through her work at Eight Wealth Management. That saved her life.

'Her best friend, Nikki White, who has a nursing background, didn't like the sound of her illness so kept pestering her to get it checked out through Vitality. Sure enough, we travelled to Guildford on the Wednesday and three days later heard from the radiologist who was concerned about something they had discovered. Days after, the surgeon who was to deal with it rang to confirm that Sarah had stage three bowel cancer. That was the final day in June. Sarah's operation was booked in for the following week.

'I'm not the only one whose family have had cancer. We've had so many people sending good wishes, telling us it's a good cancer and this, that and the other, which has been appreciated. I am not being disrespectful and realise it was people trying to keep me positive, but there's no such thing as a good cancer. It's a horrible word.'

McCormack had been on furlough from Pompey during lockdown, but as football resumed and the play-offs loomed, he had to decline to return on compassionate grounds. Pompey completely understood his desire to remain by the side of his wife ahead of her impending operation to remove the cancer, their empathy appreciated immensely by the kit man. Instead, kit responsibilities were handed over to assistant Clark Denford for the play-offs, another long-serving member of the back room and currently involved in his second spell at the club.

Deprived of McCormack and the shielding Barry Harris, there was a different look to the Blues' bench as they headed into their two-legged encounter with Oxford. The 53-year-old instead watched from home as Kenny Jackett's men were eliminated by a penalty shoot-out to condemn them to League One football for another campaign. Unashamedly, it was Sarah occupying his thoughts.

He added: 'My priorities have changed. Sarah is the most important thing in my life. Kenny has been great. I told him: "Listen, gaffer. I've put this club first for 21 years. I'm sorry if I'm letting you down, but I'm now putting Sarah first. I'll be back when she's better." He replied: "No problem, Kev, you take as much time off as you need." He was brilliant.

'I'll tell you something that shows the man's class. Two days after we were knocked out of the play-offs, I received a call from him at 9am. I was taking Sarah to hospital for her operation and he rang up to wish us well. He finished it by saying: "Give Sarah our love." The gaffer is a gentleman, an absolute gentleman, and his wife, Sam, is lovely too. They are good people.

'I am as loyal as they come. Work is work but life is life, and I won't forget that from him. I won't forget the people who rang. I'm no one special, but, when you go through something like this, it's nice to know you have people like that to call upon. I dropped Sarah off at the hospital in Guildford, came home and waited. I couldn't visit her because of Covid-19. She was in for a week and all we could do was FaceTime each other. It was the longest week of my life. Mentally it was tough as I worry about things – that's me.

'When I boxed, the outcome was down to me – if I didn't perform that was my own fault. With this I was helpless. I told her I wished I had the cancer instead. I needed my friends during that period and they were there for me. I knew they would be. Knightsie and Awfs were brilliant. I've known them for years, while our assistant manager Joe Gallen also kept ringing every day. As human beings, he and the gaffer are right up there.

'There was also Mark Catlin, Tony Brown and Anna Mitchell, always there for me, always offering support. I didn't ask for that but I needed it. Ellis Harrison brought a big bunch of flowers and a card round, while I had messages of support from Gaz Evans, John Marquis, Cameron McGeehan and a few others. John Kiely was ringing me every week; he's a great man. I also received a call from Paul Cook, who had heard about Sarah. I started talking to him about football and he said: "Forget about football; how's your missus?"

'A couple who follow Pompey came around to my house – I know them from chatting to supporters outside grounds up and down the country. They brought two solar light bulbs which light the garden up at night. People have been so, so kind. I am loud and brash, and people can take me the wrong way, but I'm a loyal person. I come from a loyal background – I served as a Marine and loyalty means everything to me. I don't care whether people are loyal back but I was brought up like that.'

Sarah received the all-clear ten days after being admitted to hospital for an operation to remove the cancerous growth. The process from diagnosis to conclusion took under three weeks, a remarkably rapid response from the private health sector which McCormack credits with saving his wife's life. Pompey have granted his desire to remain away from work until September, likely to rule out his involvement with their pre-season programme, once the new campaign's start date is finalised. It's a scenario the hard-working Welshman is comfortable with, as he diverts sole attention to his wife and her recovery.

He said: 'My outlook on life has changed. Sarah is my priority – she is the only thing that matters now. You cannot help but have negative thoughts. I have constantly asked myself: "If I lost her, what would I do?" I know I shouldn't think like that, but it's natural isn't it?

'She has to go for a CT scan every four months now, so we're looking at November. That's the next step in the fight. She's got the all-clear and this is the recovery state now. Cancer is strange. It's not like a broken leg, because you can't see it, but it's there on the inside. We're taking it day by day. I'm no longer going to worry about menial things. In fact, I'm going to ask the club if I can change my hours to spend more time with Sarah, perhaps cut down on away trips.

'We all have to work to live, but it's no good if your partner is no longer there to share it with you. This has massively changed my outlook on life, and I've vowed not to stress as much as I did before. I'm supposed to be coming back to work at Pompey on 1 September, but if she's not well enough then I won't. Sarah's getting there slowly which is the main thing.

'It puts everything in perspective when your partner has cancer. Let's face it, everything else is insignificant; your family comes first. My father never praised me for what I did, even when boxing and winning national titles. He would tell everybody else but wouldn't say it to me. That's just the way he was. I'm that sort of way with my son and daughter, but, let me tell you, I am so proud of them. I probably don't say it enough and I should.

'Oliver works for Portsmouth Aviation and Kimberley is a care worker looking after dementia patients. They still live at home and we've coped with this as a family. Families are more important than anything else.'

While Sarah was in hospital recovering from her operation, McCormack set about overhauling the back garden of their Waterlooville home. As well as creating a more attractive environment for his wife to recuperate in, the mission doubled up as a means of keeping the Welshman occupied, rather than contemplating the unthinkable.

Having rightly stood back and admired his handiwork, he generously volunteered his services to a 78-year-old former SAS soldier residing three doors down, whose L-shaped garden had bushes in need of trimming back. Over the course of the summer, McCormack laboured on the gardens of four of his elderly neighbours. Marks carved into his legs by belligerent thorns raise a chuckle as he reflects on his efforts. With the season over and furlough still being applied, his work is now done. Time to join Sarah in their transformed back garden.

He added: 'Do you know what? When I received that news on the golf course about Sarah getting the all-clear, it was wonderful being in the presence of friends. I've known many of them for years, and they helped and supported me through this. They picked me up off the ground and that day they picked me up off the eighteenth hole.

'I then got up off the floor, dried my tears and carried on; after all, we were playing for a few bob and I was in for a good round anyway. The adrenaline and elation took hold. My second shot landed on the green and I ended up parring a par-four hole. We were playing doubles, and that was enough for me and Neil Sillett's son, Ollie, to be crowned winners. It was a good day.

'I do get wound up at times because I get tired. People don't realise what the job entails, travelling up and down the country. I'm a worker, and I've always been a worker. I can't sit on my arse doing nothing – I have to be active. That's why I did all that gardening this summer as I needed to keep my brain busy and wanted to help people. I'm not blowing my own trumpet, but you can't blag a job for 21 years. I've had some great highs with Pompey and some terrible lows, such as relegation and periods when people were losing their jobs, which broke my heart. The friendships you make in football are unbelievable. I won't forget those who were there for me and Sarah. Not a chance.'

MARK CATLIN
17 July 2020

The scorched turf was punctuated by patches of glorious green, reminiscent of Southsea Common wilting under the height of summer's glare. The Fratton Park pitch was indistinguishable from the lush surface which last saw duty a fortnight earlier in the first-leg opener of the play-off semi-final. Eventually, League One was settled through conclusion on the playing field. Wycombe Wanderers claimed the final promotion spot, triumphing 2–1 over Oxford United at an eerily empty Wembley stadium. No date is yet set for football's return, although mid-September has been mooted among Football League circles.

In the meantime, the finishing touches are being applied to Fratton Park's North Stand renovation, while the pitch has been shorn of its emerald top to allow for the customary reseeding process to begin. Preparation for the 2020–21 campaign is under way, irrespective of the ongoing financial uncertainty provoked by the coronavirus crisis. There can be no pausing for breath as the cycle continues, with Kenny Jackett at Pompey's helm challenged to lead the side out of League One.

Similarly, Mark Catlin is plotting an eighth season overseeing a period which, financially and operationally, he considers to be the club's toughest task since emerging from their last administration.

'When I lived in Spain, we used to play five-a-side on a Sunday morning,' said the Blues' chief executive while gazing across the reconstructed Fratton pitch. 'On one occasion, we were 5–0 down. Sweat was dripping off me and my face was like an orange ready to explode, but I was still running around. I put everything into all I do. There were a couple of minutes left in the game and I pulled a goal back. I picked up the ball out of the net and shouted: "Come on, lads, we can still do it." The other nine players on the pitch just started rolling around laughing. It took me a few seconds to twig what had amused them but that's my mentality – I never quit.

'When I left Bury in 2012, it was off the back of achieving League Two promotion and one of the best league placings for years, while the club was also debt-free and turning a profit. It was the right time to go. I am a fighter by nature. I've been beaten up loads of times in my life when growing up, yet I'm not one of those to lie on the floor, cowering and covering my head, letting people kick me. I'd rather get up and at least try to fight. That's just my nature.

'Is my time at Pompey done? Not at this precise moment. I would more likely leave when everything is stable and we've topped out. I know we haven't topped out yet. There are a lot of financial challenges facing this football club and it's not in my nature to quit. The EFL are proposing a salary cap. Is it right for me to leave at the moment while we fight it? Should I be going when we are currently losing nearly £1m a month following the impact of coronavirus? Is it right for me to walk away when everyone at the club is under so much pressure from the fan base?

'Our former chairman Iain McInnes possesses a very similar type of character and resigned following promotion from League Two in April 2017. I'm more inclined to do it on the back of success than in the midst of arguably the biggest challenge football has ever faced.'

To fire Pompey's latest promotion push, they had recruited John Marquis, Marcus Harness and Ellis Harrison for significant transfer fees, increasing the playing budget to accommodate them. Marquis finished as the Blues' joint-top scorer with Ronan Curtis on fourteen goals, while Harrison was the other player to reach double figures for the season. As for Harness, who netted in the play-off second leg, his tally of nine goals, primarily from out wide, earmark him as one to watch in forthcoming campaigns. Ultimately, however, Catlin believes promotion ambition was undone by the decision to curtail the League One season when a resurgent Pompey still had nine matches left to play.

He added: 'Unfortunately, much of what happened this year was away from the pitch in terms of the pandemic and its tragic death toll. The majority of League One clubs didn't want to carry on with the season, whereas morally we thought it was the right thing to do. We had an obligation to supporters to ensure that the campaign was completed the right way, which was on the field of play.

'In terms of football, we had taken on the lessons of playing 62 games in 2018–19 and were determined not to fall away again. The policy was to have two players of equal ability for each position, rather than putting your money into one outstanding footballer. As it so happened, because of the pandemic, it backfired on us. The season was brought to an end just as I felt we were starting to grow stronger, while other clubs were picking up injuries and didn't possess the squad depth we had. We did have a couple of wobbles before the season ended, such as Peterborough United and Fleetwood Town before the break, but I felt our strength in depth would have carried us through.

'During lockdown there were heated discussions going on about whether or not clubs should carry on with the season. We believed we had an obligation to our supporter base to do everything we could safely. It has been proven by the Premier League and Championship that it wasn't about safety, it was about the money. Not finishing has probably cost us in excess of £1m in terms of refunds to season-ticket holders, work we do with sponsors and missing out on match-day income from the remaining games. That's just from not completing the matches. There are other losses incorporated as a result of having to continue spending with no additional income being received.

'Until last week we didn't know what league we were going to be in and whether we would be subject to a £2.5m or an £18m salary cap. Now we don't know when the new season is going to start and whether supporters will be allowed into grounds. There is still so much uncertainty. The one thing any business really hates, especially a football club, is uncertainty. At this moment in time, that's exactly what we've got.

'We still have staff on furlough. This is their job, their life, their family – this is what they live for. Some of them have been here since leaving school, so you have that added weight of responsibility. As I sit here now, we are losing not far short of £1m a month. People are entitled to an opinion about the manager, but I'm speaking to other clubs about problems and, in the greater scheme of things, we are living in a bit of a bubble. I am not sure people realise the level of redundancies and losses currently going on in football. At present, the main objective is trying to keep Portsmouth Football Club afloat.

'I am not a scaremonger. Ultimately we have the backing of Michael Eisner and Tornante as a safety net. However, a lot of other clubs are on the verge of bankruptcy at this moment in time. I'm aware of clubs being behind with staff and player wages, forced to make cuts all over the business. Thankfully, we're not in that position because of how well this club has been run over many years. However, the scars and memories of seven years ago seem to have just disappeared. People have their thoughts on the manager, yet there are a lot of other things going on which must be considered by myself and the board.'

The consequence of successive League One play-off semi-final defeats has once again raised the issue of Jackett's future among a fan base understandably raw over the latest promotion failure. The unflappable 58-year-old rode an uncomfortable period as Blues boss during the opening months of the campaign, when discontent led to the away support chanting for his removal during defeats at Wycombe and AFC Wimbledon.

Jackett responded by guiding his side to a club Football League record of nine consecutive victories in all competitions at the turn of the year. In 2020, Pompey recorded 27 points from a possible 39 in

League One, while their sole defeat in six fixtures in cup competitions came against Arsenal. To date, Paul Cook's replacement has overseen 167 Blues matches, registering a remarkable win percentage of 52.09, a record unparalleled during the club's last 70 years. Regardless, growing swathes of the Fratton faithful have lost belief in a manager contracted until the summer of 2021.

Catlin admitted: 'This has been my toughest season at a football club. The first year was really, really hard. In 2013–14, everyone thought we should bounce straight back from relegation to League Two, but we had a bottom half of the table budget with a completely new squad and massive debts to clear following administration.

'The club had also come off the back of three relegations in four years. So, trying to arrest that mentality without one of the bigger budgets in the league was not easy. Just being Pompey doesn't win you any game; you still have to compete, coming up against clubs whose budgets at the time dwarfed ours. During subsequent years, we've built our playing budget from little more than a million up to four to five times higher. We've achieved it sustainably, while clearing out debts, turning a club losing money into one generating profit.

'This season, off the back of a clear play-off hangover and losing our two best players, we were always on the back foot. It felt all the way through as though we were struggling to keep our head above water. Despite a club record of nine straight wins, as soon as it ended people were immediately saying: "Jackett out." They were waiting in the shadows to come out and scream it. After that run, we lost the tenth match 1–0 at Coventry City, who would go on to win the league. I then received an email saying: "Surely Jackett has now got to go." I responded along the lines of, "You do realise he's won nine games in a row?" He replied: "You can spin it all you want."

'Based on the start we had, I did the maths after ten or fifteen games and thought: "Wow. We now need top-two form just to make the play-offs." Some fans were saying Pompey were in relegation trouble but I believed the play-offs were the minimum we would achieve. The atmosphere around the club suggested everything was on thin ice due to that poor start. We were always one loss away from the pressure being heaped straight back on. We didn't have any breathing space. That never went away all season.

'It wasn't like the previous campaign where we were running away with League One and, when a match was lost, everyone shrugged their shoulders and looked to the next game. This time, a defeat arrived and you could immediately feel the pressure. But, as Kenny himself says, that's exactly why we're here – that's why we love Pompey. If you are at a club like Pompey in League One you have to accept those pressures. If you can't stand the heat, get out of the kitchen.'

Catlin's desire for Pompey to retain a strong voice on Football League issues saw him become a pivotal figure during lockdown deliberations. Along with Peterborough owner Darragh MacAnthony, the duo had been vocal advocates for the resumption of League One, sensing the opportunity for automatic promotion. After a period of infuriating procrastination, their motion was defeated, with members of League One overwhelmingly voting to curtail the campaign and push straight into the play-off programme. Still, the tireless Blues' chief executive has now switched to another cause, this time attempting to shred proposals for a salary cap which he is convinced will apply the promotion handbrake to League One's largest and most sustainable clubs.

He said: 'During lockdown, there were debates about the league continuing, the points per game model, a mini-tournament concept flying around, while discussions brewed about salary caps. It has been a really, really stressful few months. For the first time in my life it took its toll and business affected me from a health point of view.

'There were six to eight weeks where the doctors were telling me I had to stop talking. I'd strained my vocal cords and was in danger of doing permanent damage to my voice. It took a real toll on me and I was struggling to sleep. Running a football club is stressful at the best of times and you require a pretty thick skin. Even for me, it really felt tough during those three months.

'However, as a football club, we pride ourselves on being at the forefront of debate, especially during conversations with the EFL about potential changes to football. I'd like to think I represent what we are as a city. If we have something to say, we voice it. We are unique here in our views and opinions. You're either a sheep or a lion, and Portsmouth, as a city, is a lion. To be the chief executive, to work here or even play, you must have that lion mentality.

'During that period it was crazy. One day I looked at my diary and, although it sounds glamorous, I had appointments with talkSPORT, Sky Sports News and the EFL. People don't realise, but I do suffer from nerves. The night before you're going live on talkSPORT it's just another thing to worry about. I'm on with Simon Jordan or I'm on with Jim White, when one wrong word or sentence live on air can have an effect. You have to be on your guard, but we are a club constantly on the front foot. If we have something to say and believe in it passionately, then we're not afraid to say it. Pompey has this wonderful us against the world mentality. I think it goes back to being an island city and I do love us for that.'

Along the season's journey, there has been no greater setback to the city than the loss of John Jenkins. The D-Day veteran's passing at the age of 100 in December was marked with an emotional memorial service at Portsmouth Cathedral. Fittingly, the 'Last Post' was performed by a military bugler. For the Fratton Park leg of the play-off semi-final against Oxford United, the Blues created a cardboard cut-out in Jenkins' image, positioning him in his customary directors' box seat. It was a touching gesture from a club that continues to mourn the passing of a man with immeasurable warmth, who touched the souls of all he encountered.

'I was so privileged to know John; he was such a lovely man,' added Catlin. 'He was always very calm, especially during the early years after coming out of administration when some of the managers were getting some stick. Even following defeat, he would smile at me, shrug his shoulders and say: "I'm already looking forward to the next game."

'Maybe that was a mentality from a bygone era, whereas now you lose a match and fans want to kill you. They lose their head; it's everything in their life. Yet John was always composed and calm, and he gave you a different perspective on things. He'd say to me: "Pressure? When you're getting off that boat and running up sand dunes with German soldiers firing guns and throwing grenades at you, that's pressure." To think I worry about going into the Chimes Bar at the end of the game in case fans have a go at me! That was John – he always put things into perspective.

'Football is my life, but, at the end of the day, it's a sport. I am not here for the money, I'm here because I love being involved in this environment. He adored my wife, Elaine, and the feeling was mutual. John always told me to look after her and our children, and to not take them for granted. Do you know what really sticks with me? It was former AC Milan and Italy manager Arrigo Sacchi who coined the phrase: "Football is the most important of the least important things in life." Sometimes when you're feeling the pressure and your world is caving in, step back and reflect. John always tried to teach me that. I hope he's looking down on us now, with a shrug of the shoulders and a smile.'

ACKNOWLEDGEMENTS

During Pompey's financial meltdown, an unlikely saviour emerged – the son of Colonel Gaddafi. Purportedly, Saadi Gaddafi held talks over becoming the Blues' latest owner. The potential entrance of an offspring of the infamous Libyan dictator provoked alarm among sections of the Fratton faithful, but not all. 'Don't worry, he's the good son,' was trumpeted by some. As it was, Saadi Gaddafi didn't manage to claim control of Pompey. Incidentally, later in life, he was cleared of murdering a footballer.

It's an episode which demonstrates how any prospective owner wielding promises of riches and success will be accepted by many football fans, irrespective of the club concerned. Distressed football clubs tend to attract interest from a certain calibre of generous benefactor. But, determined to break away from the chokehold, a fanbase united to save their football club.

Firstly, I wish to thank the 57 people who kindly granted me interviews for this book, offering honest, candid and, on occasions, heartbreaking insight into being members of the Pompey family. Some are no longer with us, yet their souls remain at Fratton Park.

I was extremely fortunate that the Eisner family, chief executive Mark Catlin and manager Kenny Jackett enthusiastically bought into this project, allowing me unrestricted access to the club across the 2019-20 campaign. Such a free pass is largely unheard of in modern football and reflects a progressive club rebuilt on foundations of transparency and openness.

Many thanks to Ian Darke for contributing the foreword to this book, wonderful words penned during a flight after covering a Champions League fixture in Europe.

A special mention to Pompey's media manager Neil Weld, who will not enjoy this spotlight being shone on him, nonetheless his trust, assistance and encouragement have proven invaluable.

Others immensely worthy of mentions are Mike Vimpany, Sarah Ferre, Bobby Bacic, Ollie Marsh, Mark Coates, Harry Kavanagh, Duncan Turnbull, Taylor Seymour, Andy Johnston, Gemma Raggett, Anna Mitchell, Tony Brooks, Dave Tiller, Micah Hall, Tony Brown, Habibur Rahman, Pete Blackman, Colin Farmery and Joe Pepler.

To my family, Emma, Abi and Greg, thank you for your patience. Writing two books in a year is not advisable. Apologies – we'll go to Walt Disney World as soon as we're allowed.

As ever, I owe much to my parents, Keith and Daisy, and Tony Parratt, my adopted godfather.

Finally, a hearty thanks to Michael Sells and everyone at Icon Books for offering me the opportunity to write this book. It became an epic tale, doubling in size and word count, but we got there.

ABOUT THE AUTHOR

Neil Allen is *The News'* chief sports reporter covering Portsmouth Football Club. He has won the award for Regional Sports Journalist of the Year at the British Sports Journalism Awards two years running. He is the author of *Played Up Pompey* (2015), *Played Up Pompey Too* (2017) and *Played Up Pompey Three* (2020).